Uncovering their Names and Stories:
300+ years of a German-Jewish family 1697-2024

by **David Henry Marlow**

A Publication of JewishGen
Edmond J. Safra Plaza, 36 Battery Place, New York, NY 10280
646.494.2972 | info@JewishGen.org | www.jewishgen.org

JewishGen is the Genealogical Research Division of the Museum of Jewish Heritage – A Living Memorial to the Holocaust

Uncovering their Names and Stories:
300+ years of a German-Jewish family 1697-2024

Copyright © 2025 by David Henry Marlow. All rights reserved.
Published by JewishGen
First Printing: March 2025, Adar 5785

Author: David Henry Marlow

Cover Design: Irv Osterer

This book may not be reproduced, in whole or in part, including illustrations in any form (beyond that copying permitted by Sections 107 and 108 of the U.S. Copyright Law and except by reviewers for public press), without written permission from the copyright holder.

JewishGen is not responsible for inaccuracies or omissions in the original work and makes no representations regarding its accuracy.

Library of Congress Control Number (LCCN): 2024950240

ISBN: 978-1-962054-18-8 (softcover: 408 pages, alk. paper)

About JewishGen.org

JewishGen, is a Genealogical Research Division of the Museum of Jewish Heritage - A Living Memorial to the Holocaust, serves as the global home for Jewish genealogy.

Featuring unparalleled access to 30+ million records, it offers unique search tools, along with opportunities for researchers to connect with others who share similar interests. Award winning resources such as the Family Finder, Discussion Groups, and ViewMate, are relied upon by thousands each day.

In addition, JewishGen's extensive informational, educational and historical offerings, such as the Jewish Communities Database, Yizkor Book translations, InfoFiles, Family Tree of the Jewish People, and KehilaLinks, provide critical insights, first-hand accounts, and context about Jewish communal and familial life throughout the world.

Offered as a free resource, JewishGen.org has facilitated thousands of family connections and success stories, and is currently engaged in an intensive expansion effort that will bring many more records, tools, and resources to its collections.

Please visit https://www.jewishgen.org/ to learn more.

Vice President for JewishGen: Avraham Groll

About JewishGen Press

JewishGen Press (formerly the Yizkor Books-in-Print Project) is the publishing division of JewishGen.org, and provides a venue for the publication of non-fiction books pertaining to Jewish genealogy, history, culture, and heritage.

In addition to the Yizkor Book category, publications in the Other Non-Fiction category include Shoah memoirs and research, genealogical research, collections of genealogical and historical materials, biographies, diaries and letters, studies of Jewish experience and cultural life in the past, academic theses, and other books of interest to the Jewish community.

Please visit https://www.jewishgen.org/Yizkor/ybip.html to learn more.

Director of JewishGen Press: Joel Alpert
Managing Editor – Peter Harris
Publications Manager - Susan Rosin

Cover Photo Credits

Cover designed by Irv Osterer

Front Cover:
Alfred Neufeld (1933-1944), cousin of the author's father, in Fröndenberg - courtesy of Heinz Marowilsky's childhood photo album.
Photo taken about 1935. Alfred was murdered with his parents and sister in Auschwitz.

Back Cover:
Photo of the author's great (x3) grandfather Moses Steinthal (about 1760-about 1840) - courtesy of Dan Rotman. Photo taken around 1835.

Photo of the author David Henry Marlow - courtesy of the author.

Endorsements

"It's the astonishing, curious and sometimes terrifying details in this history of David Henry Marlow's German-Jewish family that make it so moving and impressive. Highly recommended!"

- Richard Zimler, author of The Last Kabbalist of Lisbon and The Incandescent Threads, Portugal

"This sweeping and engaging historical account is more than just an overview of the author's family history – it is a testament to what a person might discover, given the time and the tenacity to do so. David Marlow has written a compelling and humanising account of three centuries of Jewish German history that will hopefully inspire others to engage likewise with their own family's past."

- Dr Simon Holloway, Manager of Adult Education and Academic Engagement, Melbourne Holocaust Museum

"Weaving together a broad web of intersecting and connecting families, your text does justice to the nature of the German-Jewish experience. You are showing how Jews were establishing networks, and thus for whoever reads your story will discover either connections with their own stories or come to understand the far-flung nature of their own family."

- Dr. Frank Mecklenburg, Mark M. and Lottie Salton Senior Historian, & Director of Research and Chief Archivist, Leo Baeck Institute, New York

"I always appreciate works like yours, as they provide very important information about the lives of people in our region, particularly regarding the people persecuted and murdered by the Nazis, just because they were Jews. Thanks to your work the lives of the victims remain in our memory."

- Dr Joachim Schröder, President, Old Slaughterhouse Memorial Centre, Düsseldorf

"Through this panoramic family history, David Marlow invites us to consider how history reverberates in the present. At a time when liberal democratic ideals are under increasing threat, works that sharpen our knowledge of the past, and its injustices, are ever more vital. This is an important work."

- Dr Seumas Spark, Adjunct Fellow in History at Monash University and President, Dunera Association, Melbourne

Forward

My family's history reflects a 300-year history of Jews in German-speaking lands, finding stories about amazing individuals, Jewish village life, Protected Jews, urbanization and assimilation, antisemitism, Kristallnacht experiences, the Kindertransports, the deportation process and the Dunera story.

The story of my ancestors takes us from the Lithuanian border, through East Prussia to Hamburg, Berlin, Hannover, Hildesheim, Wuppertal, Magdeburg, Leipzig, and many small German towns and villages. I also discovered family from towns in what is now western Poland but were once German-speaking lands.

I found relatives like writer and librarian Dr Werner Kraft, banker and philanthropist Dr Max Steinthal, philologist Prof Dr Heymann Steinthal, soldier and theatre director Captain George Isenstein, and Pauline Löwenhardt nee Lennhoff whose nine sons fought in WW1.

David Henry Marlow
Melbourne, Australia
February 2025

Uncovering their Names and Stories:

300+ years of a German-Jewish family 1697-2024

David Henry Marlow

2025

"Remember the days of old; consider the years of ages past; ask your father, he will show you, your elders, and they will tell you."

- Deuteronomy 32:7

"In fact, though the two are often confused, memory is different from history. History is someone else's story. It's about events that occurred long ago to someone else. Memory is my story. It's about where I come from and of what narrative I am a part. History answers the question, "What happened?" Memory answers the question, "Who, then, am I?" It is about identity and the connection between the generations. In the case of collective memory, all depends on how we tell the story…

One of the greatest gifts we can give to our children is the knowledge of where we have come from, the things for which we fought, and why. None of the things we value — freedom, human dignity, justice — was achieved without a struggle. None can be sustained without conscious vigilance. A society without memory is like a journey without a map. It's all too easy to get lost. I, for one, cherish the richness of knowing that my life is a chapter in a book begun by my ancestors long ago, to which I will add my contribution before handing it on to my children. Life has meaning when it is part of a story, and the larger the story, the more our imaginative horizons grow. Besides, things remembered do not die. That's as close as we get to immortality on earth."[1]

- Rabbi Jonathan Sacks, Chief Rabbi of the United Hebrew Congregations of the Commonwealth, 1991-2013

---

[1] 'Do remember the past, but do not be held captive by it', Rabbi Jonathan Sacks, The Rabbi Sacks Legacy, from The Times, 17 July 2004

Uncovering their Names and Stories:

This book is dedicated to my grandparents:

Oskar and Hanni Elkan who made it to Australia, and

Hermann and Meta Marowilsky who perished in the

Holocaust.

And to my children Bradley, Joshua and Brittany,

and their children Zander, Issy and Ava.

Uncovering their Names and Stories:

Table of Contents

1.0 Why? Am I Mad?

2.0 Method in my madness

3.0 My family history research road trip

4.0 Through German Jewish history

5.0 My family tree

6.0 The Lazarus – Steinthal Family

7.0 The Marowilskys and Polleys up to Kristallnacht

8.0 The Marowilskys after Kristallnacht

9.0 The Lennhoffs and Neufelds

10.0 The Nathan – Elkan Family

11.0 The Isensteins

12.0 The Krafts

13.0 The Marlows – Australia

14.0 Glossary

15.0 Bibliography

16.0 Acknowledgements

1.0 Why? Am I Mad?

This is a book about my family, a story of 300 years of a German Jewish family, which I can now trace from 1697 to today. It follows my journey retracing the footsteps of my ancestors, taking me from knowing virtually nothing about my family's history and extended family. It speaks of the familial connections, where they came from and moved to, and the stories of many family members whose lives reflect the times in which they lived.

My parents virtually never talked about their families, life in Nazi Germany or the war. After my parents died, my mother Ilse Marlow in 1997 and my father Henry Marlow in 2002, I wanted to know more about my family background and more about my identity. I knew that Dad was from Wuppertal, near Düsseldorf and Mum was from the German capital, Berlin. The Düsseldorf connection was sometimes commented on by my father when we watched one of his favourite TV shows, Hogan's Heroes, particularly when Düsseldorf was mentioned on the program.

I started this project with the simplest of questions. Who were my grandparents? I only knew the names of my maternal grandparents, and nothing about my father's parents. As it turned out, this was not a simple question. The more I discovered online as documents and records became available, the more questions I had. I wanted to know about their hometowns, their families and ancestors, and what happened to everyone.

My first mission was to find out the names of Dad's parents, and to seek out my maternal grandfather Oskar Elkan's grave in Melbourne. Dad never referred to his parents by name, but I knew by then that Dad's original surname was Marowilsky. This sounded Polish to me, and Polish Jews I talked to in Melbourne said the same. This set an expectation, yet to be met, that I would find significant Polish-Jewish roots on Dad's side of the family.

I discovered my Marowilsky grandparents, Hermann and Meta online on the Yad Vashem victims of the Holocaust website about 15 years ago, but there was little information about them until documents became available online. Later I found pictures of them in my father's recently discovered childhood photo album, but my ancestors had

Uncovering their Names and Stories:

not written names on the back of the photos or in the photo album, to identify who was in the photos. This was a puzzle to solve.

I found Oskar's grave in the Melbourne General Cemetery in North Carlton and took photos to document this piece of family history. The details on the gravestone confirmed his dates of birth and death, as well as his very existence. Although I had never met him, he was my mother's father and the partner of my beloved Nana. He was important to me. I had also seen a photo of him with Nana, relaxing on the lawn in the Catani Gardens, opposite their apartment on Fitzroy Street in St Kilda.

Every year or so, I would check online and see what new documents or information I could find on my grandparents. This continued over the years, and I still had very little to show for it. When I retired from running non-profit organisations in 2023, I felt I had the time and the overwhelming urge to find out if I had family members I didn't know about. I was also inspired by my partner, Dr Erica Cervini, who completed her PhD writing about the life of her great grandmother. Erica has become a guru on family history in Australia, publishing a book, speaking at conferences, and being a frequent speaker on Australian public broadcaster ABC Radio discussing family history topics.

At this stage, I was a relatively new grandfather, with three grandchildren Issy, Ava and Zander, one each for my children Bradley, Brittany and Dr Joshua. I wanted to discover and document my family tree, so that they would all have some understanding of their family background, at least my side of it. That was something I never really had growing up. So, in a very great part, this is a legacy I leave for my descendants.

My paternal grandparents Hermann and Meta Marowilsky, who I discovered through my family research
(Source: Heinz Marowilsky photo album)

I started the family tree research process most seriously in the second half of 2023, after I recovered from a health scare, which may also have motivated me to document my family history. As I started putting the pieces of the family tree together, I uncovered quite a few interesting and surprising family stories, which I felt deserved documentation in a narrative form. Erica encouraged me to work towards a book, and the genealogical research and family history research continued in tandem from late 2023.

My ancestors deserve having their existence and their stories acknowledged, at least as far as possible, not to be left in the dust of time. Many do not have graves or gravestones remaining, so without a conscious effort, all trace of them could disappear. I wanted to give them the respect of recognition. Too many are lost to history. The stories of their lives also tell us so much about 300 years of German Jewish history, and the world events that impacted their lives. Their stories explain why I wasn't born in Germany, but in Australia.

Whether all my children and family members are passionately interested in their ancestry and heritage today, is questionable. But in the future, thanks to this research, it will be available to them when they or their children choose to access it. I certainly have had nephews and nieces, and new found cousins, press me with questions as my research has progressed.

And I have always had an interest in history, especially European history. I have been Honorary Secretary of the Australian Jewish History Society Victoria for about six years. My favourite subject in VCE was British History and I majored in Economic History at the University of Melbourne. I can even remember winning the Jewish history prize in Sunday school many years ago. This interest in history has certainly helped create context and provided a better understanding of key family events through time.

Gradually, I found that the family tree and stories were coming together to cover over 250 years of Jews in Germany, only ending with the Holocaust or scattered emigration around the world, including to the USA, the Netherlands, Australia, Canada and Israel. The story of my family appeared to reflect the history of German Jews across three centuries. This, I felt was a story worth telling.

I grew up with only one living grandparent, my maternal grandmother Hanni Elkan, our Nana. I am sure that Nana worked as an ally of the family dentist, as when I was growing up she brought me a small bag of lollies every week. I saw Nana every Sunday, unless we went away on holidays. Typically, Dad would pick her up Sunday morning, and we would take her out to lunch, and then lounge around back at home. She would sit on the couch and read the newspapers at our large lounge-room coffee table, adjusting her hearing aid at varying times, depending on whether she wanted to hear what was going on or not.

Her husband, my maternal grandfather Oskar Elkan had died in 1948. So, I never met him. My paternal grandparents were very rarely mentioned, but I worked out early in life that they had been killed in the Holocaust. This paucity of living grandparents and the fact that both my parents were only-children, meant that we had no uncles, aunts or cousins. Or so my siblings and I thought.

Very little family outside of our immediate family in Melbourne was ever mentioned, apart from occasional vague talk of unspecified cousins of Nana in the USA, whom she visited back in the 1960s. One of their descendants, Ralph Krongold from Los Angeles visited Australia quite a few times over the decades, and he met with family members in Melbourne, including my grandmother, my siblings and me. He had also met Nana on her visit to the USA in the 1960s. Apart from being related to Nana, I did not really understand the details of the family connection to him at the time of his visits. But I now know that his grandmother Helene Deutsch nee Kraft (1891-1970) and my grandmother Hanni Elkan nee Kraft (1897-1986) were sisters. I did always feel that Ralph looked like a young professor, with his wild longish hair and healthy beard. As it turns out, he did become a professor, and he still has his beard, though a different shade to what it was.

Uncovering their Names and Stories:

2.0 Method in my madness

Genesis

I started my research into the family by seeking out the names and details of my grandparents to start building my family tree. Initially, I found a few records and documents relating to them online. Trove, which is an online database run by the National Library of Australia, and the National Archives of Australia provided many details and documents on my maternal grandparents and my father, which were extraordinarily useful. For example, I found Dad's naturalisation records, wedding and family birth announcements in newspapers, Dad's change of name confirmation, confirmation of where Dad and Mum's family lived in Australia, and details of the ship that my maternal grandparents arrived on in Australia.

As I started to be able to populate my family tree with grandparents, and gradually beyond, I realised I needed a way to document what I found. Online genealogical online services looked very promising, and they also held a mountain of records from around the world, especially Ancestry and MyHeritage. I chose Ancestry as my master system to record my family tree, as it seemed to have the most extensive range of historical records available. But I used both, as well as a wide range of other, sometimes more specific systems, such as CompGen[2] for German records, JewishGen for Jewish records worldwide and occasionally Litvaksig.org for Lithuanian records. I use MyHeritage as my sandpit and source of records not held on Ancestry. Sometimes one system had access to a lot of records that the other systems lacked. The full list of systems I found useful is listed in the bibliography at the back of this book.

I found details of my paternal grandparents, the Marowilskys, and their parents on CompGen but they did not come up elsewhere, apart from systems providing Holocaust related records, such as the Yad Vashem database of Holocaust victims and the Arolsen Archives. I found the Arolsen Archives a very helpful source of records on family members who were deported to ghettoes or concentration

---

[2] Verein für Computergenealogie (Association for Computer Genealogy)

camps. It holds an abundance of records, such as on the deportations, Gestapo arrest records, and concentration camp records.

The genealogical systems provided access to records of birth, marriage, taxation, census, emigration by ship, death, and burial. No system had everything and much from some towns is not easily extracted, or even necessarily in existence. In Germany, record keeping tended to remain highly decentralised to city or sometimes state archives, or churches or synagogues. Unfortunately, most synagogues were destroyed under the Nazi regime, and many records were bombed out of existence (such as military service records) or just lost to the ravages time. But many records remained, and initially I did not have to rifle through boxes of paper files or scan through miles of microfiche, as most of what could be found on my family had been scanned and indexed, so it was available online. Not that long ago, I would have had to scrounge through many boxes of paper documents at many local archives, or if I was lucky, scroll through miles of microfiche.

Later, when I visited the State Archives in Dessau-Roßlau, I looked through boxes of records and record books relating to Protected Jews in Saxony-Anhalt, which included family members. These dated from the 1700s to the 1800s and provided great details on my Lazarus - Steinthal family.

Over months of research, I found seven particular pots of gold that helped me progress my family tree and understanding of my family history in leaps and bounds.

Firstly, I discovered the Lazarus - Steinthal family tree through the Berlin Jewish Museum website and the Leo Baeck Institute website in New York. This is a handwritten family tree developed over decades, originally covering 1720 to 1935, but was extended in the 1960s. It is part of the Esther Elbin Family Collection in the Leo Baeck Institute in New York. A large copy of this family tree printed on canvas now hangs on my bedroom wall.

It was interesting because some records online had suggested that my great (x2) grandfather Bernhardt Kraft from Calbe in Saxony-Anhalt may have been married to Helena Steinthal. The Steinthal family tree had a handwritten note that showed one of Moses Steinthal's nine daughters, Helene marrying a Kraft from Calbe, and Calbe is a very

Uncovering their Names and Stories:

small place. Eureka! This link provided a link to Lazarus-Steinthal ancestors back to my great (x5) grandfather Lazarus (Eleasar) Philipp, who was born in 1697.

This was an important discovery from the universe of my family history, reflecting the lives of Jews from 1697 until modern times, mostly in German speaking lands. Not just Jews, but my Jewish relatives. They included teachers, merchants, shopkeepers, rabbis, medical doctors, butchers, a librarian, tailors, furriers, barbers, cattle dealers, writers and poets, bankers, a cigar manufacturer, and even a famous German academic, Heymann Steinthal. But more on them later.

The second pot of gold I discovered was the genealogical detective work that had been undertaken over years by my cousin Dan Rotman, who also lives in Melbourne, Australia. Dan's great grandfather Theodor Kraft and my great grandfather Selmar Kraft were brothers. Dan had unearthed substantial connections in the Kraft family from at least 1820 with Selmar and Theodor's father Bernhardt Kraft to today. But thankfully Dan had also spread his family tree research more broadly than just the direct Kraft family, so this was a great boost to my family research. It was like doing a jigsaw puzzle with many of the pieces already connected.

For me, membership in Ancestry was certainly worth the cost, and it was my third pot of gold. My family history research project would not have been possible without the resources available on Ancestry.com. Ancestry had been essential in sourcing data and documents, dates, photographs, locations, and other details on many family members across the various parts of my ancestry, especially in Germany, the USA, the Netherlands, Israel, the UK and Australia, and across the many towns and cities my family lived.

JewishGen was the fourth pot of gold. It includes not just records and documentary evidence, but also histories and background information on towns and cities where Jews lived, worked and died. The special interest groups related to it on Facebook were also essential in getting advice and suggestions and learning more about undertaking genealogical research for a Jewish family. The camaraderie, support and expertise provided by a variety of people online helped develop the necessary skills and find the sources of essential records.

JewishGen is part of the Museum of Jewish Heritage and includes access to genealogical webinars and a Youtube library of presentations on many topics, some of which were incredibly useful to my research.

Pot of gold number five. CompGen is the largest genealogical system in Germany, and like JewishGen was a great help in finding details of records on many of the German Jews in my family. It was especially helpful with finding and proving connections to my Marowilsky family in Pillau, East Prussia in the 19th century. No other source seemed to have anything to prove the connections and find details, especially in linking the Pillau Marowilskys to having come from Vistytis, in what is now Lithuania.

The sixth pot of gold were census records. These came from various systems and sources but were a great way of proving who was living with which families, such as Bernhardt Kraft and his family living together in Calbe in eastern Germany in 1867, or the Wernick household where my father lived for a year in Wolverhampton in England in 1939-1940. Sometimes a genealogical system would have records on two or three children from a family and suggest maybe a third. With the addition of referring to census records, I could find that two children plus one possible child, became six confirmed children. This seriously aided completeness in putting together the story of the family. Missing siblings also feels disrespectful to their memory. They deserve to be identified and documented, wherever possible.

Number seven was a very hard-to-find interview. Wuppertal-based criminal sociologist Prof Dr Manfred Brusten interviewed my father in 1994, in German, for his research on what happened to the Jews of Wuppertal under the Nazi regime. I found a master's thesis in Wuppertal by Anna Ruhland that quoted my father from the interview. I tried for some time to find Prof Brusten or Anna. After many Google searches, asking academics and genealogists around the world for help, I eventually found the right Anna Ruhland, who is now a history teacher in Bensberg, near Cologne. Anna kindly searched her 20-year-old records, and thankfully found and sent me

Uncovering their Names and Stories:

a transcript of the interview in German. I quickly translated it and found an abundance of detail on my father's time in Germany and thereafter, which my father had never talked about with his family.

These sources of information were indispensable, but they did not provide everything. I needed more. Much more. I needed to find missing family members, find military service records, identify the birth and death dates of people with incomplete profiles on the websites. I needed to better understand their lives, and what they lived through, whether that be eighteenth century Gröbzig, nineteenth century Pillau, Wuppertal in the Weimar era, or Leipzig under the Nazi regime. But these sources of family history provided a terrific start.

To help better complete my genealogical research, I undertook a DNA test with Ancestry DNA, and then downloaded my DNA data from Ancestry to MyHeritage as a cross-check. I tested with Ancestry because it has the largest database of testers to match with, and you could download your results and upload to MyHeritage to seek matches on another database of testers. You cannot test with MyHeritage and then upload the result to Ancestry. The DNA results found my genetic ancestry to be 99-100% Ashkenazi Jewish, from central and eastern Europe. I was a little surprised, as I thought there would likely have been some intermarriage over the generations, which might have reduced that percentage, or I might find some Polish links, given the Marowilsky surname of my father. But no, none of that. I was not so interesting. Ancestry DNA did suggest 1% Aegean Islands, which would explain my love for Saganaki and Taramosalata, but 1% is probably a statistical error, and was not supported by the MyHeritage DNA analysis which found me to be 100% Ashkenazi Jewish. I certainly found intermarriage in many places in my family tree, but not in my direct line of descent.

From my desk

My desk in Elwood was the base from where I undertook a great deal of research. In parallel, I used online resources, family resources and books. For accuracy, my desk of choice is my very busy coffee table, where I worked while sitting on my couch, laptop at the ready with a pile of books, notes and copies of articles by my side, in English and

German. I work like this, with my iPhone armed with Google Translate and Google Maps; a magnifying glass for examining maps, photos and documents; and the Compact Oxford German Dictionary beside me. Two dogs asleep next to me, unless they are badgering me for a treat, a walk or dinner.

I had three main objectives.

Firstly, I wanted to further develop and understand my family tree, especially my direct ancestry as far as I could. I wanted to find missing grandparents, great grandparents and beyond. But I also wanted to understand their lives as much as possible.

Did they have to travel as traders? Did they have to stay home and look after the business and family while their spouse went off to markets or off to war? Did they serve in the military? For example, I found relatives who fought in the German unification wars of the 19th century, many who served in World War 1, and even a relative, Captain George Isenstein, who fought in the American Civil War.

Ancestry, MyHeritage, FamilySearch, JewishGen, CompGen and Litvak SIG were particularly useful online genealogical resources. I also referred several times to JRI Poland but found little link to Poland in my ancestry, apart from siblings of ancestors who may have married a Polish Jew along the way. Though, some ancestors were born in Prussian towns, which are now renamed towns in modern Poland. For example, my great grandmother Henriette Polley's hometown of Liebstadt in East Prussia, is now Milakowo, and my great (x5) grandfather Lazarus Philipp's hometown of Landsberg an der Warthe is now Gorzów Wielkopolski.

And if you are ever doing similar family research, please do not forget to Google the name of someone you are researching. I found terrific details on several people by simply Googling either their family name or the individual's full name. This is how I found the Civil War records of Captain George Isenstein, the biographies of Heymann Steinthal, the father of my great (x2) grandfather Bernhardt Kraft, and the death announcements or records of various ancestors.

Secondly, I wanted to understand how I should approach the family research and how I could find the information, records and documents I needed to better understand the story of my family. Part

Uncovering their Names and Stories:

of this was aimed at understanding the best way to record, document and communicate what was becoming an intriguing family saga. There are many books on how to trace your ancestors, including specific ones on tracing Jewish, German and Jewish German relatives. The ones I found most useful (and some which were slightly useful) are listed in the bibliography.

Thirdly, I needed to understand the history of Jews in German-speaking lands generally over the period, including in the towns and cities where my family lived. In some cases, my research required peaking over borders into Lithuania, the Netherlands, England, the USA, and the old parts of Prussia which are now in Poland or Russia. I wanted to understand the economic, social and cultural changes which they went through, their war experiences, and how these affected them. This would provide the context for what my family experienced, but also helped visualise what they went through, which may not have been specifically documented in diaries, letters or similar.

From my desk, I could access relevant archives in Australia, Germany, Poland and the USA. In particular, the Australian archives were very helpful, given their centralisation, digitalisation and completeness. The various German state and city archives, and German national archives (Bundesarchiv) were all helpful in providing family records and information, such as restitution claim documentation. The allied bombings of World War 2 destroying records, Jews possibly hiding their identity in war years, and decentralisation of archives made this a much more complex task, but there was a lot of information obtained nonetheless, which was essential to understanding the story.

The Public Records Office Victoria provided details from Victorian rates books for my parents. Electoral role records in Victoria, telephone and city residency books for Germany were very useful in determining and confirming who lived where, and when.

The Arolsen Archives, Yad Vashem Victims Database, United States Holocaust Memorial Museum, and USC Shoah Foundation provided online resources and records on my family's history through the Holocaust. There, I found the records, documents and details of family members who were murdered in Auschwitz, Izbica, Sachsenhausen, Theresienstadt, Sobibor, Riga and elsewhere.

Holocaust Survivor testimonies on video, which are often available online, provided first-hand experiences of what Jews and members of my family went through during the Holocaust. This was especially helpful in understanding their experiences during and around Kristallnacht. My Dad's first cousin Arno Heller's testimony proved the existence of many family members, as I was unsure about the full list of my grandmother's Lennhoff siblings, but also what the family went through on Kristallnacht in Germany. Arno also described escaping on the Kindertransport (the informal name of the program to rescue Jewish children from Germany in 1938-1939) with his sister, and his personal experiences in joining the US Army, including serving in North Africa and Europe. Wuppertal-born Holocaust survivor and Melbourne Holocaust Museum volunteer guide Henri Korn (1929-), provided first-hand video testimony of what it was like on Kristallnacht in Wuppertal, at the same time that my father and my Marowilsky grandparents were living there.

Family documents, pictures and artefacts were very limited. Some families have diaries, boxes of records and old papers, old passports, old postcards, photos from the 'old country', or other resources hidden away under a bed, in the family attic or at the back of a cupboard. Like many families, my partner's family had her great grandmother Rose's siddur with key family events, such as weddings and funerals, recorded inside.[3] This provided a great outline of her family's history. Starting out, I had none of that for my family. Today, you might find much of this on someone's Facebook page.

But thankfully, I discovered that my sister Helen Nathan had our father's childhood photo album from the 1920s and 1930s in Germany, as well as some photos of then unconfirmed family members on her wall at home. I had not known that the album even existed. I just hoped that the photos on the wall were not the photos that came with the picture frames.

I do have a small whiskey shot glass with caricatures of men's faces on the glass, and a small metal turtle that flips open at the top. These

---

[3] Siddur = Jewish prayer book

had belonged to my grandmother Hanni Elkan, dating back to her time in pre-war Germany. The glass was undoubtedly used by my grandmother, and possibly my grandfather, to enjoy a whisky and maybe schnapps on occasions. My grandmother used the little turtle for saccharine for her coffee, but in the more distant past it may have been used for snuff or tablets. I remember the glass in her buffet that she had in her quite dark dining room in her apartment in St Kilda when we visited in the 1970s.

Newspapers which were now available online provided many gems of information, such as the death notices for my great grandparents Selmar and Frieda Kraft in the local Jewish community newspaper in Leipzig, advertisements for Selmar's department store business in the local Leipzig newspapers over decades, the fact that my Dad was best man at his friend Ken Green's wedding in Melbourne, Australian naturalisation notices available on Trove, and information on shipping arrivals.

The Deutsches Zeitungsportal website was an excellent source of German newspaper information, providing details on various family members, such as death notices, wedding announcements, business advertisements and court proceedings. It is like Trove in Australia. And the OldNews.com website from MyHeritage provided various newspaper resources from Germany, Australia and other countries. Goethe University's library website was also a useful online source of old German newspapers and journal articles.[4] And Newspapers.com was very helpful for details that made the newspapers on my relatives who emigrated to the USA, and their descendants.

My co-conspirators

The first people I started contacting (harassing?) for information, leads, photos, documents and stories were my sister Helen Nathan nee Marlow and my brother Peter Marlow. Thankfully, both live in Melbourne, not that very far from me. We shared what we could remember from the past at various cafes and restaurants, or I worked to extricate memories from Helen in her lounge room, or Café D'Lish, while our combined three dogs played with each other

---

[4] Sammlungen.ub.uni-frankfurt.de/

around us and ate meatballs. My exuberant moodle Fred and poodle Mr Chifley had many lovely sessions playing with Helen's papillon Luis. We all agreed that our parents never talked much about their families in Germany or the past. Despite that, it was surprising how much we could recall. It was a good start.

Peter remembered the names of a one of Dad's aunts and an uncle, as well as giving me a tip on a researcher from Wuppertal who had interviewed Dad a couple of decades earlier, as part of some work he was doing researching into victims of the Nazi regime from Wuppertal. Peter's daughter Leah remembered the researcher's name, Prof Dr Manfred Brusten, as she stayed with his him in Wuppertal a few decades earlier. It turned out that I was already looking at some of Prof Brusten's work on the Jewish children on the Kindertransport from Wuppertal, for which he had interviewed my father in 1994. Thankfully, I was recently able to obtain a copy of a transcript of the interview from teacher and researcher Anna Ruhland, who cited it in her master's thesis.[5] Prof Brusten is also the driver of the Stolpersteine project in Dad's hometown of Wuppertal.

On one visit, my sister Helen dug out our father's childhood photo album with pictures of Dad as a youngster with family and friends back in Germany, and on holidays around Germany. For some relatives, it may be the only surviving photographic proof of their existence. The photos are from about 1925 to 1938, and are labelled with places the photos were taken, but little hint of who was in the photos. No names. That has required detective work, and some very helpful new-found cousins. All witnesses from before the war, such as my parents, all our grandparents and others from the time are long gone. Helen also had some photos on the wall of her home that we had assumed might be grandparents or great grandparents. The only hope was to find a distant family member who might have matching photos with clues to the names of those in the photos, or who knew them later in life.

I also need to give full credit to my other co-conspirators from around the world, who were generous with their time and helped

---

[5] 'Henry Marlow (Heinz Marowilsky)', transcript of interview with Prof Manfred Brusten, Armadale, 4 October 1994, edited version 6 - 2001

Uncovering their Names and Stories:

tremendously in the research effort. I thank those historians, researchers, archivists, museum directors, librarians, volunteers and others who helped, and who are recognised in the acknowledgements section at the back of this book. Some deserve an additional special mention here for their very kind and generous contributions.

Professor John Löwenhardt (The Netherlands) is a newly discovered cousin and expert on the Löwenhardt family. My great grandfather and John's great grandmother were siblings. My great grandfather Aron (Adolf) Lennhoff was the father of my paternal grandmother Meta Marowilsky. He was also the brother of Pauline Lennhoff who married Levi Löwenhardt. Pauline and Levi Löwenhardt were John Löwenhardt's great grandparents. John has researched his family extensively, including writing many papers on the family, and developing a website to help make the stories accessible. It has been a great experience exchanging stories, photographs (often a one-way street to me) and lessons since we discovered each other in early 2024.

Dan Rotman's (Melbourne) great grandfather Theodor Kraft and my great grandfather Selmar Kraft were brothers. They were both merchants, Selmar in Leipzig, and Theodor in Calbe and then Magdeburg. Dan has researched his family tree extensively over a couple of decades, while also collating photographs of family members. Much of his family tree is the Kraft family, which is also a significant part of my overall ancestry. The grandmother I grew up with, Hanni Elkan, was the youngest child of Selmar and Frieda Kraft. Dan's generosity and advice has been outstanding.

Ralph Salinger (Israel) is not a relative, but is an expert on Lithuanian Jewry, and thankfully especially on the town of Vistytis, which was the home of my Marowilsky ancestors for a time. I could not find much online about the Marowilskys from there, but Ralph was extraordinarily helpful in providing leads to background information on Vistytis, the town's history and access to all the cemetery records for the Vistytis Jewish cemeteries. Ralph was also instrumental in helping me connect with Prof Dr Ruth and Michael Leiserowitz of the 'Jews in East Prussia', who have also been very helpful in researching my Marowilsky and Polley ancestors.

Rodney Eisfelder (Melbourne) is not a relative either, but he is a member of the Australian Jewish Historical Society Vic, and the President and German genealogy specialist in the Australian Jewish Genealogical Society Vic. He has been very generous with his time and expertise in finding records for me, such as the death notices of my Leipzig Kraft great grandparents and uncovering details of my Hamburg Nathan/Elkan ancestors, sources of relevant newspaper advertisements and other records, and has provided very useful and productive advice. Rodney is a bulldozer who helps clear away my genealogical roadblocks, and I am greatly appreciative of his help.

Some other helpers of special note for their very kind contributions are Frau Anke Boeck, archivist from the State Archives in Dessau-Roßlau for going far beyond expectations to help with the Lazarus – Steinthal family, Mathias Hille of the Schönebeck City Archives (Elbe) for his help with the Kraft family of Calbe, and my many newly discovered cousins from around the world. The full list of all who have helped with the project are listed in the acknowledgements section of this book. Please forgive me if your name is missing.

It is also worth considering the different ways a family history can be documented and communicated. I have chosen a narrative form through this book, highlighting key individuals and stories from my family history, while also continuing to develop the family tree in parallel. But cousins I have unearthed, have used a variety of methods. Ray Sherman has created a PowerPoint type storyboard on Youtube to present his family's story over a few generations. Prof John Löwenhardt has formed a foundation and a website with himself and guest writers writing stories about the Löwenhardt clan. Dan Rotman has focused on documenting an extraordinarily extensive family tree for his Rotman-Kraft ancestors, which is a wonderful resource for the extended family. Gabriel Kahane has leveraged his musical and song-writing talents to use music to tell the story of his grandmother Hannelore Kahane nee Schaefer, based on her diaries. He wrote the Orinoco Sketches in 2011, named after the ship Hannelore fled Germany in 1939.

Uncovering their Names and Stories:

Cemeteries as a source of information

I find cemeteries very depressing, which is not surprising I suppose, but they are a great source of information when researching family history. For example, gravestones can provide information on or confirmation of the names of family members, dates of birth and death, sometimes occupations or religious information can be found, such as whether the person is actually Jewish, a Kohanim or a rabbi. Often however, in Nazi Germany Jewish graves were desecrated, gravestones stolen and used for other purposes, gravestones used for target practice, or simply left to rot and be overgrown. In more modern times, efforts are being made by many to preserve, clean-up and document Jewish cemeteries and gravestones, and this seems to be happening across many parts of Europe.

Old Jewish cemetery in Gröbzig, Saxony-Anhalt
(Photo credit: David Marlow)

I started my cemeteries research from my laptop in Melbourne, finding graves and sometimes gravestone photos through Findagrave.com; JewishGen Online Worldwide Burial Registry (JOWBR), JewishGen; Vistytis New Jewish Cemetery digitised documents, Litvak Cemetery Catalogue, Maceva; and Jüdische Friedhöfe[6] in Deutschland und Angrenzenden Ländern.[7]

Maceva is the Lithuanian Jewish non-profit organisation which maintains, cleans, photographs and records the remaining graves and gravestones in Jewish cemeteries in Lithuania. Their work enabled me to read every surviving gravestone in the Vistytis New Jewish Cemetery in Lithuania, without leaving my apartment. Maceva was formally founded by Aleksandr Avramenko and Sergey Kanovich in 2011. Their volunteers also very recently, in August 2024, went through cleaning and photographing the Old Jewish Cemetery, but none of the gravestones had surnames.[8]

In Melbourne, I visited Springvale Botanical Cemetery, Melbourne for my parents and grandmother Hanni, and Melbourne General Cemetery, Carlton North for my grandfather Oskar. Naturally, visiting my parents' and grandparents' graves was not a new experience, but it felt a little different in the context of researching the history of our family.

On my family history road trip across Germany, I visited many old Jewish cemeteries, such as the Jüdischer Friedhof Plettenberg, on Freiligrathstraße, which is the resting place of seven Lennhoffs, my paternal grandmother's family members. The gravestones in these cemeteries helped confirm birth and death dates, the names of spouses in some cases, and the location of burial. Visiting them also provided a link to the past, which made them feel more real as family members and created a longer, more concrete emotional connection.

Libraries and Museums

Libraries and museums are a researcher's heaven. They hold books, articles, exhibits, artefacts and displays relating to the places and time periods that my family lived through. Books can feed your imagination, and museums can evoke a greater understanding of the time, and the lives lived. Walking the streets of where they lived helps

---

[6] Jüdischer Friedhof = Jewish Cemetery
[7] Jewish cemeteries in Germany and neighbouring countries (online)
[8] Email from Ralph Salinger, Maceva volunteer, 20 August 2024

Uncovering their Names and Stories:

fill a piece of the puzzle, but the world changes around them. The modern-day petrol stations, e-charging stations, TV antennas and shopping malls were not in existence in the times of my ancestors, creating a very different feel from what they would have experienced. Museums help provide pieces of history from the time, such as artefacts and exhibits that help place yourself into the lives of those long-lost family members, especially when the museum is in the town or city where they lived.

At home in Melbourne, I started with the Lamm Jewish Library of Australia in North Caulfield, the newly renovated Melbourne Holocaust Museum in Elsternwick where I had taken many interfaith and non-Jewish groups for visits, and the Jewish Museum of Australia in St Kilda. I had visited them all many times before, but this time I went with a different, more personal mission in mind. The mission was to add to my understanding of my family's past.

For example, the Jewish Museum of Australia, which is in St Kilda near where I live, had exhibits and many artefacts related to Jewish immigration from Europe and the *Dunera* experience, including the internment camps for 'enemy aliens' in Australia. The Melbourne Holocaust Museum (MHM) was particularly useful in colouring in the history of the Holocaust experience. After viewing the brilliantly renovated exhibits, I sat in the MHM library and used their resources to delve deeper into a variety of relevant topics, such as the Sachsenhausen Concentration Camp and the experiences of the Dunera Boys.

Some of my research was conducted in the Lamm Jewish Library of Australia, which is located in the Jewish community's Beth Weizmann Community Centre complex, in Melbourne. I spent six years working at Beth Weizmann, mainly as the Executive Director of the Jewish Community Council of Victoria. The library combined a few former libraries and resources, including the Makor Library, and was half funded by the Australian Government with matching funding from the Lamm family. Erwin Lamm had been a Dunera Boy like my father, and a passionate Orthodox Jewish community leader over many years. His son Danny Lamm AM is a long-time colleague of mine and has been involved on the boards of a variety of Jewish community organisations over many years. Coincidently, I bumped into Danny while I was at the library which bears his family name, after rummaging amongst the library's Jewish German history books.

I also found that libraries that I accessed online provided access to a huge reservoir of books, journals, periodicals and newspapers. In particular, I found the State Library of Victoria in my hometown and the University Library of the Goethe Universität, Frankfurt am Main incredibly useful. Through them, I could access articles and e-books that provided ideas, historical perspectives such as on the Kindertransport program and the *Dunera*, eyewitness accounts, and even the business advertising over decades of my great grandfather Selmar Kraft in the local papers in Leipzig.

In Germany, I visited the Topography of Terror Museum in Berlin; the Berlin Jüdisches Museum (Berlin Jewish Museum); the Erinnerungsort Alter Schlachthof, (Old Slaughterhouse Memorial Centre), Düsseldorf; the Gröbzig Synagogue Museum; the team of the MiQua, LVR - Jewish Museum in the Archaeological Quarter, Cologne; and the Sachsenhausen Memorial and Museum. I found them all extraordinarily useful and helpful, and frequently very moving. The team at the museum in Gröbzig, where my Lazarus - Steinthal family came from, and Dr Christiane Twiehaus in Cologne, have been particularly keen to help and are very generous with their time. Their assistance is greatly appreciated.

On my road trip alone, I visited 18 libraries and museums. With some museums, you were very much on your own, even when sending emails weeks beforehand in German and chasing up. Nevertheless, for most museums, and the same goes for archives, people on the ground were very keen to be helpful and assist. Some went way beyond what you might expect.

For example, Frau Anka Boeck from the Landesarchiv Sachsen-Anhalt[9] in Dessau-Roßlau, went out of her way to source primary records on the Lazarus - Steinthal family, which helped fill in gaps, find missing family members, and prove or disprove the Lazarus - Steinthal family tree. She kindly made notes regarding documents and entries that might have been relevant to my family and tagged the documents to aid in my research. Frau Boeck also very kindly pointed

---

[9] State Archives in Saxony-Anhalt

Uncovering their Names and Stories:

me to numerous other sources of information and documentation in the state of Sachsen-Anhalt, including a couple of museums in Halberstadt, which I quickly added to my road trip schedule.

The Gröbzig Synagogue Museum is getting ready to reopen as I write, as they are completing a major renovation. The museum is inside the old synagogue complex. The Gröbzig synagogue is where my Steinthal family members would have attended daily prayers, Shabbat services and participated in the Jewish festivals, especially Rosh Hashanah and Yom Kippur. It also contained a small school for the local Jewish children.

Despite being very busy getting the museum ready for reopening, Gröbzig Museum Director Anett Gottschalk took me on a tour of the old Jewish cemetery, just out of town, highlighting known relatives buried there. Afterwards, Museum Educator Dorisz Macher took me on a tour of the old synagogue building, pointing out the many historic features, such as the large original Chanukiah and the synagogue's stained-glass windows. Dorisz had also conducted research on the Steinthal family, which she kindly shared with me, and provided copies. We drank tea in the museum offices as we shared each other's discoveries, including my first impressions of what I had unearthed in the archives in Dessau-Roßlau. The Steinthal family is important to Gröbzig, as Prof Heymann Steinthal is their most famous son, and many Steinthals were important in the town's history.

The Cologne Jewish archaeological museum (MiQua) is currently undergoing construction, a short walk from the Cologne Cathedral, and right next door to the Gothic Cologne city hall in the old Jewish quarter. It is a fascinating project, being built around and above archaeological excavations of the old Jewish quarter. In a couple of years, I look forward to returning to see the completed building and exhibits. Dr Christiane Twiehaus, Head of Department for Jewish History and Culture at MiQua, very kindly took me on a tour of Jewish Cologne, including highlighting Jewish and antisemitic elements in the art and windows within Cologne Cathedral. Christiane remains a very supportive and helpful adviser.

Gröbzig Synagogue Museum
(Photo credit: David Marlow)

Hurdles to overcome

I inherited no diaries, letters, old documents nor siddurim with milestone dates recorded inside, like some other families.[10] My parents and their parents were long gone, and my parents had no siblings. It felt like there was not much to start with.

Over generations, I found that some family members had divorced and remarried, sometimes several times, like my great (x4) grandfather Michael Lazarus (1729-1813) who had four wives (sequentially). It is hard enough to find records for a Jewish community in a small town in Germany in the 1700s, without also trying to identify four wives, and confirm which children belonged

---

[10] For example, as was common in the past, my partner Dr Erica Cervini's great grandmother Rose Pearlman wrote details of key family events and simchas inside the cover of her siddur.

Uncovering their Names and Stories:

to whom. Female divorcees could have remarried, taking a different surname, making tracing them over time almost impossible.

In Germany, many records were decentralised to churches and synagogues, and in the case of Jews, burning down synagogues on Kristallnacht did not just erase the synagogues, but the records they contained. About 267 synagogues were destroyed on Kristallnacht.[11] Also Allied bombing of cities did not help with the survival of records. In a synagogue, normally you can find plaques with names of past members, donors, presidents and rabbis, as well as registers of births, deaths and marriages. That is all destroyed if a synagogue burns to the ground.

In the records I did find, there was inconsistency with names, sometimes spelled in various ways. Surnames could also change spelling by generation. Handwriting was often very hard to read, but so was my mother's handwriting, so maybe I had a head start. Gravestones were often destroyed, missing or damaged by Nazis or the ravages of time. Many records are not yet online, borders and countries have changed frequently over centuries, there can often be typographical errors through OCR [12] scanning of records, and typographical errors from the digitisation process often due to unclear handwriting in the original, all made life complicated. (Thank you to the volunteers who give their time to photograph, record data from, and translate information from historical records and gravestones!)

And of course, virtually everything was in German, apart from some Hebrew often on my Jewish family's gravestones, but mostly German. When talking to friends about what I was doing, the first thing they asked was whether I spoke German. My usual answer was, "Ein bisschen, aber nicht so gut", meaning "a little, but not so good." I have my high school German, unused much since, but it was generally enough to identify whether a document might be useful. Google Translate and Google Lens, though imperfect, frequently helped me out, sometimes augmented by my Compact Oxford German Dictionary. When in doubt, the Genealogical Translations

---

[11] 'The Kindertransport and Refugees', Learning about the Holocaust and Genocides, Holocaust Memorial Day Trust
[12] Optical Character Recognition

Facebook Group members were very kind and professional in helping to translate genealogical or newspaper records.

Reading the script

But to get to the translation step, you first need to decipher the German handwriting and often the printed letters are not so straightforward. The use of the 'Fraktur' or 'Deutsche Schrift' font was common in German print, which has quite a gothic and very different look to the modern eye. It was created by Hieronymous Andreae in the early 1600s and became the standard in 1871 with the new German Empire. It was the first to introduce the 'eszett' (ß) and umlauts (ä, ö, ü) which characterise German script today.[13]

'Kurrent' is ironically an old form of German handwritten script, which can often be indecipherable to the inexperienced reader, like me. It was common from the 15th century until the early 20th century. Kurrent means runs together.[14]

'Sütterlin' is a more modern German script, based on Kurrent, which was created in 1911 by Ludwig Sütterlin (1865-1917), and taught in German schools from 1915 to 1941. This was in turn replaced in 1941 with 'Deutsche Normalschrift' or German normal handwriting.

Thanks to FamilySearch and its owner, The Church of Jesus Christ of Latter-Day Saints, a leader in the global genealogical space, there is information and cheat sheets on the various handwriting styles and gothic fonts available online for free. These guides help make the reading of old German print and handwriting in documents, letters and other materials a much more achievable process.[15]

Online, I also found 'Transkribus', which is a handwritten text recognition (HTR) software system that can be used to decipher historical handwritten German documents. Like anything based on

---

[13] 'The History of Old German Cursive Alphabet and Typefaces', Karen Lodder, Germangirlinamerica.com
[14] ibid.
[15] 'Handwriting Guide: German Gothic', Resource Guide, Family History Library, Salt Lake City Utah and 'Germany Handwriting', FamilySearch

Uncovering their Names and Stories:

Artificial Intelligence, you need to be careful using it, and I would not recommend relying on it 100%. Mistakes are possible, but it is useful.[16] Anything that can help clarify seemingly impenetrable handwriting is a godsend when dealing with historical documents.

Google Lens was often helpful on my iPhone in reading German, Czech, Lithuanian, Hebrew or Polish text that I found a serious challenge. It does not get everything 100% correct, but it is quick and easy. It helped identify passages of text relevant to my family history, which I could then get another eye or piece of software to review.

Jewish names

Before the 1800s, Jews in Germany tended to use the traditional Jewish naming method of a given name and the name of their father, such as David son of Chaim (David ben Chaim – my Hebrew name)[17]. This is called Patronymics, where the first name of the father is used as the surname of the children, which results in a different surname each generation, as demonstrated in my Lazarus – Steinthal family.[18] Most Jews across the German states did not adopt hereditary family names until required by law. Orthodox Jews still today use their 'Jewish names' for religious practices and when being called-up in Synagogue, while using their 'normal' or 'hereditary' name in everyday life. I am David ben Chaim when called up in shule.

By the 1820s, most German states were extending civil rights to Jews and were making hereditary surnames mandatory. It started in 1787, when Joseph II of Austria passed a law mandating family surnames for Jews in his domain and requiring official records to be maintained in German. Other jurisdictions followed suit in the early 1800s, for

---

[16] Transkribus.ai/
[17] David ben Chaim is the author's Hebrew name
[18] Jewish Surnames and Patronymics - Tracing Your Ancestors before they had Surnames, Dr Thomas Fürth, JewishGen Youtube, 2 June 2022

example, Prussia in 1811, Anhalt-Dessau in 1822, and French possessions in German lands in 1808 and 1813.[19]

Many family genealogists had assumed that virtually everyone in the Steinthal family tree held by the Leo Baeck Centre had the Steinthal family name, but the original records in the Protected Jews archives of the Dessau-Roßlau Archives show that my Lazarus - Steinthal family didn't adopt the Steinthal surname until 1821. Eleasar in the family tree was formally known as Lazarus Philipp in these official documents. His children had the surname Lazarus. In 1821, his grandson David Lazarus initiated the adoption of the Steinthal family name for the family.[20]

Without fixed surnames, identifying a person such as Moshe ben Joshua was problematic for contemporary government bureaucrats, and certainly for future family historians and genealogists. Many Joshuas could have a son named Moshe, and if you are trying to find your Moshe's father, on a grave or on marriage documents, how can you be sure. Hereditary surnames certainly help with identification. Undoubtedly, German principalities at the time were more concerned about identification for legal and taxation purposes, rather than the needs of 21st century genealogists, but I thank them for their efforts nonetheless.

Naming after family members

It was, and often is a common tradition for Ashkenazi Jews to name babies after a deceased relative.[21] In this way, a baby could be named after a deceased grandparent or aunt for example, but not the still living father or mother. This is not a Torah-based requirement, but a custom that started around 100-200 CE and was common by the 12th century. It often happened, by then, that a name would repeat every

---

[19] 'Genealogical Resources for German Jewish Ancestry', George E Arnstein Ph.D, chapter VII, Germanic Genealogy, A Guide to Worldwide Sources and Migration Patterns, Dr Edward R Brandt et.al., Germanic Genealogy Society, St Paul MN, April 1995

[20] Protected Jews archives of the LASA Archives in Dessau-Roßlau (Z 44, C 15 No. 106)

[21] 'Naming Traditions', JewishGen, slide 7 of 94

second generation, and we can see that occur frequently in my family tree over generations.

Helen or Helena, Julius, David, Elkan, Bella, Eduard, Moses and other names reappear after a generation. In the more recent generations, the babies often received a middle name in honour of a deceased grandparent, such as my nephew Michael Zev Nathan. But he is an exception in my family in recent years, as naming babies after past relatives has fallen away in my Marlow extended family. This may be because we did not know three of our four grandparents, and both our parents did not have siblings. So, we had no uncles or aunts and little to no memory of grandparents to help name babies.

It is such a common convention in Orthodox Jewish circles, that when I was preparing to get married, and I disclosed that my father's Hebrew name was Chaim ben Chaim (Chaim son of Chaim), it seriously perplexed Rabbi Sholem Gutnick who was officiating. He increased the questioning level to ensure that I really was Jewish. How could a Chaim name a son Chaim? It should be noted that their German first names were different. Dad was Heinz (later Henry), and my grandfather was Hermann. My middle name of Henry, named after my father, also made Rabbi Gutnick's brow furrow. How could I have been named after my living father? My parents were not very traditional.

Sephardi Jews, however, traditionally name babies after living grandparents, commonly in a fixed order. "The first son is named for the father's father, the first daughter for the father's mother. The next son is named in honor of his mother's father and the second girl for her maternal grandmother."[22]

---

[22] ibid.

3.0 My family history research road trip (Ausflug)[23]

Ausflug - Berlin

A key part of my research took me far away from my desk. I undertook a three-week self-drive family history research tour around Germany, visiting towns and cities which were important to the story of my family. My objective was to get a feel for the places my ancestors had lived and worked. I wanted to be where they had family dinners, gone to school, celebrated Jewish festivals, attended synagogue, visited on holidays, shopped and plied their trades. An extensive and busy road trip or Ausflug was planned and undertaken in March 2024.

Map of my family history research road trip starting and ending in Berlin:

(Map created by author in MapChart)

Early in undertaking my family history research, I thought I might end up visiting Wuppertal and Berlin, where I believed my families

---

[23] Road trip

Uncovering their Names and Stories:

were from, based on what I was told by my parents. We understood that Dad was from Wuppertal and Mum was from Berlin. But it was never going to be so simple. As I uncovered ancestors going back generation by generation, I found more hamlets, towns, and cities across northern and central Germany where my family had lived, not to mention towns in the old East Prussia and over the border in Lithuania. In the end, I undertook a three-week self-driving tour around over thirty key towns and cities where my ancestors had lived, worked and generally experienced the ups and downs of being a Jew in Germany.

I flew nearly 16,000 km from Melbourne to Berlin, 32 hours from take-off at Tullamarine Airport in Melbourne to landing at Berlin Brandenburg Airport, and then driving 3,096 km around Germany. To put the drive into perspective, the distance I drove around cities and towns in Germany is significantly further than driving from London to Istanbul, Turkiye; or New York City across much of the USA to San Antonio, Texas.

I wanted to retrace the footsteps of those ancestors, the book dealers, rabbis, merchants, traders, shopkeepers, teachers, bankers, parents, aunts, uncles, soldiers, clothes-cutters, scholars, bakers, butchers and their families who lived and migrated through German speaking lands. This involved some short visits to some very small towns and hamlets, and longer stays in bigger towns and cities.

Flying to Germany on Friday 9 March 2024, while I looked out the window of my British Airways plane, I had significant anxiety about landing in Berlin. The anxiety continued through short stops in Perth and London. I remembered that my parents and my maternal grandparents only escaped Germany by the skin of their teeth. My grandfather Oskar had been arrested by the Gestapo in Berlin and locked up in the nearby Sachsenhausen Concentration Camp. From at least 1933, it was not a happy place for my family. And Germany generally had ended badly for over a hundred of my family members.

My anxiety only increased as the plane landed at Berlin Brandenburg Airport, with me thinking about the history of my family in Berlin and elsewhere in Germany, especially through the Holocaust. I knew much had changed, but parts of history arose in my mind. As we taxied on the tarmac to the gate, we slowly passed a stationary Israeli

El Al plane. It reminded me that modern day Germany was now one of the better friends of Israel. I took this as a very good sign, and I was somewhat relieved.

I was also not embarking on a relaxing holiday. Dozens of towns and cities, researching in archives and libraries, hunting for signs of relatives in many cemeteries, and visiting Holocaust museums and memorials is not like a relaxing holiday by the pool in Bali or a shopping expedition in London, nor people-watching while sipping coffee outside a café in Paris. But I did take a couple of days off from my research focus to explore Prague. I could not resist Prague when I saw it was only a two-hour drive from Dresden, and I could visit the site of the Theresienstadt Concentration Camp and Ghetto along the way, sitting between Liebstadt in Germany near the Czech border and Prague in the Czech Republic. Theresienstadt had been an ominous end for many family members.

After fulfilling the usual administrative and immigration requirements at the airport, I picked up my Opel rental car from Europcar, which would be my research headquarters for the next three weeks. Its navigation system allowed me to easily find the smallest of hamlets and most hidden of city streets, nooks and crannies. I was not worried about driving on the 'wrong' side of the road, as I had driven on the right-hand side of the road before, in both Los Angeles and Koh Samui in Thailand. But driving around the autobahns of Germany was an education, as well as an adventure. They have their own, apparently unwritten rules and many sections of the autobahns displayed a tolerance for frightening speeds.

Berlin has much to attract visitors, in the way of shopping and fashion, nightclubs, and other activities. But I was there for the history and links to my family. Unfortunately for my anxiety levels, much of the Nazi past of Berlin are major attractions in Berlin, though most, if not all, symbols and monuments of Nazism are long gone. But visiting the remains of Hitler's Bunker which is now largely the site of a car park, the impressive Memorial to the Murdered Jews of Europe and Information Centre (Holocaust Memorial), the very educational Topography of Terror Museum, displays at the Berlin Jewish Museum, and the historically important Reichstag, made the Nazi era quite vivid.

Uncovering their Names and Stories:

I found my hotel with ease, the very comfortable NH Collection Berlin Mitte Checkpoint Charlie, close to the centre of town, despite my car navigation system not yet working. The signs on the road from the airport, pointing towards Berlin Mitte (Central Berlin) were very helpful. When I connected my mobile phone to the internet, I found an email from Frau Anke Boeck, an angel of an archivist from the Saxony-Anhalt Landesarchiv in Dessau-Roßlau. They had fabulous original records on Protected Jews from the 1700s and 1800s, which would reap wonderful new information on my Lazarus – Steinthal ancestors. Thankful for the exciting news, I immediately added the archive to my list to visit while driving between Magdeburg and Gröbzig in eastern Germany.

From the hotel, it was less than a 15-minute walk to my first stop, the historic site of Hitler's Bunker, the Führerbunker, where the madman presided over the last days of the demise of the Nazi regime. I must admit I was thinking nasty thoughts as I read the information boards at the site of Hitler's Bunker, near where he married Eva Braun and committed suicide in 1945. The Führerbunker was built in the garden of the Reich Chancellery in 1943 to provide better protection from Allied bombing, than did the then existing bomb shelter. The Bunker found itself in the Russian zone of occupied Berlin after the war. The Soviet authorities blew up the Bunker in 1947, and it was later levelled and covered with concrete rubble, and the entrance buried. As I stood there, reading the information boards, tour groups were learning the lessons of the Third Reich from tour guides in an amazing range of languages, while I thought about what devastation one evil man with his hateful and obsequious henchmen had wrought.

About a five-minute walk from the Bunker site sits the Berlin Memorial to the Murdered Jews of Europe, just near the 210-hectare Tiergarten park, the Central Park of Berlin, which also contains the Berlin Zoo. The memorial was designed by American architect Peter Eisenman and inaugurated on 10 May 2005. It is a majestic, substantial and imposing work of architecture. What you see at first is a field of rectangular concrete pillars. They are "a rigid grid structure composed of 2,711 concrete pillars, or stelae, each 95 centimeters wide and 2.375 meters long, with heights varying from zero to 4 meters. The pillars are spaced 95 centimeters apart to allow only for individual passage through the grid."[24] On average, the individual stela weigh 8 tonne, while the heaviest weighs 16 tonne. It is a massive and impressive construction.

The site it sits on used to house two palaces in the Ministerial Gardens. The area had contained over time the palace of the Count of Schwerin, various ministries, President Hindenburg's official residence and headquarters, the ministry of the Prussian royal household, and the headquarters of the Nazi Propaganda Minister Dr Joseph Goebbels. The buildings and gardens did not survive the Allied bombing of 1945, the clearance of the land by the Soviets and the construction of the Berlin Wall.

On the architect's website, it says, "In this monument there is no goal, no end, no working one's way in or out. The duration of an individual's experience of it grants no further understanding, since understanding the Holocaust is impossible."[25] I explored the memorial for quite some time, walking around and between the stelae. I wondered whether each stela, amongst the sea of stelae, represented a Jewish community lost in the Holocaust. I then looked for the entrance to the underground information centre.

The American cultural critic Edward Rothstein writing in the *New York Times* echoed my perceptions on my visit to the old Jewish cemetery in Prague two weeks after my visit to Berlin, that the pillars at the memorial are reminiscent of the "tilted gravestones of Prague's ancient Jewish Cemetery, only here they are anonymous and ominous."[26]

As I walked down the stairs to the entry of the excellent information centre underneath the memorial, I found it heartening to see so many diverse people from around the world and around Germany visiting, learning about what happened. The lessons of the past must be remembered. The exhibition typically has half a million visitors annually, who learn about the persecution and murder of European Jewry, and the places where the events took place.

---

[24] Eisenman Architects website
[25] ibid.
[26] 'In Berlin, Teaching Germany's Jewish History', Edward Rothstein, New York Times, 1 May 2009

Uncovering their Names and Stories:

Memorial to the Murdered Jewish of Europe in Berlin
(Photo credit: David Marlow)

I wholeheartedly agree with Edward Rothstein when he wrote, comparing the information centre to the striking memorial above it, that the "below-ground information centre is even more powerful. The Holocaust is historically outlined and then made personally vivid. Embedded in the floor of a darkened room are illuminated panels inscribed with letters from the period, around which you walk as if navigating the memorial's pillars, until you enter, in dazed shock, another gallery that traces the way specific Jewish families from all over Europe headed toward destruction."[27]

After walking around the underground exhibits, allowing some time for sombre contemplation, a schnitzel lunch at a local diner which seemed to be run by the cast of the Sopranos, some note-taking and a fifteen-minute walk, I found the Topography of Terror History Museum. Its internal and external exhibits were very interesting, whether you were experienced with the Nazi period, or a newbie. It is excellent, a much better museum than its name might suggest. I

---

[27] ibid.

must admit it sounds more like a carnival ride than a history museum. But it is an extremely serious and educational museum, with excellent detail focused on the history of the SS and Gestapo, covering the period from the start of the Nazi regime to the end of the war. It is built on the site of the old Gestapo, SS and Reich Security Headquarters from 1934 to 1945, on what was Prinz-Albrecht Strasse. The street is now called Niederkirchnerstrasse, named after Käthe Niederkirchner (1909-1944), the German Communist resistance activist who was shot by Nazi firing squad in Ravensbruck Concentration Camp in 1944.[28]

The outside Exhibition Trench runs along the excavated cellar wall of the old Gestapo headquarters building and provides exhibits on the history of Berlin under the Nazi regime, 1933-1945. I walked along the straight path of the exhibition, following the story of the Nazi takeover of Berlin and the various key events of the period. I wondered how the events affected my Kraft, Elkan, Steinthal and other family members at the time. This included my mother, her parents, her uncles and aunts, and various cousins.

I followed the path up to the new exhibition building. The old building on Prinz-Albrecht Strasse had been the 120-bed Hotel Prinz Albrecht before Reichsführer-SS Heinrich Himmler took it over for the SS Headquarters.[29] The original buildings were partially destroyed during the later part of World War 2 and finally completely demolished during the Soviet occupation. The new building's exhibits tell the story of the terror planned and inflicted out of this space: the elimination of political adversaries, the Aryanization programs, the expansion of the empire, and the despicable acts perpetrated in Nazi Germany and across occupied Europe. It is quite a chilling and more than a little sobering, if not depressing museum. But it is educational and comprehensive.

I took a short walk from there, investigating some Cold War era sites, such as a museum of East German cars, pieces of the old Berlin Wall and Checkpoint Charlie. The latter is now a remarkably

---

[28] 'Käthe Niederkirchner', Gedenkstatte Deutscher Widerstand
[29] Topography of Terror: Gestapo, SS and Reichssicherheitshauptamt, Reinhardt Rürup (ed.), Verag Willmuth Arenhövel, Berlin, 2000

Uncovering their Names and Stories:

commercialised tourist trap, rather than the romantic border between East and West Berlin I imagined from espionage movies. The tourists seemed unaware that the traffic, while trying to pose for a good photo or selfie, had replaced the East German border guards as the major threat in the area.

I soon arrived at the Berlin Jewish Museum on Lindenstrasse, conveniently only about a ten-minute walk from my hotel. The museum is situated on the site of what was the main office of the Central Association of German Citizens of Jewish Faith (Centralverein deutscher Staatsbürger jüdischen Glaubens).[30] The Centralverein was founded in Berlin in 1893, to combat the rise of antisemitism in the German Empire. By 1926 it had about 60,000 members.

Unlike at the Topography of Terror Museum, there were some significant security processes in place at the museum. Having worked in a couple of Jewish community buildings in Melbourne, I was very comfortable with the security.

The Jewish Museum Berlin was designed by the Polish-Jewish architect Daniel Libeskind and opened in 2001.[31] It aims to tell the story of the "social, political and cultural history of the Jews in Germany" from the fourth century to today. The new section is housed next to the site of the old Prussian Court of Justice, which was built in 1735, and is now the entrance to the new building.[32]

One of the reasons for building the museum was to 'un-erase' the contribution of German Jews from Berlin and German history.

After walking through the entrance, I locked my canvas day bag in a locker and passed through the old Baroque Kollegienhaus.[33] This building was built during the reign of Friedrich Wilhelm I and now forms the entry building for the Berlin Jewish Museum. I walked down the stairs into the underground section, which connects you to

---

[30] <u>Fatherland and the Jews: Two Pamphlets by Alfred Wiener</u>, 1919 and 1924, Alfred Wiener, Granta, London, 2022, p.62
[31] Libeskind also designed the reconstructed Ground Zero in New York City.
[32] Studio Libeskind website
[33] Kollegienhaus = college house

the new building. The stairs lead to three underground routes. I first explored the Holocaust Tower, second the Garden of Exile and Emigration, and then through to the Stair of Continuity. The exhibition spaces are long and dramatic, like the Jewish experience in German history.

This museum had been one of my major target destinations for the trip. It turned out to be artistically and architecturally very interesting, but it did not help advance my detailed knowledge or thinking as much as I would have hoped. A friend who visited the museum a few months after me expressed similar sentiments.

It would be extremely useful for the novice. Unfortunately, the library was closed on the days I was in Berlin, as were the archives which include the Leo Baeck Institute Berlin archives. My dealings online and via email with the Leo Baeck Institute were, nevertheless, very supportive and helpful to my research. The museum building complex is marvellous, including the glass courtyard. Ten out of ten to the architect.

But the museum felt emotionally stunted to me, especially given the rich history of Jews in German-speaking lands, let alone the missed opportunities presented by the history of the Nazi regime for strong emotional connections, from book burnings and Kristallnacht to the deportations. The administration at the museum could learn a great deal from Yad Vashem or the information centre at the Memorial to the Murdered Jewish of Europe.

Or even the Bebelplatz library memorial. The Bebelplatz is a square, a fifteen-minute walk east along Unter den Linden from the Brandenburg Gate. Under a glass floor, there is an installation designed by Israeli artist Micha Ullman, commemorating the Nazi book burning of 1933. Underneath is an underground room with empty bookshelves, with space for 20,000 books representing the approximately 20,000 books burned there on 10 May 1933. This memorial was opened on 20 March 1995. Text on bronze plates explains the context for the installation including the tragically prophetic words from Heinrich Heine in German, "That was a prelude, but when they burn books, they end up burning people too."

Some months after my visit to Berlin, I came across Edward Rothstein's harsh but not unreasonable comments on the Jewish

Uncovering their Names and Stories:

Museum in the *New York Times*, "There may be worse Jewish museums in the world than the Jüdisches Museum Berlin, which opened in 2001. But it is difficult to imagine that any could be as uninspiring and banal, particularly given its pedigree and promise."[34] This seemed to gel closely with my feelings during my experience of the museum.

Berlin Jewish Museum
(Photo credit: David Marlow)

One day in the museum at lunchtime, while I recharged myself with a very acceptable pastrami bagel and cup of tea, I observed many young German students being led through the courtyard. They were learning about the history of Jews in Germany. Despite my concerns about the missed opportunities with the museum, it was terrific to see young people learning about the past. Hopefully, this would help counteract the Holocaust deniers venting their nonsense online.

It was also heartening to see that on my first day in Berlin, it was International Women's Day, and it was taken very seriously in the city. Most shops were closed, and it was like a public holiday, as a

---

[34] 'In Berlin, Teaching Germany's Jewish History', Edward Rothstein, New York Times, 1 May 2009

German-speaking Chinese gentleman explained to me, as he kindly helped me use a public parking meter. There was also a very large women's protest at the Brandenburg Gate where I felt very outnumbered, despite some other tourists. While there, I thought about the Nazi rallies that used to take place in front of the Brandenburg Gate. But that did not stop me having my first Bratwurst on a small bread roll for the trip, near the Gate, which was delicious. As the poet George Herbert said, "living well is the best revenge."

The Reichstag was barely a five-minute walk north from the Brandenburg Gate. It is the home of the German Bundestag, the lower house of the German parliamentary system, and was completed in 1894. The famous Reichstag fire of 1933, supposedly orchestrated by an arson attack by communists, gave Hitler the excuse he needed to eliminate communists and socialists from the German political system. He hated communism, and they were his first major target. Many ended up in concentration camps. The building was restored and modernised in the 1960s and was reconstructed with a massive glass dome in the 1990s.

After a couple of very full days of exploration in Berlin, I planned what I thought of as a 'Beauty and the Beast' day, visiting Sachsenhausen Concentration Camp, a forty-minute drive north of Berlin, and Schwerin a further two-hour drive northwest, on the Sunday. Sachsenhausen was the beast, and lovely Schwerin was the beauty to help alleviate the emotional impact of the concentration camp. It worked. I felt terribly depressed after several hours at Sachsenhausen, walking through the heart-rending gates, and seeing the horrifying exhibits in the camp museum on how prisoners were treated, including the murders, beatings, torture, starvation and other mistreatment. Just being in the place of such enormous horrors left me in dark spirits.

One exhibit described how the prisoners, "were subject to the arbitrary and absolute power of the SS guards. Especially from 1939 onwards, the beginning of the war, hardly anyone could hope to be released. In a cynical welcome speech, the camp commander told

Uncovering their Names and Stories:

new arrivals that the only exit from the camp would be through the chimney of the crematorium."[35]

Sachsenhausen Concentration Camp
(Photo credit: David Marlow)

After driving 190 km northwest from Sachsenhausen, I found myself in picturesque Schwerin. I slowly lightened up with the fairy-tale-like old town of Schwerin. I walked around the huge tranquil lakes and magnificent castle on the expansive Schweriner See, I watched the ducks glide across the water. Walking to and around Schloss Schwerin improved my morale substantially.[36] Nevertheless, Sachsenhausen cast a shadow over my thoughts for days.

By nightfall, I had started to reach mental equilibrium. After dinner, strolling back to my hotel opposite the Ostorfer See, I passed a young man wearing a 'slap-dancing' costume. He was walking the other way. I walked just a little faster to escape the memories it brought up. It is his culture, not mine.

---

[35] Exhibit in the Sachsenhausen Concentration Camp Memorial and Museum
[36] Schloss = castle

Schloss Schwerin
(Photo credit: David Marlow)

Ausflug - Northern Germany

In the morning, I had breakfast at my hotel, the historic and centrally located Niederlandischer Hof hotel. While admiring the ducks on the Ostorfer See, I wondered how people could do such evils to other people. Given the experiences of their families, how could my parents always love so many things German. Although Dad certainly had a more positive view of Germans than Mum. Dad's school mates at his 'commercial school' supported him while Mum was forced to sit at the back of her class, as a Jew, and then was finally kicked out of school altogether. This followed her always and she resented it. Dad loved going to the Hofbräuhaus in Melbourne, as he possibly went to similar restaurants in Germany before the war, while Mum was not as keen. My mother would sometimes glare at elderly Germans, seeming to ask with her eyes, "what did you do in the war?" My daughter Brittany inherited the ability to give that look. Neither could ever play poker professionally.

As I enjoyed the view, I started to think about how my family had hundreds of years of history in German-speaking lands, and the Nazi

Uncovering their Names and Stories:

years were a relatively very short period of that time. They had holidays along German lakes and rivers; pleasant times at home with family and friends; celebrated births, barmitzvahs and weddings; exchanged pleasantries with neighbours and workmates or schoolmates; raised families; and pursued careers and developed businesses. They may have sometimes faced antisemitism and discrimination, but nothing was like 1933-1945. That was a period that decimated my family.

After breakfast, I visited the old, small Schwerin synagogue, and then drove west to Lübeck, which felt like the marzipan capital of the world. Many shops and cafes were dedicated to the sweet goodness of marzipan. Lübeck is the southern-most city on the Baltic Sea, and thus far north in Germany, taking me closer to my destination for the day, Hamburg where my paternal grandfather Oskar was born. The old gate to the city of Lübeck is very impressive and dates to the 1400s. There are also many medieval buildings still standing in the old city. I enjoyed a marzipan-flavoured coffee, before leaving for the drive to the Ohlsdorf Jewish Cemetery in Hamburg. I would be looking for traces of ancestors, particularly my grandfather's Nathan family.

The Ohlsdorf Jewish Cemetery has 18,000 graves and sits next to the general Ohlsdorf Cemetery, which is the largest cemetery in the world according to the city's marketing.[37] But billiongrave.com says it is the fourth largest cemetery in the world.[38] Either way, it is huge. There are around 1.4 million people buried in the general cemetery, spread around 4 million square metres.[39]

My great grandmother, Bella Nathan nee Hirsch (1848-1919), mother of my maternal grandpa Oskar is buried in the Ohlsdorf Jewish Cemetery. She is in section ZX-11. I found the section, which is quite large, but could not find her grave. Nevertheless, it was very moving to know that I had found the area where she rested, and I placed a pebble on a section marker. I thought about her raising her five children, including her baby Oskar.

---

[37] Ohlsdorf Cemetery, hamburg.com
[38] 'The 7 Largest Cemeteries in the World', Billiongraves.com
[39] Ohlsdorf Cemetery, hamburg.com

I also photographed some gravestones with Nathan and Hirsch surnames, just in case I would later find connections. But those surnames are a bit like Smith and Jones in Jewish cemeteries in Germany.

Ohlsdorf Jewish Cemetery, Hamburg
(Photo credit: David Marlow)

Afterwards, I drove deeper into town and later walked around central Hamburg. It felt quite emotive, knowing that I was seeing streets, rivers and buildings that Oskar would also have seen and known. I also found connection to my roots, having an excellent meal at a German fish restaurant, and Bismarck herring and herring salad from the breakfast buffet the next morning.

I was looking for the site of a particular photo I had seen online, of a very attractive old building, the Wasserschloss, sitting on the waterways of Hamburg. I showed the picture to the hotel concierge with little hope. But with detailed and excited instructions in unintelligible German from the concierge, I followed the direction of his pointed finger and walked down to the Speicherstadt.

Uncovering their Names and Stories:

The Wasserschloss building in the Speicherstadt, Hamburg
(Photo credit: David Marlow)

The Speicherstadt is an old section of Hamburg, sitting on the waterways which ultimately lead to the North Sea, providing terrific views. It is the largest warehouse district in the world and is possibly the most stunning. It was built from 1883 to 1927. The Speicherstadt forms part of Germany's 40th UNESCO World Heritage Site.[40] These very substantial buildings, standing on oak timber-pile foundations, were certainly around in the days of many of my ancestors. After an extensive walk around the area, I found the Wasserschloss.[41] I took a few photos, including a selfie, and celebrated my photographic win with a good coffee nearby.

---

[40] Speicherstadt, Größtes Lagerhausenensemble der Welt, hamburg.de

[41] Wasserschloss translates as 'water castle'

The Wasserschloss is a beautiful, moated castle-like structure, sitting on a peninsula between two canals, the Wandrahmsfleet and Holländischbrookfleet. It was built between 1905 and 1907, and is a famous, and well-photographed landmark in the Speicherstadt. It was originally used for accommodation and as a workshop for the winch-keepers, who were responsible for the maintenance and repair of the area's hydraulic storage winches. The winches were used to hoist goods up to the storage floors of the warehouses. Today the Wasserschloss houses a tea shop and café on the ground floor.[42] It was there in the time of my grandfather Oskar Nathan and my great grandfather Simon Nathan, and I wondered if they too admired the same views in their day.

During the rest of the day, I visited other places my ancestors may have seen and been, including the remains of the Poolstrasse Synagogue, the beautiful old Rathaus and surrounds, the Hamburg Municipal History Museum, and took a long walk to the very large Jewish cemetery in Altona. Poolstrasse must have been a very Jewish neighbourhood by the start of World War 2, given the large number of Stolpersteine scattered up and down the street, outside many of its buildings.

In Hamburg, I thought frequently about my grandfather, World War 1 veteran Oskar Elkan, who I never met, but whose grave I visited in the Melbourne General Cemetery, where he was buried in 1948. He was born Oskar Nathan in Hamburg and changed his surname to Elkan in 1921.

With a two-hour drive south, I travelled from the home of my Nathan ancestors in Hamburg to the home of my Isenstein ancestors in Hildesheim, just south of Hannover.

The old city of Hildesheim is full of many beautiful medieval buildings. The centre of the old city is the town hall on Rathausstraße, which is just meters from the modern city mall shopping strip. Rathausstraße dates to 1268 and used to be called Hosenstrasse. The mall features familiar stores like Aldi and Woolworths, a range of

---

[42] 'New Life in the Castle', Andy Lindemann, Quartier-Magazin, No. 16 (12/2011-02/2012), Hamburg

shops like any modern city, and a shop selling Bismarck herring rolls. My homeland.

Rathausstraße, Hildesheim
(Photo credit: David Marlow)

I then drove to the Jewish cemetery in Moritzberg in Hildesheim, a small but very well-maintained cemetery, surrounded by thick woodland and a few houses by the roadside.

From Hildesheim, I drove 30 minutes north to the city of Hannover. Both were homes to my Isenstein ancestors, who initially lived in Hildesheim and then gradually most moved to Hannover. My great grandmother Frieda Isenstein was born in Hannover and married the merchant Selmar Kraft. They settled together in Leipzig, after living for a time in Stassfurt near Selmar's birthplace Calbe.

I spent a productive couple of days visiting places in Hannover where my relatives may have lived, prayed or been buried.

Ausflug – North Rhine-Westphalia

Wuppertal Schwebebahn
(Photo credit: David Marlow)

The next city was hot on my to-do-list. Wuppertal was Dad's self-proclaimed hometown, though he was born in Pillau, East Prussia. At the breakfast buffet in Hannover, I filled my cargo pants pockets with bread rolls and mandarins for the day's journey. Wuppertal was a three-hour drive west, avoiding super-fast-moving Porsches, BMWs and Audis on the Autobahn. This was the start of retracing the footsteps of many of my father's side of the family, the Marowilskys and Lennhoffs. I had spent the first seven days on my mother's side of the family.

Parts of Wuppertal looked like they were out of a steampunk movie or graphic novel. It is highly industrialised, featuring the impressive Schwebebahn hanging monorail system, that dates to 1901. The Schwebebahn has 20 stops and is used as public transport along its 13 km route. I found several parts of the city that were very relevant to the story of my father, his Marowilsky parents and my Lennhoff ancestors.

Uncovering their Names and Stories:

That evening, I drove fifty minutes to Düsseldorf and back, to visit the Old Slaughterhouse Memorial Centre at Düsseldorf University. It had very informative exhibits and contained the old beef slaughterhouse or abattoir where my Marowilsky grandparents were held and processed after their arrest, as part of their deportation process. It was educational but appallingly depressing. It was quite overwhelming to read about what they went through. Dr Joachim Schröder, Director of the Memorial Centre requested a photo of Hermann and Meta Marowilsky, which I have since provided, once I could confirm their photos in my father's childhood photo album. Dr Schröder has provided some terrific research advice and valuable documents on my grandparents.

The next morning, from Wuppertal I drove 45 minutes south to Cologne, which sits across the Rhine River, to meet Dr Christiane Twiehaus, Head of the Department of Jewish History and Culture of MiQua. MiQua is the Jewish Museum in the Archaeological Quarter of Cologne. After seeing information about the new museum online, I had approached them by email about a visit a couple of months before my trip, but they advised me that the museum was still under construction. Nevertheless, Dr Twiehaus very kindly offered to take me on a personal tour of Jewish Cologne. And I am very thankful for the very informative tour, especially when she was to be flying overseas later the same day.

Dr Twiehaus' tour included the old Jewish quarter as well as an in depth and very informative tour of the Cologne Cathedral, a major religious and tourist mecca in Germany. A highlight, if that is the right word, was the identification and explanation of many antisemitic features within the artworks in the cathedral.

Cologne Cathedral is the most visited landmark in Germany with over six million visitors annually, and it felt like many of them were there the day I visited. It is also the tallest twin-spired church in the world, the second tallest church in Europe, and the third tallest church in the world.[43] It is no wonder that it was crowded on that cold day in March.

---

[43] '8 Tallest Cathedrals in the World' SAHC Histructural, 8 November 2018

The artworks and artefacts in place in the cathedral include a depiction of Jesus being flogged by two Jewish men in "plate-shaped funnel" hats, suggesting that Jesus was beaten by Jews and not the Romans. Other items depict opponents of Jesus being consistent with old antisemitic tropes. There is a 'Judensau' (Jew's pig) and "extremely defamatory and repulsive portrayals of a ritual murder" in the choir stalls, which date to the 14th century. The choir stall screen depicts the 'problematic' subject of Jewish conversion.[44] While some donated cathedral windows attest to the contributions of Jewish donors, they also include antisemitic stereotypes.

Contentiously, instead of removing the offending artworks, the cathedral leadership has chosen to educate. Cathedral staff in concert with the Jewish community produced a booklet to explain to visitors about the historical context of the art pieces.[45] I did not see the booklet on my visit, but I did find quite honest information on the Cologne Cathedral website and Christian Network Europe online. I just hope that the many tours and school groups receive the appropriate education.

I do worry that leaving the antisemitic artwork in place perpetuates the communication of antisemitic tropes and reinforcement of anti-Jewish myths, which could lead to antisemitic actions. Despite this, it is heartening to see that the cathedral leadership has worked with the Jewish community. Indeed, it recently hosted an exhibition under the banner of '1700 Years of Jewish Life in Germany'.

The cathedral's own website is honest and says that many of the artworks are "either in part or in total – evidence of an appalling, anti-Judaism and are quite rightly seen as highly problematic." And they admit that "Christian anti-Judaism led to the persecution of the

---

[44] 'Cologne Cathedral and 'The Jews'', Harald Schlüter, Kölner Dom (Cologne Cathedral) website, koelner-dom.de/en/tour/cologne-cathedral-and-the-jews
[45] 'Many antisemitic artefacts in Cologne Cathedral', CNE News, Christian Network Europe, 27 September 2023

Uncovering their Names and Stories:

Jewish population and its exclusion from society. It was the precursor of modern antisemitism." [46]

A stained-glass window in Cologne Cathedral
(Photo credit: David Marlow)

The cathedral's website has good intentions, and goes on to say, "Christians have the on-going task to not only uncover and reveal derogatory stereotypes, clichés, and negative connotations in the

---

[46] 'Cologne Cathedral and 'The Jews'', Harald Schlüter, Kölner Dom (Cologne Cathedral) website, koelner-dom.de/en/tour/cologne-cathedral-and-the-jews

artworks created down through the centuries, but also to remember their fatal consequences."[47]

After the personal tour, I took a lunchbreak from the education in historic antisemitism, with a rather excellent calves-liver and salad lunch, and then visited the NS (National Socialism) Documentation Centre. This museum in a dismal setting, provides a history of the Nazi regime in Cologne. It includes the general horrific Nazi story, as well as the Cologne-specific history of the rise and tragedy of the Nazi regime.

This museum is housed in EL-DE Haus on Appellhofplatz, which was the Cologne regional headquarters of the Gestapo from 1935 to 1945. Externally, it looks like many other buildings in the neighbourhood, but its harmless facade hides a terrible history of torture, interrogation and murder. It retains the old Gestapo prison cells, well-preserved in the basement. The basement spoke to me of the hideous things that were done there in the name of racial purity, and preservation of the Nazi regime. Hundreds were executed there. It was highly claustrophobic, and a place to leave your imagination at home, but that was difficult to do with the overload of details in audio stories, unsettling surroundings and scratched writing inside cells. The cells were tiny, with steel doors, and were likely at the time to have been packed full of desperate people with little hope.

If you ever visit this museum, unless your German is pretty good, get the English audio guide, as most of the written information is in German.

Later that day, I had extensive discussions over quite good coffee at The Cologne Hilton with Dr Carlo Gentile. Dr Carlo is a friend of my friend and colleague Eitan Drori in Australia, and Carlo is a specialist on the Nazi period. He works in the Martin Buber Institute for Jewish Studies, at the University of Cologne. He was incredibly knowledgeable, genial and very generous with his time.

That night I had a lot to ponder. The night before I had been at the Old Slaughterhouse in Düsseldorf, where my grandparents had been processed by the Gestapo, and during the day had seen the old Jewish

---

[47] ibid.

quarter, visited the Cologne Cathedral and had my anxieties turned up several notches in the old Gestapo headquarters. But I had also spent some lovely educational time with Dr Christiane and Dr Carlo through the day.

The next day was Shabbat, so I attended the morning service at the Roonstrasse Orthodox Synagogue, near the University of Cologne. Construction of the synagogue was completed in 1899, but it was largely destroyed on Kristallnacht. It was set on fire and additionally damaged during the war. Only the central section and burnt-out tower survived. Nevertheless, it was the only synagogue, out of the five shules in Cologne, that was not completely destroyed. It was rebuilt in 1959, and its Shabbat minyan today would be the envy of many synagogues back home in Melbourne. It is quite impressive internally and externally. It had a very good crowd, well led by Rabbi Yaron Engelmeyer.

The siddurim (prayer books) were in Hebrew and German, as you would expect, but adding a level of difficulty for this Australian state-school boy. I missed the English translation. Much of the conversation around me was in Russian, which was also not surprising given post-Soviet Union emigration to Germany. But this did not stop me having very pleasant conversations in English with several congregants.

Everyone was friendly and very welcoming, and the Orthodox service was very familiar, though without the hallmark choir and 'mellifluous' tones of Chazzan Brett Kaye at my St Kilda Hebrew Congregation back home. The Roonstrasse shule president very kindly loaned me a Tallis for the morning. It was a wonderful feeling to experience a shule service in the country and languages my ancestors would have known and recognised.

Afterwards, I drove to Dierdorf and Sessenhausen, which are very near each other, about an hour southeast of Cologne. I unsuccessfully searched for traces of ancestors, including in the old Jewish cemetery in Dierdorf. They are both small villages, surrounded by extraordinarily green paddocks. On a narrow country road along the way, as I was just driving north past Sessenhausen, a deer rushed across the road in front of my car, as a kangaroo might quickly bound across a country road in Australia. The deer and I ventured on safely in our different directions. Nevertheless, I was glad I had extensive car insurance and drove carefully.

Heading north to Plettenberg, the old home of my Lennhoff ancestors, I drove for nearly two hours climbing into the hilly countryside of the Lenne Mountains, with extraordinary winding roads and ultimately brilliant views of the very substantial Bigge River, which flows into the Lenne River. The latter or the Lenne Mountains around and to the north of Plettenberg, are the likely source of the names of the town Lenhausen and my Lennhoff ancestors.

I stopped in Lenhausen on the way to nearby Plettenberg, just 17 minutes apart. I investigated the Jewish cemeteries in both towns, as well as the streets that the Lennhoff clan would have known well. Though they would not have recognised the heavy industry now dotted around the towns.

On what was now day ten of my family history road trip, I drove north to Hennen for nearly an hour past Hemer which was home to the Löwenhardt family, a branch of the family connected to my Lennhoff side, which has been well researched by my cousin Prof John Löwenhardt.

I walked around the small marketplace in Hennen, and then drove around the corner to the small, old Jewish cemetery. The Jewish cemetery in Hennen was in use from around 1700 to 1920. Only eight gravestones remain, and a sign advises that the gravestones are probably not in their original places. People walked past with small dogs and prams on the path outside the cemetery, which only has a low fence with no gate. They all said 'Guten Morgen' pleasantly, as did I in response.

From Hennen, I headed east, visiting the towns of Fröndenberg, Werl, and Körbecke on the beautiful Möhnsee lake. These towns were all places where relatives of mine had been born and lived. I visited the Jewish cemeteries, which were all very small. I did not find any traces of relatives, but I also knew from experience now, that did not mean that relatives were not buried there, probably in unmarked graves. Nevertheless, it was a wonderful feeling, seeing the places, countryside and streets that my relatives had lived.

Uncovering their Names and Stories:

In the Fröndenberg Jewish cemetery, there are not too many gravestones remaining, but there is a large memorial stone dedicated to the Jewish citizens of Fröndenberg, who were victims of the Nazi regime, and four Jewish women who resisted in the Auschwitz Concentration Camp and were hanged publicly. The memorial stone finishes with the words, "Never lose respect for the lives and dignity of others."

The Jewish cemetery in Werl is built on the old city moat. Jews lived in the town from the 16th century, and they were buried in the cemetery from 1565 onwards. Like everywhere else in Germany, the Werl synagogue was destroyed on Kristallnacht. After walking around the centre of Werl, I found a large memorial stone in the cemetery, dedicated to the Jewish citizens of the town, who had suffered from the lack of "understanding, rejection and hatred ordered by the Nazi regime (1933-1945)". In 1946, former SA and SS men were forced to repair the damaged cemetery.

Hennen, Fröndenberg, Werl and Körbecke are close together. You can drive through all four towns from end-to-end in an hour. I took a few hours, hoping to find traces of members of the Bentheim and Neufeld families. I did not find any specific traces but was happy to explore the towns where family members Dora Bentheim (1825-1905), Rike Bentheim (1822-), Herman Neufeld (1856-1941) and Moses Neufeld (1831-1910) had lived.

Sitting outside at a small café opposite the Möhnsee, very near the Körbecker Brücke which I had just driven across, I treated myself to a coffee and bratwurst on a roll for lunch. Enjoying the beautiful view across the water, I remembered that the Möhnsee dams had been successfully bombed in a Dambusters' raid in World War 2, with devastating results.

About eighty-one years earlier, on the night of 16/17 May 1943, the RAF Bomber Command 617 Squadron used their top-secret 'bouncing bombs' to breach the Möhnsee and Edersee dams. Two hydroelectric power stations were destroyed, factories and mines devastated, and about 1,600 civilians (including 1,000 mainly Soviet slave labourers) were killed in the resultant flooding. The RAF lost 56 aircrew, with 53 dead and 3 captured. Thirteen Australians were amongst the aircrew. Two of the Australians died, and one was captured in the raid.[48]

Memorial stone in the Fröndenberg Jewish cemetery
(Photo credit: David Marlow)

Today, the Möhnsee is a very picturesque sight, tranquil and quiet. I sat there quietly eating my bratwurst, unfortunately passively smoking the pipe smoke from the two elderly German men sitting at the next table. There was nowhere else really to sit where I was safe from their exhalations, and I didn't want to leave the view.

---

[48] 'The Story of the Dambusters: Operation Chastise, May 1943', The Historic England Blog, 15 May 2023; 'Marking the 80th anniversary of the Dambusters Raid', Department of Veterans' Affairs, Australian Government, 16 May 2023; and 'Operation Chastise', Wikipedia.

Uncovering their Names and Stories:

Ausflug - Central Germany

After lunch, I drove across the Stockumer Damm and then southeast for just over an hour to Kassel, in central Germany. Kassel is a substantial city, sitting on the Fulda River and dates to 913 CE. The Brothers Grimm lived there in the 19th century, and there is a Brothers Grimm Museum in the city today.

Herz Carl Gotthelft (1817-1880) was born and died in Kassel, and he married Emilie Isenstein (1837-1890) from Hannover. Emilie was my great (x2) grandfather Julius M Isenstein's only sister. Herz and Emilie lived in Kassel and had two daughters, Julie (1878-1941) who married Dr Moses Gerson (1866-1936) from Berlin, and Henriette (1872-1943) who married Isidor Blumenthal (1861-) from Burgdorf, Hannover. Kassel was home to many Gotthelft family members and where Julius S Isenstein (1837-1882) died. This Julius was a nephew of my great (x3) grandfather Marcus Isenstein (1802-).

Spending the night in the city of Kassel broke up the long drive east to Saxony-Anhalt, the modern German state where my Kraft and Steinthal families had extensive history. It was also a place many of my ancestors may have passed through when they travelled on business or migrated from one side of Germany to the other.

In the hills above Kassel sits Schloss Löwenburg, which dates to the late 18th century. It was a good hike from my car, helping me to burn off the bratwurst, and is a lovely faux medieval castle, with beautiful views of the city. It is smaller than the marketing suggests, and is a little Disney-like, but is a lovely place to see and visit nonetheless, sitting in a beautiful woodland setting.

That evening I sat in the comfortable bar of my hotel, the Renthof Kassel in the centre of the city, updating my journal with the observations of the day. The hotel is in a beautiful building with a great history. It was founded in 1298 as a Carmelite monastery, served as a court school, a knight's academy and for a short time as a university. It retains many of its romantic, old features, including a large, dramatic spiral staircase.

Ausflug – Saxony-Anhalt

The next morning, I drove two hours east to Halberstadt, the first city I was visiting in the modern German state of Saxony-Anhalt. It has a beautiful central, old town with many cobblestone streets and historic buildings, which would well and truly have been around in the days of my ancestors.

Halberstadt has a long and important Jewish history, and is home to the Moses Mendelssohn Akademie, the Berend Lehman Museum for Jewish History and Culture on Judenstraße, the remains of the 1712 Baroque Klaus Synagogue, and the old mikveh can be seen in a 16th century building. I felt very welcomed there, and the staff of the museums went out of their way to be helpful and informative. The museums in town provided a wonderful overview of the Jewish history of Halberstadt and surrounds, from at least medieval days and through the Holocaust.

One researcher in the Moses Mendelssohn Akademie had her dog Tony with her, and missing my pooches, I gave Tony a command in German. Tony immediately sat, and we were met with a round of applause from the gathered staff in the foyer. I still do not know whether they were applauding Tony for his obedience or me for my attempt at speaking German.

The old Cantor's house at Bakenstraße 53 was built in the late 1700s, and from 1879 its gateway was the main entrance to the Klaus Synagogue. The house now is Café Hirsch, which forms part of the overall museum complex. The houses of Bakenstraße and Judenstraße hid the synagogue from public view, which was a requirement of the approval of its construction by the wealthy court Jew Berend Lehmann (1661–1730). It worked, because I walked past it twice before finding it.

Halberstadt was the birthplace of Emil Heller (1883-1942) who married Dad's aunt Paula Lennhoff (1886-1942). Emil was very fond of his Opel, which was coincidently the same brand of car I was currently driving around Germany. Emil's 1935-1936 Opel featured in my father's childhood photo album. Tragically, Emil and Paula were murdered in Auschwitz.

Uncovering their Names and Stories:

Old centre of Halberstadt
(Photo credit: David Marlow)

On the other side of the family, it was also the hometown of Elkan Leisner (1924-1976) who married my mother's first cousin Edith Krebs (1924-2010) in England. Edith's mother was Else Kraft (1892-1942), who was one of my Nana's two sisters.

I was delighted to see and climb the Peterstreppe (St. Peter's Staircase) near the museums, in the centre of town. It dates from 1278, and at the top of the stairs, sits the Domplatz (Cathedral Square), which used to hold the Jewish market in Halberstadt. The Jewish market area back in time included the Jewish butchers and small market stalls. Family members would certainly have come to this area for their shopping needs.

The Peterstreppe and adjoining building is basically on the opposite side of the Cathedral Square to the Church of St Peter and Paul, and it is one of the oldest parts of Halberstadt. The building is the old episcopal palace chapel, which has housed the Heinrich Heine City Library since 2000. The whole centre of town and the well-preserved old Jewish quarter were wonderful to explore. I walked around, feeling the history, imagining the Jewish traders, families and merchants walking around and living their lives in this area over the centuries.

As I took a photo of the library, I thought about the famous German Jewish writer and poet Heinrich Heine (1797-1856) that it is named after. As a former bookseller, I again thought about Heine's famous, and in retrospect tragic and prophetic line, "Wherever they burn books they will also, in the end, burn human beings".[49] His books were amongst many others burned by the Nazis in 1933. He was in good company. The Nazis also burnt books by Thomas Mann, Bertolt Brecht, Erich Maria Remarque, Albert Einstein, Stefan Zweig, Emil Ludwig, and many, many others.[50]

Nearby, there is a memorial on Domplatz dedicated to the Jews deported from Halberstadt during the Holocaust. Four hundred Jews from Halberstadt were deported and murdered by the Nazis.[51]

After absorbing the history of Halberstadt, I drove about 45 minutes east to the town of Calbe. This was home to my Kraft family from my great (x3) grandfather Hermann Kraft in the early 1800s, his son Bernhardt Kraft (1820-1882) to Bernhardt's eight children, including Bernhardt's son and my great grandfather Selmar Kraft (1863-1935), until Selmar moved to Leipzig. I walked around the very large Calbe general cemetery and searched for the old Jewish cemetery, eventually finding it but was unable to gain entry. I have since found out that there was nothing much to miss. I found no physical traces of the family in Calbe, but documents and records I found elsewhere helped fill in gaps on my Kraft family.

After the lack of success on the ground in Calbe, I drove 20 minutes south to the important historic large town of Bernburg. My great (x3) grandfather Moses Steinthal's brother Joseph Steinthal (1764-) was on the Bernburg Finanzrat in the 18th century.[52] It is a town more than three times bigger than Calbe, having a population of about

---

[49] The Pity of It All: A Portrait of Jews in Germany 1743-1933, Amos Elon, Penguin, 2002, p.129
[50] Amos Elon (2002) p.412
[51] 'Jewish Life in Halberstadt', Jutta Dick, Berend Lehmann Museum, Halberstadt
[52] Finanzrat = Finance Council

Uncovering their Names and Stories:

36,000, with enormous charm and character. The town developed around the 10th century (at least) Schloss Bernburg. The castle is reasonably large, and now incorporates an extremely interesting local history museum, with exhibits telling the history of Bernburg back to the dinosaur age. The museum was fascinating, with fabulous views over the Saale River valley below.

While I was walking the streets of Bernburg, the Düsseldorf Stadtmuseum and the Düsseldorf Slaughterhouse Memorial and Museum both emailed me, giving permission for me to use some new and old photos, which I had requested for this book. It was very kind of them. The photos were old and recent photos of the Old Slaughterhouse, as it would have been at the time my Marowilsky grandparents were being processed there after their arrest, as well as photos of the current memorial and museum.

Later, I visited the Jüdischer Friedhof am Rösseberg in Bernburg. It is surrounded by a very substantial and smart looking brick wall, a sign that the local Jewish community was once large and comfortably well off. It was certainly reasonably well looked after, especially compared to some of the old Jewish cemeteries which had seen much better days, such as in Calbe and Lenhausen. Though, even here, there seemed to be many gravestones missing.

The next day I drove 40 minutes north to the capital of Saxony-Anhalt, the city of Magdeburg. Magdeburg was the home of Selmar's brother Theodor Kraft and his family, and the Magdeburg City Library was very helpful. I spent some time researching upstairs in the library. A tram running past the library reminded me of my home in Melbourne, Australia which has the largest tram network in the world.[53]

Feeling on a high from touching and photographing history of my Kraft family in Magdeburg, including the Stolpersteine dedicated to Walter and Theodor Kraft, and Theodor's old home, I drove about an hour southeast to Dessau-Roßlau. Dessau was the old capital of Anhalt, before it merged into Saxony-Anhalt.

---

[53] 'The 10 Largest Tram Networks in the World', Cat Vitale, Rail.nridigital.com/future_rail_sep23/10_largest_tram_networks

Dessau was home to another brother of my great (x3) grandfather Moses Steinthal, Josua Steinthal (1764-). Josua was also known as Reb Falk. He was a teacher at the Talmud Torah School in Dessau, as it was then known. He married Sara Cohn and had three children, Ida, Falk and Heyman.

Trolley-load of 'Protected Jews' records on the Lazarus – Steinthal family in Gröbzig, in the Landesarchiv Sachsen-Anhalt, Dessau-Roßlau
(Photo credit: David Marlow)

I had a particular mission to complete at the Landesarchiv Sachsen-Anhalt in Dessau-Roßlau, studying the Duke of Saxony-Anhalt's old records on Protected Jews which related to my Lazarus – Steinthal family in Gröbzig. The fabulous archivist Frau Boeck had extracted an abundance of useful records for me in readiness for my visit. A whole library trolley-load of record books from the 1700s and 1800s were waiting for me, indexed and tagged, marking places in the records which Frau Boeck thought might relate to my family members.

The archivists also provided a large reading room, for me to be able to study the documents in a comfortable, quiet and roomy

Uncovering their Names and Stories:

environment. Most tagged pages and documents turned out to be spot on, relating to my Lazarus – Steinthal ancestors. This necessitated a couple of hours of note taking and photographing of dozens of record pages in a reading room at the Archives, followed by many more hours of translation, interpretation, cross-referencing and review when I returned home to Melbourne.

These records added about a dozen family members to my Lazarus – Steinthal family tree, including siblings, wives and children. For example, I found that my great (x5) grandfather Lazarus Philipp had four children, and not just one as I had previously thought. It also confirmed quite a few dates of birth and death, and adoption of the Steinthal family name in 1821. The family surname was Lazarus the generation before that, and Philipp the generation before that. There were also records about passing on of inherited property, the names of the children of family members, and addresses of where they lived in Gröbzig. It was a treasure trove of discoveries, and a terrific find just before my visit to Gröbzig.

While in Dessau-Roßlau, from my quite central hotel, I walked around the centre of town, visiting the very impressive new synagogue, the Cantor's House (which was actually the Rabbi's house) and the memorial to the Jews murdered by the Nazi regime. There were also quite a few impressive churches around the city centre.

Very near to my hotel, outside the Marienkirche, I came upon a statue of Leopold I, Prince of Anhalt-Dessau (1676-1747). Leopold seems to have always been destined for a military career, becoming colonel of a Prussian regiment at the age of 17. Birthright has its privileges. He was ruler of Anhalt-Dessau from 1693 to 1747, as well as a General Field Marshall in the Prussian Army. He was respected as a military leader and helped modernise the Prussian Army, by the standards of the time. He was a senior commander in the War of Spanish Succession and the Great Northern War against Sweden. He also led the Prussian Army to victory over the Saxons at the Battle of Kesselsdorf in 1745, during the Second Silesian War. His mother, the

300+ Years of a German – Jewish Family

Dowager Princess Henriette Katharina, ran the principality while Leopold was at war.[54]

Sample of 'Protected Jews' records including Lazarus – Steinthal family dated 1754, held in the Landesarchiv Sachsen-Anhalt, Dessau-Roßlau

(Source: Landesarchiv Sachsen-Anhalt in Dessau-Roßlau; photo credit: David Marlow)

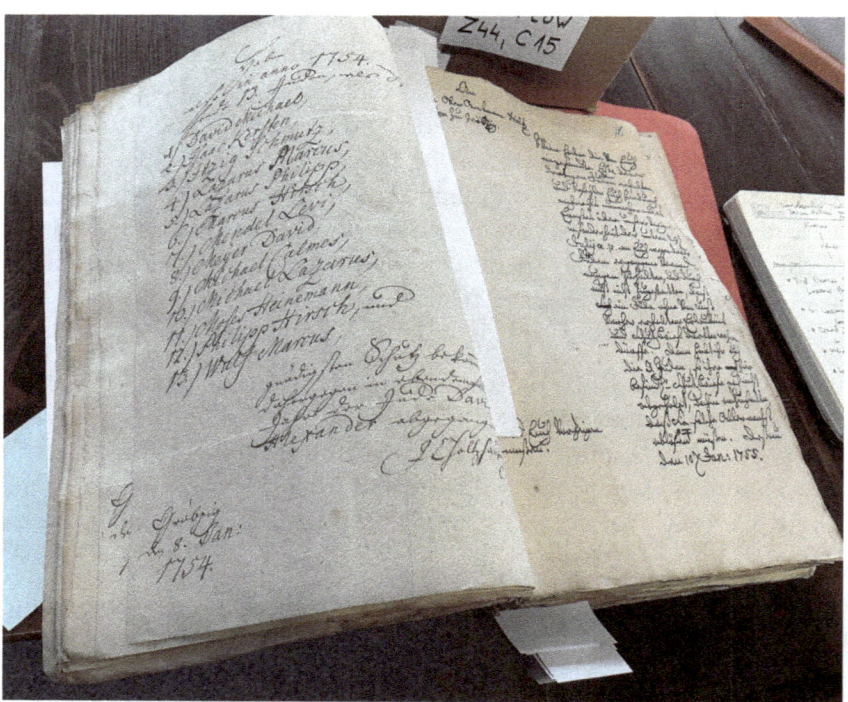

After a 45-minute drive southwest, I arrived in the small town of Gröbzig, with its population of about 3,000. I had anticipated longingly the visit to this hometown for the Lazarus - Steinthal family from 1720 to the mid 1800s. I was so excited, that I arrived about an hour early for my meeting with the museum director. So, I took a long walk around town, before I headed back to the museum to meet Anett Gottschalk.

---

[54] 'Leopold I, Prince of Anhalt-Dessau', Wikipedia

Uncovering their Names and Stories:

Inside the restored Gröbzig old synagogue
(Photo credit: David Marlow)

Overall, I walked around the old market square, the old Jewish cemetery, the street where much of the Steinthal family lived, and toured the Gröbzig Synagogue Museum. The museum comprises three main buildings, the synagogue itself, which has been lovingly restored, the main museum building which was undergoing a comprehensive renovation for re-opening late in 2024, and the office building which incorporates a reconstructed period classroom and the office for research and management.

This was a highlight of my research road trip. As I walked through the small town of Gröbzig, across the old market square and past the old Rathaus, towards the old Jewish cemetery, I thought of my ancestor Lazarus Philipp the book dealer who would have walked the same streets and marketplace in the 1700's. As would his children and grandchildren thereafter. The old buildings appear untouched by progress, but nevertheless are well maintained. There is even an ornate old hand water pump on the footpath near outside the museum. The visit made connection to my Steinthal ancestors feel very real, especially after studying the Lazarus – Steinthal family records in the Saxony-Anhalt Archives.

Ausflug - Saxony

After spending several highly informative hours in Gröbzig, I drove southeast for 45 minutes to Leipzig, the birthplace of my Nana, Hanni Elkan nee Kraft. It is a busy city, which today has a population of about 590,000, bigger in population than Baltimore, Leeds or Tasmania. It was also where my great grandparents Selmar and Frieda Kraft had their home and business. It is a sizable city, and I was delighted to find the graves of Selmar and Frieda after checking every grave in the two large Jewish cemeteries. It was also heart-warming to visit Selmar and Frieda's still existing, very smart looking home and place of business at 10 Lindenauer Markt.

Gravestones of my great grandparents Selmar and Frieda Kraft, in Leipzig
(Photo credit: David Marlow)

I visited the 1897 Brodyer Synagogue, which was not far from my Leipzig hotel. On Kristallnacht, the interior and windows were

Uncovering their Names and Stories:

destroyed, but luckily it was not set on fire. It was refurbished in 1939, because the Nazi regime wanted to put on a good show, and they had the Leipzig Fair coming up. That did not last long, and the Nazis repossessed it afterwards. After the war, it was once again used as a synagogue.[55]

I had dinner that night opposite the old town hall on Markt Platz in Leipzig and set out the next morning for Colditz.

As a youngster, I enjoyed the old movie about World War 2 prisoners of war (POWs) planning an escape from Colditz Castle. The 1971 'Escape from Colditz' movie, the one with David McCallum,[56] not the 1955 or more recent iterations. I do not know how historically accurate it was, but it is the one I remembered best. So, I could not help but stop by on the way past and see the famous castle first-hand. It has an immense presence, high above the village of Colditz. Colditz is a Renaissance castle that was once a residence for Saxon kings and was used to imprison captured Allied officers during the war. It now houses a POW museum, a youth hostel and a music academy. The latter two roles made it a hive of activity on the day I visited. A yard full of chickens is kept just below the main entrance, providing an interesting musical backdrop.

Along the way, I also passed near the town of Torgau. This is where the US 69th Division driving from the west, and the Soviet's 58th Guards Rifle Division coming from the east, met up on 25 April 1945.[57] This split Germany in half and was a major milestone in World War 2, taking place just before the fall of Berlin to the Soviets on 2 May.

By then, Hitler had already committed suicide in his bunker in Berlin on 30 April. British Prime Minister Winston Churchill described

---

[55] 'Leipzig', Jewish heritage, history, synagogues, museums, areas and sites to visit (jguideeurope.org)
[56] Yes, 'Duckie' from NCIS.
[57] <u>Berlin: The Downfall 1945</u>, Antony Beevor, Penguin Books, 2007, p424

Hitler eloquently as, "the repository and expression of the most virulent hatreds that have ever corroded the human breast."[58]

After ticking Colditz Castle off my bucket list, I drove about 90 km southeast to magnificent Dresden, walking around the old city and the old Markt, seeing the city's majestic buildings, including the historic Rathaus and Christ's Church. The latter was only metres from my hotel. Dresden has a beautiful old city section and is a very sizeable metropolis with 592,000 residents.

The city sits alongside the majestic Elbe River. Magnificent buildings, including the old royal castles, palaces, the opera house and other grand buildings have survived, and are breathtaking. There must have been a massive rebuilding and renovation effort after the destruction of World War 2. The buildings include some of the most splendid Baroque architecture you will see, most notably the Zwinger, which is a palatial complex of the best Baroque architecture in Germany. It houses museums and is a venue for musical events. The Zwinger is an amazing ornament for the country, let alone Dresden.

From Dresden, I drove 45 minutes south to the hamlet of Liebstadt, which I had thought was home to my Polley family ancestors, driving around town and walking around the cemetery. It sits very close to the border with the Czech Republic. I then drove to the nearby holiday destination and health retreat of Bad Gottleuba, spending the night at the lovely, family-owned Gasthof Hillig in the centre of town. The Hillig family provide excellent German meals and a warm welcome.

I passed many deer grazing in the forest between Liebstadt and Bad Gottleuba. It was a lovely quiet break from the hustle and bustle, and frantic traffic of Leipzig and Dresden. I have since discovered that the Polleys were actually from Liebstadt in East Prussia, now known as Miłakowo in modern Poland. Mea Culpa. It was a lovely stop in the journey, nonetheless.

---

[58] 'Hitler shot himself 75 years ago, ending an era of war, genocide and destruction', Michael E. Ruane, The Washington Post, 30 April 2020

Uncovering their Names and Stories:

Baroque details in Dresden
(Photo credit: David Marlow)

Ausflug – Czech Republic

From Bad Gottleuba, I drove south for about an hour, seamlessly crossing the Czech border and onto the Theresienstadt Concentration Camp in Terezin. I only noticed I was in the Czech Republic when the road signs were no longer in German. The history of the concentration camp and ghetto dominates the whole town of Terezin. The architecture in town felt quite Stalinist in style, though it would have pre-dated Czechoslovakia coming under Soviet control by many years. Not a joyful place. Nor did it feel an inspiring or attractive place to live. The concentration camp and related museums appeared to be the major industry in town.

My first stop was the Terezin Ghetto Museum, which once housed a school, and then visited the old Magdeburg Barracks which was the seat of Jewish self-governance during the time of the ghetto. Today it houses a museum and bookshop. The museums include a replica of what the congested ghetto housing was like, and many exhibits of musical, artistic and literary works created in the Theresienstadt

Ghetto. It was clear how over-crowded the ghetto was, and this was the accommodation that family members like my grandfather's sister Sophie Nathan and my great grandfather's brother Theodor Kraft would have experienced.

The Small Fortress is the walled concentration camp, which also houses a museum. It was built in the 18th century by the Emperor of Austria, Joseph II. He named it after his mother, Maria Theresa, hence Theresienstadt. After Germany invaded what they had not yet taken of Czechoslovakia in March 1939, they turned the Small Fortress into a Gestapo prison in 1940, and the town into a German military base.

Over 1,500 Jews were imprisoned in the Small Fortress over 1940-1945. About 500 of those were tortured to death and most of the others were murdered after being transferred to death camps.[59]

It is all as unsettling and horrifying as you would expect. The actual concentration camp is a haunting and depressing place. Surprisingly, I was surrounded by Israelis in tour groups while I walked around the concentration camp complex. Hebrew was not the language and accent I was expecting to be surrounding me, and I must admit that I found it comforting. A young Israeli woman kindly paid for my map of the camp, as I did not have the small change required and the shop did not accept credit cards.

After parking in the carpark over the road, I walked past the National Cemetery which runs alongside the path to the entrance of the fortress, and through the impressive entrance gate, which allows entrance to the walled, castle-like structure. At one end of the cemetery with its sea of horizontal gravestones, is a huge cross, and at the other end is a matching large Magen David, backed by the wall of the fortress.[60] I visited the old guardhouse, prisoner records office and commandant's office. I saw the ubiquitous and distressing 'Arbeit Macht Frei' sign. These are words that still send shivers up the spines of many Jews, not just Holocaust Survivors. I passed through the various yards of the old concentration camp, and the old

---

[59] Plaque in the Small Fortress in Theresienstadt
[60] Magen David = Star of David

Uncovering their Names and Stories:

hospital, while the 'model' barbershop, bathroom and delousing station were along the path, looking like the prisoners had just left.

An elderly Jewish woman with a New York accent had lost her tour group and was starting to panic. Being lost and alone in an old concentration camp would not be fun for anyone. I pointed her in the direction of the American-accented group that I had seen enter one of the barracks, and she calmed down.

After ensuring she rejoined her group, I walked through the seemingly unending (500m), narrow and claustrophobic tunnel (connecting corridor) to the execution yard. Though I knew the tunnel was not used during the Holocaust years, it is still a dark and eerie experience. The light at the end of tunnel was very much welcomed. Unfortunately, it opens into the execution yard, where hundreds were shot from 1943 to 1945. Mass graves were found near here in 1945, and they were reburied in the National Cemetery out the front of the Small Fortress.

I flew past the 'Death Gate', the mass cells, the pool built for fire-fighting purposes, the cinema for the guards, and the solitary cells. I meandered through the exhibits of the camp museum, which is in the old SS Barracks. I walked through the various cells and cell blocks and observed the artworks and sculptures acting as memorials to those murdered.

I could not bring myself to eat or drink in the restaurant, which is in the old officers' canteen. I could not eat in this place of cruelty. Especially after the education provided in the camp museum.

About half the prisoners who died in the Theresienstadt Ghetto died in 1942, that is 15,891 people. More than 155,000 Jews passed through Theresienstadt, and of those 35,440 died in the ghetto and 88,000 were deported to their deaths.[61] The names of more than 77,000 victims are handwritten on the walls of Pinkas Synagogue, which I later visited in Prague's old Jewish quarter.[62] The National

---

[61] 'Theresienstadt', Yad Vashem, yadvashem.org/holocaust/about/ghettoes/theresienstadt.html
[62] 'Terezin Concentration Camp: History and Overview', Jewish Virtual Library

300+ Years of a German – Jewish Family

Cemetery contains about 10,000 victims, but only 2,386 have individual graves.

I had at least twelve family members murdered or die from mistreatment in Theresienstadt, including my great grandfather Selmar Kraft's brother Theodor, as well as Polley, Steinthal, Neufeld, Lennhoff and Gotthelft family members.

After quite a few hours at Theresienstadt, I was delighted to escape. I grabbed a hotdog and bottle of water from a kiosk across the road from the Small Fortress and drove just over an hour southeast to Prague. I was taking a two day break away from the Holocaust and my family history. I had always wanted to go to Prague. It was on my bucket list, as they say. And If I was going to be so close, I could not miss it. And after more than two weeks of German museums, cemeteries, synagogues and old buildings, I needed a hiatus from my family history tour. So, I was now ready for a couple of days of Czech museums, cemeteries, synagogues and old buildings.

Pipe organ in the Spanish Synagogue in Prague
(Photo credit: David Marlow)

Uncovering their Names and Stories:

I stayed at the Hotel Josef, which I selected because it looked central on a map, and it had very good reviews and inviting views pictured online. It turned out to be called the Josef, because it was in the old Jewish Quarter called Josefov. And handily, it was only a six-minute walk to the Spanish Synagogue.

The highlights for me in Prague, included the expansive Prague Castle complex (which is a UNESCO World Heritage Site) with the imposing Gothic St Vitus Cathedral and the castle's jaw-dropping views over the city; the old Jewish Quarter with its Prague Jewish Museum which includes five historic synagogues (Spanish, Maiselova, Pinkas, Klausen and Staronova Synagogues), the Old-New Synagogue and the Old Jewish Cemetery with its overcrowded gravestones; the old town square (Staromestske namesti) with its mechanical astrological clock dating to 1410; and the 1357 Charles Bridge with its collection of historical and religious statuary spread across the Vitava River. And the goulash.

The Moorish Revival-style Spanish Synagogue, built in 1868, is especially beautiful and is still used for services for the Prague Jewish community today. It replaced the previous synagogue, which was an old schoolhouse, and was in use as a house of prayer from the 15th century when Jews arrived who had been expelled from Spain.

I also enjoyed perusing the old Judaica on display at the various sites of the Jewish Museum, which were basically the five synagogues and the Ceremonial Hall next door to the cemetery.

The Old-New Synagogue is apparently the oldest, operating synagogue in Europe, at least according to its marketing. It has been functional since the late 13th century, apart from the Nazi occupation years of 1942-45.

Ausflug – Home Stretch

After an early morning last walk through the old Jewish quarter, I drove back to Dresden to search for ancestors in the old and new Jewish cemeteries. Ironically the Alte Jewish Cemetery in Dresden is in Neustadt, and the Neue Jewish Cemetery is in Altstadt.

I walked through the old and new Jewish cemeteries but had little success. Many, if not most of the gravestones in the old cemetery in Dresden clearly had their faces shot off, despite the high walls, most likely around Kristallnacht or the Holocaust, so their names and dates are lost to history. What a disgrace! In more recent years, the local Jewish community organisation Hatikvah cares for the old cemetery, and they kindly let me in to walk around looking at the face of every gravestone. Hatikvah has an office just a few doors down the road from the old Jewish cemetery.

The gravestones in the new cemetery were in much better condition. They had not been attacked like in the old cemetery. I found a family member buried in the new cemetery, Simon Gotthelft (1848-1895), who I thought had died in Berlin, which is where he had married Gertrud Frank (1864-1951). But here he was, nonetheless. It was not such a surprise when I later discovered that his children Carl, Therese, Paula and Martha were born in Dresden. Simon is related through my Isenstein family. Young Israel Julius Isenstein (1856-1929) married Simon's sister Sophie Gotthelft. Israel was a first cousin of my great (x2) grandfather Julius Marcus Isenstein (1834-1914).

The next morning, after enjoying the marvellous hotel breakfast buffet, I drove just over two hours north from beautiful Dresden to the Wannsee Conference House in Berlin. It is now a museum, the House of the Wannsee Conference Memorial and Education Centre, telling the story of its role in turning the persecution and murder of Jews, into a full-blown, industrial Holocaust. Although the House sits in a lovely position in beautiful gardens on the water, the Großer Wannsee. I could not wait to get away from there. To me, it is a house of horrors.

Nevertheless, I was delighted to see several university groups from various countries on educational tours of the Wannsee museum. It is vital that the lessons of the past are not forgotten but are passed on to future generations. The exhibits cover the history of Nazism, the exclusion and deportations, and the horrific experiences of Jews from various countries during the Nazi era.

Wannsee is where 15 Nazi leaders met on 20 January 1942, largely well-educated men with a depraved agenda, to plan the deportation and mass murder of Jews and others at a super industrial level and pace. Most were university educated and over half held doctorates in law. It was only an hour and a half long meeting, but its ramifications were earth shattering for the Jews of Europe. Evil hangs heavy in the air in the building like humidity around the Equator.

House of the Wannsee Conference Memorial and Education Centre, Berlin
(Photo credit: David Marlow)

I then drove an hour across Berlin to the Weißensee Jewish Cemetery, to find some of my many Steinthal family ancestors who were said to be buried there. Despite it being the largest Jewish cemetery in Europe, I had great success finding Steinthals. Some had very substantial family plots, and Prof Heymann Steinthal (1823-1899) had a prominent, large gravestone in a VIP row. Altogether, I found eight Steinthal family graves, which helped provide or confirm dates of birth and death.

After photographing many relevant gravestones, and placing small stones upon them, I drove into central Berlin. I visited the Neue Synagogue, a beautiful building, dating to 1866, so it may well have been somewhere my Steinthal or Elkan family members may have attended. Albert Einstein played the violin there for a fundraising concert in 1930. Like every other operating synagogue I visited in

Germany, it had a police presence outside the building. The police nodded hello as I entered, but the security guard inside was not so welcoming.

On my last morning in Berlin, and the last day of my family history road trip, I drove and walked around the city. This included the very impressive cathedrals that are the Deutscher Dom and the Französischer Dom, Gendarmenmarkt Square which is bookended by the two cathedrals and is under major renovations, the Berlin Konzerthaus, the Baroque palace that is Schloss Charlottenburg, and several other sights of the city.

Steinthal family graves in the Weißensee Jewish Cemetery, Berlin
(Photo credit: David Marlow)

Uncovering their Names and Stories:

While I drove down Ben Gurion Strasse in central Berlin, I thought about the German streets that I had driven over the previous three weeks with Jewish-related names, such as Judenstrasse and Cantorstrasse in various towns, and streets I had come across named after famous Jews, such as Eli Wiesel, Hannah Arendt, Leo Baeck, Walter Rathenau, Albert Einstein, Heinrich Heine, and Golda Meir.

That afternoon, I headed to the airport, returned the rental car, and got ready to board the plane for the 30-hour trip back home to Melbourne.

Overall, on my road trip I visited eighteen museums, libraries and archives in Germany which could have something to say on my family's story; twenty two cemeteries where family members were buried or gravestones might provide clues; houses and apartment buildings where family members had lived; places where they had worked; two concentration camps with their horrors ringing in my ears; and more than a dozen synagogues where ancestors might have prayed and celebrated Jewish festivals. I walked the streets they would have walked and marketplaces where they would have shopped or sold merchandise.

I visited five German UNESCO World Heritage Sites, out of 52 in Germany: the magnificent but flawed Cologne Cathedral, the marzipan-obsessed Hanseatic City of Lübeck, the beautiful Garden Kingdom of Dessau-Wörlitz, the Museum Island in Berlin incorporating five museums, and St Mary's Cathedral & St Michael's Church in picturesque Hildesheim. In the Czech Republic, the whole historic centre of Prague is a World Heritage Site. I also visited the old Jewish cemetery in Altona (Hamburg) and the Small Fortress of Terezin, which are both listed for consideration as World Heritage Sites down the track.[63]

In Berlin, I walked streets that would have been familiar to my mother, thinking of her as a young Jewish girl, growing up under the Nazis, and saw the apartment building where my mother and maternal grandparents had lived. In Wuppertal, I saw the Schwebebahn my father would have travelled on, with a station barely 100m from where he had lived. I thought of him travelling on

---

[63] WHC.unesco.org

this suspended passenger train line in the 1920's with his parents and in 1930s with his school friends. In Plettenberg, I walked between the graves of my Lennhoff and Neufeld relatives, wondering about their lives, how they celebrated Jewish festivals, and how they interacted with their non-Jewish neighbours and business contacts in the area.

I walked past the homes where my parents and grandparents lived, prior to fleeing for their lives or being forced into concentration camps and ghettos. I saw the apartments where my Elkan grandparents lived in the 1930s at 53 Kniephofstrasse, Berlin. I did the same where my Marowilsky grandparents had lived at 14 Döppersberg, Wuppertal. I imagined my parents growing up there and the lives they lived in those places and the surrounding areas, such as the local markets, schools, synagogues, parks and shopping areas.

To record what I found and felt on this magical family history tour, I took over 900 photographs of buildings, gravestones and various important sites; I copied over 100 pages of documents and records; I recorded my experiences and discoveries in my journal; and posted highlights on Facebook for family, friends and my many helpers and advisers. Some of the photos I took on my family history research road trip appear in this book.

Uncovering their Names and Stories:

4.0 Through German Jewish history

German Jews

You can be Jewish and German. In fact, there is even a Yiddish term for Jews from German speaking backgrounds, 'Yekke' or 'Jekke'. Some claim the term is mildly derogatory, some say it is a term of affection or a jocular name for Jews of German background. Either way, I am happily a member of the private Facebook group 'Jekkes Engaged Worldwide in Social Networking', which has over 2,400 members. There are various claims as to the origin of Jekke, but the most common one is that it is derived from the word jacke (jacket) and was used by eastern European Jews to describe German Jews who wore short jackets, rather than the longer coats of eastern European Jews, such as worn by Chasidim.[64] Stereotypes commonly ascribed to Jekkes are the strong inclination to being punctual and pedantic. My Dad, Heinz Marowilsky, was a definitely a Jekke.

It surprises me still, that some people are themselves surprised when I tell them my parents were German Jews. "How can you be both?" they ask. I usually explain that being German is about where you were born, maybe where your parents were born and probably relates a little to language and some cultural attributes. You can be German and Catholic, German and Lutheran, and German and Buddhist, so why not German and Jewish. Being Jewish was about religion, but also to some extent is an ethnicity with its own cultural attributes.

My parents were certainly German in that they were born in what is or was Germany, Mum in Berlin and Dad in Pillau,[65] amongst German speakers. They certainly absorbed love for some cultural things German, especially Dad, such as food and music. In later life they demonstrated this to me, in their fondness for smoked eel, pickled herring, liverwurst, pickled onions, sauerkraut and polka (what I called 'oompah') music, which Dad played on long drives in the car. He even possessed a pair of very professional looking

---

[64] 'These German Jewish Baby Names Honor Yekke Heritage', Naomi Kaye Honova, Kveller, 8 August 2023

[65] Pillau was part of the eastern most part of East Prussia, near the Lithuanian border, and after the end of World War 2 became part of the USSR, and since the fall of the Berlin Wall, part of Russia.

cymbals, which he would, most embarrassingly, take with him to the Hofbräuhaus in Melbourne to play with the band. My parents went there so often, that the then owners, the Homberger family, became quite close family friends. His only non-business friends I remember, were management and band members from German-Austrian restaurants, like the Hofbräuhaus in Melbourne's CBD and the Salzburg Lodge in the suburb of Heidelberg.

Jewishness comes from your parents and family. Being religiously or halachically[66] Jewish, comes from your mother. If your mother is Jewish, you are Jewish. But both parents and your broader family, as well sometimes your local community, help create your sense of being Jewish and Jewish identity. For example, Friday night dinners, Seders during Pesach and lighting Chanukah candles. So, add in gefilte fish, matzo ball soup and a whole swag of Jewish festivals throughout the year. I certainly remember well, going to Temple Beth Israel in St Kilda with my parents for Yom Kippur and Rosh Hashanah. And they insisted I go to Sunday school there to help prepare me for my barmitzvah, despite my grumblings about it on Sunday mornings.

But growing up, we were much more likely to have rye bread, schnitzel and liverwurst at home rather than challah, gefilte fish or latkes. And my parents usually went out for dinner on Friday nights, rather than have a Shabbat dinner. Shabbas dinner was not a 'thing' for my parents, but it is much more for my siblings and me, especially my sister Helen, even if the frequency may be variable.

Choosing Temple Beth Israel (TBI) as their synagogue would have been an easy decision for my parents. Its foundation stone was laid in 1937 and their senior rabbi at the time was Rabbi Dr Herman Sanger (1909-1980) who had arrived in the community in 1936, escaping Germany just in time. Rabbi Sanger was from Berlin, and he attracted many families who had escaped Germany and Austria, like my parents. Having a German-speaking rabbi with a German accent would have made refugees like my parents very comfortable.

Although Rabbi Raymond Apple AO (1935-2024) was a leading Orthodox rabbi, he described the Progressive Rabbi Sanger as "a

---

[66] Halachically = by Jewish law

cultured, handsome, eloquent German liberal rabbi who gave firm leadership for four decades".[67]

I remember Rabbi Sanger as a great orator, as was his successor the highly respected Rabbi Dr John Levi AC who took over as Senior Rabbi at TBI in 1974. Rabbi Levi officiated at my barmitzvah in 1975, and he is the epitome of a gentleman and a scholar. When I held an author event with former Governor General Sir Zelman Cowen, Sir Zelman requested that Rabbi Levi introduce him. John is also a great historian and leader in interfaith relations. In more recent times, he has been a valued friend and colleague.

Religion and nationality are two different things. At least, that is how things work today. Sometimes in the past, being Jewish made you an outsider. You couldn't be truly German if you were Jewish, and not just under the Nazi regime. More on this later.

The Early Years of Jews in German Lands to the Thirty Years War (321–1648)

Jews have lived in what is now Germany for over 1,700 years.[68]

The documented history of Jews in what is now modern-day Germany commences with a mention in an edict issued by Roman Emperor Constantine in 321 CE. It related to Jews in the Roman colony of Cologne, like their upper-class pagan neighbors, being able to be compelled to serve on the municipal council or 'curia', which was responsible for financing and administration of the city. The edict proves that Jews were present in Cologne, and numerous and wealthy enough to share in the costly burdens of public office.[69] Helping to confirm this, there was a Jewish graveyard found in Cologne in the 1930s, which dates from the fourth century.[70]

---

[67] 'The German Rabbinate Abroad – Australia', Rabbi Dr Raymond Apple, European Judaism, Berghahn Books,
Volume 45 No. 2 Autumn 2012, p.27
[68] 1,700 years of Jewish Life in Germany, Leo Baeck Institute, 2021
[69] ibid.
[70] German Virtual Jewish History Tour, David Shyovitz and Mitchell Bard, The Virtual Jewish World, A Project of AICE, 2023

After the Romans destroyed Jerusalem and the Temple, Emperor Vespasian (70-79 CE) introduced a special tax on Jews, despite Jews being granted citizenship. This set the precedent for special taxes on Jews that continued in various shapes and forms for nearly 2,000 years.[71]

Jews served the Romans as merchants, craftsmen, doctors, soldiers and slaves, and travelled with the Roman legions to the Rhine region.[72] I may well have had far distant ancestors as part of the support team for the Romans. Archeological evidence from this early period proves that Jewish and Christian roots existed in provincial Roman society, which coexisted with paganism. This all changed with Christianity dominating the Roman Empire and was formalized in 380 CE with the Edict of Thessalonica. The first formal and documented discriminatory measures taken against Jews were introduced soon after. Synagogues and pagan temples then began to be converted into churches.

The Roman Empire existed from 756 BCE to 476 CE, including battles with many Germanic tribes to create Roman Germania. However, Rome did not fully defeat all the German tribes. Attila, King of the Huns, comes to mind. By 430 CE, the Huns had come from Central Asia and established a large empire in Central Europe. They conquered the Goths and many other German tribes. After Attila died in 453 CE, the Hun Empire collapsed. Various German successor states grew, which helped end the Roman Empire in Western Europe.[73]

Germanic peoples intermarried with members of the Roman provincial elite, merging skills. And Slavic people settled in what is modern day eastern Germany.[74]

Historical and archeological evidence suggests that Jews were an integral part of urban life in the region during the early Middle Ages

---

[71] Traveller's Guide to Jewish Germany, Billie Ann Lopez & Peter Hirsch, Arcadia Publishing, 1998, p.14
[72] Jews in Germany: From Roman Times to the Weimar Republic, Nachum T. Gidal, Könemann, Cologne, 1988, p.23
[73] Britannica.com
[74] ibid.

under the Frankish kings. An uneasy co-existence continued, while over time the wealthy cities Mainz, Worms and Speyer became centers of Jewish learning in the Rhine region.[75]

Pope Urban II sought to liberate Jerusalem from the Turkish Muslims and called for a crusade on 26 November 1095.[76] This resulted in the First Crusade starting from 1096 CE, which brought persecution and massacres of Jews. In some cases, whole communities were murdered or expelled from towns and cities. For example, about 12,000 Jews are thought to have been murdered in towns in the Rhine River region between May and July 1096.

For years afterwards, Jews across what is now Germany were subject to periodic violence and expulsion, culminating in pogroms that swept across Europe during the Black Death between 1348 and 1350, when Jews were blamed for the pandemic and massacred.[77]

The Holy Roman Empire of the German Nation eventually replaced the Roman Empire in Germanic lands from 962 to 1806, ruled by the Holy Roman Emperor. In the Middle Ages and early Modern period, power shifted from the weakened Holy Roman Emperor to the various principalities, eventually becoming more of a union of territories.[78]

As Voltaire is said to have remarked, the Holy Roman Empire was not holy nor Roman nor an empire.[79] It was more "a motley medley of more or less independent kingdoms, lay and ecclesiastical principalities and free cities".[80]

The Black Death brought tremendous social disruption and change, including revolutions in media, religion and science. The Reformation created religious upheaval, the invention and spread of

---

[75] Leo Baeck Institute (2021)
[76] German Virtual Jewish History Tour, David Shyovitz and Mitchell Bard, The Virtual Jewish World, A Project of AICE, 2023
[77] Leo Baeck Institute (2021)
[78] 'History of the Holy Roman Empire', Holy Roman Empire Association, holyromanempireassociation.com
[79] ibid.
[80] 'The End of the Holy Roman Empire', Richard Cavendish, History Today, Volume 56, Issue 7, July 2006

printing, the scientific revolution, the rise of rationalism and religious skepticism, and the increasing power of the centralised state. New thinking, ideologies and economic structures, population growth, and urbanisation were notable from the mid 1400s.[81]

Over this period, German-speaking lands were a collection of about 1,800 small states, each with its own laws and policies, including those regarding Jews. These included a variety of measures, from total banishment to discriminatory measures, such as a requirement to wear an identifying badge, exclusion from many cities or particular economic activities to 'toleration' by order of the local sovereign.[82]

From Nation States to Napoleon (1648–1806)

The Thirty Years War ended with the Peace of Westphalia in 1648. A new political system of territorial states with independent rulers was created. Jews were prohibited from living in some states, but in those areas where they were allowed, many shared and benefitted from this transformation. Provided with 'letters of privilege', a few became prosperous and powerful, although quite precariously protected by the ruler who issued the letter.[83]

Nevertheless, most Jews lived in poverty in the countryside, not helped by the imposition of Jew-targeted taxation and occupational restrictions. In fact, over 75% of Jews in the 1700s lived in poverty.[84] They lived alongside Christians and engaged in a variety of trades (such as silk, tobacco, sugar, horses, and cattle) and many peddled goods door-to-door. My great (x5) grandfather Lazarus (Eleasar) Philipp (1697-1772) and his brother were book dealers during this time, and very much travelling book dealers in their early years.

Jews and Christians were still separated by customs and language, as most Jews in German speaking lands spoke Western Yiddish

---

[81] Leo Baeck Institute (2021)
[82] ibid.
[83] ibid.
[84] <u>Jewish Life in Germany: Memoirs from Three Centuries</u>, Monika Richarz (Ed), Indiana University Press, 1991 pp.475-478

(German-Jewish dialect).[85] Though Jews were often literate, unlike most of their non-Jewish neighbors, their skills were more likely to be in the German-Jewish dialect and reading Hebrew, but not in German.

The German Jewish philosopher and theologian Moses Mendelssohn (1729–1786) was born in Dessau and moved to Berlin in 1743. He was unable to speak German when he arrived, and initially only spoke Western Yiddish and Hebrew. He was highly influential, helping to change the German-Jewish world. His work helped bring Jews closer to Germans, such as by his translation of the Torah into German.[86] However, this was not so universally popular with observant Orthodox Jews at the time. He advocated for emancipation of the Jews, greater tolerance and humanity. As such, he became the symbol of the Jewish Enlightenment (Haskalah) of the late 18th century, which brought German Jewry into modern times.[87] Secular education increased, focus on Halacha declined and German Jews started focusing on speaking German. Through this process, many Jews started to assimilate, some converted, and many became secular Jews as religious observance declined.

Napoleon to Bismarck (19th Century)

Napoleon Bonaparte defeated the Austrian army in 1800. France took the German territories west of the Rhine in 1801 under the Treaty of Luneville. The Holy Roman Empire was finally destroyed by the French under Napoleon in 1806. He presided over a committee of imperial princes who redrew the map, reducing the number of small states, organizing things in a more controllable way.[88]

The larger Prussian and Austrian states happily gained territory in the resulting reorganization of 1803. Major gains went to non-threatening states such as Bavaria, Wurttemberg and Baden. Sixteen

---

[85] Leo Baeck Institute (2021)
[86] ibid.
[87] Amos Elon (2002)
[88] 'The End of the Holy Roman Empire', Richard Cavendish, History Today, Volume 56 Issue 7, July 2006

Germanic states formed the Confederation of the Rhine, which stretched from the Elbe River to the Alps, and seceded from the Holy Roman Empire on 1 August 1805.[89]

The Holy Roman Empire of the German Nation was over. Napoleon announced it. And Emperor Francis renounced the imperial crown on 6 August 1805.[90]

Napoleon then defeated Prussia, welcomed Saxony to the Confederation and created the new kingdom of Westphalia for his brother Jerome to rule. Prussia and Austria also joined. But it only lasted seven years to 1813, after the Battle of Leipzig where a coalition including Austria, Prussia, Sweden and Russia defeated Napoleon.

The German Confederation was an association of 39 mainly German-speaking states, which was created by the Congress of Vienna in 1815.

There were pogroms throughout German lands in August to October 1819, known as the Hep-Hep riots. As a result, many German states removed civil rights from Jews and many Jews emigrated.

In 1848, there were republican revolts across Europe, including in what is now Germany. They all failed and resulted in some retaliatory repression. Many Germans, including German Jews, left German lands for places like America after the failed 1848 revolutions. My great grandmother's uncle George Isenstein (1832-1902) was one of those who emigrated, and he joined a German-dominated regiment of the Union Army in 1861, during the American Civil War.

The Prussian-dominated North German Confederation succeeded the German Confederation in 1866. It was initially a military alliance under the leadership of Prussia and formed a federal state that comprised 22 German states, including Prussia. It did not include Bavaria, Wurttemberg, Baden, Southern Hesse and Austria.[91]

---

[89] ibid.
[90] ibid.
[91] 'A Guide to the United States' History of Recognition, Diplomatic, and Consular Relations, by Country, since 1776: North

Uncovering their Names and Stories:

It was not until the creation of Austria-Hungary in 1867 and the unified Germany under Otto Von Bismarck (1815-1898) in 1871, that Jews were finally granted full equality under the law in most German-speaking lands. Despite living with their non-Jewish neighbours for about 1,500 years, it took until the 19th century for civil rights and full citizenship to be extended to Jews throughout German-speaking lands.

Bismarck was a Prussian statesman, who became the first Chancellor of the German Empire. His attitude towards Jews and Judaism varied at times. At one time, he opposed opening senior government positions to Jews. Another time, he was attacked by antisemites for passing the laws of 1869 and 1871 which abolished restrictions based on religious differences. [92] There was an element of political expediency for Bismarck to back these changes, as he was supported at the time by Jewish liberal parliamentarians. Later they became bitter opponents when he turned his allegiance to Conservatives after 1878.[93]

He was no fan of the antisemitic court preacher Adolph Stoecker, but he liked the latter's antipathy for socialism. He ignored a petition with 250,000 signatures, which called for the dismissal of Jews from all government positions in 1881.[94] Clearly the antisemitism of the Nazis did not begin with Hitler.

Meanwhile in 1885–86, Bismarck supported the expulsion of thousands of Russian and Austrian people from Prussia, including around 9,000 Jews. Bismarck, strongly disliked all things Polish and East European Jews (Ostjuden) and shared the prejudices against them with the established Jewish community in Germany.[95]

As German Jewry became more liberal in their politics and more Reform in their religion, Bismarck grew distant from them and lost

---

German Confederation', Office of the Historian, US Department of State
[92] Encyclopedia.com
[93] ibid.
[94] ibid.
[95] ibid.

much of their support. At one stage previously, he had the support of the majority of German Jewry.[96]

The Franco-Prussian War (1870-1871) arose when France attempted to reassert its dominant position in Europe. It was a war between the North German Confederation and the Second French Empire. Some historians suggest that Bismarck provoked the French into declaring war on Prussia, so the recalcitrant German states would be induced to join the Confederation. If so, he got his way.[97]

There were three wars fought towards the unification of Germany. The first was against Denmark in 1864, the second against Austria in 1866, and the third against the French in 1870. This led to most German speaking states in Europe uniting under Prussian leadership. I had relatives fight in the unification wars, including Levi Löwenhardt (1840-1898) who was the husband of my great grand-aunt Pauline Löwenhardt nee Lennhoff (1847-1933). Levi was a Private in the Prussian Army.

Germany won the wars, and the unification of Germany was completed, including establishment of the German Empire and the annexation of Alsace-Lorraine in the west. The German Empire was founded on 18 January 1871, and Bismarck consolidated what he had created. After a couple of changes of emperor, and differences of opinion between Emperor William II and Bismarck, the latter ending up having to resign in 1890.[98]

Improved political rights, partnered with enormous economic growth thanks to industrialization, unleashed tremendous creativity, energy and wealth amongst the German Jewish community. More integrated into economic, cultural, and intellectual life in Germany, many Jews adopted a German identity, including more traditional German names, as well as middle class German fashions and lifestyles.[99] For example, a Chajim might become Hermann, or unfortunately given mid 20th century events, Aron could become Adolf, like my great grandfather Adolf Lennhoff.

---

[96] ibid.
[97] Britannica.com
[98] ibid.
[99] Leo Baeck Institute (2021)

Uncovering their Names and Stories:

Jewish reformers fought for emancipation, and they also sought to reform Judaism through changes in worship, including shorter services, musical accompaniment, and German hymns. For example, at the Neue Synagogue in Berlin, German texts were introduced alongside Hebrew texts for the liturgy and prayers, and services were accompanied by an organ and choir.[100] This could well have been my mother's synagogue in Berlin, because she very much enjoyed the organ and choir at Temple Beth Israel in Melbourne in later life.

The cultural assimilation of German Jews at this time came from a long-shared history as well as increasing economic and political freedoms. But antisemitism emerged as a threat to Jews in Germany and Austria-Hungary, with political parties pursuing antisemitic policies under which Jews could not be German. They also lobbied for the exclusion of Jews from German society.[101]

Antisemitism was not new to this time. Jew hatred, pogroms and discrimination had a long history. But the word 'antisemitism' only started being used from 1860, first used by Austrian-Jewish scholar Moritz Stein Schneider (1816-1907) in the phrase 'antisemitische Vorurteile' (antisemitic prejudices). Stein Schneider used the term to describe French philosopher Ernest Renan's (1823-1892) ideas about 'Semitic races' being inferior to 'Aryan races'.[102] But the Holocaust Encyclopedia gives credit for first use of the term antisemitism to German journalist Wilhelm Marr, who founded the League of Antisemites in 1879.[103]

After 1871, freedom of domicile allowed Jews (and non-Jews who moved to a lesser extent) freedom of movement and the result was urbanisation, a shift to larger towns and cities from the villages and rural areas where they had been commonly living.[104]

---

[100] ibid.
[101] ibid.
[102] Anti-Semitism: A History and Psychoanalysis of Contemporary Hatred, Avner Falk, Praeger, Westport, 2008 p21
[103] 'Antisemitism', Holocaust Encyclopedia, US Holocaust Memorial Museum
[104] Jewish Life in Germany: Memoirs from Three Centuries, Monika Richarz (Ed), Indiana University Press, 1991 pp.7-9

300+ Years of a German – Jewish Family

This had a big impact on my family. For example, my Steinthal ancestors in little Gröbzig mostly moved to Berlin; my great grandfather Selmar Kraft and family moved from Calbe to Leipzig; many Lennhoff family members moved from Plettenberg to Elberfeld/Wuppertal; much of my great (x2) grandfather Bernhardt Kraft's family moved from Calbe to Magdeburg; most of the Polley family moved from Liebstadt in East Prussia to Berlin; and the Marowilskys moved from Vistytis to Pillau in East Prussia, and a couple of generations later to Wuppertal. These sorts of moves not only provided work, business and cultural opportunities, but also access to education, which was highly valued by Jewish families.[105] However, urbanisation also led to reduced religious observance and increased assimilation.

Map of my family's migration from hamlets, towns and villages to larger towns and cities:
(Underlying map derived from MapChart)

By the 1770s and 1780s, most wealthy Jews in Berlin no longer observed Shabbat, wore beards or kept kosher. By 1814, about half

---

[105] ibid. p.8

the Jewish community in Berlin no longer bought kosher meat. Synagogues only became full on the High Holydays.[106]

In Hamburg by 1933, the percentage of mixed marriages was 39%. This was a significant break from the tradition of marrying within the community, which had long been a key driver of retaining Jewish identity and continuity in Jewish communities.[107]

By 1925, almost one third of German Jews were living in Berlin, including many of my Steinthal, Elkan and Kraft relatives.[108] The massive Jewish population growth in some key cities relevant to my ancestors highlights the importance of urbanisation for Jewish communities, especially in Berlin, after unification:[109]

Jewish population	1871	1910	1925
Berlin	36,015	90,013	172,672
Hamburg	11,954	19,472	19,904
Leipzig	1,739	9,434	12,540
Cologne	3,172	12,393	16,093
Wuppertal[110]	40	584	750

Nevertheless, in southern and western Germany, and in the Rhine Province of Prussia and Westphalia, Jews remained largely in villages and rural towns. So, while this trend continued elsewhere, I retained relatives in small towns in what is now North Rhine-Westphalia, such as Hemer, Hennen and Körbecke.

World War 1 and the Weimar Republic

When World War 1 (1914-1918) commenced, German Jews signed up for military service in droves, in fact in a higher percentage than

---

[106] <u>Jewish Daily Life in Germany 1618-1945</u>, Marion Kaplan, Kindle File, 1970, location 2322
[107] ibid. p.7
[108] ibid. pp.8-9
[109] ibid. p.8
[110] 'Wuppertal', Jewish Virtual Library, years are 1877 (estimated), 1905 and 1926

non-Jewish Germans. Many saw an opportunity to demonstrate their loyalty to the relatively newly unified Germany and wanted to send a message to the antisemites that they were true, loyal Germans. During the war, about 100,0000 Jews served in the German army and about 12,000 were killed.[111]

At least twenty members of my family signed up to fight for the German Empire in World War 1, apparently determined to do their duty for their country. The family members I have identified so far, who served in the German (or mostly the Prussian) Army in World War 1 were:

- My grandfathers, Oskar Nathan Elkan and Hermann Marowilsky,
- Oskar Nathan Elkan's brother Hermann (wounded - lost an arm),
- Dr Bruno Hassmann was killed serving as a medical officer,
- The nine sons of Levi and Pauline Löwenhardt nee Lennhoff, most of whom were wounded:[112]
    - Salomon-Georg Löwenhardt (served in a volunteer militia artillery regiment in Russia),
    - Isidor Löwenhardt (served in a volunteer militia infantry regiment),
    - Max Löwenhardt (served in a reserve infantry regiment in Russia),
    - Hugo Löwenhardt (served in a volunteer militia artillery regiment in France),
    - Emil Löwenhardt (served in an infantry replacement regiment in France),
    - Adolf Löwenhardt (served as a medical corporal in a fusilier regiment in France),
    - Corporal Julius Löwenhardt (served in an infantry ammunition column in Russia),
    - Siegmund Löwenhardt (served in an infantry regiment in France), and

---

[111] Lopez and Hirsch (1998)
[112] 'An old Hemer Family', John Löwenhardt, Löwenhardt Foundation, The Netherlands, 9 December 2014

Uncovering their Names and Stories:

- o   Hermann Löwenhardt (served as a rifleman with a mountain machine gun unit in Serbia),
- The brothers Fritz (died in service in Palestine) and Werner Kraft,
- My maternal grandmother's brother Bruno Kraft (wounded),
- Kurt Polley (badly wounded),
- Elkan Nathan (died in service in France),
- Emil Heller, husband of Paula Lennhoff, and
- Rudolf Steinthal (died in service in Poland).

The nine Löwenhardt brothers who served in World War 1
(Source: Löwenhardt Foundation, The Netherlands)

Interestingly, I had at least one family member fighting on the other side. Walter Isenstein, a relative of my great grandmother Frieda Kraft nee Isenstein, was born in the USA and served in the US Army in a field artillery battery (Battery E 303 FA).[113]

Despite the service of so many Jews in the German Army in World

---

[113] Walter Arthur Isenstein, Abstracts of World War 1 Military Service, New York State Archives

War 1, as the war dragged on, antisemites scapegoated Jews as 'shirkers' and 'profiteers'. The German military even ordered a 'Jewish census' (Judenzählung) to attempt to show that Jews were avoiding combat service on the front line. The results of the census demonstrated otherwise and were suppressed by the authorities.[114] German Jews felt betrayed that their service and commitment were being questioned.

I am sure that the Jews in the German Army would have been surprised, if they were in action against Australian troops, that the Australians may have been led by the German-Jewish Australian General Sir John Monash (1865-1931). Monash was the grandson of printer, bookbinder and publisher Baer Löw (Loebel) Monasch (1801-1879), from Posen, Prussia.[115]

My grandfathers could well have faced Australian troops on the frontline. Unfortunately, a substantial number of old German military records were destroyed in World War 2 and the German Military Archives have been unable to help provide my grandfather's' records.

Interestingly, my good friend and Senior Rabbi of St Kilda Hebrew Congregation in Melbourne, Australia, Rabbi Yaakov Glasman AM has Sir John Monash's desk in his office, donated to the synagogue by a generous donor. Monash had a long history with the St Kilda synagogue and was on the board for over a decade after he returned from the war, from 1920 to 1931.[116]

With the defeat in 1918, the Kaiser abdicated, the German Empire ended, and Germany was recreated as a republic, the Weimar Republic (1918-1933), named for the town where the new constitution was formed. Germany had lost economically important territory, had to pay substantial reparations and suffered national

---

[114] Leo Baeck Institute (2021)

[115] <u>Jews in Germany: From Roman Times to the Weimar Republic</u>, Nachum T. Gidal, Könemann, Cologne, 1988, pp.211-212; and 'A Town in Poland remembers its past', Caroline Durre & Rafael Witkowski, <u>Australian Jewish Historical Society Journal</u>, November 2004, Vol XVII, Part 3, p364-374

[116] 'Annual report', St Kilda Hebrew Congregation, 1932

humiliation, at least from the German perspective. This, combined with a variety of post-war economic issues followed by the global Great Depression (1929-1939), provided fertile ground for right-wing extremists to take political advantage.

Persistent antisemitism during the Weimar Republic did not prevent a remarkable Jewish renaissance in Germany. The Weimar constitution made the country a democracy, where civil rights were guaranteed regardless of your religion. Women also gained full rights, including voting rights. Jews rose to positions of unprecedented political prominence. The first draft of the new constitution was drafted by Interior Minister Hugo Preuß, who was Jewish. However, the case of the Jewish chairman of AEG Walter Rathenau, who became Germany's Foreign Minister but was assassinated in 1922, highlighted the danger of public prominence for Jews.[117] Ironically, he had at one time called for Jews to avoid prominence in the public space.

As a prominent Jew, Rathenau was a particular target for the far-right. Fanatics chanted, "Shoot down Walther Rathenau, the goddamned Jewish swine!" And that they did. On 24 June 1922, assassins from a far-right group threw a hand grenade at his car and sprayed him with automatic gunfire.[118] Rathenau was dead before a doctor could arrive.[119]

At peak, during the Weimar Republic, about 3% of the 600 Reichstag delegates were Jewish. But by 1932, the trend had reversed with only one Jewish Reichstag member.[120]

There were many wealthy and middle-class Jews in Germany, but by 1930, a quarter of the German Jewish community needed support from community welfare programs.[121] The stereotypes being

---

[117] Leo Baeck Institute (2021)
[118] <u>Fatherland and the Jews: Two Pamphlets by Alfred Wiener</u>, 1919 and 1924, Alfred Wiener, Granta, London, 2022, p.19
[119] Amos Elon (2002) p.385
[120] <u>The Routledge History of the Holocaust</u>, Jonathan C Fredman (ed.), Routledge, Oxford, 2011, p.14
[121] "1815-1933: Emanzipation und Akkulturation I bpb", Prof. Em. Dr. Arno Herzig, Budeszentrale fur politische Bildung, bpb.de

promulgated by the Nazis were not true. Many struggled financially. Antisemitism surged with the Great Depression from 1929, amid false claims of Jewish betrayal in World War 1 and ridiculous lies that Jews controlled the world. The libelous and fraudulent 'The Protocols of the Elders of Zion' (1920) was widely circulated and contributed to the conspiracy theories. I was disgusted when the same book was in piles, proudly and prominently displayed at bookshops in Malaysia, generations later in 2002-2003, when I ran call centres in Singapore and Malaysia.

The German Workers Party was founded in 1919 and was renamed the National Socialist German Workers Party (Nationalsozialistische Deutsche Arbeiterpartei, known as the Nazi Party) the following year. Adolf Hitler (1889-1945) became party leader in 1921, and he established the SA in 1921 and the SS in 1923.[122]

The former World War 1 corporal and leader of the Nazi Party, Adolf Hitler, manipulated President Paul von Hindenburg (1847-1934) through Hindenburg's advisers, into appointing him to the position of Chancellor in 1933.[123] When the respected national hero of World War 1 and second President of the Weimar Republic, the elderly Field Marshall Hindenburg died from lung cancer in 1934, Hitler leveraged a loophole in the Weimar Constitution and anointed himself with the powers of the Chancellor and President within a day. He did not need to manipulate Hindenburg any longer. He made himself de facto Hindenburg, with the new titles Führer and Reichskanzler.[124]

The Nazi Regime and the Holocaust

Until 1933, Jews had become very prominent in certain professions, most notably lawyers and doctors, thanks to urbanisation and the pursuit of education disproportionately compared to non-Jewish

---

[122] <u>The Routledge History of the Holocaust</u>, Jonathan C Fredman (ed.), Routledge, Oxford, 2011, p.39
[123] Hindenburg was also a veteran of the Franco Prussian War of 1870-71.
[124] Leader and Chancellor of the Empire

Uncovering their Names and Stories:

Germans.[125] But, the overall Jewish population in Germany in 1933 was only 505,000, or 0.75% of the total German population of 67 million.[126]

Profession	Number of Jews in the profession	Jews as % of profession
Lawyers, notaries	3,030	16.2%
Judges	286	2.7%
Doctors	5,557	10.8%
Dentists	1,041	8.6%
University teachers	192	2.6%
Secondary teachers	317	0.8%

These professions were also amongst the first to be targeted by the Nazi regime, and Jews were gradually banned from practicing their professions.

Any fantasies of freedom, belonging and assimilation were destroyed when the Nazi Party came to power in 1933. German Jews had sought and gained rights over centuries. These were being quickly removed and far worse. Legal persecution and violence against Jews were ramped up over the following five years, depriving Jews of employment, confiscating property, and dramatically narrowing their social opportunities. In November 1938, the persecution culminated in a massive nation-wide pogrom against Jews.[127] Hundreds of thousands emigrated by the end of the 1930s, including my parents, but most of those who remained were murdered in the Holocaust, including my paternal grandparents and many other members of my family.

A range of discriminatory laws and regulations were brought in, targeting Jews. For example, medical treatment by Jewish doctors was

---

[125] Jewish Life in Germany: Memoirs from Three Centuries, Monika Richarz (Ed), Indiana University Press, 1991 p.15
[126] 'Germany: Jewish Population in 1933', Holocaust Encyclopedia, United States Holocaust Memorial Museum
[127] Known as Kristallnacht in Germany

no longer reimbursed by the City of Berlin's public health insurance company from 1 April 1933.[128]

The Nuremberg Race Laws which were passed in September 1935, forbade intermarriage or intercourse with Jews, and forbade employment of German women aged under 45. From then also, Jews were no longer German citizens. The Laws also excluded Jews from the civil service and government regulated professions, such as medicine and education.

The Nazi regime officially encouraged Jewish emigration until October 1941. But the Nazi leadership knew how to plunder and pillage. They increasingly taxed Jewish emigration (90% of their wealth) and restricted the amount that could be taken out of German banks.[129]

When Adolf Hitler came to power in 1933, there were about 523,000 Jews in Germany. This was less than 1% of the German population, and they were mainly urban dwellers. One third of them lived in Berlin, a result of decades of urbanisation. Initially about 37,000-38,000 Jews fled Germany, but many did not flee far enough, and were caught up as Germany expanded into nearby countries, such as the Netherlands, France and Czechoslovakia. Many countries, including the USA and British Commonwealth countries, were hesitant to take many Jewish refugees, which resulted in many, including many of my family members, being murdered by the Nazis. Their immigration restrictions slowed the escape from Germany.

The Nazi ideology was founded upon poisonous antisemitism and Hitler created and promulgated a narrative scapegoating Jews (and Jews as surrogates for Bolsheviks) for all the woes of Germans. Many, if not most, Germans were passive bystanders to Nazism and its evils, but this should not absolve anyone from any guilt. Without the indifference of so many, the Nazis could not have gotten away with what they did.

As the German Lutheran Pastor and anti-Nazi dissident Dietrich Bonhoeffer (1906-1945) wrote, "Silence in the face of evil is

---

[128] Exhibit, Melbourne Holocaust Museum
[129] 'German Jewish Refugees, 1933-1939', Holocaust Encyclopedia, United States Holocaust Memorial Museum

Uncovering their Names and Stories:

itself evil: God will not hold us guiltless. Not to speak is to speak. Not to act is to act."[130] This could easily also be applied to the lack of response to rising antisemitism today.

Bonhoeffer is often quoted, but I am not sure his fate is as well remembered. He was initially imprisoned by the Gestapo in 1943 for nearly 18 months, and eventually re-arrested in February 1945 and imprisoned in Buchenwald near Weimar. He was then transferred to Flossenbürg concentration camp in Bavaria and hanged at the age of 39 on 9 April 1945.[131]

Jews were prevented from being able to receive academic degrees from 15 April 1937.[132] This affected my father who could not go to university because of this discrimination. He then chose to go to what he called 'commercial school', and when the authorities wanted to kick him out because he was a Jew, Dad said his classmates stood up for him. This commercial school, 'Berufkolleg Elberfeld', still stands in Wuppertal, conveniently within 100m of where his apartment building stood. For my mother, the Nazi regime stopped her even attending school.

The opportunity for the regime to put their foot on the throttle against the Jews came, when a Nazi and German diplomat, Ernst vom Rath was assassinated in Paris by Polish Jewish teenager Hershel Grynszpan on 9 November 1938.[133] This was the pretext that the Nazi leadership needed to accelerate the departure of Jews from Germany.

The Minister for Public Enlightenment and Propaganda, Joseph Goebbels (1897-1945) orchestrated the Kristallnacht pogrom. He wrote in his diary, "The Jews are to experience the rage of the people. That's right. I immediately issue appropriate instructions to police and party... Now the people will act."[134] In the resulting massive

---

[130] Goodreads.com/quotes/601807-silence-in-the-face-of-evil-is-itself-evil-god
[131] 'Friedrich Bonhoeffer', Holocaust Encyclopedia, United States Holocaust Memorial Museum
[132] Exhibit, Melbourne Holocaust Museum
[133] The Holocaust, Laurence Rees, Viking, London, 2017, p139
[134] loc.cit.

national pogrom, the SA and SS and their supporters destroyed "more than seven thousand Jewish businesses and two hundred synagogues". This was Kristallnacht 9-10 November 1938.[135] It was not so much the 'people', but organised and implemented by the Nazi SA and SS. When I visited Germany, many sites of destroyed synagogues are marked with memorials to the lost synagogues and Jews murdered on Kristallnacht.

Over 30,000 German Jewish men were arrested on Kristallnacht and sent to concentration camps.[136] My grandfather Oskar Elkan was arrested and sent to Sachsenhausen Concentration Camp, where people were subject to terrible brutality and mistreatment. The name Sachsenhausen translates as houses of the Saxons.

Kristallnacht changed everything. With synagogues burned down across the country, Jewish businesses destroyed or stolen, thousands arrested and forced into concentration camps, the fire was under every Jew to get out. If they could find a way. In 1938, 36,000 Jews escaped Germany and Austria. Another 77,000 fled in 1939.[137] Overall, about 304,000 Jews emigrated from Germany from 1933 to 1939.[138] This included my parents and my maternal grandparents.

The resultant refugee crisis led to an international conference on the problem, the Evian Conference, which was held in France in July 1938, four months before Kristallnacht. It had been prompted by the Nazi takeover of Austria, the so-called 'Anschluss', which resulted in a spike of Jewish refugees. No real solution was found, though 32 countries were represented at the conference. By the end of 1939, 202,000 Jews were still in Germany and 57,000 in Austria.[139] Eight months after Evian, the Nazis invaded Czechoslovakia, threatening

---

[135] The Monuments Men: Allied Heroes, Nazi Thieves and the Greatest Treasure Hunt in History, Robert M Edsel with Brett Witter, Random House, 2013, p8
[136] Exhibit, Melbourne Holocaust Museum
[137] ibid.
[138] 'German Jews During the Holocaust', Holocaust Encyclopedia, United States Holocaust Memorial Museum
[139] ibid.

Uncovering their Names and Stories:

357,000 more Jews.[140] The start of World War 2 in September closed the door to many places, such as Britain, Palestine and Australia.

The British were so concerned that Palestine might be seen as a potential target for Jewish emigration at Evian, that they ensured that the President of the Jewish Agency for Palestine, Dr Chaim Weizmann, did not address the Evian delegates.[141]

The doors closed completely when the regime banned Jewish emigration in October 1941, with 163,000 in Germany still waiting to escape.[142] Most of these Jews, which included many of my relatives who were unable to get out earlier, were murdered in concentration camps and ghettos. Some delayed leaving because they were World War 1 veterans and unwisely thought they were safe, some kept thinking it would all blow over until escape became impossible, some could not afford the emigration tax after years of being unable to work, and some just could not find a safe haven that would take them. Visas were not easy to get.

The Nazis thought they had a problem with Jews with 525,000 Jews in Germany in 1933. But by 1942, the Nazis controlled Europe. And there were nine million Jews across Europe, including three million in Poland alone. To address this Nazi perceived problem, on 20 January 1942, fifteen Nazi leaders met at the Wannsee Villa in Berlin to discuss implementation of the 'Final Solution to the Jewish Question'. This was the formal launch of the industrial extermination of European Jewry. Over half the Wannsee attendees held doctorates in law, most were university educated, and half were World War 1 veterans.[143] So, where did this savage and evil intent come from?

The Wannsee Conference was organised by SS Obergruppenfuhrer Reinhard Heydrich. At the conference, he outlined plans for the Final Solution. He was assassinated by Czech resistance agents four

---

[140] Aliens: The Chequered History of Britain's Wartime Refugees, Paul Dowswell, Biteback Publishing, London, 2023, chapter 4
[141] The Holocaust and Australia: Refugees, Rejection and Memory, Paul Bartrop, Bloomsbury, London, 2022, chapter 4
[142] 'German Jews During the Holocaust', Holocaust Encyclopedia, United States Holocaust Memorial Museum
[143] Wannsee Villa exhibit, Melbourne Holocaust Museum

months later. Hundreds of men, women and children were murdered in the SS reprisals.

As an outcome of Wannsee, five death camps were established at Auschwitz-Birkenau (which had multiple purposes), Chelmo, Belzec, Sobibor and Treblinka. These camps had the key role in the industrial scale extermination of European Jewry. Zyklon B gas had already been trialed on Soviet POWs at Auschwitz in September 1941. Gas was seen to make it easier on the SS 'exterminators'.[144]

Apart from these specific death camps, there were over 1,000 Nazi concentration camps and sub-camps during the Holocaust, acting as transit and/or labour camps. The death rates from brutality, torture, summary execution, mistreatment, starvation and disease at these camps was extreme, but nothing compared to the murderous efficiency of the death camps. During Operation Reinhard (1942-1943), 25% of the Jews murdered in the Holocaust (horrifyingly, about 1.47 million Jews, young and old), were murdered in a three month 'surge' due to the creation of the death camps.[145]

The Nazi leadership, especially Heinrich Himmler, were keen to not have details of their plans written down, but they were not too shy to talk openly to their fellow Nazis. Hans Frank, Governor-General of the General Government, told top officials in Kracow in 1941, "I want to say to you quite frankly that we shall have to finish with the Jews one way or another. About the Jews of Europe, I have only one point of view – the Jews have to disappear. They must go. I have begun negotiations to send them to the east...We were told in Berlin: Why all this trouble? We can't use them either, liquidate them yourselves."[146]

---

[144] Belzec, Sobibor, Treblinka: The Operation Reinhard Death Camps, Yitzhak Arad, Indiana University Press, Bloomington, 1987, p.11

[145] 'Quantifying the Holocaust: Hyperintense kill rates during the Nazi genocide', Lewi Stone, Science Advances, January 2019

[146] ibid. p.12

Uncovering their Names and Stories:

In October 1943, Himmler himself said to a group of senior SS and police officers in Posen, "I refer to the evacuation of the Jews, the annihilation of the Jewish people."[147]

Between 160,000 and 180,000 German Jews were murdered by the Nazis and their collaborators, mainly in camps and ghettos. Like my German Jewish ancestors, the victims had been German citizens, with rights since the time of Napoleon. They had assimilated over centuries, many had served in the Prussian or German armies, especially in World War 1, spoke German, and were heavily immersed in German culture. A few thousand survived in hiding, with the rest spread around the world, in a German Jewish diaspora.[148]

Amongst my family alone, we lost over one hundred mothers, fathers, aunts and uncles, cousins, children, salesmen, merchants, businessmen, bankers, butchers and veterans.

Apart from the over 1,000 Nazi concentration camps and sub-camps under the Nazi regime, they also created 1,143 ghettos in their occupied eastern territories. These were meant to be temporary. From late 1941, the Nazis destroyed the ghettos and either directly shot the Jewish inhabitants or deported them to death camps.[149]

List of major Nazi concentration camps:[150]

Concentration Camp	Location	Operational period
Auschwitz – Birkenau*	Poland	1940-1945
Belzec	Poland	1942-1943
Bergen-Belsen	Germany	1943-1945

---

[147] <u>Belzec, Sobibor, Treblinka: The Operation Reinhard Death Camps</u>, Yitzhak Arad, Indiana University Press, Bloomington, 1987, p.16

[148] <u>The Jews of Germany</u>, Ruth Gay, Yale University Press, New Haven, 1992, p.xiii

[149] 'Ghettos', <u>Holocaust Encyclopedia</u>, United States Holocaust Memorial Museum

[150] 'List of major Nazi concentration camps', Simon Wiesenthal Center via Jewish Virtual Library: A project of AICE

Buchenwald *	Germany	1937-1945
Chelmo *	Poland	1943-1945
Dachau	Germany	1933-1945
Dora-Mittelbau	Germany	1943-1945
Flossenbürg	Germany	1938-1945
Gross-Rosen	Poland	1940-1945
Janowska	Ukraine	1941-1943
Kaiserwald	Latvia	1943-1944
Majdanek	Poland	1941-1944
Mauthausen*	Austria	1938-1945
Natzweiler-Struthof	France	1941-1944
Neuengamme	Germany	1940-1945
Oranienburg	Germany	1933-1935
Plaszow	Poland	1942-1945
Ravensbruck	Germany	1939-1945
Sachsenhausen*	Germany	1936-1945
Sobibor*	Poland	1942-1943
Stutthof *	Poland	1939-1945
Theresienstadt/Terezin*	Czech Republic	1941-1945
Treblinka *	Poland	1942-1943
Westerbork	Netherlands	1939-1945

The bolded camps in the table above were death camps, which were set up for the intention of the mass murder of as many Jews and other targeted people as possible, noting that Auschwitz-Birkenau had multiple purposes.[151] Concentration camps marked with an asterix (*) were where members of my family are confirmed to have been murdered during the Holocaust.

I believe that naming my family members murdered by the Nazis and their henchmen, pays respect to the memory of my lost family members, and ensures that they are not forgotten. So far, I have identified over 100 family members murdered in the Holocaust:

---

[151] Belzec, Sobibor, Treblinka: The Operation Reinhard Death Camps, Yitzhak Arad, Indiana University Press, Bloomington, 1987, Preface

Uncovering their Names and Stories:

Auschwitz: Walther Kraft, Peter Hess, Kurt Polley, Hugo Neufeld, Nathan Neufeld, Rita Neufeld, Hertha Neufeld, Paula Neufeld, Libertha Neufeld, Werner Neufeld, Johanna Neufeld, Doris (Dorit) Neufeld, Alfred Neufeld, Eduard Hans Steinthal, Wolfgang Gotthelf, Elizabeth Gotthelf nee Düsterwald, Ernst Adolf Gotthelf, Julius S. Brunn, Paul Gotthelf, Heinrich Manasse, Fritz Joseph, Adolf Löwenhardt, Julia Löwenhardt nee ten Brink, Emil Löwenhardt, Klara Löwenhardt, Ursula Löwenhardt, Siegmund Löwenhardt, Margarete Löwenhardt, Eva Löwenhardt, James Simon, Walter Rosenberg, Ruth Rosenberg, Evelyn Rosenberg, Julius Bernd Isenstein, Otto Hans Isenstein, Anna Daus, Hertha Heller, Emil Heller, and Paula Heller nee Lennhoff; (39)

Buchenwald: Dr Paul Sander; (1)

Chelmo: Sarah Anne Lennhoff; (1)

Mauthausen: Günther Ehrenfried; (1)

Müngersdorf: Emilie Lennhoff; (1)

Sachsenhausen: Bruno Kraft and Elkan Nathan; (2)

Sobibor: Margarethe Käthe Ehrenfried, Saly Löwenhardt, Jeanne Löwenhardt, and Elly Löwenhardt; (4)

Stutthof: Hertha Löwenhardt, Selma Neufeld, and Werner Neufeld; (3)

Treblinka: Sophie Nathan Elkan, Hugo Löwenhardt, Josephine Löwenhardt, Henriette Löwenhardt, Manfred Löwenhardt, Günter Löwenhardt, Max Krebs, Natalie Krebs nee Salzman, and Emma Neufeld nee Steeg; (9)

Zamosc: Nathalie Neufeld, Paul Neufeld, and Hedwig Lennhoff; (3), and in ghettoes -

Izbica: Hermann and Meta Marowilsky; (2)

Łódź (Litzmannstadt): Olga Bachrach nee Neufeld, Julius Bachrach, and Meta Lievendag; (3)

Minsk: Frieda Marx nee Lennhoff, Rosa Lennhoff, Leo Löwenhardt, Manfred Löwenhardt, Max Löwenhardt, Hildegard Löwenhardt and Günter Löwenhardt; (7)

Riga: Emmi Kraft nee Simon, Oskar Isenstein, Valeska Isenstein nee Waldbaum, Hertha Henriette Düsterwald, Else Löwenhardt, Selma Löwenhardt, Isidor Löwenhardt, Heinz Löwenhardt, Emilie Löwenhardt, Martin Brunn, Arthur Jägers, Emma-Irma Jägers, Paula Jägers, Hermann Lievendag, Emma Lievendag, Else Krebs nee Kraft, and Fedor Krebs; (17)

Theresienstadt: Theodor Kraft, Natalie Polley, Lona Irene Steinthal, Anna Steinthal, Herz Neufeld, Bertha Neufeld, Sally Simon Lennhoff, Regina Lennhoff, Pauline Steinthal, Hedwig Eckstein, Regina Lennhoff nee Thalberg, and Henriette Gotthelft; (12) and

Warsaw: Betty (Betti) Silberberg nee Neufeld; (1).

There were undoubtedly many other family members for whom we do not have details of their fate. And there are many others who are related, but for whom I am a small blip on the radar of their distant family connections.

They all had thought they were Germans who just happened to be Jewish. The Nazi philosophy was not consistent with that worldview. Hitler made being Jewish incompatible with being German. And the Nazis wanted to make sure that everyone knew that Jews were separate and something different, dehumanising them at every opportunity. Jews did not fit with Hitler's vision of racial purity.

Hitler saw the Holy Roman Empire as the First Reich and the period of the German Empire from 1871 to 1918 as the Second Reich.[152] Hitler's Third Reich, as he envisaged it, commenced with his becoming Chancellor in 1933 but it ended in 1945. It did not last his promised thousand years but cost 15 to 20 million lives in Europe alone, including at least six million Jews murdered in the Holocaust.[153]

---

[152] 'Why was Nazi Germany called the Third Reich?', Michael Ray, Britannica.com
[153] 'The blast of World War II', britannica.com

Uncovering their Names and Stories:

Identification of Jews

Hitler and the Nazi regime were paranoid about the identification of Jews. To the extent, that they even published a children's propaganda book in 1938, called 'Der Giftpilz' (The Poisonous Mushroom). I first saw information about it when I visited the Melbourne Holocaust Museum. It was popular and used in German schools. The book likened the difficulty in identifying Jews from other Germans, to identifying poisonous mushrooms from other mushrooms. It was pure hate, created for a children's market.[154]

The German propaganda book 'The Poisonous Mushroom'
(Source: German Propaganda Archive, Calvin University)

The Nazis certainly wanted to make sure that Jews were highly identifiable. On 17 August 1938, an executive order was issued requiring all German Jews with non-Jewish first names to add 'Israel' for men or 'Sara' for women to their names. This had to be completed by 1 January 1939, and personal records across Germany

---

[154] Der Giftpilz exhibit, Melbourne Holocaust Museum

were updated, effectively giving every Jew a new middle name. When you peruse records from Germany for my family from this time, you can see the amendments, including 'Israel' and 'Sara' middle names.

Under these new rules, Jews had to carry identity cards that highlighted their Jewish heritage, and Jewish passports were marked with a big red 'J'.[155] The 'Israel' and 'Sara' middle names were later removed from German record cards in the 1950s.

The next step to increase identification was in September 1941, when the 'Police ordinance on the identification of Jews' made the wearing of the yellow six-pointed star (Star of David) with the word 'Jude' in black mandatory, for all Jews in Germany aged six and above. It had to be worn when out in public.

The same regulation required Jews to obtain police permission to travel beyond their community and forbade the wearing of medals and decorations. The last part was aimed at Jewish veterans of World War 1, who often wore their medals, notably on Kristallnacht, hoping that their service to Germany would garner public support and help protect them. The official punishment for violations was a fine of up to 150 Reichsmarks or imprisonment for up to six weeks.[156]

Despite the myth spread in Hollywood movies, the only concentration camp to tattoo prisoners was the Auschwitz concentration camp complex, and then only if they were being kept alive, such as for forced labour. If they were being killed immediately, there was no need for tattooing numbers on the prisoners. This was implemented by the SS, and was another step in the dehumanising of Jews, which started in Hitler's speeches and the German media. It continued with various rights stolen away, and then in deportation in cattle cars to concentration camps and ghettos. The tattooing allowed the camp guards to identify the bodies of dead Jewish prisoners.[157]

---

[155] 'Law on Alteration of Family and Personal Names', Holocaust Encyclopedia, United States Holocaust Memorial Museum
[156] 'Polizeiverordnung Uber die Kennzeichnung der Juden', Verfassungen der Welt, 1 September 1941
[157] 'Tattoos and Numbers', Holocaust Encyclopedia, United States Holocaust Memorial Museum

Uncovering their Names and Stories:

Many of my relatives who were lost, would have had the concentration camp tattoo, as they were murdered in Auschwitz. Over forty were lost there. But most of my family were murdered at other concentration camps like Treblinka, Sachsenhausen and Mauthausen, or in ghettos such as Theresienstadt, Izbica, Minsk and Riga. For example, Kurt Polley from Liebstadt might have been tattooed, as he was deported to Auschwitz-Birkenau. Kurt was murdered there in April 1943, aged 45. His paternal grandparents, Moses and Dorothea Polley, were my great (x2) grandparents.

Post World War 2

The horrors and industrial magnitude of the Holocaust made the terrible pogroms of medieval times seem very small by comparison. Most of the few surviving Jews emigrated, if not immediately after World War 2, then to Israel after its founding in 1948.

After the War, Germany was split between totalitarian East Germany (the Russian controlled German Democratic Republic) and democratic West Germany (Federal Republic of Germany, influenced by the Western European powers and the USA), as was Berlin itself. The division between east and west Berlin was set in concrete with the Berlin Wall in 1961. Berlin was the capital of East Germany. Bonn became the capital of the Federal Republic in the west through the Cold War.[158]

This split, and the Cold War of which it was a microcosm, defined much of the second half of the twentieth century. The Berlin Wall and the so-called 'Iron Curtain' officially fell on November 9, 1989. Then began the difficult process of reunification of the two Germanys, and the return of Berlin as the unified capital of Germany, which took place in October 1990.

The small Jewish community that remained in Germany in the post-war period, was bolstered dramatically when about 200,000 Jews emigrated there from the former Soviet Union in the 1990s, as well as absorbing the arrival of a small but significant wave of Israelis,

---

[158] <u>Germany for the Jewish Traveller</u>, German National Tourist Board (GNTB), Frankfurt am Main, p7

particularly to Berlin.[159]

The renaissance of German Jewry was formalized when the Chancellor of Germany Gerhard Schröder signed an agreement with the Central Council of Jews in Germany, which brought the legal status of Jews to the same level as the Catholics and Lutherans. This took place on 27 January 2003, the anniversary of the liberation of Auschwitz. The anniversary of its liberation is commemorated on January 27 as International Holocaust Remembrance Day. The agreement committed the German government to funding the Jewish community and to nurturing Jewish cultural heritage.[160]

There are now about 125,000 Jews living in Germany, the eighth largest Jewish community by country in the world, one position above Australia with 117,200.[161] And nearly half of those Jews in Germany live in Berlin. There are now also 110 synagogues scattered around the country.[162]

---

[159] Leo Baeck Institute (2021)

[160] German National Tourist Board (GNTB) loc.cit.

[161] 'Global Jewish population hits 15.7 million ahead of new year, 46% of them in Israel', Times of Israel Staff, Times of Israel, 15 September 2023; and German Virtual Jewish History Tour, David Shyovitz and Mitchell Bard, The Virtual Jewish World, A Project of AICE, 2023

[162] German Virtual Jewish History Tour, David Shyovitz and Mitchell Bard, The Virtual Jewish World, A Project of AICE, 2023

Uncovering their Names and Stories:

5.0 My Family Tree

Through my family history research, I have identified family members going back as far as 1697, when Lazarus (Eleasar) Philipp was born in Landsberg an der Warthe (Gorzów Wielkopolski) in what was then part of Prussia and is now in western Poland. But my family did not drop to earth from another planet with the ancestors I found in my family history research. They had to have come from somewhere. The ancestors I name and describe had ancestors before them in places like western Lithuania, the German speaking principalities, and in what is now Poland.

Before that, there may have been ancestors from elsewhere in Europe, and possibly some travelling as support workers with Roman Legions as they conquered lands for the Roman Empire. And prior to that, there would have been ancestors living in the Holy Land, in the times of the Temple in Jerusalem, sharing a history with so many Jews who trace their ancestry to the times of the Maccabees, the biblical Hebrews and the slaves of the time of the Pyramids.

Map highlighting the towns and cities which were most important in the history of my family, for good or bad

(Map created by author in MapChart)

What I have uncovered in the family, is about 300 years of German Jews with roots in various parts of central and eastern Europe, notably what is now western Lithuania, western Poland, and northern and central Germany.

In the following part of this chapter, you will find the family trees of my ancestor families that I have uncovered through my research. They are in summary, with further description and stories in chapters to follow. My complete discovered family tree is available on Ancestry.com, while I use MyHeritage as my research sandpit. My family tree on MyHeritage is where I can play with unconfirmed suggestions from MyHeritage and explore still-to-be-proven hypotheses.

My family tree on Ancestry is far more reliable, trustworthy and based on evidence. To access my family tree on Ancestry, if you have an Ancestry account or open a free Ancestry guest account, you can use the following QR code with your camera phone:

Much of the family is yet to be discovered, especially before the 1700s, and many family members have been sadly lost to time. Records have been lost to fire, bombardment, other war damage or some other tragedy, or family connections have been lost through administrative mishaps, remarriage, changes of name or similar events which have broken the chain of documentation.

Following this chapter are the chapters covering the stories and details of my family and ancestors through each clan or branch of the

Uncovering their Names and Stories:

family, dating back through three centuries. Some family members have a more detailed story of their life described, where they were specifically important to me, where I find their stories particularly interesting or poignant, or where I believe their story is useful in illustrating a particular period and era my family lived through. While others are mentioned out of respect for their memory - to ensure that they are not forgotten.

My Parents, Grandparents and Great Grandparents

When I started my family history research, I did not even know the names of my paternal grandparents. Now I know the names and at least some details about all my grandparents and great grandparents, and have visited places where many of them lived, worked and were buried. My parents, Henry Marlow and Ilse Marlow nee Elkan, were born during the Weimar Republic, in post-World War 1 Germany. My grandparents were all born in the German Empire after 1870, and all my great grandparents were born in German-speaking states prior to unification.

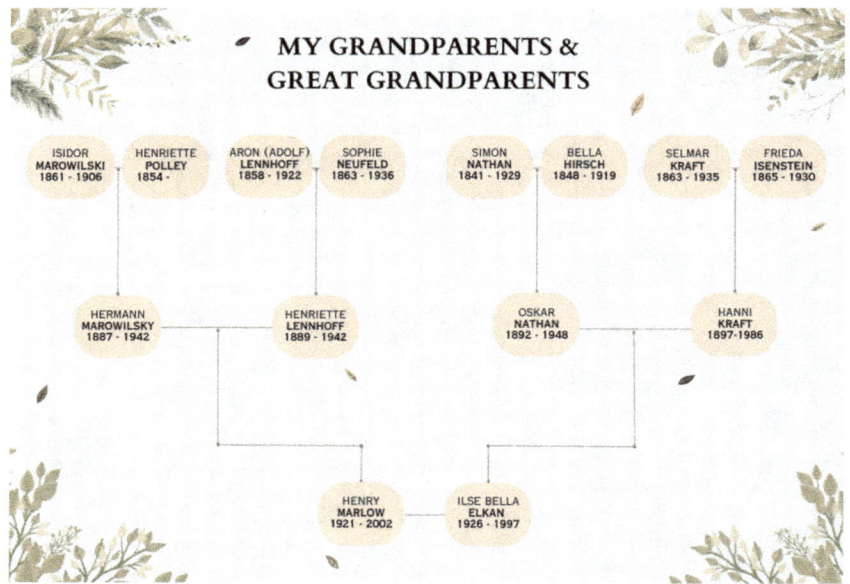

(Design: Kim Gasperino; Sourced from Ancestry, MyHeritage, JewishGen, Compgen, Dad's photo album, Yad Vashem, FamilySearch, gravestones and elsewhere)

Uncovering their Names and Stories:

My Marowilski and Polley Family Tree

My father Henry Marlow's Marowilsky/Marowilski family came from Vistytis, Lithuania via Pillau in East Prussia, and then moved to Wuppertal which is in modern day North Rhine-Westphalia. Dad's grandmother Henriette Polley's family came from the small village of Liebstadt in East Prussia, now named Miłakowo in modern Poland.

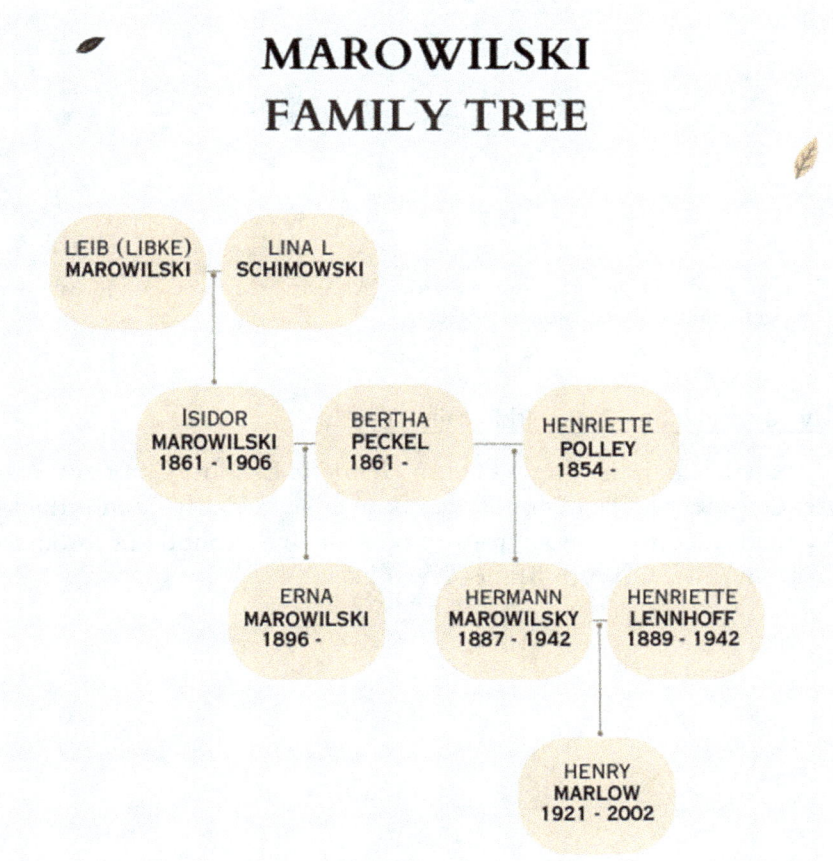

(Design: Kim Gasperino; Sourced from Ancestry, MyHeritage, JewishGen, Compgen, FamilySearch, gravestones and elsewhere)

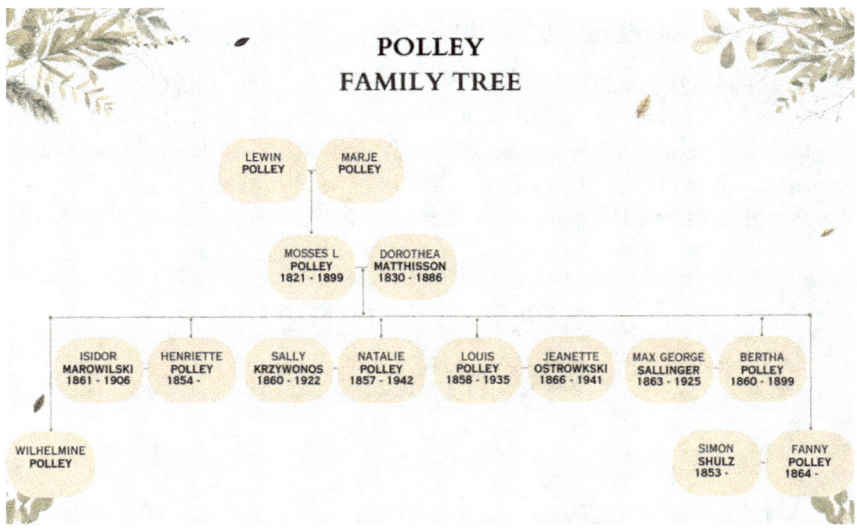

(Design: Kim Gasperino; Sourced from Ancestry, MyHeritage, JewishGen, Compgen, FamilySearch and elsewhere)

My Lennhoff and Neufeld Family Tree

My paternal grandmother was born Henriette Lennhoff, and my great grandmother Sophie Lennhoff was born a Neufeld. My Lennhoff and Neufeld ancestors came from various towns around the modern German state of North Rhine–Westphalia.

Uncovering their Names and Stories:

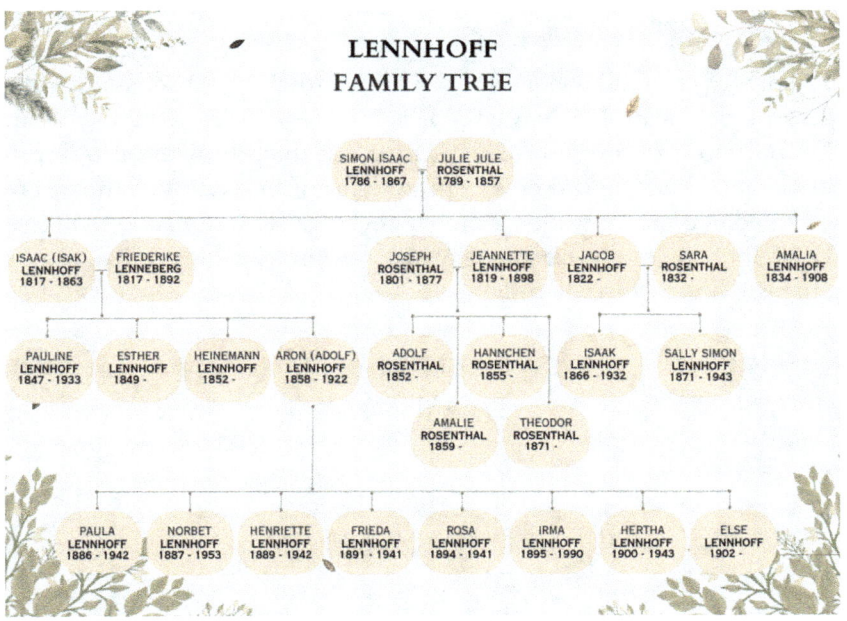

(Design: Kim Gasperino; Sourced from Ancestry, MyHeritage, JewishGen, Compgen, FamilySearch, gravestones, Löwenhardt Foundation – Netherlands, Yad Vashem, Arno Heller's Holocaust testimony and elsewhere)

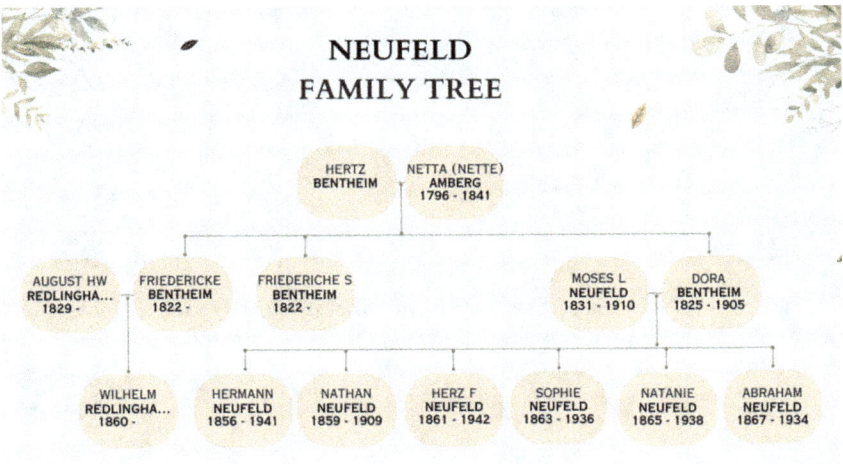

(Design: Kim Gasperino; Sourced from Ancestry, MyHeritage, JewishGen, Compgen, FamilySearch, gravestones, Löwenhardt Foundation - Netherlands and elsewhere)

My Nathan - Elkan Family Tree

My maternal grandfather was Oskar Nathan, later changing his surname to Elkan. My Nathan - Elkan ancestors came mainly from Hamburg in northern Germany, with most then moving onto Berlin between the wars, and then escaping to far distant lands, if they were not killed in concentration camps or ghettoes. They escaped to places like Melbourne, Australia and Cleveland, Ohio. We have Elkan family cousins living in Florida today.

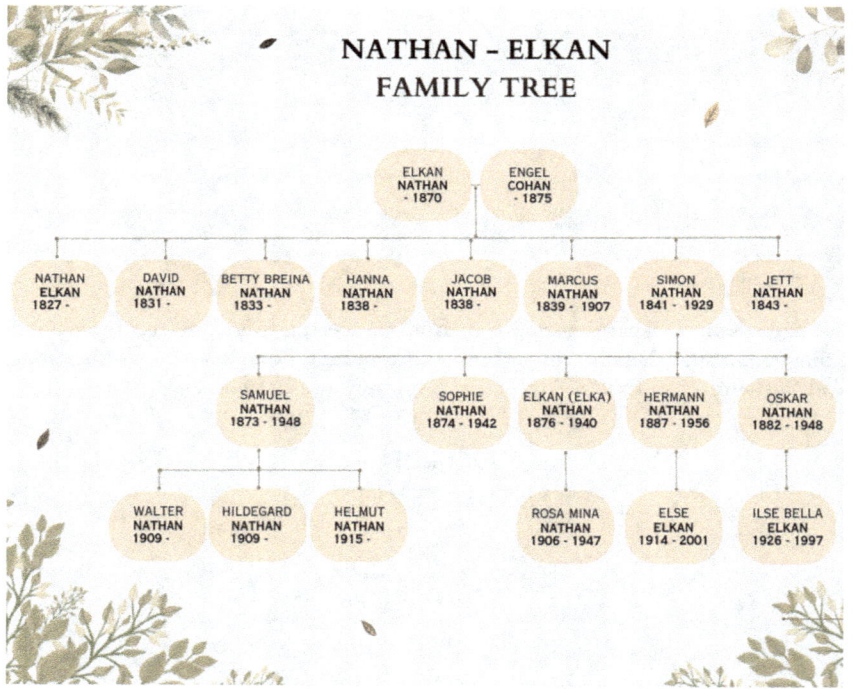

(Design: Kim Gasperino; Sourced from Ancestry, MyHeritage, JewishGen, Compgen, FamilySearch, gravestones, Staatarchiv Hamburg and elsewhere)

Uncovering their Names and Stories:

My Kraft Family Tree

My Nana, my mother's mother, Hanni Elkan was born Hanni Kraft in Leipzig. My Kraft family ancestors came from towns and cities in eastern Germany, in places that are in modern day Saxony-Anhalt and Saxony, including Calbe, Magdeburg, Stassfurt and Leipzig. The Holocaust did great damage to the family, but we have various cousins living today, who are descended from the Kraft family living in Melbourne, Los Angeles, New York, New Jersey, Toronto, Berlin and The Netherlands.

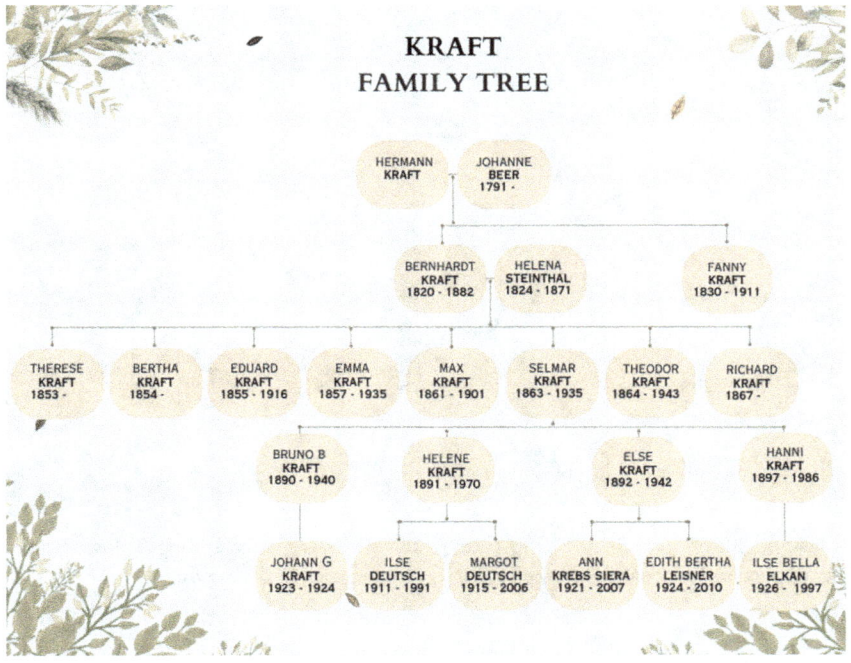

(Design: Kim Gasperino; Sourced from Ancestry, MyHeritage, JewishGen, Compgen, FamilySearch, gravestones, Dan Rotman family tree and elsewhere)

My Isenstein Family Tree

My great grandmother Frieda Kraft, wife of Selmar Kraft, was born Frieda Isenstein in Hannover. My Isenstein ancestors came from Hildesheim and Hannover in northern Germany. The earliest ancestor on my Isenstein family tree is Marcus Salomon who would have been born in the early 1700s.

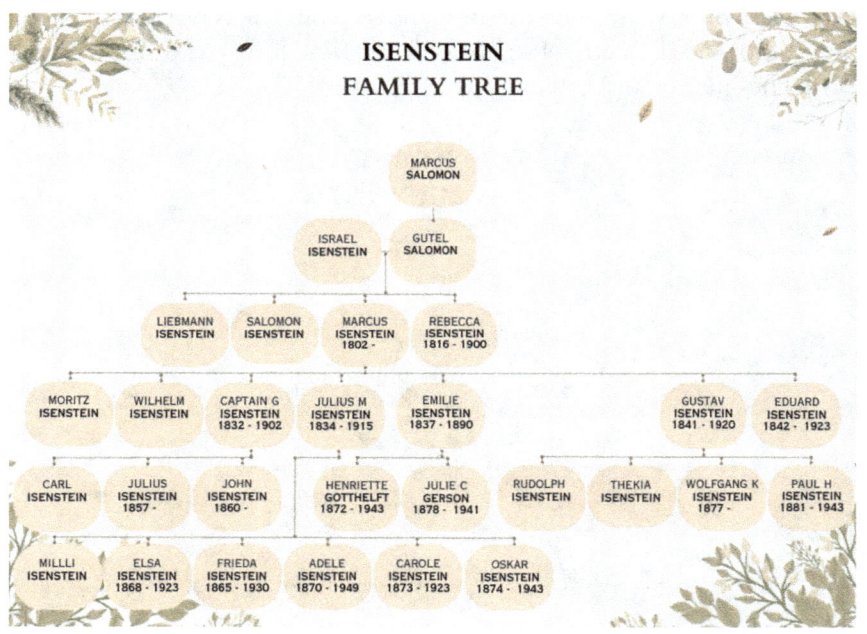

(Design: Kim Gasperino; Sourced from Ancestry, MyHeritage, JewishGen, Compgen, FamilySearch, Shapell Roster, gravestones and elsewhere)

My Lazarus – Steinthal Family Tree

My great (x2) grandmother Helena Kraft was part of the Lazarus - Steinthal family from Gröbzig. My Lazarus - Steinthal family tree starts with the book dealer, my great (x5) grandfather Lazarus (Eleasar) Philipp (1697-1772) who was born in Landsberg an der Warthe in eastern Prussia, in what is now western Poland, and his wife Rochel Philipp (1701-). They raised a family in the small town of Gröbzig, in what is now the German state of Saxony-Anhalt in eastern Germany.

Uncovering their Names and Stories:

Lazarus and Rochel's four children helped build a very large family, very much thanks to their son and my great (x4) grandfather Michael Lazarus (1729-1813), who had eight sons from four wives. The family had a diversity of descendants, becoming for example teachers, merchants, shopkeepers, factory owners, academics, doctors and bankers. As the family grew, it spread around Saxony-Anhalt, and many ended up in Berlin, very middle class and very assimilated into German culture.

The Steinthal family is connected to my Kraft family through my great (x3) grandparents Moses Steinthal and Chaichen Steinthal nee Samson's daughter Helena marrying Bernhardt Kraft from Calbe. Moses and Chaichen had nine daughters in total.

There is a variety of evidence to show that the Steinthal and Kraft families were connected via Helena's marriage to Bernhardt Kraft. Firstly, Helena's marriage to a Kraft from Calbe is noted on the Lazarus – Steinthal family tree kept in the Leo Baeck Institute. And there were not many Krafts in the small town of Calbe at the time. Secondly, many of my distant DNA matches have Steinthal connections in their family trees, typically linking back to my great (x4) grandfather Michael Lazarus. And various documents show that Bernhardt was married to a Helena, though she may have been using the 'Lichtenstein' surname for some time before she married Bernhardt.

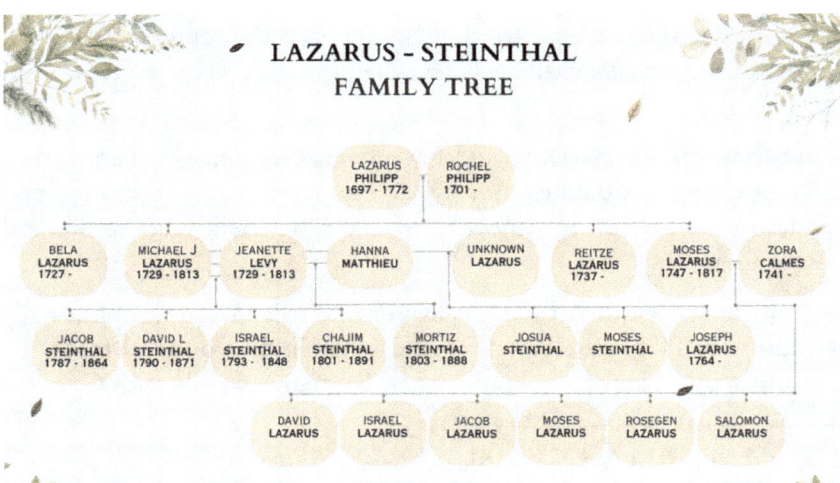

(Design: Kim Gasperino; Sourced from Lazarus-Steinthal Family Tree held by the

Leo Baeck Institute – New York, and the Protected Jews Archives, LASA – Dessau-Rösslau, Saxony Anhalt and Ancestry)

What language did my ancestors speak?

My ancestors were predominantly from German speaking lands, especially in what is modern day Germany, so one might have assumed they always spoke German. After all, my parents spoke no Yiddish. But that is not the case.

For the sake of this research, I have distinguished between Western Yiddish, which was spoken in German speaking lands, and Eastern Yiddish, which was enormously popular from Poland eastwards. What most people around the world think of as 'Yiddish' today, is Eastern Yiddish.

My Marowilski great grandparents and beyond from what is modern day Lithuania, would have spoken Eastern Yiddish, and when the family moved to East Prussia, they would have adopted German as their new standard language, at least in inter-relationships outside the family.

Most of my ancestors from all over what is now Germany, would have spoken Western Yiddish until at least the late 18th century. German Jews started shifting from Western Yiddish to German in the late 18th and early 19th centuries thanks to the Jewish Enlightenment. So much so, that by the early 20th century, Western Yiddish was virtually extinct. It had died out as a written language in the 1820s.[163]

After that, my ancestors would have been German speakers across the many towns and cities they lived. Part of this transition involved sending the children to schools or having teachers who spoke and taught German.

Both forms of Yiddish are basically Germanic languages, traditionally written with Hebrew characters. Western Yiddish derived from the combination of Hebrew, Aramaic and Romance words with German

---

[163] 'Yiddish', BJE: NSW Board of Jewish Education, bje.org.au/knowledge-centre/jewish-languages/non-hebrew/yiddish/

Uncovering their Names and Stories:

dialects around 1000 – 1250 CE.[164] I can remember in my younger days, copies of the Australian Jewish News being printed in Yiddish with Hebrew characters, as well as the main English edition.

Eastern Yiddish was the language of the author and playwright Sholem Aleichem, famous for his stories about 'Tevye the Dairyman', which was the basis for 'Fiddler on the Roof'. Half of Eastern Yiddish speakers were murdered in the Holocaust, but the language continues to thrive amongst Ultra-Orthodox Jews and other cultural inheritors of Yiddish, particularly amongst many descendants of Polish Jews.

Missing women

One the most disappointing aspects I found with this research was the invisibility of Jewish women through the years. Amos Elon has also noted this in <u>The Pity of It All: A Portrait of Jews in Germany 1743-1933</u>, "Sadly, very little is known of Jewish women in nineteenth-century Germany; most available sources deal exclusively with men."[165]

Until the 20th century, these women had generally been mainly homemakers, responsible for raising the children in the German Jewish household for centuries. It was certainly an important role, especially where they often had quite a few children, and the husband could be away for extended periods, travelling around towns trading their wares. This would also have included being responsible for religious observance at home, keeping a kosher home and often community involvement. This became easier as travelling merchants settled into shops or professions in larger towns or cities, so the husband could be home more, contributing to the household work needs, and housekeepers and nannies for the family became possible for some wealthier families.

Nevertheless, many women ran the business when the husband was away, and some ran their own businesses. Often the woman had to take over when the husband died. And when eventually husbands

---

[164] ibid.
[165] Amos Elon (2002) p.270

were locked up in concentration camps after Kristallnacht, women stood up in the most trying of times, taking charge and dealing with the Gestapo, emigration processes and the Nazi bureaucracy.

Jewish women only really started attending Jewish universities in the 1900s, which started to make entering various professions possible.[166] Jewish men obtained freedoms in the 19th century, but Jewish women would have to wait much longer. As it says in the 'The Shalvi/Hyman Encyclopedia of Jewish Women', "Jewish men did finally achieve full political and civil rights with the unification of Germany in 1871."[167]

When women were finally allowed into universities in Germany around 1900, a third of students were women.[168] German women could not vote until 1918 and were banned from joining political organisations until 1908. German Jewish women were doubly discriminated against as women and Jews, despite being citizens.

Women were also often missing from the family tree. Records would identify, say my great (x5) grandfather Lazarus Philipp (1697-1772), but not his wife. I only found her name, Rochel Philipp (1701-), in the records of the Protected Jews in the record books from the 1700's in the LASA Archives in Dessau-Roßlau.

Sometimes there were multiple wives not recorded, such as for Michael Lazarus. He had four wives that we know of, but we only know the names of two of them, Jeanette Levy (1767-) and Hanna Matthieu. No information has emerged on Moses Steinthal's wife Chaichen Samson. Frequently they were just ghosts hidden behind their husbands.

The husbands had employment, built businesses and once free to do so, professions, but this came later. Businesses promoted the names of their male owners, such as Selmar Kraft or Theodor Kraft, but not their wives Frieda and Kathinka. For many years, women were not

---

[166] 'Germany: 1750-1945', Associate Professor Sharon Gillerman, The Shalvi/Hyman Encyclopedia of Jewish Women, Jewish Women's Archive, 31 December 1999

[167] ibid.

[168] 'Women's Lives: Work and Impact of Jewish Women in Hamburg', Hamburg key documents on German-Jewish history, Institut für die Geschichte der Deutschen Juden, 2016

Uncovering their Names and Stories:

free to pursue careers, from which recognition and maybe some independence could be derived. They became shadows in history, rather than being able to stand out like today in such roles as journalists, doctors, solicitors, dentists, surgeons, teachers, professors, artists and in business.

While German Jewish men assimilated in the later 19th century into German society through professions, academia and business, middle class and upper class German Jewish women created many voluntary associations and became significantly involved in non-Jewish associations. These were often in the areas of health and self-help societies.[169] For example, an advertisement on page 6 of the Israelitisches Familienblatt (Jewish community newspaper) on 12 September 1912 lists my great grandmother Henriette Marowilsky (nee Polley) as a donor to a Jewish homelessness charity, amongst many other donors.

There were also prominent upper class Jewish women who ran salons in Berlin, notably Rachel Levin Varnhagen, Henriette Herz and Dorothea Schlegel Mendelssohn, hosting social and intellectual gatherings at their homes, including Jews, non-Jews, noblemen and commoners. Count Alexander zu Dohna even made an unsuccessful marriage proposal to the widowed Henriette Herz. These salons did not exist for long, but they crossed the pre-existing barriers of religion, social status and gender.[170]

The roles of poor and working-class Jewish women, who often had to work to support the family, are usually neglected in the histories of the period. Given the number of men killed or severely injured in wars, or dying well before the wife, as frequently happened in my family, women often had to find ways to continue the family business, take in boarders to make ends meet, or find paid work.

Women were increasingly in the German workforce, but German Jewish women were proportionally significantly less in the formal workforce. In 1882, eleven percent of German Jewish women in Prussia were in the workforce, compared to 21% for non-Jewish

---

[169] Sharon Gillerman (1999)
[170] ibid. and <u>Jews in Germany: From Roman Times to the Weimar Republic</u>, Nachum T. Gidal, Könemann, Cologne, 1988, p.15

women. By 1907, these numbers had increased to 18% and 30% respectively.[171]

Emigration counseling office in Berlin in 1936, such as my grandmother Hanni Elkan would have worked with to get her family to safety in 1938
(Source: Sueddeutsche Zeitung Photo via Alamy Stock Photos / public domain)

Unfortunately, the 19th century Jewish Reform Movement did not bring the religious equality for women we might have expected, given where the Reform Movement is today. Women often remained seated separately to men, they could not be counted in a minyan, nor be called to the Torah. At that stage, it had been more about prayers, prayer books and sermons in German.

By the time of the Nazi regime, a significant proportion of Jewish women received doctorates from German universities, often in medicine or philosophy. Many pursued careers in social work and teaching. Though wherever they went or worked, being Jewish and female, they faced significant discrimination in the workplace and social settings.

---

[171] Sharon Gillerman (1999)

Uncovering their Names and Stories:

The removal of rights and institutional racism under the Nazis affected men and women. Many women had to work, who had not worked before, as their husbands lost their careers and employment, or worse. Jewish women also often had to defend their husbands with the authorities, many raising their husband's World War 1 service. They had to seek to get their husbands released after arrest and find an escape avenue from Nazi Germany. I can picture my Nana going to an emigration office in Berlin to get her family out of Germany, while her husband was in Sachsenhausen. I can imagine her booking the ship to Australia and dealing with the authorities to get Oskar released. She would also have had to find a country that would take them, arrange passports (if they did not already have them), go through the bureaucratic process with the Gestapo and police, arrange certification with the Finance Office, send petitions to Sachsenhausen and the Gestapo to arrange release and sell whatever property she could.[172]

---

[172] The Routledge History of the Holocaust, Jonathan C Friedman (ed.), Routledge, Oxford, 2011, p.97

6.0 The Lazarus – Steinthal Family

My Lazarus – Steinthal family ancestry dates back to at least 1697 starting with the birth of Lazarus Philipp, and has a long and important history in the small town of Gröbzig, and in later years in the German capital Berlin:

Lazarus Philipp (1697-1772)
Father of
V
Michael Lazarus (Reb Jechiel) (1729-1813)
Father of
V
Moses Steinthal (circa 1760s-mid 1800s)
Father of
V
Helena Steinthal (1824-1871)
Mother of
V
Selmar Kraft (1863-1935)
Father of
V
Hanni Elkan ("Nana") (1897-1986)
Mother of
V
Ilse Marlow (1926-1997)
Mother of
V
David Marlow (1962-)

The bookseller from Gorzów Wielkopolski

My earliest ancestor that I have identified through my family research is Lazarus (Eleasar) Philipp (1697-1772), who in some online family trees has been erroneously identified as Eleasar Steinthal, but Lazarus died in 1772, decades before the family adopted the Steinthal surname in 1821.[173]

---

[173] Protected Jews archives in the LASA Archives in Dessau-Roßlau

Uncovering their Names and Stories:

All records agree he was a book dealer, as was his older brother, whose first name is yet to be identified. According to Lazarus' great grandson Heymann Steinthal, the brothers bought and sold new and used Hebrew books. Coincidently, or possibly due to genetics, I had my own bookshop business in Australia from 2003 to 2012 with stores in the suburbs of Hampton and Toorak in Melbourne, Australia. But I do not think that Lazarus ever had to worry about competition from Amazon, e-books or a Borders bookshop opening down the road.

The Lazarus-Steinthal Family Tree held in the Esther Elbin Family Collection of the Leo Baeck Institute – New York indicates Lazarus Philipp was born in 1697, and this is supported by the Protected Jews record books in the Dessau-Roßlau Archives. To put this timing in perspective, this was a year before the Glorious Revolution in England, when Catholic King James II was replaced by his Protestant daughter Mary, and her husband William of Orange. Or from another perspective, 72 years before Napoleon Bonaparte was born.

Lazarus – Steinthal Family Tree from Esther Elbin Family Collection
(Source: Courtesy of the Leo Baeck Institute – New York)

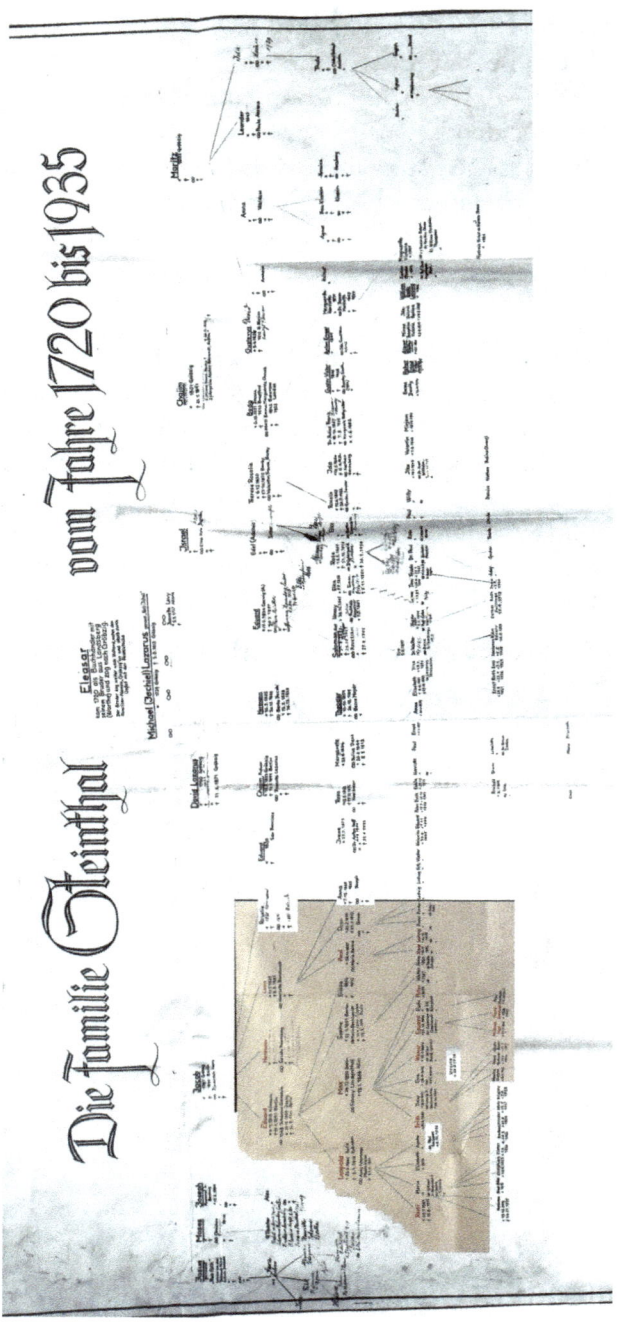

Uncovering their Names and Stories:

This Lazarus – Steinthal Family Tree is held in the Esther Elbin Collection in the Leo Baeck Institute in New York, provided by Esther Elbin nee Cohn (1918-1984). Esther was the great (x4) granddaughter of Michael Lazarus, who is my great (x5) grandfather. Esther is descended through Michael's son, Israel Steinthal (1793-1848), Israel's son Eduard (1824-1897), Eduard's daughter Henriette (1865-1949), and Henriette's daughter Elka Buchholz (1994-1973). Elka is Esther's mother. Esther had a twin sister Ruth Franziska Cohn Unger-Kempinski (1918-1984). Coincidently, both Ruth and Esther died in 1984, but quite a few months and kilometres apart, Esther in California and Ruth in Rotterdam.

Mistakenly, I had thought that Lazarus Philipp came from Landsberg an der Warthe, near Sessenhausen in what is now western Germany. This was indicated in several family trees on genealogical websites. The managers of those family trees had mistakenly assumed that Lazarus had come from the Landsberg an der Warthe near Sessenhausen in modern day Germany, which is basically a truck stop and restaurant, rather than the town to the east. The truck stop comes up if searching on Google Maps. That was why I visited Sessenhausen and the wrong Landsberg an der Warthe on my research road trip. But with further research, I have discovered that is not the case.

Many towns in and around Germany have the same or similar names, which is why they sometimes use the name of the river flowing through the town or city to help distinguish the town they are talking about, such as Frankfurt am Main, Frankfurt an der Oder, Calbe (Saale) and Landsberg an der Warthe.

Lazarus Philipp was actually born in Landsberg an der Warthe in what was Prussia but is now in the west of modern Poland, or Gorzów Wielkopolski as it has been known since the end of World War 2. It is not far from the modern border with Germany.

Furthermore, Prof Heymann Steinthal (1823-1899) wrote in an article on his childhood memories, about his great grandfather

Lazarus (Eleasar) and Lazarus' brother travelling from Landsberg an der Warthe to Amsterdam, stopping in Gröbzig along the way.[174]

This only makes sense if the brothers were travelling from the direction of Poland, as Gröbzig sits on virtually a straight line westward from Landsberg an der Warthe (Gorzów Wielkopolski) to Amsterdam in the Netherlands. It would be completely the wrong direction to travel from the speck of Landsberg an der Warthe in Germany.

This is clear when you view the map below. Lazarus' origins in Gorzów Wielkopolski were further confirmed in a presentation on Heymann Steinthal by Prof Dr Wolfgang Behr in 2009.[175]

The Jewish community of Gorzów Wielkopolski dates to the 14th century, but all the Jews were expelled in 1573, gradually building back the community to 21 Jewish families by 1690. Lazarus was born just a few years later in 1697. In 1701 the town became part of the Kingdom of Prussia. Its Jewish population had reached 417 by 1717, when all Jews "without right of domicile" were again expelled, with only 96 remaining.[176] It peaked at a Jewish population of 450 in 1910.[177]

Gorzów Wielkopolski currently has a population over 125,000, and reportedly no Jews remain. The old Jewish cemetery is in very poor condition, with only seven or eight gravestones remaining out of up to 100 graves there originally.[178]

---

[174] 'Aus den Jugenderinnerungen Steinthals mit einer Vorbemerkung von Leo Baeck', <u>Der Morgen</u>, Heymann Steinthal, pp. 141-146, 8. Jahrgang, June 1932, 2. Heft, p.141

[175] 'Avant la letter: Chajjim Steinthal (1823-1899) as a linguist of Chinese revisited', Wolfgang Behr, keynote presentation, 6th Conference of the European Association of Chinese Linguistics, Adam Mickiewicz University, Poznan Poland, 26 August 2009

[176] 'Virtual Jewish World: Gorzów Wielkopolski, Poland', Jewish Virtual Library, Encyclopaedia Judaica, 2008

[177] 'Landsberg an der Warthe (Brandenburg Neumark) – today in Poland', Benjamin Rosendahl, Germanysynagogues.com

[178] 'Gorzów Wielkopolski: Lubusz', International Jewish Cemetery Project, International Association of Jewish Genealogical Societies

Uncovering their Names and Stories:

Map comparing travelling from Landsberg an der Warthe (Germany) to Amsterdam compared to travelling from Landsberg an der Warthe (Gorzów Wielkopolski, Poland) to Amsterdam

(Map created by author in Google Maps)

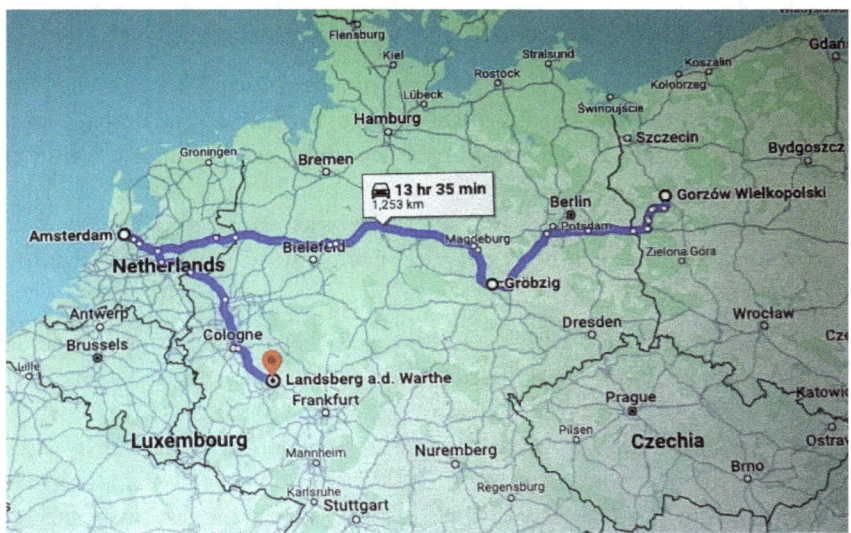

The Lazarus - Steinthal family of Gröbzig

The book dealers Lazarus Philipp and his older brother arrived in Gröbzig from Gorzów Wielkopolski in 1720, likely having been expelled along with most of the Jewish population of the town in 1717. They bought and sold new and used Hebrew books along their travels.[179]

In the time of Lazarus, there were Hebrew printing presses around Anhalt-Dessau, notably in Köthen (only a three hour walk north from Gröbzig), Dessau (until 1704), and Jeßnitz (which is halfway between Gröbzig and Bernburg). This would have helped generate supply for their book trading. Books Lazarus might have dealt in include Maimonides' Code with commentaries (1739–42),

---

[179] 'Aus den Jugenderinnerungen Steinthals mit einer Vorbemerkung von Leo Baeck', <u>Der Morgen</u>, Heymann Steinthal, pp. 141-146, 8. Jahrgang, June 1932, 2. Heft, p.141

Maimonides' 'Guide for the Perplexed' (1742), the 'Sifra', and the Jerusalem Talmud, 'Seder Mo'ed'.[180]

Lazarus decided to stay in Gröbzig, reportedly tired of travelling, and became a successful and respected citizen of the small town. His brother's first name remains unknown, but we know he moved to the Netherlands and there took the surname Gröbzig.[181]

After he left Gröbzig, Lazarus' brother continued his journey to Amsterdam, and the family did not hear from him for many years. Years later Lazarus travelled to Amsterdam in his "old age". While in the synagogue in Amsterdam to commemorate the festival of Tisha B'av[182] he told a local servant where he was from, and the servant responded that a member of the community had the surname Gröbzig.

The synagogue may well have been the Great Ashkenazi Synagogue in Amsterdam, which was inaugurated in 1671, and now forms part of the Joods Historisch Museum (Jewish Historical Museum).[183] From the early 1500s, Amsterdam was populated by Sephardi Jews from Portugal, but in the early 1600s Jews from Central Europe started moving to the city, overtaking the Sephardim in numbers by 1700. In 1676, Amsterdam was home to 5,000 Ashkenazi Jews and 2,500 Sephardim.[184]

The community member also had the same first name as Lazarus' brother, and despite his brother initially not recognising him, Lazarus had found his long-lost sibling. His brother said since he had no family in Amsterdam, he wanted to move to Gröbzig in the following Spring. Unfortunately, he never made it. As he was travelling back to Gröbzig from the Netherlands, his stagecoach overturned, and he

---

[180] 'Anhalt, Germany', Jewishvirtuallibrary.org

[181] Guide to Die Famalie Steinthal von Jahre 1720 bis 1935, 1935-1961, AR1393, Leo Baeck Institute

[182] Tisha B'av (Ninth of the Hebrew month of Av), commemorates the destruction of the first and second temples in Jerusalem in 586 BCE and 70 CE respectively.

[183] 'Great Ashkenazi Synagogue in Amsterdam', Religiana.com

[184] 'History of the Jews in Amsterdam', Wikipedia

Uncovering their Names and Stories:

died in the accident.[185] You had to be careful on the roads even then. Unfortunately, the older brother never married and had no children. He would have enjoyed having the large family network in Gröbzig.[186]

The small town of Gröbzig has a population today of about 3,000, and is located between what was Saxony and Prussia, in the current state of Saxony-Anhalt. In Lazarus' time, it provided Jewish traders a convenient home base for business trips. Most importantly, it was close for the trip to the Leipzig trade fair which is a reasonable distance for the local merchants to travel to and from. You can walk it in a day or two, and much faster by coach, horse or cart. Traders could stop overnight in Halle (Saale) or Landsberg (Saale) along the way.

By the end of the 1600's, Anhalt had established more favorable living and economic conditions for Jews, and more Jewish families gradually settled in Gröbzig. While there were only three Jewish families in 1713, by 1763 there were 40 Jewish families in the town, which was at least 15% of the population. The community included Jews from very different German speaking countries, including Prussia, Hesse, Saxony, and Bohemia. Nevertheless, the Protected Jews in Gröbzig still had to pay 10 thalers in protection money every year.[187]

It became a very Jewish town. In the 1700s and 1800s, 15% to 20% of the town's population were Jewish. In the mid-1800s, they had a Jewish mayor and largely Jewish city council for two council terms.[188]

Lazarus was one of the Gröbzig Jews who traded in Leipzig. Among the Jews of Gröbzig, there were some wealthy merchants, but also

---

[185] 'Aus den Jugenderinnerungen Steinthals mit einer Vorbemerkung von Leo Baeck', <u>Der Morgen</u>, Heymann Steinthal, pp. 141-146, 8. Jahrgang, June 1932, 2. Heft.
[186] ibid. pp141-142.
[187] 'Chajim Steinthal' by Friedrich Ekkehard Vollbach on Sachsen-Lese
[188] 'Provenance Research on Judaica and other holdings in the Museum Synagogue Gröbzig since 1933', Tim Schauer, Museum Synagogue Gröbzig, 29 June 2020

small traders, cattle dealers, a doctor, a schoolmaster and a butcher. The Jews at the time lived mainly on Lange Strasse and around the market area. Unusually for the time, the Jews in Gröbzig were allowed to freely choose their place of residence. They owned houses and were able to operate shops and stores. They were only forbidden from practicing a craft or from working in a factory, but during the Napoleonic Wars these restrictions were also lifted.[189]

Lazarus and his wife Rochel (1701-) had two sons and two daughters. Their sons were Moses Lazarus (1747-1817) and Michael (Jechiel) Lazarus (1729-1813). Michael was also known as Reb' Jehel or Jechiel, indicating he was a respected married man. Both sons were born in Gröbzig,[190] as were Lazarus and Rochel's daughters Bela Lazarus (1727-) and Reitze Lazarus (1737-).[191]

Lazarus Philipp became a Protected Jew on 6 February 1754, paying a special tax (Schutzgeld) of 10 thaler per year to the Duke of Anhalt for protection. In time, his sons Michael and Moses also became Protected Jews.[192]

Protected Jews or 'Schutzjuden' were provided letters of protection (Schutzbriefe) from the Duke and paid the annual tax for the privilege. The record books for the Anhalt 'Schutzjuden' from the 1700s and 1800s are preserved at the Archives in Dessau-Roßlau, and I was able to review the treasure trove of original documents during my visit there in March 2024. The archivists very kindly extracted the record books that held the records for my Lazarus and Steinthal family ancestors. A library trolley-load of boxed original record books from the 1700s and 1800s welcomed me when I arrived at the Archives, which provided a gold mine of information on the Lazarus – Steinthal family, including family members previously unidentified,

---

[189] ibid.
[190] Guide to Die Famalie Steinthal von Jahre 1720 bis 1935, 1935-1961, AR1393, Leo Baeck Institute and Protected Jews archives in the LASA Archives in Dessau-Roßlau (Z 44, C 1c No.23) and (Z 44, C 1c, No. 23 p27v and p28r)
[191] Protected Jews archives in the LASA Archives in Dessau-Roßlau
[192] ibid.

Uncovering their Names and Stories:

milestone years, some addresses and confirming many family details, such as the date they adopted the Steinthal surname.

The 'Schutzjuden' concept originated under the Holy Roman Empire, and the rights over Jews were later transferred from the Emperor to local princes and free cities.[193] The status of 'Schutzjuden' was highly sought after and were restricted in number. They also appear to have been limited to male heads of households. They generally provided a right of residence and travel, as well as various trading rights, which were required for commercial activities. They were allowed to buy houses or farms.[194]

Schutzjuden document mentioning Lazarus and Rochel Philipp

(Source: Schutzjuden documents from the Landesarchiv Sachsen-Anhalt in Dessau-Roßlau; photo credit: David Marlow)

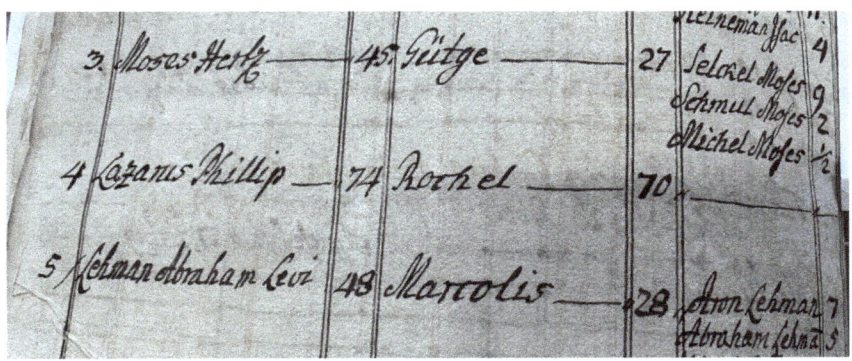

Lazarus' eldest son Michael Lazarus had eight sons – Josua (Reb Falk), my great (x3) grandfather Moses, Joseph (1764-), Jacob (1787-1864), David (1790-1832), Israel (1793-1848), Chajjim (1801-1891), and Moritz (1803-1888), with four wives (hopefully sequentially), including Jeanette Levy (1767-) and Hanna Matthieu.[195]

---

[193] 'Schutzjuden', Encyclopedia.com
[194] 'Aus den Jugenderinnerungen Steinthals mit einer Vorbemerkung von Leo Baeck', <u>Der Morgen</u>, Heymann Steinthal, pp. 141-146, 8. Jahrgang, June 1932, 2. Heft, p.141
[195] <u>Guide to Die Famalie Steinthal von Jahre 1720 bis 1935, 1935-1961</u>, AR1393, Leo Baeck Institute and 'Aus den Jugenderinnerungen Steinthals mit einer Vorbemerkung von Leo

Lazarus Philipp's other son, Moses Lazarus married Zora Calmes (1741-), and had five sons and a daughter, Rosegen who married Aron Abraham. Moses and Zora's sons were David, Israel, Jacob, Moses and Salomon Lazarus.[196]

Moses Lazarus became a Protected Jew on 17 June 1761.[197] Michael was also a Protected Jew, and his son David became one on 30 March 1816, most likely replacing Michael who had died in 1813. Eduard Steinthal became a Protected Jew on 10 August 1841. The Lazarus – Steinthal family appears to have largely lived on Hallesche Straße in Gröbzig, one of the major streets in town, until the family gradually left for other towns or Berlin.[198] Their presence in town involved a couple of houses and at least for some time a farm. Michael bought a house next to his father's property in 1776.[199]

I drove into Gröbzig along Hallesche Straße, which is one of the town's major streets, and walked along it on my visit. I was able to amble along where my ancestors had walked and lived, and the town looked largely the same size as it had been in my ancestors' days. Except cars have replaced horse drawn carts and carriages. Many of the old buildings remain.

One of Michael's sons David Lazarus, arranged for the family to change their surnames to Steinthal in 1821, as permanent surnames became compulsory. David later became co-leader of the Jewish community in Gröbzig with Gerson Rosenbaum in 1823 and 1825.[200]

Baeck', Der Morgen, Heymann Steinthal, pp. 141-146, 8. Jahrgang, June 1932, 2. Heft, p.142

[196] Protected Jews archives in the LASA Archives in Dessau-Roßlau, and Family Research notes on Steinthal family in register books of 'Protected Jews' in Gröbzig, Anke Boeck, Landesarchiv Sachsen-Anhalt, Dessau-Roßlau, 19 March 2024

[197] Protected Jews archives in the LASA Archives in Dessau-Roßlau (Z 44, C 15 Nr. 103)

[198] ibid. pp.16ff

[199] Family Research notes on Steinthal family in register books of 'Protected Jews' in Gröbzig, Anke Boeck, Landesarchiv Sachsen-Anhalt, Dessau-Roßlau, 19 March 2024

[200] Protected Jews archives in the LASA Archives in Dessau-Roßlau (Z 44, C 15 Nr 104 Bl. 1 u. Bl. 60)

Uncovering their Names and Stories:

David died at the age of 42 in 1832, from the flu while on a business trip. His wife Henriette Heinemann (1785-1871) continued to run the shop, with the help of Eduard Steinthal (1820-), their eldest son (age 12). David was also the father of the famous German philologist[201], philosopher and linguist Prof Dr Heymann (Chajim) Steinthal (1823-1899). Their youngest son Hermann Heinrich Steinthal (1825-1899) became a medical doctor. Unfortunately, Henriette had to close the business because her debtors reportedly failed to pay their debts. Sadly, after that, they lived in what Heymann Steinthal later described as poor conditions.

Fritz Jahrmarkt wrote in his book about Gröbzig, that Heymann's birthplace was, "a tiny, unsightly one-storey house, yet imposing by Gröbzig standards."[202] The home also housed David's store. When he extended two small windows on the street side of the building into one large window, it became the first shop window in the town. There was a sign above the window, which proudly stated, "David Steinthal – Manufaktur-, Weiss-und Wollwaren". He sold fabrics, which were measured and cut to customer order, underwear and woollen goods.

Heymann Steinthal wrote two essays about the local school and the synagogue in his hometown. Heymann's work, "The Jewish elementary school in Anhalt from 1830-1840" is about his school and the lessons he experienced there. The rich Jewish families had their children taught by a private tutor, and the wealthy families jointly financed a teacher for their children, whose lessons children of the poor families could also attend.

School fees for the poor students were raised by an association of the Jewish community, called the Chewro, which helped support poor Jews. Most Jewish men in Gröbzig could read and write German and understand mathematics. Heymann also wrote that, on orders from the government, the Anhalt Jewish rural communities had to fire

---

[201] (Yes, I had to look it up too.) "A *philologist* is someone who studies the history of languages, especially by looking closely at literature." (Vocabulary.com)
[202] 'Aus der Geschichte der jüdischen Gemeinden im deutschen Sprachraum', Gröbzig (Saxony-Anhalt), Gröbzig Synagogue Museum

their Polish teachers (due to their lack of education) and hire teachers who had been educated at the renowned Dessau Jewish French School.[203]

The Gröbzig synagogue was built in 1788-92, a community centre was added in 1832, and the synagogue was rebuilt in 1858-59.[204] As part of the 1858 renovation, a women's gallery and pulpit were installed. Above the original synagogue entrance was written in Hebrew, "This is the gate of the Eternal, the righteous shall enter through it."[205] It is a classicist sacred building and was much later opened as the Gröbzig Synagogue Museum in 1988.

Lazarus had died by the time the current synagogue was built, but his children and grandchildren would all have attended. With the small size of the synagogue building, it would have been full of Lazarus' children and grandchildren for many years for education, prayers and celebration of festivals.

Whilst walking through the old synagogue in March 2024, I noticed money slots in one of the internal pillars. It is where congregants would have made charitable donations for Tzedakah. It is customary for Orthodox Jews to give charity before morning (Shacharit) and afternoon (Minchah) prayers, except on Shabbat or Jewish holydays. I can remember, as Executive Director of St Kilda Hebrew Congregation, helping Rabbi Yaakov Glasman manage and distribute the collected donations for those in need.

The current museum complex includes an entry portal, the synagogue, a reconstructed classroom, a coach house designed for the hearse, and a house for the cantor and shochet (ritual slaughterer of animals).[206]

---

[203] 'Chajim Steinthal' by Friedrich Ekkehard Vollbach on Sachsen-Lese

[204] Traveller's Guide to Jewish Germany, Billie Ann Lopez & Peter Hirsch, Pelican Publishing, 1998, p234

[205] Psalms 118:20

[206] 'Provenance Research on Judaica and other holdings in the Museum Synagogue Gröbzig since 1933', Tim Schauer, Museum Synagogue Gröbzig, 29 June 2020

Uncovering their Names and Stories:

The synagogue building survived the Holocaust, because the local Jewish community had reduced in numbers drastically after 1871, as Jews became free to live in any city they chose. Big city living was cheaper and provided more employment and business opportunities than a small town.

The Gröbzig Jewish cemetery is about a 30-minute walk out of town from the Gröbzig Synagogue Museum and sits along the Fuhne River. The cemetery began with the founding of the community and expanded early in the 19th century. It was desecrated repeatedly under the Nazis but was restored after World War 2. Many older gravestones are in poor condition.[207] There are many Steinthal family members buried there, though not all are easily identifiable. The Director of the museum, Anett Gottschalk, very kindly took me on a personal guided tour of the cemetery, pointing out known Steinthal family gravestones. It was also very pleasing to see how well the cemetery has been maintained in recent years.

By 1903, the town had a population of 2,001 people, but only 39 Jewish community members. By 1934, the Jewish community handed over the synagogue to the city of Gröbzig for use as a museum. It may not have been as voluntary as some since have tried to make it sound. The ritual objects of the synagogue were transferred to nearby Dessau, which was the main town in the Duchy of Anhalt but were destroyed during Kristallnacht.[208] Some items were later found to have been concealed in the Gröbzig Synagogue, such as the large Chanukiah in the hidden attic. These items survived the war, and are now exhibited in the synagogue, including the Chanukiah and a Torah scroll.

When the war commenced, hairdresser Friedrich Fuchs was the museum's administrator. After virtually all the Jews had 'left town' by 1939, Fuchs retrieved objects from Jewish properties in town and moved them to the museum. He claimed that this was an "act of salvage". The fact that people left things behind, suggests that the departure of the Jews was not so voluntary. When Nazi thugs from Köthen came to town in 1938 to burn down the synagogue, the town

---

[207] Traveller's Guide to Jewish Germany, Billie Ann Lopez & Peter Hirsch, Pelican Publishing, 1998, p235
[208] Billie Ann Lopez & Peter Hirsch (1998)

mayor stopped them, arguing it was (by then) town-owned property. Nevertheless, he removed all the symbols and wording from the premises that referred to Jews. The mayor reported to the district administrator of Köthen that Gröbzig was 'Judenfrei' (free of Jews) on 1 October 1940.[209]

However, the team at the Gröbzig Synagogue Museum told me that nine Jews remained in the town by the start of World War 2, and they were all eventually deported into the maelstrom of the Holocaust. They were Henriette Löwenthal, Rosalie Meyerstein, Berthold and Marie Karger, their daughter Johanna Karger, Ernst Blumenthal, Emmi Blumenthal, Johanna Salazin and Henriette Schlesinger.[210] It does not look like any of my family were left in the town by World War 2.

Heymann Steinthal had learned German and Hebrew in the modest one room school in a small building adjoining the Gröbzig Synagogue.[211] That building is long gone, but the schoolroom has been recreated in a room next to the offices of the Gröbzig Synagogue Museum. It looks as Heymann describes it in the story he wrote of his childhood memories, including the bare walls.[212]

Heymann moved to Bernburg to study at the Carlsgymnasium in 1836. He quickly caught up on Greek and Latin, though they were new to him. In Bernburg, he lived with a distant relative, very likely his uncle Joseph who was on the Finanzrat in Bernburg. Simultaneously, Heymann attended a Jewish religious school, where he studied Hebrew and the Talmud.

He graduated from high school in 1842. At his high school graduation ceremony, he gave a lecture on "Romeo and Juliet" in English. He originally planned to study theology but commenced studying linguistics at the University of Berlin in 1843. He attended

---

[209] 'Chajim Steinthal' by Friedrich Ekkehard Vollbach on Sachsen-Lese
[210] Anett Gottschalk, Director, Gröbzig Synagogue Museum
[211] 'Aus den Jugenderinnerungen Steinthals mit einer Vorbemerkung von Leo Baeck', <u>Der Morgen</u>, Heymann Steinthal, pp. 141-146, 8. Jahrgang, June 1932, 2. Heft
[212] ibid.

Uncovering their Names and Stories:

lectures and seminars on many languages, including Old Slavonic, Persian, Chinese, Turkish, Mongolian, Tibetan and Japanese. It has been said that he was proficient in 24 languages.[213]

Recreated classroom at the Gröbzig Synagogue Museum
(Photo credit: David Marlow)

He received his doctorate in philology at the University of Tübingen in 1847 with his thesis on the relative pronoun. Heymann was appointed Private Lecturer (Privatdozent) of philology and mythology at the University of Berlin in 1850. He lived in Paris from 1852 to 1855, studying Chinese and was appointed Assistant Professor at Berlin University in 1863.

He met the philosopher and historian Moritz Lazarus (1824-1903), and they became friends and collaborators, and co-founded the "Magazine for Ethnology" in 1860. They worked and wrote together. By then, Moritz was already an honorary professor in Bern. Heymann

---

[213] 'Chajim Steinthal' by Friedrich Ekkehard Vollbach on Sachsen-Lese

even married his friend's sister, Jeanette Lazarus (1840–1925) in 1861.[214]

Heymann and Jeanette had three children, David Steinthal (1864-1870), Agathe Steinthal (1866-1873) and Lona Irene Steinthal (1873-1943). Unfortunately, David and Agathe died very young, David at age 6 and Agathe at age 7. Their youngest child, Lona married Dr Anton Hess (1867-1933), having five children, Heinrich (1905-1995), Eduard (1906-), Peter (1908-1943), Erich (1911-1924) and Estella Rosa (1913-). Lona was murdered in Theresienstadt, while her son Peter was also deported to Theresienstadt and then deported to Auschwitz where he was murdered in 1943.

Heymann had maintained a lifelong interest in and devotion to Judaism and Jewish life. He often lectured and wrote newspaper articles as spokesperson and director of the "Deutsch-Israelitischer Gemeindebund" (German - Israeli Community Organisation). He defended Jews and Judaism against antisemitism.[215]

Prof Dr Heymann Steinthal
(Source: Gröbzig Synagogue Museum)

Prof Dr Heymann Steinthal died on May 14, 1899. He is buried prominently in the 'Honour' Row of the Jewish Weißensee Cemetery

---

[214] 'Chajim Steinthal' by Friedrich Ekkehard Vollbach on Sachsen-Lese
[215] Encyclopedia.com

Uncovering their Names and Stories:

(Jüdischer Friedhof Weißensee) in Berlin, where I found him quickly when I visited. It is the largest Jewish cemetery in Europe with 115,000 graves spread over 42 hectares. He was an important academic, thinker and researcher. Recently, the Gröbzig Synagogue Museum held an exhibition focused on Heymann, the town's most famous son, a grandson of my great (x4) grandfather Michael Lazarus.

It was fortunate that he was not buried in Gröbzig, because the old Jewish cemetery there was desecrated in 1940, the 1980s and in 2013-2014.[216] Thankfully now, the Gröbzig Synagogue Museum helps preserve and protect it.

Moses Steinthal from Gröbzig [217]

Of my great (x4) grandfather Michael Steinthal's eight sons, the most important to me was Moses Steinthal (1760s to mid-1800s). He was my great (x3) grandfather. I use the surname Steinthal for him, but it is uncertain which surname he used during his lifetime. He was one of Michael's three older sons. Thanks to my cousin Dan Rotman, I have a photo of Moses, showing what appears to be a religious, older Jewish gentleman. With a serious demeanour, white hair and sideburns, and wearing a large cap or yarmulke. Being born in the 1760s, he was probably in his eighties when the photo was taken. This is consistent with his looks in the photo. So, we know from the photo that Moses lived a long life, and we know from the Steinthal family tree that he fathered nine daughters, including my great (x2) grandmother Helena Kraft nee Steinthal.

Moses was a contemporary of Napoleon Bonaparte, who was born in 1769, but Napoleon died in 1821, so there were no photos of him.

---

[216] 'Aus der Geschichte der jüdischen Gemeinden im deutschen Sprachraum', Gröbzig (Saxony-Anhalt), Gröbzig Synagogue Museum

[217] We are not certain of the surname he used during his lifetime. It could have been Michael, Lazarus, Lichtenstein, or Steinthal after 1821.

Moses lived long enough for the technology of photography to be available.

My great (x3) grandfather Moses Steinthal
(Source: Dan Rotman)

The early photographer Nicéphore Niépce captured an image with a camera in 1826, but it took between eight hours and days of exposure, with imperfect results. The most viable and successful photography process was invented by Louis Daguerre, who invented 'daguerreotype'. This was the first public and commercially operating photographic process. It only required minutes of exposure in the camera. Daguerre demonstrated it to the Chamber of Peers in Paris on 2 August in 1839 and made the technical details public on 19 August to the Academy of Sciences.[218] Other photographic processes started to replace daguerreotype from the 1850s.

---

[218] Seizing the Light: A Social & Aesthetic History of Photography, 3rd edition, Robert Hirsch, Routledge, 25 April 2017

Uncovering their Names and Stories:

It is undoubtedly daguerreotype that allowed the photo of Moses, so we know his photo must have been taken in the 1840s at the earliest, when Moses would have been in his eighties.

Josua (the oldest of the eight sons) and Joseph (1764-) were Moses' full brothers, while the other five sons of Michael, including David mentioned above, had other mothers. The mother of Moses, Joseph and Josua is currently uncertain. Not much is known about Moses, but we do know that Josua was also known as Reb Falk, studied in Fürth, became a lecturer at the Talmud Torah Jewish School in nearby Dessau and was a member of the Beth Din. Given 'Falk' is German for falcon, he may have resembled a falcon in some way, such as in eyesight or personality. Joseph was on the Finanzrat (Finance Council) in the nearby major town of Bernburg.[219]

Moses Steinthal had nine daughters with his wife Chaichen Samson: Amelia, Bertha, Debora, Henriette, Johanna, Rahel, Sara (1830-1885), one daughter still to be identified and my great (x2) grandmother Helena Steinthal (1824-1871). Chaichen must have been much younger than Moses, as he was likely in his fifties or sixties when Helena was born.

The family had a couple of cousins marry. Moses and Chaichen Steinthal's daughter Sara married Eduard Steinthal (1824-1897) from Coswig, near Dresden. Eduard was the son of Moses's half-brother Israel Steinthal (1793-1848) and Elka Herz (1787-1830). Both Sara and Eduard were grandchildren of Michael Steinthal, and they had two children together, Elka (1856-1930) who married Victor Simon (1831-1901), and Dr Salomon (1859-1927) who married Rosa Elkes (1865-1909). However, Sara and Eduard divorced by the early 1860s, and Eduard married Irma Rosenberg (1830-1898). Eduard and Irma had two children, Rosa (1864-1918) who married Abraham Düsterwald (1855-1930), and Henriette (1865-1949) who married Jacob Julius Buchholz (1861-1942).

---

[219] Guide to Die Famalie Steinthal von Jahre 1720 bis 1935, 1935-1961, AR1393, Leo Baeck Institute; and 'Aus den Jugenderinnerungen Steinthals mit einer Vorbemerkung von Leo Baeck', Der Morgen, Heymann Steinthal, pp. 141-146, 8. Jahrgang, June 1932, 2. Heft

Helena Steinthal married Bernhardt Kraft (1820-1882) from Calbe in the current German state of Saxony-Anhalt. Bernhardt and Helena had eight children, Therese (1853-), Bertha (1854-), Eduard (1855-), Emma (1857-1935), Max (1861-1901), Selmar (1863-1935) who is my great grandfather, Theodor (1864-1943) and Richard (1867-). Helena and Bernhardt's family group is confirmed by the Bernhardt Kraft family census of 1867.

Dr Max and Fanny Steinthal

With urbanisation and increased upward social and financial mobility, which came with education, new freedoms and financial progress, Jews continued to move to larger towns and cities. This was very true of the Steinthal family. Little Gröbzig was home for the family from 1720, but by the mid to late 1800s they had moved to larger cities, notably Berlin.

Probably the most financially successful of the Steinthal family was Dr Max Steinthal (1850-1940), who was born in Berlin. He married Fanny Lindenthal (1866-1941) in Vienna in 1889 and they lived in Berlin, raising seven children. Their children were Erich (1890-1963), Daisy (1891-1980), Eva Korala (1892-1993), Jakob (1894-1972), Eduard (1896-1943), Ruth Berthe (1898-1974) and Peter (1899-1972).

Max's father was wholesale merchant Eduard Steinthal (1815-1896), whose father was Jacob Steinthal (1787-1864), whose father in turn was Michael (Reb Jechiel) Lazarus (1729-1813). Michael was also my great (x4) grandfather through his son Moses.

Max Steinthal grew up with his siblings Leopold (1849-1919), Amalie Sophie (1851-1937) and Elvira (1854-1916) in the family home at Neuen Friedrichstraße 22, Berlin. The street was renamed Littenstraße in 1951 and is very near Museuminsel (Museum Island) and Alexanderplatz in central Berlin.

Max's brother Leopold married Anna Neumann (1864-1943) in Mannheim. They had five children, Maria (1888-1945), Rudolph (1889-1915) who fell in World War 1 at the age of 26, Franz (1893-1893), Agathe (1894-1958) and Elizabeth (1896-1981). Anna died in Theresienstadt.

Uncovering their Names and Stories:

Max's sister Amalie Sophie (1851-1937) married Neuropathologist Prof Dr Martin Bernhardt (1844-1915) in Berlin in 1877. They had two children together, Walter (1879-1966) who married Friederike Neukranz (1875-), and Dr Hans Herman (1882-1957). Walter died in Berlin in 1966, and Hans died in a Kibbutz in northern Israel in 1957. Hans married Irma Scheyer in 1914, and they had two children in Berlin, migrating in 1935 to a Kibbutz in Palestine. In Berlin, Hans worked in a hospital as a pediatrician, until the Nazi regime forced him out of his job. Their children were Renate (1915-1991) and Martin (later Moshe) Theodor (1919-2012). Young Martin migrated to Palestine in 1933.

Martin's uncle Dr Max Steinthal, who did not believe in the Zionist movement, paid for his nephew's tuition to study agriculture in Palestine at the Mikveh Israel school. The Mikveh Israel school was established in 1870, and was the first agricultural school in what is now Israel.[220] In Israel, Martin met and married Sarah bat Yakov (Jacobson) (1917-1965), who was born and died in Kibbutzim. Through my research, I have discovered and met online Martin and Sarah's daughter Judith Roudman (1949-), who still lives in a Kibbutz in Israel, and has herself been researching her family history. Judith found mentions of her Steinthal and the Lazarus ancestors in her grandmother Irma's siddur (prayer book).

As a young adult from 1876, Max lived at Vonnstrasse 31 in central Berlin. When Max married Fanny, they moved into Roonstrasse 9 in Berlin-Tiergarten, which is a 15-minute walk from the Botanical Gardens, and a 35-minute walk from where my Elkan grandparents lived. It was a very upmarket part of central Berlin. Max and Fanny's house today houses a child-care centre. In the early years of his career, Max's work was very successfully focused on the stock market and arbitrage business at Deutsche Bank.

Max eventually became one of the ten richest men in Berlin, the capital of the German Empire. He started off home-schooled, before attending the Königgstädtische Realschule. He was an apprentice banker at the A Paderstein Bank where he built a successful banking

---

[220] Mikve Israel Encyclopedia of Zionism and Israel, Raphael Patai, 1971

career, and he became a board member at 21. Max joined the board of directors of Deutsche Bank in 1873, where he served until 1905. He joined the supervisory board, and later became chairman from 1923 to 1932.

Max was also co-founder, promoter and chairman of the supervisory board of the Berlin elevated and subway railway. It became immediately profitable and a great asset to the city, especially since Max managed to gain an exemption from traffic tax.[221]

Memorial plaque for Dr Max Steinthal in Berlin's Alexanderplatz S-Bahn and U-Bahn station

(Source: Deutsche Bank AG Historical Society)

In his private life, he supported the Jewish Hospital and was a member of the charity Society of Friends, as well as supporting other charitable causes. For example, he donated 100,0000 gold marks in 1905 to the City of Charlottenburg to build a forest school.[222]

Through his career, Max amassed a fortune, including real estate and a substantial art collection. His and Fanny's private art collection included works by Manet, Pissaro, Munch, and Picasso. After being stolen by the Nazi regime, 60 of the pieces were recovered years later

---

[221] 'Max Steinthal', provenienzforschung.zlb.de/en/restitutions/max-steinthal/
[222] 'Max Steinthal', Wikipedia (German version)

Uncovering their Names and Stories:

and exhibited in the Berlin Jewish Museum. Fanny's miniature collection was never found.[223]

Plaques commemorating Max's work as co-founder and supporter of the first elevated and subway railway in Berlin, were installed at the Klosterstrasse subway station in 1913 and the Alexanderplatz subway station in 1930. The latter plaque was removed by the Nazis in 1933, but was replaced in 2002.[224]

Max was forced off the Deutsche Bank supervisory board in 1935, because being Jewish was incompatible to being a director of a major bank, or any bank for that matter, in Nazi Germany.

In 1938, he was forced to sell his real estate assets, at heavily discounted values. Other assets were simply confiscated. He was forced to sell his home to the Luftwaffe in 1939, and his remaining assets were seized in 1940. Their son Eduard (1896-1943) was murdered in Auschwitz in January 1943, but their other six children all escaped the Holocaust, emigrating to various countries.

Max died on 8 December 1940 in his room in the Eden Hotel on Kurfürstendamm, at nearly ninety years of age. After a hugely successful career and being a generous philanthropist, he was penniless and homeless. Max and Fanny had been married for 51 years. Fanny died the following year, aged 76, awaiting emigration in the same hotel.[225]

The Eden Hotel was built in 1912 near the Berlin Zoological Gardens, which is in the large Tiergarten park in west Berlin. In its heyday, the hotel saw patrons like actress Marlene Dietrich, author Erich Maria Remarque and film director Billy Wilder. However, it is most famous for the murders of former Reichstag member Karl Liebknecht and socialist Rosa Luxemburg. They were illegally arrested and assassinated by the military on 15 January 1919. They were taken to the hotel for interrogation, which at that time was under control of the military. Liebknecht was then taken to

---

[223] ibid.
[224] ibid.
[225] Certified Award on the Account of Max Steinthal, Claim Number 501712/HB/AC, Claims Resolution Tribunal, 12 October 2007

300+ Years of a German – Jewish Family

the Tiergarten to be shot, and Luxemburg was beaten with a rifle butt and shot in the head in a car outside. Their bodies were dumped in a canal.[226] In later years, the hotel became a meeting place for Nazi officials and was virtually destroyed by British bombing in 1943.

Dr Max and Fanny Steinthal celebrating Max's 80th birthday with family, friends and colleagues in better times (1930) at the family home on Uhlandstraße in Berlin
(Source: Deutsche Bank AG Historical Society)

---

[226] 'The Murder of Rosa Luxemburg', Verso Books Blog, 15 January 2019; 'Murder Rewarded: how the killers of Rosa Luxemburg avoided punishment in the Weimar Republic (and beyond…)', rosaluxemburgblog, 23 April 2012; 'Hotel Eden', Weimarberlin.com/2021/03/hotel-eden.html?m=1; and Berlin's Grand Hotels and the Crisis of German Democracy, Adam Bisno, Perspectivia.net/servlets/MCRFileNodeServlet/pnet_derivate_00002120/27_bisno_hotels.pdf

Uncovering their Names and Stories:

```
Geheimer Kommerzienrat Max Steinthal, ein Senior des deutschen
Bankwesens, Aufsichtsratvorsitzender der Deutschen Bank und Disconto-
Gesellschaft, feierte dieser Tage seinen 80. Geburtstag. Unser Bild
wurde bei der Geburtstagsfeier aufgenommen. Von links nach rechts,
erste Reihe sitzend: Frau Fehr, Frau Wassermann, Frau Urbig, Geheim-
rat Max Steinthal, Frau Steinthal, Frau von Gwinner, Frau Solmssen,
Frau Schlitter. Zweite Reihe: Blinzig (DD-Bank), Dipl.-Ing. L. F.
Reichenheim, S. Fehr (DD-Bank), Dr. Frank (DD-Bank), Dr. Bierwes
(Mannesmann), Konsul Vollmann-Dresden, Wassermann (DD-Bank), Werner
Steinthal, Frau Dr. Frank, Dr. von Stauß (DD-Bank), Arthur von Gwinner
(DD-Bank), Frau Russell, Peter Steinthal, Dr. Schlitter (DD-Bank),
Max von Schinckel (DD-Bank), Dr. Silverberg (Rheinische Braunkohlen),
Frau Mosler, Dr. Russell (DD-Bank), Urbig (DD-Bank), Dr. Boner (DD-
Bank), Dr. Millington-Herrmann (DD-Bank), Hugo Markus (Wiener Bank-
verein), Dr. Solmssen (DD-Bank).
```

The Meyer and Boss families

Jacob Steinthal also had a daughter Rosalie Steinthal (1820-1881), who married Herman Aron Meyer (1816-1887), who together raised seven children in Berlin, Max (1842-1912), Amalie (1847-1910), Martin (1849-1942), Felix (1851-1880), Bernhard (1853-1917), Therese (1854-1920) and Anton Aron (1859-1940).

Bernhard Meyer married Rosa Behrend (1858-1928) and raised three daughters in Berlin, Helene (1865-1919), Edith (1887-1944) who died with her husband Hans Lindenberg (1887-1944) in Auschwitz, and Alice Clara (1890-1942) who married the pharmacist George Boss (1884-1961). The Boss couple raised three children in Berlin, Axel (1912-1995), Ewald Heinz (1914-1998) and the sadly short-lived Ingeborg (1917-1917). Alice was murdered in the Holocaust. Ewald Boss married Caroline Hess and moved to Brazil where his descendants, my recently uncovered cousins, are thriving in Sao Paulo.

It has been wonderful contacting Ewald's son Gunther Boss, who brought me up-to-speed on the Boss family and pointed me to the Holocaust testimony of his cousin (and mine more distantly) Brigitte Steele nee Meyer.[227]

---

[227] Brigitte Steele nee Meyer's Holocaust testimony, Holocaust Museum Houston, 9 July 2004

7.0 The Marowilskys and Polleys up to Kristallnacht

My Marowilsky family were from just inside the border of what is now Lithuania. They migrated to East Prussia (the part which is now part of Russia) and then moved onto Wuppertal in western Germany, in what is now North Rhine-Westphalia:

Leib Marowilski
Father of
V
Isidor Marowilski (1861-1906)
Father of
V
Hermann Marowilsky (1887-1942)
Father of
V
Heinz Günter Marowilsky (Henry Marlow) (1921-2002)
Father of
V
David Marlow (1962-)

The Marowilskis of Vistytis

My father Henry Marlow was born Heinz Günter Marowilsky (1921-2002). He used to tell us that he and his family were from the city of Wuppertal. This is an important industrial city near Düsseldorf, in the current German state of North Rhine-Westphalia. It is true that he grew up in Wuppertal and spent a lot of time living and holidaying around western Germany, but he and his father were actually born in Pillau in East Prussia, near what is now the Lithuanian border. And his (Marwilsky / Marowilski) ancestors for a couple of generations prior, came from Vistytis, a very small town in Lithuania on the border with what was East Prussia.[228]

I can trace the family back there to my great (x2) grandparents Leib Marowilski and Lina Marowilski nee Schimowski. The family appears to have lived in Vistytis from at least the early 1830s, but possibly much earlier, until the 1860s-1880s.

---

[228] Wyshtyten in German, Vishtinets in Yiddish and Wisztyniec in Polish.

Uncovering their Names and Stories:

Vistytis was established in the early 1500s, on the border of the then Duchy of Prussia. The town grew, as it was settled by Lithuanian, Russian, German and Polish people. It declined when the railroad line by-passed it to the north, and many of its Jewish population emigrated to the USA, Germany and South Africa from the 1850s.

Vistytis was part of the Kingdom of Poland and the Grand Duchy of Lithuania (Polish – Lithuanian Commonwealth) from 1569 to 1795, though by 1768 the Russians considered the Commonwealth a protectorate of the Russian Empire.[229]

Jews in town were required to have surnames, once they were under Prussian control from 1797.[230] It is possibly due to the strong Polish influence in the area until at least 1795, that my father's ancestors chose a very Polish sounding surname, Marowilski.

The Marowilsky/Marowilski surname most likely derives from the small village of Marwille, near Vistytis.[231] Marwille sits on the eastern shore of Lake Vistytis, 3 km southeast of Vistytis. It is about a ten minute drive or two hour walk north from the modern Polish border. Today it is known as Žirgėnai in modern Lithuania and is a tiny hamlet with a population of about 16.[232] In 1798-1800, it belonged to Prussia and was what was known as a 'Vorwerk' or farm on the outskirts of a town.[233] It has also previously been known as Marville, Marivilis and Marvilius.

It is quite possible that my ancestors came from Marwille before moving to the larger town of Vistytis. I have found numerous Marwilskys born in Marwille, in online family trees belonging to some of my DNA matches. I have not been able to confirm the familial connections, but quite a few Marwilskys who lived in Vistytis, had been born in Marwille. The DNA matches make some sort of connection of those Marwilskys to my Marowilsky family likely.

---

[229] 'Polish-Lithuanian Commonwealth', Wikipedia
[230] ibid.
[231] Email from Prof Dr Ruth Leiserowitz, Jews in East Prussia, 16 August 2024
[232] 'Zirgenai', Mapcarta.com
[233] Email from Prof Dr Ruth Leiserowitz, 20 August 2024

Jews had begun to settle in Vistytis in 1589, and a lot was allocated for building a synagogue and another lot for a Jewish cemetery.[234] The local Jews would have spoken Eastern Yiddish, as did most of the Jews of Eastern Europe. Gradually the Jews of Vistytis built all the trappings of a regular Jewish community, synagogues, a kehilla (Jewish community governing body) until 1844, a Jewish cemetery, a mikveh, and an elementary religious school from 1878.[235]

Jacob Hyam Rubenstein (1890-1963) was born in Vistytis and described it as a picturesque small town, "The town, Vishtinetz, was laid out symmetrically with the market square as the hub. The square was actually a rectangle; the side running from north to south was about twice as long as that running from east to west. The streets radiated from each of its four corners at right angles to each other. A beautiful lake, one of the largest in the region, formed a semicircle about the town to the south and partly to the west. It formed part of the international boundary. The land boundary extended to the rest of the limits of the town. To the north, the town was bounded by hills, which the inhabitants dubbed "The Red Mountains". At the foot of the hills meandered a creek which used to go dry in the summertime."[236]

The Vistytis-born author Dr Vilius Kočiubaitis described the exotic smells of the town, and notably those emanating from the many Jewish owned bakeries, "One can imagine the aroma- everywhere; emanating from bakeries different types of bread - bagel (bread in the shape of a small flower, sprinkled with poppy seeds), the aroma of challah (braid-shaped bread) mingles with the smells of groceries, where there are huge barrels of cucumbers and herring (Baltic herring), where borscht (Russian beetroot soup) is sold."[237]

The few main streets and square had cobblestones and no sidewalks. Houses were mainly built of timber and bathrooms were outside, which would not have been very friendly on a cold winter's night.

---

[234] 'Vistytis' chapter, <u>Encyclopedia of Jewish Communities in Lithuania</u>, Josef Rosin, Yad Vashem, 1996
[235] <u>Jews of Vistytis</u>, Dr Vilius Kočiubaitis, translated by Ralph Salinger
[236] ibid.
[237] ibid. p580

Uncovering their Names and Stories:

Water was drawn from wells and cleaning of the streets was left to roaming pigs. The Jewish community had a public bathhouse, largely thanks to its ritual 'mikveh' required by Jewish law. Houses did not have plumbing, baths or showers. But each household did tend to keep chickens and have a vegetable garden, often having a cow or two.[238]

Vistytis was devastated by fire in 1901. More than half the town burned to the ground. Kaiser Wilhelm II visited on Yom Kippur, as he had been hunting in the nearby Rominta Forest when he heard about the tragic fire. He donated 10,000 marks (US $2,500) to the town, and he called on Tsar Nicholas of Russia to do the same, to help fund restoration. The Kaiser's visit and donation were reported in the *New York Times* newspaper on 24 October 1901.[239]

Afterwards, straw and shingle-roof houses were banned. Many people, Jews included, left town rather than rebuild.

Russian troops devastated Vistytis in 1915, and all the Jews left town, with only a few returning after the war. There were 1,482 people in Vistytis in 1923, of whom 222 were Jewish. At its peak, the town had almost 1,500 Jews.[240] Intolerance and pogroms in Lithuania, as in neighbouring Poland, often led Jews to emigrate. This was a sad decline for a town that in 1570 had two breweries and two taverns. Pig bristle brushes used to be the town's major business, but that industry and the pigs have long since disappeared. At peak, there were two synagogues and a Jewish school, but they are also long gone.[241]

Lithuanian historian and member of the Seimas (unicameral parliament) Emanuel Zingeris wrote, "Before the war, the Jew was part of the Lithuanian landscape: wherever you would go, it was possible to see a cow, a peasant, a horse, a Jew and the bicycle."[242]

---

[238] ibid.
[239] ibid.
[240] 'Vishtinetz, Lithuania: A visit to Vistytis', 1994, Bert Oppenheim, JewishGen
[241] ibid.
[242] Jews of Vistytis, Dr Vilius Kočiubaitis, translated by Ralph Salinger

During World War 2, all remaining Jews in Vistytis were murdered. The German army took over the town on 22 June 1941 after an artillery barrage. Persecution of the Jews commenced immediately, starting with the wearing of yellow stars on 23 June. All 200-300 Jews in Vistytis were murdered, apart from possibly two young girls who were hidden. All Jewish property was handed over to those who collaborated with the Germans.[243] By 2011, the population of Vistytis had declined to 436 people, and no Jews.

Today, nothing is left of the synagogues apart from one wall of the old synagogue, which now forms part of a barn. But the Lithuanian citizens of Vistytis erected a stone plaque in 1993, commemorating the lost Jews the town.[244]

The Vistytis New Jewish Cemetery still exists, as does the old Rabbi's house at 6 Taikos Street. Over 200 gravestones have been counted, photographed, digitised and translated by volunteers for the volunteer-based Maceva organisation. Over 600 graves are registered online. At least half the gravestones are missing or illegible, many just partially legible. Yet, some are in near perfect condition. Not too many have clear surnames. Reviewing all the gravestones did not find any of my ancestors, but some may well be among the graves where the gravestones are missing or illegible.[245]

Leib and Lina's son Isidor Marowilski (1861-1906) was born in Vistytis. Many of the Jews of Vistytis migrated to East Prussia in the middle of the 19th century, and largely to rural areas around Labiau and Seckenburg.[246] The historian of the 'Jews in East Prussia'

---

[243] 'Vistytis' chapter, Encyclopedia of Jewish Communities in Lithuania, Josef Rosin, Yad Vashem, 1996, and Jews of Vistytis, Dr Vilius Kočiubaitis, translated by Ralph Salinger

[244] ibid.

[245] Vistytis New Jewish Cemetery digitised documents, Litvak Cemetery Catalogue, Maceva

[246] Labiau is now known as Polessk and Seckenburg is Zapovednoe, Russia. They are just over an hour's drive apart from each other.

organisation told me that "in the second half of the 19th century, every Jewish shopkeeper in this region had roots in Vistytis."[247]

By 1886, the Marowilski family had emigrated to East Prussia and Leib was working as a tradesman in Labiau, and for some time as a merchant. His son Isidor married twice, firstly to my great grandmother Henriette Polley (1854-) in 1886 in Liebstadt. Their marriage did not last long, and they divorced in the Königsberg District Court in 1891. Records indicate that Henriette became an independent trader and a member of the Jewish congregation in Königsberg from 1893 to 1899.[248] Königsberg, now called Kaliningrad, is only 45 minutes by car from Pillau, and at the time was the capital of East Prussia.

Isidor's second marriage was to Bertha Peckel (1861-) in 1894. He worked as a tradesman in Labiau, not far from Pillau[249] until 1886, and became a product dealer and merchant in Pillau from 1887. Isidor and Bertha had a baby Erna Marowilsky in Seckenburg, East Prussia in 1896. Isidor died in 1906 in the village of Lappienen in East Prussia, about a one hour drive from Labiau, at the age of 45. According to the German Minority Census, Bertha and Erna were still living together in Elchniederung near Labiau in May 1939, long after Isidor had died. The 'Jews in East Prussia' told me, "They were probably deported to Minsk via Königsberg in 1942."[250] This would have been the Maly Trostenets death camp, near Minsk in Belarus, where they were likely shot on arrival. Bertha would have been 82 and Erna 45.[251]

I have suspicions that some of the Marwilskys, and possibly Marwitzkis in Pillau may also be related to my Marowilsky ancestors. Prof Dr Ruth Leiserowitz, Chairwoman of the 'Jews in East Prussia', told me, "It was also widespread in the 19th century to change one's

---

[247] Email from Prof Dr Ruth Leiserowitz, Jews of East Prussia, 16 August 2024
[248] ibid.
[249] Pillau in German, Pillawa in Old Prussian, Baltiysk in Russian, and Pilave in Yiddish.
[250] Email from Prof Dr Ruth Leiserowitz (2024)
[251] 'Deportation train from Königsberg', Jews in East Prussia; and 'Königsberg', Wikipedia

family name again to distinguish oneself from other branches of the family. Too many families in Vistytis called themselves Marwitzki; later, Marwilsky appeared, and then Marowilsky."[252] I also found a relatively close DNA match who is descended from the Marwilskys from Vistytis. Absence of records has made these familial connections difficult to prove.

The Marowilskys of Pillau

Isidor and his first wife Henriette Polley had one child together, Hermann Marowilsky (1887-1942), who was my paternal grandfather. Hermann was born in Pillau, East Prussia in 1887, and he attended the Königliche Realschule (Royal Secondary School) there for six and a half years. The Polley family was originally from Liebstadt, in southern East Prussia.

But how did a Jewish couple find each before the times of online dating sites, especially when they came from geographically dispersed towns? Parents found matches for their treasured children through matchmakers, business relationships and relatives. I can imagine conversations in synagogues where prayers were three times per day, or taverns, where fathers might discuss pairing up children or nephews or nieces. Mothers might do the same in markets, while working in the family business, or over the fence.

Mostly the father led the matchmaking search, as he was head of the household. One of the first steps of the matchmaking process was the need to agree the marriage and inheritance contracts. This established the financial baseline for the newly married couples. Many couples lived with one or other parents for a year or so.[253] I did find that my maternal grandmother's sister Else Kraft lived with her new husband Fedor Krebs, in the beginning of their marriage, with

---

[252] Email from Prof Dr Ruth Leiserowitz (2024)
[253] 'The history of Jewish families in early modern and modern times', Mirjam Thulin & Marcus Krah, in Jewish Families and Kinship in the Early Modern and Modern Eras, (PaRDeS; 26), University of Potsdam, Potsdam, 2020, p.19

Uncovering their Names and Stories:

my great grandparents Selmar and Frieda Kraft in their home at 10 Lindenauer Markt, Leipzig.

The towns of Pillau and Vistytis are over 220 km apart, with Labiau sitting in between, slightly closer to Pillau. Vistytis sits beside Lake Vistytis, on the border to the current Russian held Kaliningrad Oblast.[254] It had a population around then of 2,449[255], while Pillau sits on the coast and had a population of 3,434 by 1886.[256] Pillau was a slightly larger town but would have looked promising from the point of view of economic and work prospects. Pillau had shipyards and a relatively new railway connection, making it a gateway to nearby Königsberg, now known as Kaliningrad, the easternmost large German city until World War 2.

The Jews of Vistytis conducted a lot of trade with East Prussia, often travelling by foot or horse to do business across the border. Travel in those times could also be by coach or wagon, for those with the money to afford it. They would have seen German customs and economic development as they traded across the border. So, over the 19th century, "an unusually high total number of Wyshtyten Jews settled in nearby East Prussia and acquired Prussian nationality",[257] as did the Marowilsky family.

Pillau was originally an old Prussian fishing village, founded on the Vistula Spit in the 13th century. It became an important port in the Duchy of Prussia with fortifications starting to be built in 1550. It was occupied by the Swedes after the Thirty Years War, who handed it over to the Elector of Brandenburg for 10,000 thalers ransom. It

---

[254] Kaliningrad was known as Königsberg when it was part of East Prussia
[255] 'Vistytis' chapter, <u>Encyclopedia of Jewish Communities in Lithuania</u>, Josef Rosin, Yad Vashem, 1996
[256] <u>Geographical dictionary of the Kingdom of Poland and other Slavic countries</u>, Tom VII, Warsaw, 1887, p 156
[257] 'The Traders of Wystiten: The Border as a Modernization Factor for Litvaks in Transnational Space in 19th Century', Dr Ruth Leizerowitz, pp319-331, <u>Central and European Jews at the Crossroads of Tradition and Modernity</u>, Jurgita Siauciunaite-Verbickiene and Larisa Lempertiene (eds.), Vilnius: Centre for Studies of the Culture of East European Jews, 2006

was at various times occupied by the Russians, Prussians and Napoleon's French.

Pillau was in the part of East Prussia, north of modern Poland, which was absorbed by the USSR after World War 2. The German inhabitants were expelled by the Soviets under the Potsdam Agreement. Under the USSR's Russification campaign, Pillau was renamed Baltiysk in 1946.[258] It had a population of 3,434 in 1886, and now has a population of over 30,000.[259]

My grandfather Hermann learned the merchant trade in nearby Königsberg. After completing his apprenticeship in Königsberg, he obtained a job in Wuppertal at the Gebr. Kaufman department store where he met Meta Lennhoff, who was also working at the store. They married in 1918, most likely after Hermann's military service, and then moved to Pillau to take over Hermann's mother Henriette's small grocery store.[260] Henriette would have been aged 64 at the time. Their house at Gouvernementstrasse 5, Pillau was my father's first home as a baby and young child, after being born in Pillau in 1921.

Dad never mentioned Pillau to his family in Australia. On the rare occasions when he did talk about his past, generally with a little liquid priming, he talked about Wuppertal.

The Marowilskys in Wuppertal

In 1925, when Dad was four years of age, the Marowilsky family sold the grocery store business and moved back to Wuppertal, where Hermann and Meta both got jobs back at the Gebr. Kaufman department store. The family moved into a large apartment building at Döppersberg 14 in Elberfeld, Wuppertal which my father remembered was very close to the train station. This was the same

---

[258] Encyclopedia of Russian Cities: Moscow: Great Russian Encyclopedia 2003, p36

[259] 26. Number of permanent population of the Russian Federation by municipalities as of January 1, 2018, Federal State Statistics Service, Russia, 23 January 2019.

[260] Henry Marlow interview with Prof Manfred Brusten, October 1994

Uncovering their Names and Stories:

building that Dad's Lennhoff grandparents Sophie and Adolf lived in, though on a different floor. They went to synagogue regularly and lived the lives of a fairly liberal Jewish family.

Herman Marowilsky with his son Heinz Marowilsky
(Source: Heinz Marowilsky childhood photo album)

By 1926 Hermann was in financial difficulties and went through bankruptcy. [261] He certainly had a tumultuous life. But things improved temporarily, and between 1930 and August 1938 he was head of the made-to-measure department at Gebr. Kaufman. From 1938 onwards, thanks to the Nazis, both Hermann and Meta were unemployed until their deportation in April 1942.

During the early 1920s, inflation in Germany increased to ridiculous levels, largely due to the huge debt the country had amassed to finance its Great War effort. The hyperinflation was triggered by France and Belgium occupying Germany's Ruhr valley industrial region in January 1923. They did this because Germany had fallen

---

[261] Deutscher Reichsanzeiger und Preußischer Staatsanzeiger, Saturday 6 February 1926, page 25 and Berliner Börsen-Zeitung, Abendausgabe, Tuesday 9 February 1926, page 8

behind in reparation payments due to them, which was compensation for the French and Belgian losses in World War 1.[262]

Hyperinflation caused great financial difficulties across Germany and was the likely cause of Hermann's financial problems. "By mid-1923 the German mark was losing value by the minute: a loaf of bread that cost 20,000 marks in the morning would cost 5,000,000 marks by nightfall; restaurant prices went up while customers were eating; and workers were paid twice a day. When economic collapse finally came on November 15, it took 4.2 trillion German marks to buy a single American dollar."[263]

"A lifetime of savings would no longer buy a subway ticket",[264] so many people's entire wealth became worthless. People had to sell their possessions to pay for food. This may well be what drove my grandfather to bankruptcy, even though the economy had improved a little by 1926. The occupation of the Ruhr had ended by then, and a more realistic reparations payment schedule had been agreed and implemented. Though people who had lost everything, had to rebuild. The economy was still far from perfect. By the end of 1925, unemployment had hit one million people, and increased to three million by March 1926.[265]

Soon after losing their savings in the early 1920s, Germans had to come to terms with the Great Depression from 1929, which hit the country and undoubtedly my grandparents hard.

Dad had his barmitzvah at the synagogue close to home in Wuppertal in 1934, undoubtedly surrounded by his grandmother Sophie Lennhoff, and his many Lennhoff aunts and Uncle Norbert, as well as possibly a few cousins. I do wonder what it was like having your barmitzvah in a country where roaming gangs of Nazi youth and Brownshirts looked to create trouble for Jews, signs in shops denigrated and scapegoated Jews for all the problems of the world,

---

[262] "Germany: Years of Crisis 1920-23", Britannica.com
[263] ibid.
[264] ibid.
[265] The Coming of the Third Reich: How the Nazis Destroyed Democracy and Seized Power in Germany, Richard J Evans, Penguin, London, 9 August 2012, p.178

Uncovering their Names and Stories:

symbolism in churches reinforced antisemitic tropes, newspapers spread hate and lies about Jews, Christian neighbours avoided you, and many avoided looking you in the eye or were downright antagonistic. 'Social death' was a real thing under the Nazi regime.

Nevertheless, there were still some good times, at least until the early 1930s. Dad attended 'Haus Berta' in 1935, and his childhood photo album features several photos from there. He looks like he had a great time, and one photo has another boy on his shoulders, as he is smiling broadly underneath. Haus Berta was like a youth-group-in-a-box. It was opened in July 1934 as a Jewish holiday and training home for children of members of the Reich Association of Jewish Front Soldiers (RjF), and Hermann was a veteran of World War 1. It offered Jewish children an opportunity for fun and recreation, where most German options for children had been removed by the Nazi regime.

Haus Berta was in Dorsten near Schermbeck, about an hour's drive north of Wuppertal. It included leisure activities, occupational-oriented training, religious activities, and had a Zionist orientation.[266]

Its founder and director Leo Gompertz wrote, "For the short period of its existence since 1934, the home was associated with some hope for the future for the Jewish community and was a lively, lively place with charisma beyond the region ... For three years - from 1934 to 1937 - the house was a refuge for Jewish young people and a response to the exclusion and disenfranchisement of the National Socialists."[267]

Its administrator Leo Auerbach wrote later, "Haus Bertha was ideally located in the geographical centre of Rhineland-Westphalia, in a piece of heath and forest. It was easy to reach for all West Germans and was mainly visited by groups from Cologne, Aachen, Düsseldorf, Essen, Dortmund, Münster, Hamburg, etc. But groups from further away also came every year from Berlin, Bremen, Breslau, and not to forget: the southern Germans, the Frankfurters. The composition of

---

[266] 'Jüdisches Ferien- und Schulungsheim "Haus Berta" bei Schermbeck', Franz-Josef Hügel, Digital Cultural Heritage LVR, 2023, kuladig.de/Objektansicht/KLD-345341
[267] Gelsenzentrum.de

the groups was also diverse. Most belonged to the youth association of the R.J.F. but many members of other youth organizations came: Makkabi, Bar Kochba, Kadimah, Mizrachi and others."[268]

Dad (standing - second from left) with friends at Haus Berta
(Source: Heinz Marowilsky childhood photo album)

To rub salt into the wounds, the Nazis closed Haus Berta in 1937 during Friday night services, which was apparently a "festive highlight". On Kristallnacht, the building was burned to the ground, and the property was 'Aryanized' thereafter.[269]

Other photos in my father's photo album show him having fun on holidays, and with friends and family in a wide variety of places around Germany, including along the Rhine, and in Bremen, Hamburg, Fröndenberg, Oberdollendorf and Burgholz. There are also photos of him with his middle school class, gym class, sporting groups, and at a music camp. There are photos of various family members, including his parents Meta and Hermann, his maternal

---

[268] Dorsten-unterm- Hakenkreuz.de

[269] 'Jüdisches Ferien- und Schulungsheim "Haus Berta" bei Schermbeck', Franz-Josef Hügel, Digital Cultural Heritage LVR, 2023, kuladig.de/Objektansicht/KLD-345341

Uncovering their Names and Stories:

grandmother Sophie Lennhoff, and various aunts, uncles and cousins.

One small photo of particular note, shows my father as a youngster with an equally young buddy wrapped in what looks like a giant pretzel, standing in front of a very high bridge in the background. It looks like what might be a studio photo. The bridge is the Müngstener Brücke, which is the highest railway bridge in Germany.

Heinz and Arno Heller in front of the Müngstener Brücke around 1933
(Source: Heinz Marowilsky childhood photo album)

It still stands, spanning the River Wupper, only 18.4 km south of Wuppertal. Dad's buddy in the photo has turned out to be his first cousin Arno Heller (1920-2016), who must have been visiting on holidays from Hamburg. Arno's son Peter helped me confirm the identity of his father in the photo. Arno had a very interesting life, escaping the Holocaust on the Kindertransport with his sister Ingrid, ending up raising a family in New York City.

Not much more than a decade after the photo was taken, both Dad and Arno lost their parents to the Holocaust, along with many other family members. And they escaped Nazi Germany separately on the Kindertransport. Dad to England and Arno with his sister Ingrid to the USA. Arno ended up in the US Army, serving in North Africa and Normandy from D+1, and Dad spent three years in internment in Australia. The cousins would never see each other again, but both boys named their first child Peter.

Dad did not have many first cousins. Dad's father Hermann Marowilsky had no siblings, apart from his half-sister. Of Dad's mother Meta's seven Lennhoff siblings, Norbert, Irma and Else did not have children. Frieda and Rosa were murdered by the Nazis in the Minsk Ghetto in 1941, and Hertha was murdered in Auschwitz in 1943. It was only Meta's sister Paula who had children that we know of, Arno and Ingrid Heller. Meta and Paula must have been close, as there are several pictures of Paula in Dad's childhood photo album, including a lovely photo of sisters Paula and Meta standing together in their hats and coats in Wuppertal. Paula and her husband Emil Heller were murdered in Auschwitz.

This photo was taken on 22 May 1936 at the funeral of their mother Sophie Lennhoff nee Neufeld, who died at the age of 73 after a long illness. She is buried in the Jewish cemetery on Weinberg Strasse, next to her husband Aron (Adolf), who died in 1922. The death notice for Sophie in the Jewish newspaper was placed by Sophie's daughter Hertha.[270] I placed pebbles on Sophie and Aron's gravestones when I found their graves in March.

---

[270] Israelitisches Familienblatt Vol 38, 4 June 1936, Issue 23, p.23

Uncovering their Names and Stories:

Meta Marowilsky nee Lennhoff and her sister Paula Heller nee Lennhoff

(Source: Heinz Marowilsky childhood photo album)

The Polleys of Liebstadt

My great grandmother Henriette Marowilsky nee Polley was born in Liebstadt in 1854. Liebstadt was a small town in the Mohrungen district, East Prussia. The town had a population of 2,394 in 1871 and 2,609 in 2017.[271] Liebstadt was founded in 1302, under control of the Teutonic Order, until 1525 when it became part of the Duchy of Prussia. It was destroyed by Swedish troops in 1659 and invaded by Napoleon's troops in 1807.

---

[271] Dokumentacja Geograficzna (in Polish), Vol. ¾, Warszawa: Instytut Geografii Polskiej Akademii Nauk, 1967, p30

After World War 2, East Prussia was split into three parts. A small northern sliver became part of Lithuania, most of the northern half became part of the USSR and is now part of Russia, and the large southern section became part of Poland. Liebstadt is in the south west, now renamed Milakowo, in Poland.

Henriette's parents were Moses Lippmann Polley (1821-1899) and Dorothea Matthissohn (1830-1886). Her siblings were Wilhelmine, Natalie (1857-1942) who married Saly Krzywonos (1860-1922), Louis (1858-1935) who married Jeanette Ostrowski (1866-1941), Bertha (1860-1899) who married Max George Salinger (1863-1925), and Fanny (1864-) who married Simon Shulz (1853-). All the Polley siblings were born in Liebstadt.

Moses Lippmann Polley was a merchant in the town, and the son of teacher Lewin Polley and his wife Marje Polley, who would have been born in Liebstadt in the late 1700s. Lewin and Marje were my great (x3) grandparents.[272] Napoleon Bonaparte was quartered in the town on 18 to 21 February 1807. Lewin and Marje Polley, were living in Liebstadt at the time,[273] and if they did not see Napoleon themselves, they would certainly have seen many of his troops in and around town.

One history suggests that Jews first settled in Liebstadt in the 1820s,[274] but by then my great (x3) grandparents were already living there. Their son Moses was born in town in 1821. By the 1840s, there were over 130 members of the local Jewish community. A Jewish cemetery was built in the south end of town, and a synagogue established in the centre of Liebstadt. The synagogue was confiscated in 1938 and Aryanized. By then, most if not all of Henriette's Polley family had moved to Berlin.

At least eight people born in Liebstadt were murdered in the Holocaust. My Polley relatives made up at least two of that number.

---

[272] Compgen German genealogy database
[273] 'Milakowo', Wikipedia
[274] 'Milakowo', Virtual Shtetl, Polin Museum of the History of Polish Jews, Sztetl.org.pl/en/towns/m/743-milakowo/99-history/137684-history-of-community

Uncovering their Names and Stories:

Henriette's sister Natalie was murdered in Theresienstadt in 1942.[275] Louis and Jeanette's son Kurt Polley (1898-1943) was murdered in Auschwitz.

Today, the local Jewish cemetery has been destroyed, and most of it has been covered over by Christian graves and a monument to a plane crash. No Jewish gravestones are in their original positions. Only six gravestones remain, and they were repositioned together and relocated to a separate area in 1989. None of the gravestones relate to my family members.[276]

Map of East Prussia (1938)
(Source: Alamy Stock Photos – Interfoto – framing of mentioned key towns by author)

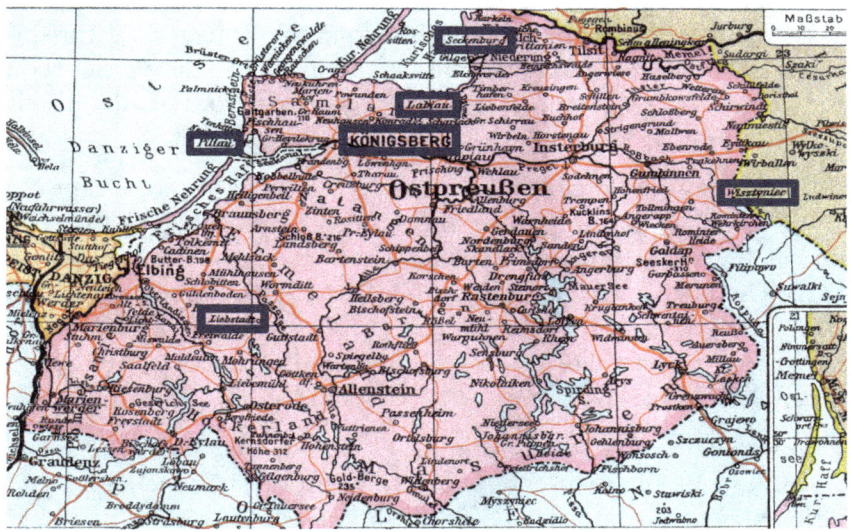

---

[275] Compgen German genealogy database
[276] 'Milakowo Jewish Cemetery', ESJF Cemeteries, Esjf-cemeteries.org/survey/milakowo-jewish-cemetery/; and 'List of preserved tombstones a the Jewish cemetery in Milakow', K. Bielawski, Cmentarze-zydowskie.pl/Milakowo.htm

The tide turns against the Marowilskys in Wuppertal

Hermann Marowilsky and Henriette (Meta) Lennhoff (1889-1942) married in Elberfeld (Wuppertal), and their only child and my father Heinz was born in Pillau in 1921. In 1925, they moved back to Wuppertal, as Henriette was born in Barmen-Elberfeld, and they were returning to her hometown. Before they were married, Henriette had worked as a saleswoman in Elberfeld. Henriette for most of her life went by the shorter name Meta, even on her Gestapo deportation records, most likely because Hermann's mother was also Henriette. Two Henriette Marowilskys in one family would have been confusing.

Dad always called Wuppertal his hometown, even though he was born in East Prussia. Wuppertal was where he was brought up, and he would have remembered holidays along the Rhine River, trips to Düsseldorf and the culture of the region, including the music, food and wine. These holidays certainly featured prominently in his childhood photo album.

Jews lived in Wuppertal from the late 16th century, but were expelled in 1794, only returning under the French in the early 1800s. The formal Jewish community in Wuppertal traces its history back to 1852. There were 87 Jews in Elberfeld out of a population of 18,783 in 1810. Barmen had 10 Jews out of a population of 16,289. The population of the towns reached 170,000 by 1910, with 1,918 Jews in Elberfeld and 643 in Barmen.[277]

Wuppertal was actually formed in 1929, with the merger of the towns of Elberfeld, Barmen, Beyenberg, Ronsdorf, Cronenberg and Vohwinkel.[278] The initial amalgamation was called Barmen-Elberfeld and was renamed Wuppertal ('Wupper Valley') in 1930.[279] It sits on the River Wupper which winds though the city, and though narrow, is a defining feature of the city. It is very noticeable as you walk or drive around. Wuppertal has a population today of about 365,000, situated not far from the cities of Düsseldorf to the west and Cologne

---

[277] Alte-synagoge-wuppertal.de/museum/gebaeude-und-geschichte
[278] 'Wuppertal', Jewish Virtual Library: A Project of AICE
[279] 'Wuppertal', Britannica.com

Uncovering their Names and Stories:

to the southwest. It is well known for its historic Schwebebahn or suspension monorail system, which commenced operating in 1901.

The Schwebebahn is the oldest electric elevated railway system with hanging cars in the world. The tracks and stations were built between 1897 and 1903, an amazing engineering achievement for its time. It certainly helped with the integration of the original component towns of Wuppertal.[280] It is still an important part of the local transportation system, having new cars introduced into service in 2015, and as of 2008 transporting 25 million passengers annually.[281]

It was such an innovation in its day, that Theodor Herzl discussed the benefits of the electric overhead train running from Barmen to Elberfeld in his utopian novel 'Alteneuland' which was published in 1902.[282]

Wuppertal is also known for Aspirin, as it originated there, being patented by Bayer in 1897.[283] Wuppertal became and remains a centre for manufacturing, very different to the small towns of Pillau and Vistytis where the Marowilskys came from. The co-founder of modern Communism, Friedrich Engels[284] (1820-1895) was born in Barmen, and there is a museum focused on his life in his father's old family home.[285]

It is ironic that Wuppertal was such a large and modern city, because my mother, a Berliner, used to tease my father for coming from the provinces, because he was from Wuppertal. If she had known about his roots in Pillau and Vistytis, Dad would have never heard the end of it.

A synagogue was built in 1865 on Genügäßstrasse (now Genügsamkeitstraße) with small numbers of Jews growing to 3,500 in 1933, but the community had declined to just over 1,000 by 1939.

---

[280] 'Facts and Figures', Schwebebahn, 21 November 2015
[281] '2008 Annual Report', WSW Group of companies, p44
[282] The Alteneuland (The Old New Land), Theodor Herzl, Sakuramachi shoin, 2017
[283] Friedrich Bayer (1825-1880) was the founder of the Friedrich Bayer paint factory, later Bayer AG.
[284] Engels co-wrote The Communist Manifesto with Karl Marx.
[285] Engels-Haus, Wuppertal

The Begegnungsstätte Alte Synagoge is now a memorial, museum and library with only one original wall remaining. Christine Hartung, Deputy Head of the Alte Synagoge has been very helpful in providing and pointing me towards information on the Jewish history of Wuppertal, including Kristallnacht and the Kindertransport,

A second synagogue was built on Zur Scheuren Street in 1897. Both synagogues were destroyed on Kristallnacht 1938, and many Jews were deported to Dachau. Those who did not escape Germany were murdered by the Nazi regime during the Holocaust, with the remaining Jews deported to Łódź, Minsk, Theresienstadt and Izbica through 1941-42, including my paternal grandparents.

In total, 1,428 Wuppertal Jews were murdered during the Holocaust.[286]

Site of the Begegnungsstätte Alte Synagoge in Wuppertal
(Photo credit: David Marlow)

The Jewish community regrew to only 89 by 1989 but increased significantly to 2,293 by 2004 thanks to immigration by Jews from

---

[286] Alte-synagoge-wuppertal.de/museum/gebaeude-und-geschichte

Uncovering their Names and Stories:

the former USSR. A new synagogue, the Bergische Synagogue and community centre was completed on Gemarker Street in Wuppertal in December 2002, with a capacity for 300 people.[287]

Though Germany is a very different place than in the 1930s, I was shocked in July 2014, when the Bergische Synagogue was attacked with Molotov cocktails, as it was discovered later, by three Palestinian men.[288] German courts later decided it was not an antisemitic attack,[289] but in the 1930s the culprits would probably have been awarded medals by the state.

I expressed my concerns after the 2014 attack on Twitter, including how it was a throwback to the burning down of the old Wuppertal synagogue on Kristallnacht. A journalist and writer based in Wuppertal, Fabian Maruschat,[290] was touched by what I wrote, and contacted me to obtain my feelings about this modern attack. He quoted me in a local newspaper, "I was horrified by this memory of Kristallnacht and am afraid that something much worse could happen again in Europe. The incident in Wuppertal affected me deeply."[291] I was very concerned that far-right and Islamist extremism were once again creating hostile and unsafe conditions for Jews in Europe. It has only become more worrisome since.

Fabian has since become a good friend, and when we caught up over a coffee recently at the popular Café Moritz in Wuppertal, he presented me with a signed copy of his graphic novel on local boy Friedrich Engels, 'Engels – Entrepreneur and Revolutionary'. We had a lovely casual chat about all things German and our various writing escapades.

---

[287] 'Wuppertal', Jewish Virtual Library: A Project of AICE
[288] 'Palestinians admit attack on Wuppertal synagogue', DPA/The Local Germany, 14 January 2015
[289] 'German court affirms ruling synagogue arson not anti-Semitic', JTA, The Time of Israel, 15 January 2017
[290] Fabian Maruschat is a freelance journalist and author, based in Wuppertal.
[291] 'Über Botschaften', Sophie Blasberg, Fabian Maruschat et.al., Zeit Fur Wuppertal, July 2014

From about 1925 to 1939, the Marowilsky family lived at 14 Döppersberg Strasse, Wuppertal.[292] On my visit to Wuppertal, I walked around the street to see the area where my father, Marowilsky grandparents, and Lennhoff great grandparents lived. The old apartment building appears to be gone, and the area is a transport hub including the Wuppertal Bus Station, the Wuppertal Hauptbahnhof (Wuppertal Central Station), and is about 100m from the closest Schwebebahn station.

In Wuppertal, the family became more middle class. Hermann was by then a businessman, working for a clothing manufacturer.[293] He also liked to play his violin after dinner. Years later, my Dad's Aunt Elsa Dauk nee Lennhoff, who had married a very nice Catholic man, our 'Uncle' Heinz Dauk, and survived the war because of him and his family, presented my father with the violin which he hung in his den in Melbourne. Elsa had arranged the rescue of the violin after her sister Meta and her husband Hermann Marowilsky were arrested by the Gestapo and deported via Düsseldorf near Wuppertal, to Izbica in Poland to be murdered, on 22 April 1942.[294]

Elsa and Heinz Dauk kept in contact with my parents after the war, and I can remember as a child phone calls from them at all times of the night from "Aunt and Uncle", as they forgot about the time differences between Germany and Melbourne. They visited the family in Australia at least twice, including at least once when I was a toddler. In September 1963, when I was one year old, they came to Australia on the *M.S. Wolfsburg* to visit my family in Melbourne and stayed until February 1964. Unfortunately, I have no memory of the visits. But I do remember that in 1975 Elsa and Heinz very kindly sent me a gold medallion necklace engraved with Michelangelo's David, as a gift for my barmitzvah. It was a treasured possession until it disappeared in a house move many years later.

Dad once told the story to a friend over drinks, with a very young me listening intently with my glass of Coke, about seeing his dentist

---

[292] Confirmed via address book entries thanks to the Stadtarchiv Wuppertal.
[293] Datenbank Judische Verfolgte in Wuppertal, Bergische Universität Wuppertal
[294] 'Mapping the Lives' online

Uncovering their Names and Stories:

murdered by Nazi thugs from his window at home in Wuppertal. I always thought he was exaggerating or making up stories, until I came across a paragraph in Sir Martin Gilbert's extraordinary book on the Holocaust, "On the day before the book-burning, Dr Meyer, a Jewish dentist in Wuppertal, was mutilated by Stormtroops, and then drowned."[295] How many Jewish dentists were beaten to death in Wuppertal in the 1930s? When I stood on the site where Dad's home had been, I did wonder where the dentist had been murdered. It sent a shudder down my back as I thought about it. I have since discovered that the dentist was Dr Alfred Meyer who was murdered on 15 May 1933.[296]

Life in Wuppertal, like in the rest of Germany, gradually became worse and worse for its Jewish community.

Dad attended an elementary school in Döppersberg and in 1930 started at the Boys Middle School South in Wuppertal, 31 Pfalgrafenstrasse. The school was founded in 1910 as the 'Graf-Adolf-Schule' and today houses the 'Bergisches Kolleg'. This was a 20 minute walk from home. Dad completed middle school, obtaining his intermediate school leaving certificate in March 1937. There is a photo of him standing with a group of young students, all about the same age, in his childhood photo album, where he looks happy with his middle school class. He enjoyed his time in school and got on well with his teachers, especially his class teacher Karl Buchborn and the headmaster Otto Ritter, who Dad said was a very friendly man. Dad was assigned to take the school news book to each class in the school and had to shout "Heil Hitler" in every class.[297]

He was prevented, as a Jew from attending university. But he said that he attended a commercial or vocational school, where his fellow students stood up for him against the authorities who wanted to kick him out. The other students said they would not go there if young Heinz was not allowed to attend as well. They all attended until

---

[295] <u>The Holocaust: The Jewish Tragedy</u>, Sir Martin Gilbert, Harper Collins, London, 1987, p38
[296] Prof Brusten notes to Henry Marlow interview with Prof Manfred Brusten, October 1994
[297] Henry Marlow interview with Prof Manfred Brusten, October 1994

Easter 1938. Dad attended the class reunion in June 1938, but he did not participate in the Rhine trip that followed, as he did not want to get the others into trouble.[298]

Jews were not allowed to go to the cinema, but one of his classmates used to pick him up to attend with them. Dad, a Jew, and his classmate in his Hitler Youth uniform.

A letter from an old school friend of Dad's, Günther Grasse, is illustrative of his positive relationship with his schoolmates in a very dangerous environment, "One day, it was 1937 and we had already left school, I had to go to Elberfeld for some reason. I came from the train station and walked along the railway tracks at Döppersberg in the direction of Barmen. Suddenly I saw my classmate Heinz Marowilsky, whom we called Maron for short, coming towards me."

Dad with his Boys Middle School South classmates (Dad is third from left)
(Source: Heinz Marowilsky childhood photo album)

"So, I went towards him; but he turned away, but on the other hand he remained standing. When I finally came closer, he warned me with the words: 'Günther, be careful! You can see what's going on!' Then he turned fully towards me, and I saw the Star of David. 'I don't care,'

---

[298] ibid.

Uncovering their Names and Stories:

I replied, 'after all, you're my schoolmate and that's how it's going to stay!' But Heinz was actually right; after all, I was a member of the Hitler Youth myself and even had a rank there, and I was also a 'youth administrator' in my training company, the Homann Works. Nevertheless, today I am of course happy about my reaction at the time, with which I put my schoolmate above the constraints of the time, without being put off by Heinz Marowilsky's well-intentioned warning."[299]

Dad's commercial school was very likely the Berufskolleg Elberfeld (Elberfeld Vocational College), which is one of the largest vocational schools in Wuppertal and has a campus off the same street where the Marowilskys lived. The College's main building is on Bundesallee, with a side entrance on Döppersberg, the street where Dad lived with his parents. He would have had a five minute walk from home, at most. The College is within 100m of where their apartment building was sited. I walked the path from where his home had been to the college and around the surrounding area between the Schwebebahn, the Wuppertal Institute nearby, and the bus station.[300]

The College was founded as a commercial vocational school in 1903. Its current marketing materials promotes it as "preparing our students in the best possible way for the requirements and challenges of the working and professional world of tomorrow."[301]

After finishing at the commercial school, young Heinz worked as a commercial apprentice at the Jewish company Ferber & Hecht at Hofaue 91 from Easter 1938 to learn about fabrics for suits. The company was Aryanized, taken over by Albert Schlieper in October 1938, with all the employees, including just the one Jewish staff member, Dad. Hofaue 91 was only a 2-minute walk from home for young Heinz.

---

[299] Günther Grasse letter dated 2 March 1995 cited by Prof Brusten in notes to Henry Marlow interview with Prof Manfred Brusten, October 1994
[300] The Wuppertal Institute for Climate, Environment and Energy undertakes research into sustainable development.
[301] Berufskolleg-elberfeld.de/bk-wuppertal/bk-elberfeld/

The world changed forever for the Jews of Wuppertal on Kristallnacht in November 1938.

Holocaust Survivor and Melbourne Holocaust Museum volunteer Henri Korn, who I have met many times and is also from Wuppertal, described seeing the immediate aftermath of Kristallnacht with his own eyes in 1938. The pogrom ran for two days starting on 9 November. He saw his synagogue burning. The Nazis had tried to burn it down on the first day but failed. They had to return on the second day to finish the job. The streets were littered with glass, fragments of Torah scroll, items from Jewish homes such as bed sheets and even an upright piano that had been thrown down to the street.[302]

Arrests took place in huge numbers on Kristallnacht and the days that followed. Not of the perpetrators, but of the Jewish victims. On Kristallnacht, about 267 synagogues across Germany were destroyed, 91 Jews murdered, and 30,000 Jewish men taken to concentration camps, such as Dachau and Sachsenhausen.[303]

Dad never talked to anyone in the family about his experience on Kristallnacht. However, in 1994 he was interviewed by Wuppertal-based researcher Prof Manfred Brusten about his Kindertransport experience, which included talking about Kristallnacht. The interview was in German.

He told Prof Brusten, "After the 'Night of Broken Glass' I saw that all over the city the windows of Jewish shops had been smashed, things had been thrown onto the street and the shops themselves had been pretty much devastated; but nothing was destroyed for us. I also saw the burned-out synagogue."[304]

His father, Hermann, was arrested and locked up in Elberfeld. Hermann was held for two weeks, and then released to the relief of the family. I hate to think what brutality and mistreatment he may

---

[302] Henri Korn Holocaust Survivor testimony, Melbourne Holocaust Museum, 2012

[303] 'The Kindertransport and Refugees', Learning about the Holocaust and Genocides, Holocaust Memorial Day Trust

[304] Henry Marlow interview with Prof Manfred Brusten, October 1994

have received while imprisoned. However, Dad said that "people in prison knew him and that's why they tried to get him out."[305] The family were, as yet, unable to escape Germany.

He explained to Prof Brusten that he hid while the Gestapo was looking for him, and his colleagues at work helped conceal him. He said, "I myself was hidden by the employees of the Albert Schlieper cloth wholesaler, where I was working as an apprentice at the time. When I was supposed to be picked up, I simply couldn't be found because I was hidden in the middle of a roll of cloth about two meters high. All the company's employees knew this, but no one ratted me out. I stayed there hidden for about a week and everyone, from the boss to the woman in the office, were very nice to me and did everything they could for me. During the whole week they denied me to the Nazis. Then I went home again because they were apparently no longer looking for me."[306]

The Marowilsky's neighbour living on the same floor as them at 14 Döppersberg was a senior police officer named Pohlkehn and his family. They were good people and good friends, and Dad remembered on the Christmas soon after Kristallnacht, "Even though our immediate neighbor was a policeman, he was a very decent man and I can still remember when he came to us at Christmas 1938, after Kristallnacht (!), and said: 'We haven't invited anyone else this evening, why don't you come over to dinner with us?' We thought we couldn't do that, because if anyone came, we'd be lost. But then he locked everything up and said: 'Just come, no one's coming in here.' Then my father and I got our violins out of the apartment to play them."[307]

After Kristallnacht, Hermann and Meta worked quickly to get young Heinz out of the country as soon as possible, with a view to them following close behind. In February 1939, he obtained the necessary police certificate, which was like a modern-day police check, and

---

[305] ibid.
[306] Die Kindertransporte 1938/39: von Wuppertal nach England, Anna Ruhland, unpublished master's thesis, Universitat zu Köln, Cologne, 29 July 2005
[307] Henry Marlow interview with Prof Manfred Brusten, October 1994

medical certificate towards the paperwork he needed to escape to England. His medical certificate recorded that he was healthy, 161cm or 5'3" tall, and weighed 55 kg. Dad's friend Heinz Holstein had already escaped to England and Holstein's brother worked at a factory in England that built airplanes.

If any Jews left had any thought that this was just like the antisemitism of old, that it would blow over or that they would be safe because they served in World War 1, those thoughts were destroyed on Kristallnacht. The remaining Jews in Germany now tried to escape wherever and however they could. Those who could not effectively flee or hide, perished in the camps.

The Central British Fund for German Jewry, known as World Jewish Relief since the 1990's, was founded in 1933. It provided a welfare system to help German Jewish refugees emigrate to Britain, and find employment, housing and medical care. The charity helped transport about 65,000 Jewish refugees (from Germany and Austria) to Britain and arranged economic support. The charity also helped instigate schemes such as the Kindertransport, which rescued 10,000 children including my father, a young Heinz Marowilsky.[308]

Britain's King Charles III has been patron of World Jewish Relief since 2015. He has been involved with the organisation since he visited Krakow's Jewish community in 2002.

World Jewish Relief retains case files, which are its administrative records. Its staff at the time noted requests for assistance and detailed the support provided. Some files contain photographs, letters and various other records. Some record the financial aid provided. Unfortunately, not all the original paperwork survived. The files they have today were found by lucky accident in the garage of a care home in the 1980s. These were digitized in 2015. Each refugee was issued a registration card, which was held at Bloomsbury House (previously the Palace Hotel) in London, and detailed names, date of birth, date of arrival, addresses, family members, case file number, and a movement number for children who arrived on the

---

[308] World Jewish Relief

Uncovering their Names and Stories:

Kindertransport.[309]

World Jewish Relief has registration slips for most of the 65,000 Jewish refugees helped by World Jewish Relief, but only about 35,000 of the original case files. The records are 'matter-of-fact' in tone but demonstrate the wide range of support provided, from accommodation to employment, medical attention to cinema tickets. In the absence of any Government support, World Jewish Relief provided an unofficial welfare system.[310]

When I approached World Jewish Relief for information, they advised that the case files for my father Heinz Marowilsky had not survived but were able to provide the registration cards for Heinz, and his parents Hermann and Meta Marowilsky. Dad's card confirmed a lot of what I already knew, such as where he lived in Wolverhampton after he arrived and suggested he was to be a textile apprentice, like he had been in Wuppertal. However, he actually became an apprentice electrician. This always amused me, as I remember my mother would not even let Dad fix a fuse at our home in Melbourne in the 1970s. The card also provided a new piece of information, being the date he arrived in the UK, 10 March 1939, just four months after Kristallnacht.

By providing the registration cards for Hermann and Meta, it proved that they were trying to flee Germany in 1939. It helped confirm the story that Dad told me, that his parents were planning to follow him to England, but the war broke out the day before they had planned to leave, so they could not get out.

Once in England, Dad obtained British visas for his parents, but that was not enough. In his interview in Melbourne with Prof Brusten on 4 October 1994, Dad said, "So I got signed applications from the theatre in Wolverhampton stating that they had work for my parents there, for my mother as a cook, for my father as a gardener. I then received the English permit for both of them to enter England, but not the German exit permit. This only came on September 3, 1939." The war had started on 1 September after Germany invaded Poland,

---

[309] Bloomsbury House opened in 1938 and was the headquarters of eleven aid organisations aimed at helping refugees.
[310] ibid.

and the gates were closed.³¹¹

Heinz Marowilsky's registration slip with World Jewish Relief
(Source: World Jewish Relief archives)

```
No. 17592        SURNAME    MAROWILSKY
                 CHRISTIAN NAME    Heinz         PTO
ENGLISH ADDRESS  4/127 Wolverhampton Rd Wolverhampton 11.9.39
HOME ADDRESS     Wuppertal              NATIONALITY German
DATE OF BIRTH    11.7.21    PROFESSION  textile apprentice
GUARANTOR-NAME and ADDRESS
ARRIVAL DATE     10.3.39
LEFT U.K. FOR                            CROSS REFERENCE
DATE
```

Meta and Hermann were eventually arrested by the Gestapo in April 1942, as Gestapo records in Düsseldorf document, and deported to the ghetto in Izbica in Poland. There is a relatively recent German documentary on Izbica with a title that translates as 'Izbica - The Turnstile of Death'.³¹²

Plundering the Jews

I wondered what happened to their possessions? And for that matter the possessions of all my relatives that fled with a single suitcase each if they were lucky, or were deported to camps and ghettos, possibly with a promise that their cases would be onforwarded. A large part of the answer came from another German documentary, called 'The

---

³¹¹ Die Kindertransporte 1938/39: von Wuppertal nach England, Anna Ruhland, unpublished master's thesis, Universitat zu Köln, Cologne, 29 July 2005; and 'Henry Marlow (Heinz Marowilsky)', transcript of interview with Prof Manfred Brusten, Armadale, 4 October 1994, edited version 6 - 2001

³¹² Izbica – Drehkreuz des Todes, Frank Gutermuth and Wolfgang Schoen, 2007

Uncovering their Names and Stories:

Auctioneers: Profiting from the Holocaust'.[313] This was very well researched. They dug deeply into the records of the auctioneers who made huge profits from selling off the possessions of the deported Jews. It explained the process by which the Nazi regime auctioned off all Jewish possessions confiscated, stolen and left behind.

This included clothing, shoes, suitcases, furniture, cooking pots, homewares, musical instruments and children's toys. They were openly auctioned to the public, in advertised 'Jewish Auctions', where the German public could get a bargain from the sale of the belongings of departed Jews. The auctioneers made 10% and the rest went into the government's taxation coffers. Typically, the auctions were held two to three weeks after the deportation.

These auctions were not hidden, but well-promoted, well-attended and well-photographed. The public attending these auctions, if not accomplices, were in the very least complicit in this process. They sold their souls for a bargain.

The auctions started around 1933, but increased dramatically as Jews were forced to flee or forced into camps and ghettos. Even belongings left behind when families were forced into a smaller Judenhaus, were targeted. Ultimately, the sales also happened in other countries invaded by Germany. In Germany alone, the auctions sold off around 450,000 beds, 900,000 cupboards, 1.8 million chairs, 7 million plates, and millions of other items.[314]

But that was just chump change, compared to the big items. On 26 April 1938 all Jews in Germany and Austrian were directed by law to register any assets valued at more than 5,000 Reichsmarks (about USD $34,000 today). That included everything from artwork and shares to real estate property. By the end of July 1938, 700,000 Jews had declared 7 billion Reichsmarks (about USD $47.6 billion today) of wealth.[315] This made the eventual confiscation or 'Aryanization' of

---

[313] The Auctioneers: Profiting from the Holocaust, Jan N. Lorenzen and Michael Schönherr, 2018

[314] ibid. based on 1933 German census data

[315] 'A 1938 Nazi Law Forced Jews to Register Their Wealth – Making It Easier to Steal', Smithsonian Magazine, Lorraine Boissoneault, 26 April 2018

all those assets much easier. The Nazis now had a complete list of what to steal, and they did so without remorse or hesitation.

Of course, not everything registered ended up in the coffers of the Nazi taxation office. Notably, many previously Jewish-owned artworks ended up in the private collections of senior Nazi leaders. Gold, money from dormant Jewish bank accounts and unclaimed insurance policies ended up in Swiss bank accounts.

Not everything has been accounted for since, as the meticulous accounting was clearly not universally followed, especially if it benefitted certain powerful people for the assets to simply disappear.[316] Adolf Hitler and Herman Göring were the masters in building collections of stolen art but many other Nazi leaders and German officers followed their example.[317]

There was more. The Nazis were loaded with excesses of chutzpah,[318] because after Kristallnacht they charged a 'reimbursement tax' on the German Jewish community, to reimburse the regime for the catastrophic damage caused by the Nazis on 9-10 November 1938.[319]

---

[316] 'Nazi Looted Art: The Holocaust Records Preservation Project', Anne Rothfeld, Prologue Magazine, National Archives, Summer 2002, Vol. 34, No. 2

[317] ibid. and Monuments Men, Robert M. Edsel with Bret Witter, Arrow Books, 2013

[318] Chutzpah = extreme self-confidence or audacity, or what my mother would call "a bloody cheek"

[319] 'I can't forget what the Nazis did to my family, but I can be grateful to a repentant Germany', Rabbi Michael Meyerstein, JTA, 12 April 2023

Uncovering their Names and Stories:

8.0 The Marowilskys after Kristallnacht

Heinz Marowilsky on the Kindertransport

Dad was one of forty children who escaped Wuppertal on the Kindertransport to England. He departed Wuppertal by train on 6 March 1939.[320] Of those, 24 were girls and 16 were boys. Twenty stayed in the UK, nine ended up in the USA, four went to Australia, two to Canada, one to Denmark and two went to what is now Israel.[321]

The rescue of Jewish children officially under the age of 17 from Germany, and their transportation to the UK, commenced soon after Kristallnacht. Five days after Kristallnacht, British Jewish community leaders lobbied the British Prime Minister Neville Chamberlain to permit temporary admission of children and teenagers, who would later emigrate. They hoped many would be able to travel onwards to the USA, if and when the country accepted more refugees. The highly optimistic intention was that the children would eventually be joined by their parents.[322]

The British Cabinet debated the issue the very next day. The Jewish community had promised to provide guarantees for the refugee children, and with the support of Cabinet, the Home Secretary announced the program in the House of Commons.

The British response to Kristallnacht is in stark contrast to the poor response from the USA. A Kindertransport type program was proposed to the US Senate, for the country to rescue 20,000 Jewish refugee children. The plan (the Wagner-Rogers Bill) was proposed by

---

[320] <u>Zerbrochene Zukunft: Der Pogrom Gegen Die Juden in Wuppertal Im November 1938</u>, Dr Ulrike Schrader, Begegnungsstätte Alte Synagoge Wuppertal, Wuppertal, 2018, p.163

[321] <u>Retterwiderstand in Wuppertal während des Nationalsozialismus</u>, Inauguraldissertation zur Erlangung des Grades eines Doktors der Philosophie in der Philosophischen Fakultät (Fach Geschichte) der Heinrich-Heine-Universität Düsseldorf vorgelegt, von Frank Friedhelm Homber

[322] 'Kindertransport', Jewish Virtual Library: A Project of AICE, and 'Kindertransport 1938-1940', <u>Holocaust Encyclopedia</u>, US Holocaust Memorial Museum

Democrat Senator Robert F Wagner and Republican Senator Edith Nourse Rogers. Anti-immigrant and antisemitic sentiment trumped compassion, and the bill was defeated.[323]

Meanwhile, in Britain representatives were sent from the Movement for the Care of Children from Germany (later the Refugee Children's Movement) to Germany and Austria to organise transportation to England.[324]

Quite a few agencies and organisations were involved in the Kindertransport program in various cities in England, Germany and elsewhere, most notably the Refugee Children's Movement, but also the Children's Inter-Aid Committee, B'nai B'rith Care Committee for Refugee Children, the Chief Rabbi's Religious Emergency Council (CRREC), and a number of Quaker organizations.[325] There were many others who helped arrange funding, foster-carers, selection of the children in Europe, and travel across Germany and the Netherlands.

Nazi Germany at that stage was happy to force Jews out of the country, especially those under working age. However, the children could only take a single suitcase, a pocketbook and 10 Reichsmarks. No capital or jewellery were allowed to be taken.[326]

The program became known as the Kindertransport,[327] and it rescued about 10,000 children from Germany, Austria and Czechoslovakia prior to Germany invading Poland in September 1939, when the

---

[323] Aliens: The Chequered History of Britain's Wartime Refugees, Paul Dowswell, Biteback Publishing, London, 2023, chapter 4; and 'Representative Edith Nourse Rogers: A Beacon of Light in America's Darkest Moral Hour', Elazar Cramer, 2019 Winning Essay John F Kennedy Profile in Courage Essay Contest for High School Students, jfklibrary.org, 2019

[324] "The Kindertransport and Refugees", Learning about the Holocaust and Genocides, Holocaust Memorial Say Trust

[325] The Kindertransport: Contesting Memory, Jennifer Craig-Norton, Indiana University Press, Bloomington, 2019, p.37

[326] 'Kindertransporte (Children's Transports) 1938/39', Jüdisches Museum Berlin, jmberlin.de/en/topic-kindertransport-1938-39

[327] Kindertransport = children transport

program ended. My father was one of them, though he was aged 17 by then, rather than under 17.[328] There actually seems to have been many who slightly breached the upper age limit, and my father's height may have helped make him appear younger.

How traumatic and stressful must separation of children and parents have been? But at least parents could feel that their children were now safe. Jewish children were often housed with non-Jewish foster parents, frequently losing connection with their religion and culture, and in some cases they converted. Kosher food was also unlikely to have been provided in most cases. For the children, they were facing an alien culture, so many strangers, a foreign language, and not knowing if and when they might see their family again.

The people who organized and approved the Kindertransport program are heroes. This includes an extraordinarily large number of selfless people and organisations in Germany and Austria, the Netherlands and the UK. Though many were Jews, non-Jews and notably the Quakers were vital to the total Kindertransport effort. Even the British Foreign Office became useful, once wakened from its slumber by Kristallnacht and Jewish community pressure. They did not just save one life. They did not save just 10,000 lives. They saved the generations that followed, and their descendants to come. Me, my siblings, our children and our grandchildren included.

This brings to mind the often quoted phrase from the Talmud, "Whoever saves a single life, it is as if he had saved the whole world."[329]

The BBC Home Service radio program appealed for foster homes for the children to be rescued on 25 November, and there were soon 500 offers. There was no requirement that Jewish children went to Jewish homes, as long as the homes were clean and respectable. Networks were established in Germany to create priority lists, such as children in concentration camps or those at risk of being arrested.

The process was organized very quickly. Only a few weeks after Kristallnacht, the first Kindertransport departed Berlin on 1

---

[328] There were certainly a number of seventeen-year-olds who escaped on the Kindertransport, including my father.
[329] The Talmud, Sanhedrin 4:5

December 1938 and arrived in Harwich in the UK on 2 December 1938. It rescued 200 children from a Jewish orphanage in Berlin, which had been destroyed on Kristallnacht.[330] A letter from the Netherlands Legation to the British Foreign Office, indicates the 200 children were accompanied by eight adults. They traveled in two special train coaches, which met up with the night boat from the Hook of Holland to England. The Hook of Holland is on the southwest coast of the Netherlands near The Hague. Typically, the Kindertransports went through there on the way to England.[331]

The first transport from Vienna departed on 10 December. Next was Czechoslovakia, triggered by the German invasion of March 1939.[332]

Dad's parents had applied to get him to England a few days before Kristallnacht, and reasonably quickly obtained permission to enter England, but did not receive permission for Dad to leave Germany until 6 March 1939. He was on the Kindertransport train later that day. His parents saw him off at the Elberfeld train station in Wuppertal. They never saw each other again.

Dad arrived in Harwich on the steamship ferry from The Hook of Holland, after taking the train from Germany. He would then have been transported to London to meet his sponsor, if there was one. Or he would have been housed in the summer camp in Dovercourt Bay, which was used temporarily for Kindertransport children, until his housing and apprenticeship in Wolverhampton were finalised. This could have been coordinated by World Jewish Relief, but also possibly with the help of his friend Heinz Holstein.

The Dovercourt Camp is in Harwich, on the east coast of England, nearly a two-hour drive northeast of London. It is one of the closest parts of England to the Netherlands, so was very handy for children coming by boat from across the English Channel.

---

[330] 'Kindertransport', Holocaust Encyclopedia, US Holocaust Memorial Museum
[331] Report on the Dovercourt Camp from N. de Selincourt and letter from Jonkheer E. Teixeira de Mattos held in the National Archives (UK)
[332] 'Kindertransport', Jewish Virtual Library: A Project of AICE

Uncovering their Names and Stories:

One former Kindertransport child remembered, "We disembarked at Harwich and were taken out into some fields. The sun was shining, the air clean, the grass greener than any I had ever seen, and if ever freedom was a tangible thing, it was so that morning in Harwich."[333]

Many young Jewish refugees from Germany, up to 4,000, were housed at the Kitchener Camp, which had a much more relaxed environment than any internment camp. They were not technically interned. Kitchener was a former military camp near Sandwich in Kent, which was used to house male Jewish refugees in the late 1930s. It was organised by World Jewish Relief and contained mainly adult men from Germany and Austria.[334] When the war commenced, 887 of the Kitchener men volunteered for the Pioneer Corps, which did everything from regular infantry work and guarding of bases to light engineering, such as mine clearing.

However, when I checked their lists, Dad was not amongst the Kitchener men.[335] He most likely went straight from Harwich to Wolverhampton. I initially thought he may have gone to Kitchener, because it was used to educate young men in employable skills, especially trade skills, and Dad became an apprentice electrician.[336]

The World Jewish Relief archives are invaluable. But the volunteer archives service is just one small part of what World Jewish Relief does today. They still work supporting refugees in the UK as they did over 80 years ago, but also provide care services to vulnerable older Jewish people in Eastern Europe, responding to disasters around the world, and providing training and employment support to young Jewish people.

---

[333] Rabbi John Rayner, The Harwich Kindertransport Memorial and Learning Trust Ltd, kindertransport-memorial.org/

[334] 'The forgotten haven: Kent camp that saved 4,000 German Jews', Harriet Sherwood, The Guardian, 24 August 2019

[335] Kitchenercamp.co.uk/list-of-names/

[336] Get the Children Out!: Unsung Heroes of the Kindertransport, Mike Levy, Lemon Soul, London, 2023, p.200

Example of a Kindertransport ferry ticket – like what my father would have used in 1939 to travel from the Hook of Holland to Harwich in England

(Source: Tim Locke, Ephraims and Neumeyers website, Lewes, East Sussex)

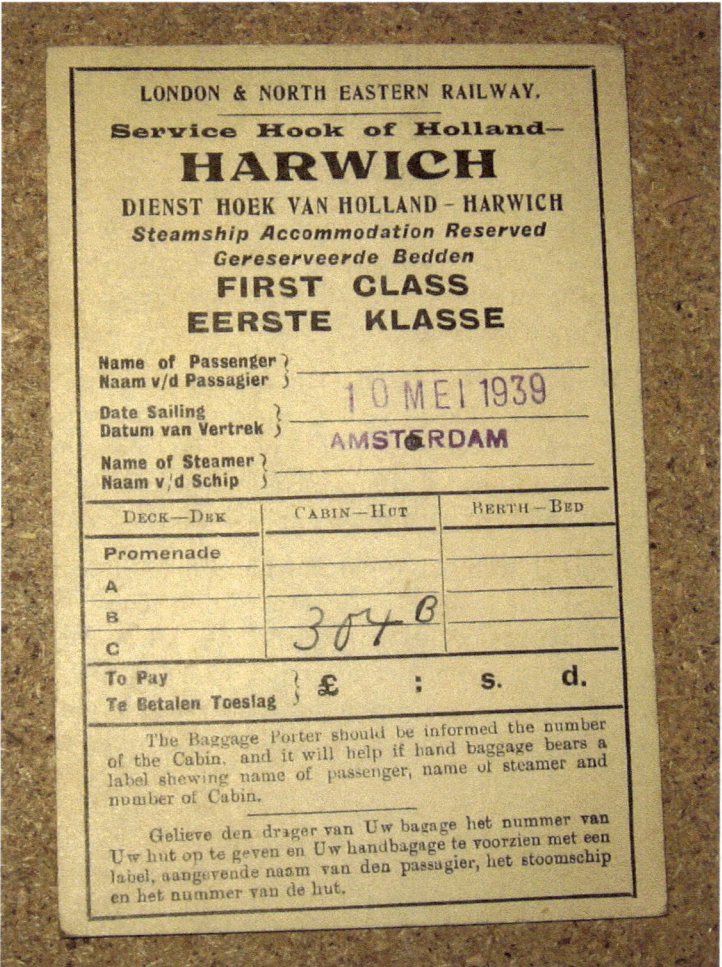

Heinz Marowilsky in Wolverhampton

World Jewish Relief confirmed to me that Dad arrived in England on 10 March 1939, just four months after Kristallnacht and four days after leaving his parents in Wuppertal.[337] His life was saved. He was found work as an electrician's apprentice, and a home with a Jewish family at 127 Waterloo Road, Wolverhampton.[338]

The British Home Office gave permission on 14 March 1939 for Dad to work as an apprentice electrician in England, writing, "The Under Secretary of State is directed to inform the German Jewish Aid Committee with reference to their letter … regarding Mr Heinz Marowilsky that the Secretary of State does not desire to raise objection to his taking the post of trainee with Messrs. J. H Blount & Co. Ltd., until 10th March, 1940."[339]

Wolverhampton is a city in central England, 19 km northwest of Birmingham, or about 200 km northwest of London by road. It has a population today of about 263,700.[340] Over its history, the city developed from being a market town specializing in the wool trade, at one time a centre for bicycle manufacturing (1868-1975), to installing the first automatic traffic lights in England in 1927.[341]

In Wolverhampton, Dad worked for Blount & Co Electrical Contractors, who today proudly promote on their website that they have been "Serving the UK and Midlands for 85 years", which means that the business started in the year that Dad was working for them.[342] He worked on electrical installations at theatres and hotels. Staff there asked if they could help find work for his parents or his girlfriend at the time, Edith Kahn (1920-1942). Edith was also from Wuppertal and Dad visited her, and her parents, at the Westerbork refugee camp in the northern Netherlands on his way through to England. Once

---

[337] World Jewish Relief
[338] Australian Army Report on Internee form and 1939 Uniting Kingdom Census
[339] Die Kindertransporte 1938/39: von Wuppertal nach England, Anna Ruhland, unpublished master's thesis, Universität zu Köln, Cologne, 29 July 2005
[340] 'How the population changed in Wolverhampton, Census 2021 – ONS', ons.gov.uk
[341] 'Traffic Control and Traffic Signals', Wolverhampton City Council, 20 September 2008
[342] Jhblount.co.uk; and Heinz Marowilsky's 'Male Enemy Alien Exemption From Internment – Refugee' form

the Nazis invaded the Netherlands, Westerbork was turned into a Nazi transit camp for deportations. Edith was sadly murdered in Auschwitz.[343]

Dad noted that he was not highly paid in England but earned one pound per day of work, of which he paid one pound per week for accommodation and one pound per week for living expenses. His parents sent him little parcels from home, including biscuits and other treats. He was asked about these packages coming from Germany when he was being assessed by a tribunal after Dunkirk. "Don't we have these things in England", he was asked. "Don't you have a mother?", Dad responded. The judges laughed and released him.[344]

At 127 Waterloo Road in Wolverhampton, Dad lived with Sam (1889-) and Bertha Wernick (1889-) who were a Polish Jewish husband and wife, who had emigrated to the UK just before World War 1. Sam ran the family shed construction business from their house, which has a big backyard. The Wernicks were a similar age to Heinz's parents and had several children around his age. Also living in the house in 1939, according to the Census that year, were the Wernick children Joseph (1920-), Joan (1923-) and Lionel (1928-2023), as well as three other people (Mark and Yetta Nieman, and Markus Ziegler), who may well have also been refugees from Nazi-threatened Europe. The Wernick's four oldest children had already left home.

The house is still standing and is only a six minute walk to the home ground of the Wolverhampton 'Wolves' football team.[345] The Wernick boys were all big Wolves fans. If Dad did see any football games during his time on Waterloo Road, it did not last. As a boy, he did play some football or soccer as we call it in Australia, but he converted to supporting Australian Rules Football in Australia. His team was the Essendon 'Bombers' during his life in Australia, rather

---

[343] Prof Brusten note to transcript of Henry Marlow interview with Prof Manfred Brusten, October 1994; and Collections.yadvashem.org/en/names/14951031
[344] Henry Marlow interview with Prof Manfred Brusten, October 1994
[345] Wolverhampton Wanderers Football Club

Uncovering their Names and Stories:

than the round ball game. His choice of team would have been an easy decision at the time, as Essendon won the 1942 grand final and was runner-up in both 1941 and 1943.

The house at 127 Waterloo Road, Wolverhampton where Heinz lived 1939-1940
(Source: David Wernick)

The Wernick family business was building portable buildings, such as poultry sheds, garden sheds, garages and greenhouses. It was founded by Sam Wernick in 1934, after trying his hand working at his uncle's bakery in London as a youngster, and as a butcher and a poultry dealer. The family found business and surviving financially a big struggle through the 1930s, and still tough into the 1940s. The extended family shared one car for quite some time, and Sam's son Lionel said he would get a new shirt each year for his birthday. It was not unusual for the Shabbat candlesticks to be pawned and retrieved between Shabbats, as a form of temporary overdraft. The business held its first annual general meeting in the house in 1947.[346]

Today, the Wernick Group operates from 34 sites around the UK, has annual revenue over £200 million, and employs over 800 people.

---

[346] Accommodating People Since 1934: The Story of the Wernick Group, Nigel Watson, St Matthew's Press, Leyburn, 2023

It is still 100% owned by the family, with Lionel's son David as Chairman, and David's son Jonathan as CEO.[347]

David Wernick told me, "My father, Lionel Wernick, who was the last of that generation, passed away last November. However, I do remember that he often used to talk about the refugees that stayed at Waterloo Road and how his mother would cook for them." 'His mother' was Bertha Wernick, who was known as a good cook, and had retained her Polish accent, and cooked meals for the family and their refugee guests. I am sure the house smelled very pleasantly of good Jewish food, likely including cholent, knishes, kugel, latkes, kreplach and holishkes (cabbage rolls).

It is a shame that Lionel passed before I contacted the family, as you never know what stories he may have remembered of Dad's time living with them. Now, we can only imagine.

Dad would have found staying with the Wernick family comfortable, with a family atmosphere, and a welcoming Jewish household. They would also have had no problem with his Marowilsky surname, as it sounds very Polish, and Sam and Bertha Wernick were Polish born.

It would also have enhanced his English language skills, which would have been very useful when he later arrived in Australia. Having other, possibly Jewish refugees in the household, with the Wernicks having come from Poland, would have helped him fit in. He was lucky. Not all Kindertransport children were housed with Jewish families. Having a Jewish family host, made it easier to retain contact with the Jewish community and observance of festivals, though he was never overly-observant.

The Wernick's local synagogue was the Wolverhampton Hebrew Congregation on the corner of Fryer and Short Streets, just a 17 minute walk from the house. The synagogue building has now become a church. Manchester-born Rev. Ephraim Shine (1916-1984) was the young rabbi of the synagogue at the time. One of the Wernicks was actually Co-Vice President of the synagogue from 1954 to 1956, and with their attachment to their Shabbat candlesticks, they must have been at least a little observant at the time.

---

[347] ibid. p.6 and p.102

Uncovering their Names and Stories:

But Dad's Waterloo Road life did not last. England declared war on Germany on 3 September 1939 in response to Hitler's invasion of Poland, which made my father and 70,000 other people from Germany and Austria 'enemy aliens'. Tribunals were established to classify these 'aliens' into various classifications, 66,000 'C' not so dangerous and not interned; 6,700 'B' to be monitored by police; and 569 'A' to be interned as 'enemy aliens'. As the German Army marched through Belgium and into France, and fears of invasion were raised, these classifications were reviewed and 12,000 additional Germans, Austrians and Italians were interned in May 1940.[348]

Winston Churchill later described the arrest, internment and deportations of suspect Austrians, Germans and many Italians as "a deplorable and regrettable mistake". The fear was that they might be enemy agents, possibly helping with 'Operation Sealion', the much-feared Nazi invasion of Britain.[349]

Dad was eventually arrested as an 'enemy alien' by the British on 10 July 1940, with the arrest order dated 6 July. After about 16 months of freedom, Mrs Wernick's cooking, and escape from Nazi persecution, he was locked up. All he had in the world were the things he carried in his suitcase. On some of his official documents, the printed phrase 'POW' was overwritten with 'Enemy Alien'. On others, much later, 'Enemy Alien' was replaced with 'Jewish Refugee'.

Dad described the arrest this way, "On the evening of July 9, 1940, two nice policemen who I knew very well came to me and said: 'Tomorrow morning at seven o'clock we'll pick you up. Everyone has to go to a camp on the Isle of Wight.'[350] The next morning I was actually picked up at seven o'clock and taken to the camp; but on the same day I was told that there was a transport to Canada and that anyone who wanted to go to Canada could go. That was the day before my 18th birthday, on July 10, 1940, and I didn't know what to do. Stay in England, where I knew practically no one, or go to Canada and then make contact with friends in America. Since Canada seemed to be the better alternative, I applied immediately and got on the ship

---

[348] <u>Dunera Boys</u>, Defining Moments, National Museum Australia
[349] 'The Dunera Incident', Albert Isaacs, presentation prepared for U3A Banyule, 18 May 2022
[350] I believe he meant the Isle of Man.

the same day - it was the *'Dunera'* - ...and then several weeks later... arrived in Australia."[351]

Dad had family in New York, including his Uncle Norbert, Aunt Lili and close cousins Arno and Ingrid Heller, and it was more easily accessible from Canada. In a letter to his parents, Arno mentions sending items to Heinz, when he would have been interned in Australia.[352]

The Marowilskys' deportation to Izbica

As for Dad's parents, he never saw them again. They were left behind in Wuppertal with no avenue of escape and no ability to work. Up to 1939, they lived at 14 Döppersberg Strasse but by 1942, like many Jews in Germany at that time, they were forced to move into a 'Judenhaus' (Jew-house), a tenement building where Jews were concentrated together like in a mini ghetto.[353]

The Ordinance on the Use of Jewish Assets of 3 December 1938 mandated that Jewish homeowners sell their properties. On 28 December 1938, President of the Reichstag and Prime Minister of Prussia Hermann Göring said that the priority was the "Aryanization" of companies and businesses, and that the "Aryanization" of home ownership should be "placed at the end of the overall Aryanization." It is desirable "in individual cases, if possible, to proceed in such a way that Jews are grouped together in one house, as long as the tenancy conditions would allow this."[354] So,

---

[351] Henry Marlow interview with Prof Manfred Brusten, October 1994
[352] Text from letter provided by Arno Heller's son Peter Heller.
[353] Gedenkbuch Wuppertal
[354] Memorial plaque on the house at Brühl 6 in Weimar - Document 215 in: Susanne Heim: 'German Reich 1938 - August 1939', Documents, Series: The Persecution and Murder of European Jews by National Socialist Germany 1933–1945 Volume 2 (Dokumente, Reihe: Die Verfolgung und Ermordung der europäischen Juden durch das nationalsozialistische Deutschland 1933–1945 Band 2), Munich, 2009, p. 583

Uncovering their Names and Stories:

Jews first lost their businesses and then their homes.

The Marowilsky's Judenhaus was as 11 Zollstrasse, Wuppertal. Zollstrasse 11 is close to Döppersberg and is now an office building and has several Stolpersteine in the footpath outside the front door to the building. Concentrating the homes of Jews made it easier for roundups for deportation to concentration camps and ghettos. There in April 1942, they were arrested by the Gestapo. Hermann had a heart attack on the day of deportation, so he was carried out on a stretcher. After an investigation much later, the Red Cross advised my father that his "parents had been taken directly to the gas chamber."[355]

From Wuppertal, they were taken to be processed at the beef abattoir or slaughterhouse in Düsseldorf, and then deported to the Izbica Ghetto in Poland.

The building of the old slaughterhouse still exists. "The footings for the cattle pens are still visible as are the cattle troughs, stone drinking troughs in which the Jews laid their babies" to keep them off the dirty floors.[356] The building is now part of the Old Slaughterhouse Memorial Centre in the Düsseldorf University of Applied Sciences, which I visited on my research road trip. Dr Joachim Schröder developed the concept for the Memorial Centre and is its current Director.

Düsseldorf is close to both Wuppertal and Cologne. The three cities form a triangle just east of the Dutch border. The Old Slaughterhouse is the former Düsseldorf-Derendorf livestock market hall, which was built in 1896-1899 and is now dedicated to the commemoration of the crimes committed there during the Holocaust.

---

[355] Henry Marlow interview with Prof Manfred Brusten, October 1994

[356] <u>Erinnerungsort Alter Schlachthof Ausstellungskatalog /Alter Schlachthof Memorial Centre Exhibition Catalogue,</u> Dr Joachim Schröder, Droste-Verlag, Düsseldorf, 2019, p17

The slaughterhouse remains on Rather Straße in the suburb of Derendorf, largely as it was at the time, and the museum exhibits include detailed explanations of what happened there during the Holocaust. Seeing the slaughterhouse is a dreadful experience. How can human beings 'process' people in such a place and load them onto cattle cars, sending them to be expunged from the earth. How dehumanising and inhumane.

The description of the processing and treatment of the Jewish victims, including my grandparents, at the Old Slaughterhouse Memorial Centre is harrowing and most disturbing. It was a most haunting experience reading the external exhibits as darkness fell on my visit.

The Old Slaughterhouse in Düsseldorf, which was used by the Gestapo as the assembly point for deportations
(Source: © Stadtmuseum Düsseldorf F 9755)

One exhibit describes the process, "On arrival at the abattoir the deportees were left in no doubt as to the utter hopelessness of their situation. The Gestapo officials treated them like cattle, meting out kicks and blows if they took too long to follow instructions. They were forced to hand over documents and house keys, and to sign a declaration of assets. They were subjected to body searches for valuables during the course of which officials shamelessly robbed them. Finally, they had to spend the night in the cattle market hall, a

Uncovering their Names and Stories:

particular ordeal in the winter of 1941. The next day they were marched to the Derendorf freight station."[357]

The museum's website says, "Almost 6,000 Jewish men, women and children from the entire Düsseldorf administrative region had to gather in this hall for a total of seven transports. They were registered, searched and robbed and had to spend a night in the livestock market hall, full of uncertainty about what was to come. The next morning, they were deported from the nearby Derendorf freight yard to ghettos in occupied Eastern Europe: to Łódź, Minsk, Riga, Izbica and Theresienstadt (today: Terezín). The ghettos were often just stopovers on the way to further concentration and extermination camps. Only a few survived the Shoah."[358]

Old Slaughterhouse Memorial Centre - outside exhibits
(Source: Old Slaughterhouse Memorial Centre; photo credit: (c) Eric Fritsch/HSD)

---

[357] Old Slaughterhouse Memorial and Museum exhibits
[358] 'Erinnerungsort Alter Schlachthof', (Old Slaughterhouse Memorial Centre), Düsseldorf University, erinnerungsort-duesseldorf.de/

"The carriages were overcrowded and poorly heated. Families were often forcibly separated... After several arduous days travel, they delivered the deportees to places they had never heard of."[359]

On arrival, "Their remaining luggage was confiscated and, as they came face-to-face with screaming SS guards with dogs, beatings and killings, they realized the utter hopelessness of their situation. The ghettoes were surrounded with barbed wire and were grossly overcrowded. German police guards shot anyone trying to climb the fence."[360]

This is what my paternal grandparents went through. Hermann (aged 55) and Meta Marowilsky (aged 53) were processed there in 1942, and were on one of the seven transports, departing on 22 April 1942.[361] They were amongst 942 deportees sent to Izbica that day and none of them survived.[362] From there they met their fates in Izbica, Poland.

The Old Slaughterhouse was also used to store furniture looted from deported European Jews in 1943.[363]

Izbica is a small town in eastern Poland, about 44 km southeast of Lublin, not far from the Ukrainian border. It is a nearly 16-hour train ride from Wuppertal to Izbica today, but we know the journey in 1942 took days longer, and was tortuous in an unheated, overcrowded cattle car. The journey would almost certainly have taken them through Hamburg, Berlin and Warsaw. But there would have been no windows, no seating and no stops for snacks. In fact, there is unlikely to have been much in the way of stops for food or water, if any.

---

[359] Old Slaughterhouse Memorial Centre exhibits
[360] ibid.
[361] Memorial Book: Victims of the Persecution of Jews under the National Socialist Tyranny in Germany 1933-1945, Bundesarchiv, and the Gestapo deportation records for Meta and Hermann Marowilsky in the Arolsen Archives
[362] Erinnerungsort Alter Schlachthof Ausstellungskatalog / Alter Schlachthof Memorial Centre Exhibition Catalogue, Dr Joachim Schröder, Droste-Verlag, Düsseldorf, 2019, p126
[363] Old Slaughterhouse Memorial Centre exhibits

Uncovering their Names and Stories:

The town dates to the 15th century, and until World War 2, the population of Izbica was almost 100% Jewish. The main language was Eastern Yiddish. By 1921, it had a population of 3,085 of which 93% were Jewish. Tragically, only 15 Izbica Jews survived the war.[364]

Germany invaded Izbica in September 1939, and the SS turned it into a 'transit ghetto' in 1941, initially transporting 1,000 Jews from Lublin. Over time, tens of thousands of Jews were transported from there to the Majdanek and Sobibor death camps. For thousands of others, they were murdered by the Gestapo in Izbica.

The town became the Gestapo district headquarters, and the former Gestapo prison still stands there today, built during the German occupation using gravestones from the Jewish cemetery. Under Operation Reinhardt, in March 1942, Izbica became the main transit ghetto for Jews from Germany, Austria, and Czechoslovakia. From March to May 1942, about 11,000-15,000 European Jews were transported to Izbica, including my grandparents.[365]

The exhibition catalogue of the Old Slaughterhouse Memorial Centre notes, "Conditions inside the Ghetto were catastrophic. Between 12,000 and 15,000 Jews were packed into a constricted space, the synagogue served as a makeshift sick bay and there were few opportunities to work. Deprived of their belongings, most of the deportees had almost no opportunity to (illegally) barter for food. Starvation and disease claimed numerous victims. The SS used additional "operations" to select people for transports to the extermination camps."[366]

A recent booklet aimed at attracting Jews to visit Izbica for Holocaust commemoration tourism,[367] says, "The liquidation of the transitory ghetto in Izbica took place on November 2nd, 1942. About 1,000 -

---

[364] <u>Izbica: A Story of a Place</u>, Robert Kuwałek and Weronika Litwin, Foundation for the Preservation of Jewish Heritage in Poland, Poland, 2012
[365] ibid.
[366] Dr Joachim Schröder (2019) p126
[367] Funded by the Foundation for the Preservation of Jewish Heritage in Poland and the Embassy of the Federal Republic of Germany in Warsaw

2,000 Polish and European Jews were gathered by force into a small firehouse in Izbica, taken to the Jewish cemetery, and then executed and buried in two or three mass graves. The victims were recruited from those, for whom there were not enough places in the transports to the death camps."[368] This could have been the fate of Hermann and Meta.

Ernst Krombach was deported from Düsseldorf to Izbica on the same transport as Hermann and Meta. In August 1942, he wrote a secret letter to his fiancée in Germany, describing life in the ghetto. He managed to sneak the letter out of the ghetto, and it provides a harrowing account of life in Izbica:

"Everything is forbidden, the penalty for everything is death....Many transports have left here. Of the approximately 14,000 Jews who arrived, only 2,000 to 3,000 are still here. They go off in cattle trucks, subject to the most brutal treatment....No week goes by without something happening: evacuation, round-ups of people on the street for work in the vicinity, visits from outside SS, house searches, confiscation of particular items. Regarding living conditions, hygiene is a joke. Everything is filthy, lice- particularly clothes lice – that spreads typhus, fleas, bugs...There are few latrines. Sewage flows through unpaved streets (stench, illness) ..."[369]

It became far worse. The Leo Baeck Institute paints the following brutal and tragic picture of some of the events in the months following this letter:

"On 19 October 1942, more than 5,000 Jews were deported from Izbica in the largest of the resettlement 'Aktions.' The Germans used the Polish (Blue) police to round up the Jews. The policemen received monetary rewards for finding Jews in hiding. This 'Aktion' was particularly bloody. At least 500 Jews were shot on the platform of the railway station in Izbica. The Germans liquidated the orphanage in Izbica by shooting all the children there. The Jews were deported to the Sobibor death camp. During the 'Aktion' some

---

[368] ibid. p.12
[369] Holocaust Historical Society of the United Kingdom via Leo Baeck Institute New York; The Encyclopaedia of Camps and Ghettos 1933-1945

Uncovering their Names and Stories:

Polish Jews escaped from Izbica, hiding in the nearby fields, returning afterwards. On 2 November 1942, more than 4,000 Jews were deported to Belzec and Sobibor death camps. The trains for the deportations shuttled back and forth nonstop."[370]

The Polish Underground courier Jan Karski described the loading of Jews into the train cattle cars in Izbica to take them to the death camps, "a freight wagon was intended for eight horses or forty soldiers in transit…The Germans ordered to pack one hundred and thirty people, but they were cramming in an additional ten. When the door would not close, they smashed people blindly with their butts, fired inside the wagon, and shouted at the unfortunate Jews. To make room for others, some of the Jews climbed up on the shoulders and heads of those already inside. From the depths of the wagon came some howl and roar of damnation."[371]

Hate Ends Now is a non-profit organisation in the USA that transports a mini museum in a cattle car around the country, to educate people about the Holocaust and the evils of hate and hate crimes. The cattle car provides a physical reminder of what happened, making the history feel more real.

Karski wrote further, "After one hundred and forty people had been crammed in, the guards proceeded to close the door. They were heavy, made of wood upholstered with iron. They crushed outward limbs amid screams of pain. After sliding the door closed, it was secured with an iron bar and bolted."[372] From his description, you can almost hear the cries and sounds of the iron bar being bolted to seal the poor victims in cattle car.

We know that Hermann and Meta were murdered, but we don't know one hundred percent whether they were murdered in town, in

---

[370] ibid.

[371] 'You can't run away from Izbica. Jan Karski's story', Przemyslaw Batorski, The Emanuel Ringelblum Jewish Historical Institute, Warsaw, p.4

[372] 'You can't run away from Izbica. Jan Karski's story', Przemyslaw Batorski, The Emanuel Ringelblum Jewish Historical Institute, Warsaw, p.4

the cemetery or transferred to a death camp.[373] Red Cross advice to my father suggests that they were probably transferred to a death camp. Indeed, they could have died of starvation or disease, as did many others in the overcrowded ghetto. Their son would not know of their fate until much later, when the full truth of the Holocaust became clearer after the end of the war.

Cattle car similar to what was used to transport my paternal grandparents and other Jews to ghettos, transit camps and death camps
(Source: Todd Cohn, Hate Ends Now)

Hermann and Meta were not alone in failing to be able to get out of Germany. The USA was still a possible escape path until it entered the war in 1942. Journalist and foreign correspondent William L.

---

[373] Memorial Book: Victims of the Persecution of Jews under the National Socialist Tyranny in Germany 1933-1945, Bundesarchiv, and the Gestapo deportation records for Meta and Hermann Marowilsky in the Arolsen Archives

Uncovering their Names and Stories:

Shirer[374] wrote in his diary in March 1940, that there was a quota of only 27,000 Germans to enter the USA. About 248,000 names were on the waiting list at the US consulate, of whom 98% were Jewish. This was about half the remaining Jewish population left in Germany at the time, who were desperate to escape to freedom across the Atlantic.[375]

As the biochemist and future President of Israel Dr Chaim Weizmann said in 1936, "The world seemed to be divided into two parts – those where the Jews could not live and those where they could not enter."[376]

Part of the reason Jews did not get out earlier was that German Jews had strong ties to the country, and to leave meant separating from the language and culture with which they were connected and comfortable. They were home. Clearly, other countries were also not lining up to take refugees, and in the early years of the regime, many felt the Nazis would not last long in government. Also, it can argued until very late, and for many that means until Kristallnacht, who could have foreseen the terrible evils of the industrial level exterminations to come. Antisemitism was not new for German Jews, and many felt that they could ride this wave out, like they and their ancestors had done before. How wrong they were. Regime language and priorities had been about getting the Jews to leave, but unfortunately many could not find somewhere to go. Further, many victims like my grandfather Hermann as a veteran of World War 1, felt that they were protected by their years of military service. This turned out to be a tragic mistake for thousands.[377]

There was only ten months between Kristallnacht in November 1938 and the exit doors closing with the start of World War 2 in September 1939. If people did not move quickly, or could not put the requisite

---

[374] William L. Shirer was the author of the classic <u>The Rise and Fall of the Third Reich.</u>
[375] <u>Berlin Diary: The Journal of a Foreign Correspondent</u>, William L Shirer, Hamish Hamilton, London, 1942, p230
[376] <u>Aliens: The Chequered History of Britain's Wartime Refugees</u>, Paul Dowswell, Biteback Publishing, London, 2023, chapter 4
[377] <u>Bound upon a Wheel of Fire</u>, John V. H. Dippel, Basic Books, New York, 1996, p.xxii and throughout

money, visas and paperwork together, then all was lost. And many lived in poverty, after years of being banned from so many jobs and professions, and having their businesses stolen. They did not have the financial resources to qualify for a visa for many countries, including the USA.[378]

In a statement from Meta's sister Else Dauk nee Lennhoff in 1960, attached to my father's restitution claim, she wrote about her brother-in-law Hermann Marowilsky, "Until August 1, 1938, he was head of the measurement department at Gebr. Kaufmann in Wuppertal. I don't know when he started there, but he was there for many years. He was then unemployed until his deportation. The couple lived in an apartment on Zollstrasse[379] consisting of a kitchen, living room and bedroom, which was well-furnished. I value all of the couple's property as at least 25,000 to 30,000 DM. The Gestapo took over the property. I also advise that his wife had particularly valuable jewelry, consisting of a necklace, bracelet and ring, a gift from her mother-in-law. Of course, this had all disappeared too."[380]

Heinz Marowilsky on the *Dunera* and Interned

Because of overcrowding in English internment camps, 7,500 internees in the UK were shipped to Australia and Canada between 24 June and 10 July 1940. But not everyone survived the journey. Disaster hit the converted passenger liner, the *Arandora Star*, one of the transport ships headed for Canada, when it was torpedoed and sunk by German U-boat *U47*, off the coast of Ireland on 2 July 1940. There were more than 1,100 internees, 86 German prisoners of war and 300 crew on board. More than half of those on board, 805

---

[378] ibid. p.188
[379] the Judenhaus address
[380] Else Dauk letter in Henry Marlow restitution claim, 1960, Wuppertal City Archives

passengers and crew, were lost.[381] *HMCS St. Laurent* rescued 868 survivors, including 586 detainees.[382]

Just a week later, my father and 2,541 fellow detainees, aged 16 to 66,[383] were boarded onto the *Hired Military Transport (HMT) Dunera* in Liverpool on 10 July 1940. It included some survivors of the *Arandora Star*. All would have been hoping that lightning did not strike twice. Also on board, were 450 German and Italian prisoners and a couple of dozen fascist sympathisers. This was a popular situation on board (sarcasm intended), as most of the internees were decidedly anti-fascist and in fact about 80% were Jewish.[384]

Sitting next to two sons of Dunera Boy Werner Haarburger at a Dunera Association luncheon a few years ago, they showed me Werner's handwritten log of the voyage to Australia. They pulled the original document out of a protective envelope. The log tells us the ship sailed that night, the day before Dad's nineteenth birthday. It stopped at Freetown, Sierra Leone on 24 July; Takoradi, Gold Coast on 27 July; Cape Town, South Africa on 8 August; and Fremantle, Western Australia on 27 August.[385]

The ship was overcrowded with most sleeping wherever they could find space. The toilets overflowed. "Food was poor and fresh water was only given to the men two or three times a week. There were

---

[381] ibid. and 'Maritime tales – tragedy of the Arandora Star', Stephen Guy, National Museums Liverpool

[382] 'The Dunera Incident', Albert Isaacs, presentation prepared for U3A Banyule, 18 May 2022

[383] Dunera Association

[384] Email from Dr Seumas Spark, Adjunct Research Fellow in History at Monash University and President, Dunera Association, 7 September 2024

[385] Dunera News, No.105, Dunera Association, February 2019, pp.8-9 which includes copies of Werner Haarburger's two-page log of the Dunera voyage, the original of which Werner's sons Paul and Dean showed to me at a Dunera Association reunion luncheon in 2018.

only ten toilets available for the passengers, which resulted in waste overflowing across the deck."³⁸⁶

Seasickness affected many poor internees. My father recalled spending most of the voyage near the bathrooms, "throwing up". To the best of my knowledge, he never travelled by boat or ship again. When my mother later in life wanted him to go on cruises with her to the Pacific, he always refused.

Timing is everything. The evacuation of British troops from France at Dunkirk had taken place only a month or two before the *Dunera* departed (May-June 1940), and the British guards on board included troops who had a very recent and terrible experience in Dunkirk. At this stage, I suspect many did not understand the difference between Nazi-led German soldiers and German-speaking Jewish refugees who were seeking refuge from the former. On the other hand, *Dunera* expert Dr Seumas Spark suggested to me that, "Some of the British guards had fascist sympathies, so may have understood very well."³⁸⁷

The influence of Dunkirk on the guards, resulted in a terrible situation on board for the internees. Some were beaten and verbally abused, many had their possessions looted and others were threatened with bayonet-fitted rifles. Several internees were stabbed with bayonets. One internee reported that soldiers smashed beer bottles on board and forced internees to walk across the broken glass.³⁸⁸ Some suitcases and belongings, which is all most had, were thrown overboard or stolen. The British Government eventually agreed to pay thirty-five thousand pounds in compensation, and three guards were court-martialled, including the ranking officer on board, Lieutenant Colonel William Scott.³⁸⁹

---

[386] Aliens: The Chequered History of Britain's Wartime Refugees, Paul Dowswell, Biteback Publishing, London, 2023, chapter 8
[387] Email from Dr Seumas Spark, Adjunct Research Fellow in History at Monash University and President, Dunera Association, 7 September 2024
[388] Dunera Boys, Defining Moments, National Museum Australia
[389] ibid.

Uncovering their Names and Stories:

Excerpt from Werner Haarburger's handwritten log of the *Dunera* journey
(Source: The Haarburger brothers)

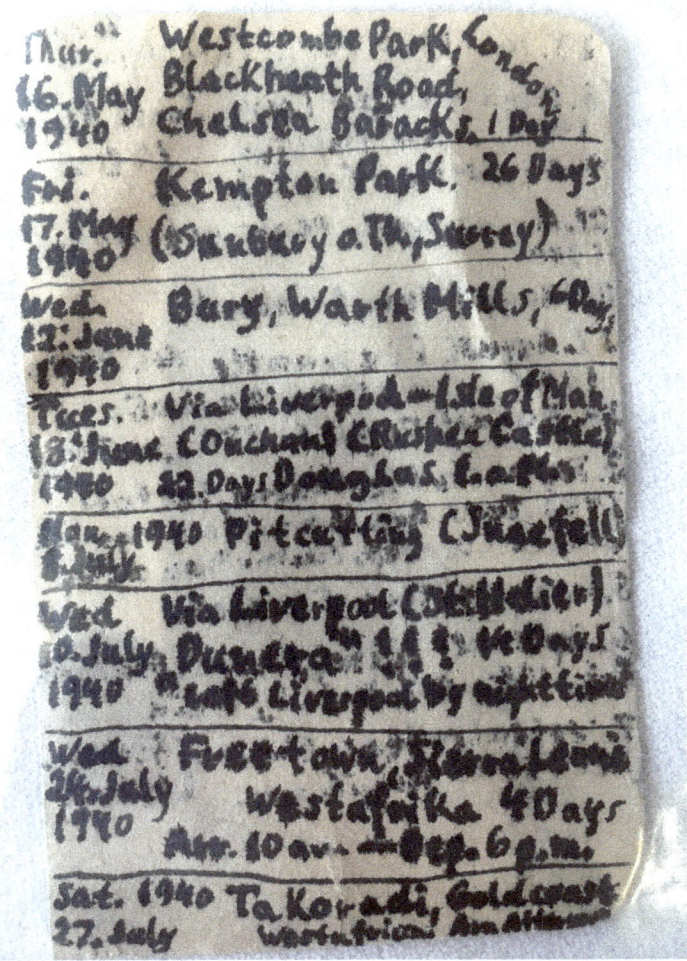

Dunera Boy Albert Süsskind wrote afterwards, that despite being almost all classified as refugees, "Everything carried in hands or loose in pockets was taken off internees. All less valuable effects like gloves, toilet articles, eatables, pipes, etc. were thrown disorderly on the ground. Valuables were stuffed into sacks, or disappeared openly into pockets of the searching soldiers. Soon rows of empty wallets were lying on the floor… Valuable documents identity and emigration papers, testimonials of all kinds were taken away, or even deliberately torn up before the eyes of the owners."[390] One poor internee committed suicide by jumping overboard, after his hard fought for papers were destroyed in front of him.

My father remembered it this way, "On the very first day the English soldiers on the ship threw all our suitcases into the sea. They had all been in Dunkirk before and were therefore very hostile towards foreigners. Not only had they seen the cruelty of war, but they also didn't know who we were on this ship. They thought we were foreign prisoners of war like the Italians, and not refugees. Many of us had already held very good positions in England - e.g. actors, rabbis, bankers, etc., but because they were not English, they too had been taken to the camp on the Isle of Wight (Sic)."[391]

"Three or four passengers got into particularly big trouble on the *Dunera*. For example, I remember that Dr. Weiss was stabbed in the back with a bayonet. Fortunately, he was not critically injured. In addition, all of our personal belongings, such as ID cards, were taken away. Personally, I was lucky. A little soldier came into our room in the evening, where we were crammed together with 220 other people, and said: 'Hey, aren't those your things lying there? I'll go and get them for you.' I was the only one who at least got his personal belongings back, while my suitcase - along with all the others - had long since been thrown overboard by the English soldiers. The British government paid for everything afterwards, but today I don't even have a picture of my parents and no documents about our family in Germany, because all my personal belongings were lost in England or on the *Dunera*."

"In South Africa, the medical officer and the captain disembarked and telegraphed to England what had happened on the ship. When we arrived in Sydney at the beginning of September 1940, we were met by the police, who arrested all the soldiers who had behaved badly. Otherwise, there was not much to see on this voyage, because

---

[390] Refugeemap.org/map/routes/albert-susskind
[391] I believe he would have meant the Isle of Man.

we were practically in the same room the whole time and were hardly allowed to get any fresh air."[392]

Victorian Jewish community leader Benzion Patkin in his book on the *Dunera* wrote, "The *Dunera* was a 'hell-ship' which led not to freedom, but to a new exile."[393]

But others in the Jewish community were not as empathetic or supportive of the Dunera Boys, or German Jewish refugees generally. Part of this, was a rabbinic ideological divide between the German rabbis on board and the local British rabbis, who looked to the Chief Rabbi in London for leadership. Rabbi Dr Raymond Apple, former Senior Rabbi of the Great Synagogue in Sydney, wrote, "The Jewish community had little time for the German Jewish (or any other) ideology".[394]

The most prominent of these British rabbis in Australia, was English-born and educated Rabbi Jacob Danglow, who warned the existing Jewish community about the dangers of the German Jewish refugees. Many of the Dunera Boys already were non-plussed about his wearing a clerical collar, like an Anglican minister, but when the Orthodox internees sought his support in getting kosher food, as a senior rabbi in Melbourne and a chaplain in the Australian Army, he refused.[395] Rabbi Loebenstein wrote regarding Rabbi Danglow's refusal, "Our request to him to arrange the supply of kosher food for the orthodox religious Jews was flatly refused. Such an attitude by a Jewish

---

[392] Henry Marlow interview with Prof Manfred Brusten, October 1994
[393] The Dunera Internees, Benzion Patkin, Cassell Australia, 1979, p.29
[394] 'The German Rabbinate Abroad – Australia', Rabbi Dr Raymond Apple, European Judaism, Berghahn Books,
Volume 45 No. 2 Autumn 2012, p.27
[395] The Dunera Internees, Benzion Patkin, Cassell Australia, 1979, p.88

rabbi was most frustrating and we could never understand the reason for it."³⁹⁶

According to Rabbi Apple the newcomer rabbis from Europe "called Danglow 'Anglo-Danglow' and said that when he shortened his name from Danglowitz he lost his wits. Though officially orthodox, Cohen and Danglow were both rather elastic in their observance."³⁹⁷

It must be mentioned, however, that Rabbi Danglow did appeal to Prime Minister Menzies and various ministers for release of the Jewish internees.³⁹⁸

Although the Dunera Boys, and especially the German Orthodox rabbis amongst them, were not fans of Rabbi Danglow, the same cannot be said of his congregation. Rabbi Danglow is fondly remembered and respected at the St Kilda Hebrew Congregation, where he was Chief Minister for 52 years (1904-1957). Amongst his many innovations, he introduced Bat Mitzvahs for girls, 'Danglow's Own' 3ʳᵈ St Kilda Scouts and extended voting rights to female members. The Danglow Centre at the shule is named in his honour, and quite a few pictures and paintings of Rabbi Danglow are prominent in the Danglow Centre and the boardroom in the main synagogue building. I was also a member and leader of the Scout group named in his honour, as was my brother-in-law Graeme Nathan and some of my nephews.

Dad always remembered that there had been a Reform Rabbi on board, but could not remember his name. He was adamant when we watched the Dunera Boys movie that he did not remember an Orthodox rabbi in the camp, only a Reform rabbi. He was probably thinking of Rabbi Moritz David from Bochum, who was a Reform

---

³⁹⁶ "Be patient and reasonable!': The internment of German - Jewish refugees in Australia', Konrad Kwiet, Australian Journal of Politics & History, Vol. 31, Issue 1, 1985, p.71

³⁹⁷ 'The German Rabbinate Abroad – Australia', Rabbi Dr Raymond Apple, European Judaism, Berghahn Books, Volume 45 No.2 Autumn 2012, p.26; Rabbi Francis Lyon Cohen in Sydney

³⁹⁸ 'Be patient and reasonable!: The internment of German - Jewish refugees in Australia', Konrad Kwiet, Australian Journal of Politics & History, Vol. 31, Issue 1, 1985, p.71

rabbi already aged 65, and he seems to have been the only rabbi in Dad's camp, camp 8. There was also another Reform rabbi in camp 7, Rabbi Dr Erich Bieheim.[399] Joseph Asher, who was the same age as my father, became a Reform rabbi later, and after release became an assistant to Progressive Rabbi Herman Sanger in Melbourne for a short time.

Dad did not seem to know that one of his shipmates was Orthodox Rabbi Dr Jonah Ernst Ehrentreu (1896-1981). Rabbi Ehrentreu was the Orthodox religious leader amongst the Dunera Boys. He had been Chief Rabbi and on the Beth Din in Munich.[400] Like my father, he had escaped to England and was shipped to Australia on the *Dunera*. After a brief time on the Melbourne Beth Din, he returned to the UK in 1947. There were also other Orthodox rabbis on board, including Rabbi Elchanan Loebenstein, Rabbi Shaul Schaffer, Rabbi Blumenthal, Rabbi Feuchtwanger and Rabbi Dr Hirsch Jacob Zimmels.[401]

Leading Australian Progressive rabbi and Emeritus Rabbi at Temple Beth Israel, Rabbi Dr John Levi AC also told me about Rabbi Fabian, Rabbi Gunther Hirschberg, George Reuben, and Joe Asher, writing "Fabian who became traditional. Hirschberg started off as a Cantor, Asher likewise, Reuben was 'made' a rabbi in Perth." They all largely became Reform rabbis some time after release from internment.[402]

After a harrowing journey, about 450 internees disembarked from the *Dunera* in Melbourne on 3 September 1940. The vast majority, including my father, sailed on to Sydney and disembarked on Pyrmont Wharf on 6 September. They were then taken on four

---

[399] German Rabbis in British Exile and their influence on Judaism in Britain, D. Phil thesis, Astrid Zajdband, University of Sussex, December 2014, p.133 and p.151; and email from Dunera researcher Carol Bunyan, 6 March 2024.
[400] The Dunera Internees, Benzion Patkin, Cassell Australia, 1979, p.52
[401] 'Spiritual Heroes of the Dunera Affair', Debbie Maimon, Yated Ne'eman, 13 April 2022; and 'Rabbi Zimmels and the Dunera', Rabbi Raymond Apple, Australian Jewish Historical Society Journal, 2022, Vol 26, Issue Part 1, p9
[402] Email from Rabbi Dr John Levi, 8 March 2024

trains, through the Blue Mountains to outback New South Wales (NSW), about 719 km west to the internment camp in Hay, in regional NSW. It was a nineteen-hour train ride, arriving in an area that was in drought, dry and dusty. It was hot, and the internees were attacked by flies. It was not the climate they were used to in Germany.[403]

The internees included many professionals, tradesmen and artists. They established their own 'university' in the camps, and arranged concerts, choirs and theatrical events.[404] Camp newspapers were published, and the internees printed a number of camp currencies.[405] The camp environment, though stark and far from freedom, was clearly a more pleasant place than was the voyage to get there. Dad remembered that they had a full band and cultural events. He said, "I was responsible for the coffee house there myself and baked cakes."[406]

Dad's Report of Internment form, which is just a POW form with the words 'Prisoner of War' crossed out, describes Heinz Marowilsky as 5'5", blue eyed, fair-haired with a fair complexion. That is taller than I remember him, and the little hair he had in later life was black, but it does confirm his becoming an apprentice electrician in England and his address in Wolverhampton, at 127 Waterloo Road. It also notes his date of 'capture' as 6 July 1940, just four days before the *Dunera* sailed.[407] In reality, he was actually picked up on 10 July and taken straight to the ship for boarding.

The *Dunera* internees became known as the Dunera Boys, and have been the subject of many books, and a television mini-series / movie

---

[403] 'Enemy Aliens', Kate Garrett, Andrew McNamara & Seumas Spark, State Library of NSW, 2022; and Email from Dr Seumas Spark, Adjunct Research Fellow in History at Monash University and President, Dunera Association, 7 September 2024.
[404] ibid.
[405] Email from Dr Seumas Spark, Adjunct Research Fellow in History at Monash University and President, Dunera Association, 7 September 2024
[406] Henry Marlow interview with Prof Manfred Brusten, October 1994
[407] National Archives of Australia, MP1103/2 E40192

Uncovering their Names and Stories:

'The Dunera Boys' in 1985, which starred the British actors Warren Mitchell and Bob Hoskins, as well as many Australian actors like John Mellion. Some of my friends in the Melbourne Jewish community, including my old university buddy Danny Shavitsky, worked as extras on the movie. When watching the movie on TV, Dad said, "It wasn't like that." He was concerned about the accuracy of the movie, which I reminded him was not a documentary. Ironically, one of his favourite TV shows, was 'Hogan's Heroes'. I am pretty sure that German POW camps were not really like Stalag 13.

Coincidently, I body-surfed as a teenager along-side Warren Mitchell at the beach in Surfers Paradise, Queensland for two years in a row. He holidayed at the same hotel as our family, The Sands, which was a regular summer holiday destination for our family in the late 1970s and into the 1980s. The Sands was the first 'high-rise' apartment building in Surfers Paradise, built across the road from the beach in the 1960s, although it is not very tall by modern hotel standards.

Heinz Marowilsky's Report of Internment Form
(Source: National Archives of Australia)

Uncovering their Names and Stories:

My father told me a couple of times that he was responsible for a 'kiosk' (canteen), or coffee house as he told Prof Brusten, in an internment camp, and was rebuked at one stage when he became over-comfortable with his life in the camp and ordered bottles of wine for the kiosk. Alcohol was evidently forbidden. Clearly, you can take the boy out of the Rhineland but not the Rhineland out of the boy. Dad had a fondness for wine all his life, and maybe a tipple of whisky at night.

The British Government had second thoughts about the internments and the treatment of the Dunera Boys. This turnaround was prompted by the Australian Governor-General Lord Gowrie, who wrote to King George VI, advising that "some real injustices have been committed."[408]

Major Julian Layton, who had experience with Jewish refugees in the Kitchener Camp, was sent to Australia by the British Home Office in early 1941 to investigate and deal with possible repatriation of internees. Most were released by the end of 1942, but certainly not all.[409] On release, many became engaged in manual labour in the 8th Australian Employment Company, which was established in April 1942, as did my Dad's good friend and fellow Dunera Boy Kurt Grünbaum.[410] While others returned to England to pursue their careers, return to family, or join the British Army to join action against Nazi Germany. Only 900 of the Dunera Boys, including my father Heinz Marowilsky, remained in Australia by the end of the war.

---

[408] 'Defining Moments: Dunera Boys', National Museum Australia, Nma.gov.au/defining-moments/resources/dunera-boys
[409] ibid.; and Email from Dr Seumas Spark, Adjunct Research Fellow in History at Monash University and President, Dunera Association, 7 September 2024
[410] Trove online database, National Library of Australia. Kurt later changed his name to Ken Green. Many other Dunera Boys also changed their names to better fit in amongst the Australian community. In that way, Heinz Gunther Marowilsky became Henry Marlow.

Many more returned to England or elsewhere after the war, with only about 630 remaining in Australia for the long term.[411]

After about seven months in Hay, Dad and other internees were transferred to Orange NSW.[412] His 'Internees – Service and Casualty Form' notes that on 18 June 1941, Dad was moved to an internment camp in Orange. It was much greener and was a relief after the dry climate of Hay. But it was only a stopping off point for the internees. About six weeks later, on 30 July 1941, they were transported by train to the Tatura internment camp, near Shepparton in Victoria. Tatura is much closer to Dad's eventual home in Melbourne, just over a two-hour drive away.

During World War 2, Tatura was the centre of a group of seven internment camps. The camps housed between 4,000 and 8,000 internees and prisoners of war (POWs). Camps 1 and 2 in Tatura were for single male internees, mostly German and Italian. Camp 3 was mainly for German family groups and Camp 4 was for Japanese family groups, both in Rushworth, which is 20 minutes down the road from Tatura. Dhurringile Mansion in Murchison, also near Tatura, housed POW officers. The Graytown camp was 48 minutes closer to Melbourne, and was used for Italian, German and Finnish POWs. Camp 13 was for Italian, German, and Japanese POWs who were transferred there after the Cowra Breakout. None of the sites of the camps can be easily visited today, as they are now on private property, and Dhurringile Mansion is part of a minimum-security prison, HM Prison Dhurringile.[413]

Dad spent over two years in Tatura, finally being released to Melbourne on 21 October 1943.[414] But refugees with German

---

[411] 'Enemy Aliens', Kate Garrett, Andrew McNamara & Seumas Spark, State Library of NSW; and Email from Dr Seumas Spark, Adjunct Research Fellow in History at Monash University and President, Dunera Association, 7 September 2024

[412] Heinz Marowilsky Internee Service and Casualty Form, National Archives of Australia. It was really a POW form over-stamped with the word "Internees".

[413] Tatura irrigation & Wartime Camps Museum, Taturamuseum.com/world-war-2-camps

[414] National Archives of Australia, MP1103/01, E40192

accents were not so universally loved in Australia during the war, or soon thereafter. To try to help improve public opinion, a pamphlet was produced by the Jewish Council to Combat Fascism and Antisemitism in 1944, titled 'Refugees: Hitler's Loss, Our Gain'. Along with the pamphlet, 'Australia and the Jews: The Facts about Jewish Influence, the Facts about the Refugees', the pamphlets argued that the refugees were skilled professionals and scholars, so their presence benefited Australian society.[415]

I first found a copy of 'Refugees: Hitler's Loss, Our Gain' on display in the Jewish Museum of Australia. Like my father, many refugees anglicised their names to become better accepted and integrated into the community in Australia, and to attempt to avoid being a target. Experience of antisemitism back in Europe would have made the Jewish refugees particularly sensitive to discrimination.

Dad could have been released much earlier if he had enlisted in the 8th Employment Company, but years ago he told me that he had been examined and deemed medically unfit. Records show that he also had permission in December 1941 to return to Britain to have his case for release considered. I do not know why he did not return to the UK, but he was lucky he didn't. The first ship to depart after his approval was in July 1942. Two of the next three ships returning with *Dunera* internees were sunk with 42 out of 43 internees on one ship, and six out of eleven on the other ship killed.[416] This may have discouraged his (and undoubtedly others) return, and his terrible experience coming over on the *Dunera* originally, may not have encouraged a repeat voyage.

British records tell us that Dad was released to do 'work of national importance', which were jobs that helped the war effort, even if not directly related to war production.[417]

---

[415] Exhibit in the Jewish Museum of Australia.
[416] Email from Carol Bunyan 3 June 2024
[417] ibid.

'Refugees: Hitler's Loss, Our Gain', Brian Fitzpatrick & Noel Counihan, 1944[418]

(Reproduced courtesy of the Jewish Museum of Australia)

So why were internees released to civilian jobs? Acting Australian Prime Minister Frank Forde explained in Parliament on 29 November 1944, "Internees released are medically examined, and those found fit are enlisted in the Civil Aliens Corps. It is the Government's policy not to release any internees for whom suitable employment and living conditions cannot be found."

---

[418] Published Melbourne, Australia, Ink on paper, 214 x 135mm, Jewish Museum of Australia Collection 13574

Uncovering their Names and Stories:

"Former internees are employed on work of national importance because of the grave shortage of manpower. It is far better that they should be usefully employed if no security risk is involved, rather than that they should remain in internment camps and be a charge upon the nation. They are not depriving any person of employment, because our man-power shortage is so great that employment exists for tens of thousands of additional persons."[419]

Frank Forde later became Prime Minister (PM) of Australia, although briefly. He was PM for eight days from 6 July to 13 July 1945, from the death of John Curtin, until Labor elected Ben Chifley as leader. Our miniature poodle is named 'Mr Chifley' in honour of the former Prime Minister.

Dunera researcher Carol Bunyan found that Dad was specifically released to work at W H Wells Pty Ltd in North Melbourne.[420] Records from 1931 suggest that they were "manufacturers of electrical and mechanical stampings, tool makers, engineers etc."[421] I remember Dad telling me that he helped make parts for bombers for the Royal Australian Air Force (RAAF). He told Prof Brusten that he made switch boxes for aircraft. They were probably parts for Beaufort bomber aircraft, which were manufactured at Fisherman's Bend in Melbourne, South Australia and Sydney.[422]

The Beauforts were twin-engine bomber aircraft designed by the Bristol Aeroplane Company which could carry bombs or a torpedo. Each aircraft required 39,000 manufactured parts. The Beaufort Division of the Department of Aircraft Production had 8,500 employees and tens of thousands more worked for 600 private subcontractors who made parts and sub-assemblies for the Beaufort. Seven hundred of the aircraft were manufactured in Australia from 1941 to September 1944.[423]

---

[419] Hansard, Parliament of Australia, 29 November 1944, p.2372
[420] 'Weekly Intelligence Report No 41 Tatura Internment Camps', 17 October 1943 (NAA MP70/1, 37/101/185 Tatura Part 3)
[421] Trove.nla.gov.au/newspaper/article/160599190/17254421
[422] Email from Carol Bunyan 3 June 2024
[423] 'Conservation Project Beaufort', Australian War Memorial

Dad, like other released internees who chose to remain in Australia, built a life and career in Australia, and established a family. The Dunera Boys who remained in Australia after release, made tremendous contributions in the academic, economic, business, scientific, artistic and cultural worlds of their new country.[424] The Dunera Boys included people like Hans Buchdahl (physicist), Fred Gruen (economist), Hans Kronberger (nuclear physicist), and Richard Sonnenfeldt (chief interpreter for the US prosecution at the Nuremberg trials after the war).[425]

If you read some stories on the *Dunera* internees, one might think everyone was an artist, academic or famous individual. But there was a great diversity amongst them. A 1941 survey of the internees, "found 20 doctors and 21 motor mechanics, 27 lawyers and 30 leather workers, 20 journalists and 22 textile workers, 27 artists and 28 butchers."[426] And one 5'5" apprentice electrician.

Dad had very eventful older teenage and young adult years. He was 17 years of age when he lived through Kristallnacht and escaped on the Kindertransport to England. He was 18 working in Wolverhampton and when he boarded the *Dunera*. He turned 19 on board, and turned 20 interned in the camp in Orange, just before being transferred to Tatura. He turned 21 interned in the Tatura Camp in Victoria. I wonder if his fellow internees arranged any celebration for his 21st birthday. He was aged 23 when he was finally released from Tatura to Melbourne.

---

[424] 'Dunera Boys', National Museum of Australia
[425] 'HMT Dunera', Wikipedia
[426] 'From Berlin to the Bush', Ken Inglis, The Monthly, August 2010

Uncovering their Names and Stories:

9.0 The Lennhoffs and Neufelds

My Lennhoff ancestry has a long history from the 1700s to the mid 20th century, in what is now the state of North Rhine-Westphalia, in western Germany. This included, most notably, family members living in Plettenberg, Wuppertal, Hemer, Hennen, Fröndenberg and Körbecke. Many Lennhoffs and Neufelds were lost in the Holocaust, but I have found living Lennhoff cousins in The Netherlands, San Diego, New York and Los Angeles. We are all descended in some way from Simon Isaac Lennhoff (1786-1867) and Julie Lennhoff nee Rosenthal (1789-1857), who both lived and died in the small town of Plettenberg:

Simon Isaac Lennhoff (1786-1867)
Father of
V
Isaac Lennhoff (1817-1863)
Father of
V
Aron/Adolf Lennhoff (1858-1922)
Father of
V
Henriette (Meta) Marowilsky nee Lennhoff (1889-1942)
Mother of
V
Heinz Günter Marowilsky (Henry Marlow) (1921-2002)
Father of
V
David Marlow (1962-)

The Lennhoffs of Plettenberg

There were Jews in Plettenberg from at least 1725. But Jewish presence was inconsistent until the 1800s. I had family amongst those early Jews in town, from at least 1786. The earliest family members that I have found so far in my Lennhoff family line are my great (x3) grandparents Simon Isaac Lennhoff (1786-1867) and Julie Rosenthal (1789-1857). Simon was born in Plettenberg, and he and Julie married in the early 1800s, and lived in the town, in what was then part of Prussia and is now in the North Rhine-Westphalia region of

Germany. Plettenberg was the home of many Lennhoffs for generations.

Around this time, the population of Plettenberg was about 1,000 while more recently it had a population of over 26,000 people.[427] Plettenberg sits on the south end of the Lenne Mountains, which reach up to Hemer in the northwest and Altena in the west. The Lenne River is the longest river in the region.

Until the early to mid 1800's, most Jews in town lived a moderate life as traders, butchers and peddlers. It became a subsidiary community of the Altena synagogue community from 1853. Even in 1900, they still only had a prayer room in a private house. They never had their own Jewish school, and children were educated at the Protestant elementary school, while parents provided the children's Jewish education. It was always a small Jewish community.

Simon and Julie Lennhoff nee Rosenthal had four children, my great (x2) grandfather Isaac (1817-1863), Jeanette (1819-1898), Jacob the butcher (1822-), and Amalia (1834-1908).

Isaac was the oldest child, and he stayed in Plettenberg while his siblings appear to have moved elsewhere in Germany, probably after marrying spouses from other towns. There would have been small pickings for life partners in the modest Plettenberg Jewish community. Isaac married Friederike (Rike) Lenneberg (1817-1892) from nearby Lenhausen in the mid 1800s. The town of Plettenberg and the hamlet of Lenhausen are only about 15 km of hilly roads apart, and on my road trip across Germany, I drove this short distance between the two towns several times.

Isaac and Rike Lennhoff had four children, all born in Plettenberg, Pauline (1847-1933), Esther (1849-), Heinemann (1852-), and my great grandfather Aron (Adolf) Lennhoff (1858-1922).

The Lennhoff and Rosenthal families were heavily intertwined over a few generations. My great (x3) grandmother Julie Lennhoff was a Rosenthal. Julie and Simon Lennhoff's son Jacob married Sara Rosenthal (1832-), and their daughter Jeanette married Joseph Rosenthal (1801-1877). Joseph and Jeanette had four Rosenthal

---

[427] 'Plettenberg', Wikipedia

Uncovering their Names and Stories:

children, Adolph (1852-1927), Hannchen (1855-), Amalie (1859-), and Theodor (1871-). My great (x2) grandparents Isaac and Rike Lennhoff's daughter Esther married Abraham Rosenthal (1843-). The Rosenthals were merchants from various towns around the current state of North Rhine – Westphalia, but mainly lived in the town of Ibbenbüren north of Münster, near the Dutch border.

On my drive to hilly Plettenberg, I stopped and walked around tiny but beautiful Lenhausen, which is where my Lenneberg relatives were born. On the walk, I unexpectedly saw a small signpost for the Jewish Cemetery of Lenhausen, which was not marked on Google Maps, paper maps or anywhere I had looked. It needed to be investigated. So, I walked up the narrow street towards the very small cemetery. As I drew close, I stopped and froze. There was a deer feasting on grass in the tiny cemetery, about the size of a one bedroom apartment. In a blink, the deer looked up, saw me and ran off at speed, disappearing well before I could get my camera phone out. The low fence was no barrier to its rapid departure. My feet crunching the fallen leaves underfoot had probably not helped.

There were no gravestones to be seen in the Lenhausen cemetery, but there was a large memorial stone erected by the municipality of Finnentrop for the Jews of Lenhausen murdered by the Nazi regime 1933-1945. The memorial states that the cemetery was probably built around 1843-1844, but may have been in use much earlier.

Later, I easily found the Jewish Cemetery in Plettenberg, which contains about 34 graves, with largely well preserved gravestones. A sign says it was not attacked in the Nazi era. It is in a residential area, surrounded by a medium height hedge. I could not open the locked gate, and there was no number to call, so I tried climbing over the hedge. As I was about half way over, with twigs sticking into me, a local woman in her car stopped and good-naturedly called out to me in German from behind the wheel. I had no idea what she said in detail, but clearly she was trying to help and seemed to suggest that there was a more sensible, hidden entry point. I thanked her, brushed the leaves and twigs off my trousers and found the 'secret' entrance where she had pointed. The yarmulke on my head probably indicated that I did not have evil intentions in a Jewish cemetery.

300+ Years of a German – Jewish Family

The Plettenberg Jewish Cemetery on Freiligrathstrasse was opened in 1787. Of the 34 graves, seven have the surname Lennhoff, and several others are related to the Lennhoffs through marriage, such as the Neufelds and Bachrachs. It is here that my Netherlands-based cousin John Löwenhardt was the first in recent times to discover that our mutual great (x2) grandfather Isaac Lennhoff was a Kohen, from the priestly lineage. John and I are descended through Lennhoff women, and the Kohanim lineage is passed from father to son, so neither of us are Kohanim.[428]

Isaac Lennhoff's gravestone in the Plettenberg Jewish cemetery
(Photo credit: David Marlow)

---

[428] 'Blessing hands in Plettenberg', Prof John Löwenhardt, Löwenhardt Foundation, The Netherlands; and <u>Tracing your Jewish ancestors: A guide for family historians</u>, Rosemary Wenzerul, Pen & Sword, 2008, p25

Uncovering their Names and Stories:

The two big blessing hands on Isaac's gravestone were the give-away. It is a traditional symbol of Kohanim. Kohanim are the patrilineal descendants of the priests of the Temple in Jerusalem, and they still retain a special ceremonial role in synagogue and various Jewish religious services, such as giving the priestly blessing and being the first to be called up to the Torah on Shabbat.

I quickly found my great (x2) grandfather Isaac Lennhoff (1817-1863). It was wonderful to see his grave in person, and I placed a small stone on his gravestone, noting the fanned hands symbol on the gravestone. I also placed stones on the gravestones of other Lennhoff and Neufeld relatives. The text on Isaac (Isak) Lennhoff's gravestone is quite poetic and translates as, "Here rests in the peace of God, Isak Lennhoff, born in November 1817, deceased on 1 March 1863. Rest gently without worries until resurrection morning."[429]

As I walked around the cemetery several times, I reviewed every gravestone, finding Nathan Neufeld (1859-1909), who was the brother of my great grandmother Sophie Lennhoff nee Neufeld, whose grave I found in Wuppertal a few days beforehand. The gravestones in Plettenberg also identified Nathan's wife Rosa (1858-1931), who I had not yet identified, and I found her dates of birth and death. There is also a large memorial stone, listing 36 names of former Jewish citizens of Plettenberg, who were victims of the Third Reich. It lists the names of seven Lennhoffs and two Neufelds. Before Plettenberg, the Neufelds had come from Fröndenberg, 39 km to the north.

Local Jews Hugo Neufeld (1892-1944), Julius Bachrach (1879-1942) and Sally Sternberg all opened department stores around the same time. The families were also all inter-related through marriage, and through various marriages related to the Lennhoff family. There are seven Sternbergs, two Neufelds, and two Bachrachs on the memorial in Plettenberg.

The Jewish and non-Jewish communities seemed to have been close and welcoming of each other. The fact that the Plettenberg cemetery had not been desecrated like many other Jewish cemeteries across Germany, was a good sign. But things changed dramatically for the

---

[429] 'Blessing hands in Plettenberg', Prof John Löwenhardt, Löwenhardt Foundation, The Netherlands

300+ Years of a German – Jewish Family

Jews of Plettenberg under the Nazi regime and its antisemitic propaganda.

Holocaust memorial in the old Jewish cemetery in Plettenberg
(Photo credit: David Marlow)

The Bachrach family was also related. I found a separate memorial stone in the Plettenberg cemetery, which shows that Julius Bachrach mentioned above, was married to Olga Neufeld (1889-1942). Olga and her husband Julius were killed in the Łódź or Litzmannstadt Ghetto in central Poland. I found confirmation and the places of death through the Yad Vashem website. Olga was the daughter of Rosa and Nathan Neufeld. Nathan was an older brother of my great grandmother Sophie Lennhoff nee Neufeld. Olga and Julius had a daughter Marianne Bachrach, who was born in Plettenberg in 1921, and luckily escaped to New York in January 1939.

Overall, 36 Jews from Plettenberg were murdered in the Holocaust, which sadly would have been nearly all of them.[430]

Many years after the Holocaust, a street in Plettenberg was named Hugo-Neufeld-Straße in Hugo's honour in 2000.[431] The street is less than a ten minute walk from the Plettenberg Jewish Cemetery on Freiligrathstraße. There are also a number of Stolpersteine around the town, commemorating the murdered Jews of the Nazi era.

After visiting the cemetery, I drove to my small Plettenberg hotel to think about all I had seen and found and wrote up my journal for the day. The hotel did remind me a little of Fawlty Towers, but thankfully the manager was not at all Basil Fawlty. He was welcoming, cheery and helpful. Though he spoke no English at all, we made do with my toddler-level German. In my room that night, I watched Hogan's Heroes in German. A weird experience in itself, but my Dad would probably have been pleased.

It seems likely that the family names of Lennhoff and Lenneberg, and the hamlet of Lenhausen all derive their names from the nearby Lenne River and the Lenne Mountains. For example, existing businesses in Lenhausen include the Lennemann bakery and the Lennegrill.

The Neufelds of North Rhine-Westphalia

The Neufeld clan are equally as important to my family history as the Lennhoffs, and the two families are forever intertwined. The Neufeld family history includes family living in Hennen, Fröndenberg and

---

[430] 'Plettenberg (North Rhine-Westphalia)', Aus der Geschichte der jüdischen Gemeinden im deutschen Sprachraum, xn--jdische-gemeinden-22b.de/index.php/gemeinden/p-r/1582-plettenberg-nordrhein-westfalen

[431] ibid.

Körbecke in northern North Rhine-Westphalia to Plettenberg in the south, and then north to Wuppertal.

Today, you can drive through all three towns Hennen to Fröndenberg to Körbecke in less than an hour. These are all places I visited on my road trip. Hennen is a small town, and currently has a population of about 4,360. Körbecke is a small village like Hennen with 3,590, but Fröndenberg is a more sizeable town with about 20,668 people.[432]

Although Körbecke is small, it sits on the picturesque Möhne Reservoir, a tourist attraction, which was artificially created when a dam was built between 1908 and 1912, damming the Möhne and Heve rivers. During World War 2 on 16-17 May 1943, the dam was breached by RAF bombers using 'bouncing bombs' as part of the RAF's Operation Chastise, well known as the 'Dambusters' raid. The massive flooding caused by the breach killed about 1,579 people, including many foreign POWs and forced Russian labourers.[433]

I can trace my Neufeld family ancestors back to the late 1700s, like for the Lennhoffs:

Netta Bentheim nee Amberg (1796-1841)
Mother of
V
Dora Neufeld nee Bentheim (1825-1905)
Mother of
V
Sophie Lennhoff nee Neufeld (1863-1936)
Mother of
V
Henriette (Meta) Marowilsky nee Lennhoff (1889-1942)
Mother of
V
Heinz Günter Marowilsky (Henry Marlow) (1921-2002)
Father of
V
David Marlow (1962-)

---

[432] Citypopulation.de
[433] 'Möhne Reservoir', Wikipedia.org

Uncovering their Names and Stories:

My great (x3) grandparents Herz Bentheim and Netta Amberg (1796-1841) were born in the late 1700s around Körbecke. They would have enjoyed the green landscapes and the views and tranquillity of the nearby rivers, well before the Möhne Reservoir existed. They married around 1820-1825 and had three children, Friedriche Selig (1822-), Friederike or Rike (1822-), and my great (x2) grandmother Dora (1825-1905).

Rike married a Christian, August Herman Wilhelm Redlinghaus (1829-) in the late 1850s, and had a son Wilhelm in 1860. Rike's brother Friedriche was baptised in Hennen in 1858.

Dora Bentheim married Moses Neufeld (1831-1910) from Hennen. Dora and Moses had six children in the larger town nearby of Fröndenberg: Hermann (1856-1941), Nathan (1859-1909), Herz (1861-1942), my great grandmother Sophie (1863-1936), Natalie (1865-1938), and Abraham (1867-1934).

Moses and Dora's son Nathan married Rosa Sternberg (1858-1931), and master painter Herz married Bertha Vyth (1871-1943). Natalie married Herman Lievendag (1868-1941) from the small town of Schüttorf, which is in northwest Germany on the Dutch border. Abraham married Emma Steeg (1865-1942) and had a son Felix (1896-1969).

Moses and Dora's third son Herz and Bertha Neufeld had nine children in Fröndenberg: Nathan (1887-1943), Betty (1890-1942), Hugo (1892-1944), Wilhelmine (1894-1900), Nathalie (1895-1942), twins Johanna (1897-1898) and Viktor (1897-1899), Emma-Carola (1899-1940) and Paul (1901-1942).

The Holocaust decimated the Neufeld clan, taking Emma Neufeld nee Steeg in Treblinka. Herz (1861-1942) and his wife Bertha (1871-1943) were murdered in Theresienstadt. Herz and Bertha's children Nathan and his wife Libertha Neufeld nee Denneboom (1884-1943), Hugo and his wife Johanna Neufeld nee Heine (1892-1944), Nathalie, and Paul were murdered in Zamosc and Auschwitz. Betty's married name was Silberberg, and she was murdered in the Warsaw Ghetto.

Nathan and Libertha's daughters Hertha (1915-1942) and Rita (1921-1942), and Hugo and Johanna's children Doris (Dorit) (1925-1944) and young Alfred (1933-1944) were all murdered in Auschwitz.

Dad's young cousin Alfred Neufeld in Fröndenberg in 1936 – Alfred was murdered in Auschwitz, aged 11

(Source: Heinz Marowilsky childhood photo album)

As I progressed in researching and writing about my family, I was worried that I had started to become a little desensitized to the Holocaust's devastation of my relatives. However, when I discovered a photograph of three year old Alfred Neufeld smiling at the camera, I was deeply affected. Alfred was a cousin of my father, and I soon also found a photograph of Dad and Alfred together in 1936. The photographs and connection to my father, made the relationship real and the impact on me more visceral. I do wonder how the loss of so many family members affected my father.

Herz's younger sister Sophie Neufeld married Aron Lennhoff, and they became my great grandparents. Five of their eight children were lost in the Holocaust, Paula and Hertha in Auschwitz, my grandmother Meta in Izbica, and Frieda and Rosa in the Minsk

Uncovering their Names and Stories:

Ghetto. My father said there were twelve Lennhoff siblings, but I have only found records of eight siblings to-date.[434]

Heinz Marowilsky with his young cousin Alfred Neufeld in Fröndenberg 1936
(Source: Heinz Marowilsky childhood photo album)

Herman Lievendag and my great grandmother's sister Natalie (Natanie) Lievendag nee Neufeld had five daughters, Johanna (1894-), Clara (1896-), Meta (1897-1942) who worked as a sales manager, Emma (1899-1941) and Mathilde (1901-).

Meta Lievendag was murdered in the Łódź Ghetto, and her father Herman and sister Emma were murdered in the Riga Ghetto.[435] In the Plettenberg Jewish cemetery, Meta is remembered on a memorial stone, along with Julius Bachrach and Olga Bachrach nee Neufeld. Meta's sister Clara migrated to San Francisco, married and became Clara Rosenbach.

---

[434] Henry Marlow interview with Prof Manfred Brusten, October 1994
[435] Thanks to Yad Vashem

My great grandmother Sophie Lennhoff nee Neufeld in Wuppertal 1935-1936

(Source: Heinz Marowilsky childhood photo album)

Immediately after the war, Clara was passionately busy trying to trace her sisters, and I found numerous records in the Arolsen Archives and the Israel Genealogy Research Association website documenting her search. Mathilde married and became Mathilde Weiss, and Johanna married and became Johanna Wardien. Mathilde survived the Holocaust, as Clara's search discovered both Mathilde and her husband alive. She may have survived Theresienstadt, as there is a Mathilde Weiss listed as a Jewish Survivor of Theresienstadt.[436] I have not confirmed whether Johanna survived the Holocaust.

The Lennhoffs in Wuppertal

My great grandfather Aron (Adolf) Lennhoff married Sophie Neufeld (1863-1936) from Fröndenberg in the early 1880s. They had at least eight children, Norbert (1884-1953), Paula (1886-1942), my

---

[436] List of Jewish Survivors Found in Theresienstadt on 10 May 1945, Israel Genealogy Research Association

Uncovering their Names and Stories:

grandmother Henriette (1889-1942), Frieda (1891-1941), Rosa (1894-1941), Irma (1895-1990), Hertha (1900-1943), and Else (1902-). Aron and Sophie's children were born and raised in Wuppertal.

Aron and Sophie died before the Holocaust and are buried beside each other in the Weinbergstrasse Cemetery in Wuppertal which is where I found their graves. A newspaper death notice from 1936 advises that Sophie died after a long illness. There are photos of their gravestone in my father's childhood photo album, and the gravestone looked much the same when I visited it in March. Dad would only have been a baby aged one when Aron died in 1922, but he would have known his grandmother Sophie, as he was aged 15 when she died.

Dad's photo album shows him seeing many unidentified family members, while on holidays in various parts of Germany. An elderly looking Sophie is pictured in the album sitting on a wooden chair on what appears to be a rooftop, as is Aron's gravestone while Sophie was still alive. Both photos would date to about 1935. The places relating to the photos in the album are labelled but not the people, though my newly discovered cousins across the USA have been helping to identify the other people in the photos. They include fathers, uncles, aunts and grandparents of my various cousins.

Sophie and Aron's daughter Irma married the factory owner Walter Robert Dörrenhaus, probably in the 1920s. They lived in Düsseldorf, and Irma lived to be 95 years of age in Germany.

Dad's aunt Else survived the Nazi regime, married to a Catholic tailor, Heinz (sometimes Heinrich) Dauk (1903-), and he and his family helped keep her safe from the Nazis. He went as far as damaging his foot so he could not serve in the army, so he could stay home to help protect Else. Many Jews who married Christians were not so lucky. Else described herself as a businesswoman.[437]

Dad's uncle Norbert served in the German army in 1907 but was probably too old for World War 1. He lived for some time in Bremen but was wise and left with his wife Lili (1891-1965) for the USA in 1937, escaping the fate of half of his siblings. Norbert and Lili left Germany for New York on the *SS President Harding* on 4 August 1937.

---

[437] Else Dauk statement attached to Henry Marlow restitution documents, April 1960

They initially lived with Lili's older brother Leo Feilmann (1885-1951) who had arrived in New York in 1909. Norbert lived in New York working as a shipping clerk until his death in 1953, and Lili until 1965.

Aron and Sophie Lennhoff's graves in the Weinberger Jewish Cemetery in Wuppertal

(Photo credit: David Marlow)

Norbert's sister Paula and her husband Emil Heller (1883-1942) remained in Germany and were murdered in Auschwitz in 1942. There are several pictures of Paula and Emil in Dad's photo album. Thankfully, the Heller children, Arno (1920-2016) and Ingrid (1922-1991) escaped together to New York as soon as their parents could get them out after Kristallnacht. Their uncle Norbert was their contact in the USA, and he helped look after them in New York.

Uncovering their Names and Stories:

Dad's aunt Frieda married Louis Marx. Sadly, Frieda and her sister Rosa Hesse nee Lennhoff were deported on the same day on 10 November 1941 to the Minsk Ghetto, where they were murdered. Hertha Mendelsohn nee Lennhoff was deported from Cologne on 29 January 1943 to Auschwitz. My paternal grandparents Henriette (Meta) and her husband Hermann Marowilsky were arrested and deported to Izbica on 22 April 1942, where they were murdered.

Aunt Else and Uncle Heinrich

The only aunt or uncle that my father said he heard from after he left Germany was his Aunt Else and her husband Uncle Heinrich (or Heinz).

Else was married to the Catholic tailor, Heinrich Dauk, who helped keep her hidden from the Gestapo from 1943. She survived the war, finding sanctuary in many hiding places in small villages with Heinrich's relatives. He was a talented and well-known tailor who exhibited in many German cities before the war. When he was drafted into the army, he deliberately shot himself through the foot so that he wouldn't have to continue serving in the war. He wanted to be able to protect his Jewish wife. Dad said, "Even after his discharge from the army, he didn't reveal where his wife was hiding. Then, at the end of 1944, the Nazis threw all the furniture out of the window of the apartment in search of my aunt; I think it was on what is now Friedrich-Ebert-Str. 77, then called the SA Strasse and before that: Königstrasse."[438] It is now the Kings Head pub in Wuppertal.

Dad spoke about their first visits to Australia, "After the war - around 1947/48 - they both came to visit me in Melbourne and brought me my violin. The violin had been stolen from our house on Döppersberg and, along with all the furniture we had, was put in the storage room of an empty shop. My uncle's sister, Mrs. Schirdewang, broke in one evening and took the violin out and took it home with her. A year later, they both came to Melbourne again. My uncle would have liked to stay here, even though he was German, but my aunt didn't want to. They couldn't tell me anything about my parents

---

[438] Henry Marlow interview with Prof Manfred Brusten, October 1994

either, since my uncle had been in the war and my aunt had survived in hiding for years."[439]

Prof Brusten did some follow-up research on Else and Heinrich, which he largely found in their 'Reparation Files' in the Wuppertal City Archives, finding Else stating, "After four of my sisters and three brothers-in-law were sent to concentration camps as Jews in the years 1941-42 (none of whom returned), I left Wuppertal to avoid the same fate."[440]

Else also described some of her experience hiding out from the Gestapo, "From July 1943 to the end of August 1944 I stayed in Arnold Stratmann's inn in Anröchte, Lippstadt district. In September 1944 the Gestapo wanted to pick me up from my apartment here (in Wuppertal) to take me to a concentration camp. At that time I was freshly operated on - in the hospital in Anröchte and was warned there by a phone call from Düsseldorf and then - with a fever of 40 degrees - I fled from the hospital (quietly overnight)."

"First to Anton Gottschalk in Siedinghausen near Büren (master wheelwright, related to Heinrich Dauk). But when the SS moved in there, I fled again for 8 months to Adam Bürger in Belecke/Möhne, Beukenbergstrasse 12a. There I had to hide without ration cards and without any support. Because: although my husband had reported me missing here in Wuppertal, a Gestapo officer was constantly instructed to search for me."

"It was impossible for me to stay in Wuppertal. My husband was a soldier and my sisters had already been deported. I felt constantly threatened by a neighbor who worked for 'Der Stürmer'.... I continued to get food stamps in Wuppertal so that no one would notice that I was illegal (i.e. was staying somewhere else illegally). My sister-in-law picked them up, but they were not usable for her because they had the letter 'J' printed on them."[441]

Heinrich Dauk was forced to close his business when he was called up for military service on 1 February 1941. He was only able to

---

[439] ibid.
[440] Prof Brusten notes to the Henry Marlow interview with Prof Manfred Brusten, October 1994
[441] ibid.

reopen 4.5 years later. He endured substantial harassment in personal and business relationships because of his marriage to Else. He also had difficulties in obtaining goods, arranging transport, destruction of advertising signs, and even the refusal for him to purchase a car.

The Löwenhardts of Oberhemer

The town of Hemer in North Rhine–Westphalia was created from the merger of Upper Hemer (Oberhemer) and Lower Hemer in 1910. Oberhemer was a very small town, with only 2,614 residents by 1904-5.[442] Today, the combined town of Hemer has a population of 34,984.

Many Löwenhardts were born in Oberhemer, but they did not start there. Jehuda Löwenhardt is the first in the family that I have identified. He is the father of Salomon Levy Löwenhardt (1792-1864), who was born in Würzburg, in what is now central Bavaria.

Salomon Löwenhardt married Mina Steinberg (1806-1897) in 1839.[443] It was Mina's second marriage, and she already had a son Ruben Moses Steinberg (1830-). Mina was either from Wachmecke, which is only 6.4 km south of Oberhemer, or Oberhemer itself. Mina and Salomon built their home together in Oberhemer to be close to her family. Salomon and Mina had three sons, Levi in 1840, Moses in 1841 and Joseph in 1843. Salomon Levy died in 1864 at the age of 72.

Pauline Löwenhardt nee Lennhoff (1847-1933) was one of three siblings of my great grandfather Aron Lennhoff. Aron's other siblings were Esther (1849-) and Heinemann (1852-). Pauline's great grandson Prof John Löwenhardt, who lives in the Netherlands, has helped ensure that his family's history is recorded, and he has been a great help to me in understanding the history of that branch of the family. He is the founder of the Löwenhardt Foundation.[444]

---

[442] 'The Löwenhardt Sisters, I', Prof John Löwenhardt, Löwenhardt Foundation, The Netherlands

[443] In numerous family trees Mina is identified as Prinz Moses Steinberg or Sternberg. She clearly adopted Mina as a first name at some stage.

[444] Prof John Löwenhardt, Löwenhardt Foundation, The Netherlands

My great grandaunt Pauline Löwenhardt nee Lennhoff
(Source: Löwenhardt Foundation, The Netherlands)

Pauline married Levi Löwenhardt (1840-1898) in September 1872 in Pauline's hometown of Plettenberg, but they lived 30 km north of there in Levi's hometown of Oberhemer, where they had twelve children. They had nine sons, merchant Salomon Georg (1873-1923); Isidor (1874-1942); worker Max (1876-1942); foundry assistant Hugo (1877-1942); master painter Emil (1879-1943); Adolf (1883-1944); Julius (1887-1978); menswear shopkeeper Siegmund (1889-1945); and Herman (1892-1972); and three daughters Clara (1880-1964); cashier Julie (1882-1941); and shopkeeper Johanna (1885-1972). In Oberhemer, Levi set up business as a butcher. His son Adolf followed his father's example and also became a butcher.[445]

After Levi died in 1898, Pauline sent her three youngest children to the Jewish Orphanage for Westphalia and Rhineland in Paderborn, which sits between Hemer and Hannover. Julius and Siegmund went to the orphanage in 1899, and the baby of the family Hermann followed in 1900. Pauline must have had trouble coping with twelve children and the death of her husband. The financial situation may have been a

---

[445] ibid.

major contributor to the problems of the family. The three boys remained in the orphanage until they turned 14.

Jews began settling in the town of Oberhemer in the Middle Ages, but they were driven out during the plague pogroms. Permanent Jewish settlement only rose again with the emancipation of the Jews at the beginning of the 19th century thanks to Napoleon.

Generally the Jews in the area lived in simple circumstances. There were 32 Jews in Hemer in 1871, and 37 in 1925.[446] With the increase in antisemitism and persecution during the Nazi era most Jewish shops were closed. After Kristallnacht, some families emigrated. Of those who remained, most died or were murdered in Theresienstadt, most likely from the terrible conditions, such as through malnutrition, exhaustion or disease.[447]

When some returned to Hemer after the war, they continued to be confronted with antisemitism. It took until the 1980s for the town to confront its past. A pastor called for remembrance, and in 1988 a public commemoration of Jewish victims of the Holocaust took place. This turnaround culminated in a memorial being erected in the Hemer cemetery in 1990.

All of Pauline and Levi's nine sons served in the German army in World War 1. Pauline's husband Levi Löwenhardt had a distinguished record of service in the Prussian army, having fought in the battles of Münchengrätz and Königgrätz in 1866. Levi was born in Oberhemer on 1 July 1840. On 15 October 1863 he enlisted in the army as an active soldier. He was a frontline soldier in three wars – 1864, 1866 and the Franco-Prussian War in 1870-71.[448]

His military record includes: "7th Army Corps, 2nd Battalion infantry, 7th Westphalian Landwehr Regiment Nr. 56. Levi Löwenhardt from Oberhemer, entered the standing army on 15 October 1863 as replacement in the 8th Company. Released into the

---

[446] 'Hemer, Germany', JewishGen Communities Database, Jewishgen.org/Communities/community.php?usbgn=-1790146
[447] 'Hemer: Jüdische Leben', Jüdische Friedhöfe in Deutschland und Angrenzenden Ländern
[448] 'Achnebbisj, a self-analysis', Prof John Löwenhardt, Löwenhardt Foundation, The Netherlands

300+ Years of a German – Jewish Family

reserves on 26 September 1866 to Oberhemer, Iserlohn District because of military duty fulfilled. Medals and decorations: E.K. 66 R. [Iron Cross 1866]. Further has participated in the 1866 campaign against Austria, in the battles of Münchengräz and Königgräz. Private First Class Löwenhardt has participated in the campaign of 1870-71."[449]

Levi Löwenhardt - husband of my great grandaunt Pauline
(Source: Löwenhardt Foundation, The Netherlands)

Levi's military passport (or military record book) was passed down through the generations of Löwenhardts from Levi's son Adolf, to Adolf's son Heinz, to his son John. In May 2023 John Löwenhardt donated it to the Jewish Museum of Westphalia in Dorsten.[450]

Levi Löwenhardt's end was very sad for an old, proud soldier. Though only aged 51, he was admitted to the Psychiatric Hospital in Niedermarsberg, about an hour and a half drive east from Hemer. He was diagnosed with Paralytische Seelenstörung (paralytic mental disorder), or what was known later as dementia paralytica, on 5 May 1898 and died only nine days later. It is evidently a very painful late stage of syphilis. Syphillis was difficult to treat in the 19th century, but is easily treated today in the early stages with penicillin.

---

[449] ibid.

[450] A scanned copy is available online thanks to the Löwenhardt Foundation, with a short description, at loewenhardtfoundation.org/en/levi-lowenhardt-military-id/.

Uncovering their Names and Stories:

When former Private First Class Levi Löwenhardt, who was a veteran of three German unification wars, died in 1898, he left his widow Pauline with nine sons and three daughters. All of the boys fought on the frontline during World War 1. Six were wounded. Max and Hermann were wounded four times each, Hermann suffering serious gas poisoning which affected him for life. Adolf was a paramedic and was 'severely disabled'.[451]

Six of the nine brothers were awarded the Iron Cross.[452] Their mother Pauline, a widow, also deserved a medal for what she went through. A husband who would have borne the physical and mental scars of serving on the frontline in three wars himself, followed by having nine sons serve in World War 1, always in danger. I can imagine her waiting for news of her sons from the front. Plus, she had three daughters to raise at home. In 1917 she received a letter from the Kaiser, thanking her for her sons' efforts on the front.[453]

After the war, several of the boys became members of the RjF (Reichsbund Jüdischer Frontsoldaten), the association of former Jewish soldiers who served on the frontline in World War 1.[454] Pauline's son Siegmund Löwenhardt was co-founder of the local branch in Essen, which is 36 km west of Dortmund where he appears to have been living at the time.[455]

The RjF had 55,000 members across about 500 local groups. It was the largest Jewish community organisation during the Weimar Republic. The RjF members saw themselves as patriotic Germans, and the RjF ardently defended its members against the antisemitic lies about lack of Jewish support for and frontline involvement in

---

[451] ibid.
[452] The Iron Cross was a Prussian military decoration, instigated by Prussia in 1813, revived in 1870 for the Franco Prussian War and recreated in 1914 by the Kaiser for World War 1. (Britannica.com)
[453] 'Vater und neun Jungen', <u>Der Schild</u>, Journal of the German Union of Jewish Front Soldiers (*Reichsbund Jüdischer Frontsoldaten*, 1922-1938), 6 March 1936
[454] German Union of Jewish Frontline Soldiers
[455] "Siegmund Löwenhardt in Dortmund-Hörde is co-founder of the local branch in Essen", from 'Father and Nine Boys', Löwenhardt Foundation, The Netherlands

World War 1. The organisation was banned from any political activity in 1936 and was closed down by the Nazis in 1938.

The Kaiser's appreciation for their family did not carry over to the Nazi administration. Of the seven brothers who still lived in Germany in the mid-1930s, the Nazi regime murdered six, often with their families. Hermann emigrated to the United States in 1921. Salomon-Georg died in 1923 of severe injuries from World War 1. The butcher, Adolf escaped the Nazis by fleeing to The Netherlands in 1936, although the regime eventually caught up with him, and he was murdered in Auschwitz in October 1944. The remaining six brothers continued living in Germany, probably thinking that their frontline service in World War 1 might protect them. If it did, it didn't for long. Of the Löwenhardt brothers who remained in Germany, only Julius survived the Holocaust.[456]

When Pauline died in Dortmund in 1933, she was buried in the Jewish section of the General Cemetery in Dortmund-Wambel, a 35 minute drive from Hemer. By then, Pauline and several of her sons and daughters had been living in Dortmund for many years.[457] Her grave was found more recently by her great grandson John Löwenhardt in 2010.

I have also met Pauline's great (x3) grandson Sebastian Zimmer online. Sebastian, who lives in Berlin, is the great (x2) grandson of Salomon–Georg and Selma Löwenhardt (1870-1942). Salomon–Georg ran a bed spring specialist shop in civilian life. They had four children, Edith (1904-), Gerda (1907-1939), Käthe (1908-2000) and Heinz (1910-1942) in Berlin. Gerda married the non-Jewish Kurt Eischleb (1894-1964), and they owned a typewriter shop. Kurt and Gerda had a daughter Ursula (1939-2002), whose daughter Karola Zimmer-Montag (1960-) is Sebastian's mother. Sebastian is a contributor to the Löwenhardt Foundation, writing and translating stories of the Löwenhardt family.[458]

---

[456] Löwenhardt Foundation, The Netherlands
[457] Email from John Löwenhardt, Löwenhardt Foundation, The Netherlands, 27 June 2024
[458] Löwenhardt Foundation, The Netherlands

Uncovering their Names and Stories:

John has also searched the Jewish cemetery in Hemer looking for Löwenhardt ancestors, but without success. Despite all the Löwenhardts born and raised in the town, and 25 gravestones remaining intact, there were no Löwenhardt marked graves in the cemetery.

One of the last remaining direct connections with the twelve Löwenhardt children died while I was writing this book in July 2024. Pauline Maria Löwenhardt (1934-2024) was the first-born child of the youngest Löwenhardt sibling Hermann, and his Catholic wife Elizabeth Ring (1898-1953). Hermann was employed as a factory worker and welder and converted to Catholicism in the USA.

Pauline Maria was named after her grandmother Pauline Löwenhardt nee Lennhoff, being born the year after the elder Pauline died. Hermann had emigrated to the USA in September 1921, following his sister Johanna who migrated to Detroit, Michigan in 1910. The younger Pauline was born in Detroit and was close to her Aunt Johanna. Pauline married Henry Klobucar in 1957 and had three children, Mary/Morgan, Joseph and Peter. She worked as a nurse, wrote textbooks and after retiring became a writer, especially writing creative non-fiction. She suffered from polio, but loved the outdoors and was a 'lover of life'.[459]

Pauline's siblings were Lucy (1936-) who also became a nurse, Hubert (1938-) and Joseph (1942-). Hubert and Joseph became submariners in the US Navy. Of Hermann's children, only Hubert is still alive, living in Connecticut.

The Hellers of Hamburg

One of my grandmother Meta's sisters was Paula Lennhoff (1886-1942). She married Emil Heller (1883-1942) from Halberstadt in Frankfurt am Main in 1917, but they raised their family at 19 Loogestieg, Hamburg. They had two children Arno (1920-2016) and Ingrid (1922-1991), who escaped together on the Kindertransport in 1939. They managed to enter the USA, with the assistance of their

---

[459] 'Pauline Löwenhardt, 1934-2024', John Löwenhardt, Löwenhardt Foundation, The Netherlands

uncle Norbert Lennhoff who escaped with his wife Lili to the USA in 1937. Unfortunately, both Emil and Paula were murdered in Auschwitz in 1942, so Arno and Ingrid never saw their parents again. Arno's son Peter told me that the only time he remembers seeing his father cry, was when he and his father drove together into Hamburg.

Arno Heller was interviewed as a Holocaust Survivor for his testimony by the USC Shoah Foundation in 1996.[460] It is a valuable testimony, as a family member under the Nazi regime and experiencing Kristallnacht, but also as an eyewitness who was a close cousin of and a very similar age to my father. Arno was born in Hamburg in 1920 and my father Henry was born in Pillau in 1921. They lived through a very similar time in Germany.

Arno's father Emil had been a sales representative for men's clothing and bedding. Arno had his barmitzvah in 1933 and did not have any non-Jewish friends during his time in Germany. He had wanted to become an engineer. Emil fought in World War 1 like my grandfathers, and he had lost a brother in that war. After the Nazis came to power, Arno's life changed. He could not attend the school of his choice and there was no chance of becoming an engineer. Discrimination and restrictions kept getting worse, and they could see there was no future for them in Germany.

By Kristallnacht, Arno was 18 and was working as a baker in his uncle Max Freimark's bakery in Frankfurt am Main, Café Freimark. He also attended a trade school two hours per week to learn baking. Most of their customers were Jewish, but he experienced racism in trade school. Max was the husband of Emil Heller's sister Friedericke Freimark nee Heller.

Arno's parents had started making plans around 1937/38 for him and Ingrid to travel to the USA, and they thought that they would be able to follow. Arno said conditions were not too bad until Kristallnacht. Things became far worse, very quickly.

On Kristallnacht, Nazis entered the bakery in Frankfurt, beat up Arno and made him throw bricks through the café window. He was

---

[460] <u>Arno Heller Holocaust Survivor testimony</u>, Interviewed by Ellen Adler, Rego Park New York, USC Shoah Foundation, 12 September 1996

Uncovering their Names and Stories:

"beaten with a whip" and the bakery was "smashed up". He and his cousin Fritz Freimark escaped into the woods, and they slept out there for several nights.[461] Arno's son, Peter Heller, visited Frankfurt several years ago, and found the café building still standing, but now housing a Vietnamese restaurant.[462] The destruction and horror of Kristallnacht were frightening and distressing.

Arno and his younger sister Ingrid fled Germany on a Kindertransport train, aged 18 and 17 respectively, sailing on the *SS New York* to the USA. Arno is listed on the passenger list as a confectioner and Ingrid is listed as a domestic servant.[463] Like my mother, her education would have been cut short due to the Nazi regime.

When he arrived in the USA, Arno had four dollars in his pocket. Arno and Ingrid saved money in the USA to pay for their parents to escape to New York, to be with them. They had also made plans and payments to arrange travel for their parents to Cuba, but that plan did not come to fruition. They sent money back to their parents in Germany every month. But their parents never made it out.

Initially in his adopted country, Arno worked for Mother's Pie Company in the Bronx, New York, as shown on his US Army draft registration card. His contact on his registration card was his closest relative, his uncle Norbert Lennhoff. Arno and his sister at that stage lived with Norbert and Lili at 559 West 156 Street in Upper Manhattan. Lili's widowed mother Elise Feilmann (1859-1943) also lived with them, until she died in 1943. The building is Robert Fulton Court, named after the engineer and inventor of the first steamship, and was built in 1909. It still stands today on the corner of 156 Street and Broadway. In Arno's last letter to his parents, he tells them that he and Inge gave Norbert "a couple of house slippers for his birthday

---

[461] <u>Arno Heller Holocaust Survivor testimony</u>, Interviewed by Ellen Adler, Rego Park New York, USC Shoah Foundation, 12 September 1996
[462] ibid. and email from Peter Heller, 4 May 2024
[463] National Archives and Records Administration

and a box of cigars." Clearly, they were appreciative of their Uncle Norbert.[464]

Arno enlisted in the US Army in 1942, serving in North Africa, Sicily, England preparing for the invasion, and then he landed in France the day after D-Day. This was his chance to fight back against the forces that persecuted his family, destroyed their lives and took away their identity. Not to mention murdering his parents and many members of his extended family. As Arno put it, he wanted "to serve the country that gave me refuge."[465]

He was a sniper, and he had said that he was "pretty good at it".[466] One of his other tasks was questioning German prisoners, given his German language capability. He was discharged after the war, at the end of 1945.[467] He belatedly received his Bronze Star Medal in 2012 at age 91.[468] It is awarded in the US military for "heroic achievement, heroic service, meritorious achievement, or meritorious service in a combat zone."[469]

He was not alone in joining up. Around 10% of Jewish refugees in the US at the time volunteered for the US Army, with about 9,500 German-Jewish US soldiers serving in World War 2.[470]

---

[464] Email from Peter Heller, 7 September 2024, providing details of the last letter from Arno Heller to his parents
[465] 'US-Auszeichnung für deutschen Einwanderer: Wie Arno Heller gegen Hitler kämpfte', Johannes Korge, Der Spiegel, 3 February 2012
[466] Email from Peter Heller, 3 May 2024
[467] Arno Heller Holocaust Survivor testimony, Interviewed by Ellen Adler, Rego Park New York, USC Shoah Foundation, 12 September 1996
[468] 'US-Auszeichnung für deutschen Einwanderer: Wie Arno Heller gegen Hitler kämpfte', Johannes Korge, Der Spiegel, 3 February 2012
[469] Foxholemedals.com.au/products/us-bronze-star
[470] 'US-Auszeichnung für deutschen Einwanderer: Wie Arno Heller gegen Hitler kämpfte', Johannes Korge, Der Spiegel, 3 February 2012

Uncovering their Names and Stories:

Arno met Ruth Neuberger (1920-2016) at a singles retreat in the Catskills, and they married in November 1947. They had a son Peter Heller (1950-) and two daughters.

Naturalisation certificate of Arno Heller with picture of him in his US Army uniform
(Source: Peter Heller)

After a couple of jobs, including as a baker in the Bronx, Arno bought into a delicatessen on 6th Avenue and 59th Street in New York. He had the business there for 25 years, and was very proud of the business he built. Together Arno and Ruth created a wonderful life together. They had both been born in the same year, and both died in the same year, 2016, aged 96. Arno's sister Ingrid Pfeffer nee Heller lived until 1991, aged 69.

I discovered and met Arno's son Peter Heller online after he was my top DNA match on Ancestry DNA. Peter has become a good friend, as well as a cousin, and he has helped me with Heller family history. For example, Peter told me that Arno's sister Ingrid married Rudolph Pfeffer (1921-1980) and they had two sons, Ronald and Jeffrey

Pfeffer. Jeffrey married Helayne Oppenheimer (1954-). They have two children together, Raquel and Russell, and they live in New Jersey. Peter and I have remained in contact, swapping photos, documents and family stories. He told me more about his father Arno, and helped confirm a photograph of a young Arno in my father's childhood photo album.

I met my cousin Jeffrey Pfeffer through Peter Heller, and Jeff mentioned that he remembered Lili Lennhoff (1891-1965), wife of Norbert Lennhoff (1887-1953), living in the building next to them when he was very young. Norbert was the only brother of Jeffrey's grandmother Paula Heller nee Lennhoff and my grandmother Meta Marowilsky nee Lennhoff. From family photos, Norbert looks a very well-dressed gentleman.

Through Jeff, I also found a surprising familial connection through the Pfeffer family, especially for an old bookseller like myself. Jeffrey's father Rudolph Pfeffer had an uncle, the dentist and jaw surgeon Dr Fritz Pfeffer (1889-1944) from Gießen, which is about an hour's drive north of Frankfurt. Fritz was surprisingly Anne Frank's roommate, one of the eight people who hid in the secret annexe with Anne Frank's family in Amsterdam during the war. When they were betrayed to the Nazis, Fritz was sent to Auschwitz, then Sachsenhausen and then Neuengamme concentration camp near Hamburg, where he died on 20 December 1944.[471]

Over 43,000 men, women and children were killed in Neuengamme, between its conversion from a brickworks in 1938 and its liberation by the British in 1945. The victims died from "disease, exhaustion, hunger, or violence".[472]

Anne Frank gave Dr Pfeffer the pseudonym Dr Albert Dussel in her original diary. By naming him 'Dussel', she was basically calling him a blockhead, or a dope. As Anne writes it, they did not get on, and as with any adult male in his forties, he may have had difficulty rooming with a young girl during extraordinarily stressful times.[473]

---

[471] 'Fritz Pfeffer', Anne Frank House, Annefrank.org/en/anne-frank/main-characters/fritz-pfeffer/
[472] 'Neuengamme Memorial', Hamburg.com
[473] The Diary of Anne Frank, Anne Frank, Avarang Books, 2023

Uncovering their Names and Stories:

Fritz's second wife Charlotte Kaletta was not Jewish, and they could not marry before the war because of the Nuremburg Laws. After the war, they were deemed by decree to have been married in May 1937.[474] Charlotte, and Fritz's only child Werner Peter Pfeffer (from his first marriage) both survived the war, and were very critical of how Fritz was portrayed in Anne Frank's Diary, and the theatrical and movie versions that came later.

Arno and Ruth's son Peter Heller married Ruth Dallal (1951-) from Israel, and they have two daughters together, Susan (1979-) and Sharon (1982-). Susan in turn has three children, Jacob (2007-), Owen (2010-) and Hannah (2015-). Sharon has a son, Levi (2007-). Peter Heller, Jeffrey Pfeffer and I have been sharing family information and photos to put together a better combined understanding of our inter-related ancestors. And I am very appreciative of their support and friendship.

Jacob Lennhoff's descendants

Thanks to a family tree connection discovered online, I met distant cousins Steven Sasso and his wife Patricia Sasso from San Diego, California. Steve's great (x2) grandfather Jacob Lennhoff (1822-) and my great (x2) grandfather Isaac Lennhoff (1817-1863) were brothers from Plettenberg, both sons of Simon and Julie Lennhoff.

Jacob the butcher had two sons, Isaak Lennhoff (1866-1932) and Sally Simon Lennhoff (1871-1943). Sally married Ida (Henny) Rosenbach (1875-1955) from Soltau-Fallinbostel in 1900. Soltau is a town of about 22,000 people, about halfway between Hamburg and Hannover, which I drove through on my road trip. Sally built a mercantile and textiles business in the town, and later in nearby Bremen.

Isaak was a butcher in Plettenberg, like his father Jacob. He married Jettchen (Lina) Thalberg (1865-1896), from Wetzlar north of Frankfurt, in Plettenberg, and they had three children, Sarah Anne (1893-1942), Siegmund (1894-1908) and Emilie (1896-1942).

---

[474] Anne Frank House

When Jettchen died in 1896, at the age of 31, Isaak married Jettchen's sister Regina (Franziska) Thalberg (1864-1942) and had three children together in Plettenberg, Rosalie (1898-1900), Hedwig (1900-1942) and Hermann (1907-).

Isaak's family was decimated by the Holocaust. Emilie was murdered in Müngersdorf in Cologne, Hedwig in Zamosc in Poland, Sarah Anne in Chelmo in Poland, and Regina in Theresienstadt. On my road trip, I found Regina (Franziska), Sally Simon, Hedwig, and Sarah Anne all listed on the Holocaust memorial stone together in the Jewish cemetery in Plettenberg. There are seven Lennhoff names on the memorial. I also found the grave of Jacob's brother Isaac Lennhoff (1817-1863) in the same old Jewish Cemetery in Plettenberg.

Isaak Lennhoff's son Hermann became a cattle dealer and farmer. He escaped the Nazi regime, fleeing to England, and ended up interned in the Kitchener Camp, at Sandwich in Kent.[475] He emigrated to Toronto to be a farmer according to his internment card, and he lived the rest of his life in Canada where he married and lived with his wife Helen Lennhoff (1912-1970). I do not know when Hermann died, but in the 1960s he was working as a salesman and still living with Helen in York, Ontario, Canada.

Jacob's other son Sally lived with his wife Ida in Soltau and they raised two daughters, Paula Lennhoff (1900-1967) and Selma Lennhoff (1901-1984). Selma married Bruno Leiser in 1958, and Paula married Harry Feilmann (1891-1946) in 1928. Harry had served in the German Army and had been wounded in World War 1, fighting in the Battle of the Marne and in Champagne, France. He was captured by the French and released in 1920. After the war, he became a bookkeeper for a metalworks company. Two decades after World War 1 ended, Harry Feilmann was a prisoner in Sachsenhausen, like my grandfather Oskar, after Kristallnacht in November 1938. He managed to get released, and quickly emigrated to New York, where he arrived on 26 January 1939. He had to wait over ten months until he would see his wife and daughter.

---

[475] Kitchener Camp – 1939 Register, Kitchenercamp.co.uk

Uncovering their Names and Stories:

Paula and Harry's daughter was Ursula Rae Feilmann (1929-2017), born in Soltau. Ursula went on the Kindertransport to England via Holland in 1938-early 1939, staying with the Morpugo family in Amsterdam. Paula and her daughter Ursula sailed together to the USA in November 1939, arriving in New York on 2 December 1939. They could then finally meet up with Paula's husband Harry.

Paula's sister Selma moved to Hamburg in 1936, then Bremen on 22 January 1939, emigrating to England on 4 April 1939, and then migrating further to Milwaukee, Wisconsin after the war in 1946. She finally settled in New York City in 1958, and lived to the age of 83.

Paula's daughter Ursula married Irvin Arturo Sasso (1922-2003) from Panama City in 1952. Irvin's father's family was from the US Virgin Islands, while his mother's family was from Jamaica. Ursula and Irvin lived together in La Jolla, San Diego, where they raised four children together, Eric (1953-2023), Philip (1955-2007), Jenifer (1961-1980) and my new friend and family history collaborator Steven Sasso (1957-). Irvin died in La Jolla in 2003, aged 81. They had been married for 51 years. Ursula lived until the age of 88 in seaside La Jolla, California, which is very far from and much warmer than her old home in northern Germany.

10.0 The Nathan – Elkan Family

My Nathan - Elkan family history developed in the seaport city of Hamburg in northern Germany for several generations, before the family set forth for Berlin:

Natan
Father of
V
Elkan Nathan (Elchanan bar Natan) (-1870)
Father of
V
Simon Nathan (1841-1929)
Father of
V
Oskar Nathan Elkan (1892-1948)
Father of
V
Ilse Bella Marlow nee Elkan (1926-1997)
Father of
V
David Marlow (1962-)

The Nathans of Hamburg

Hamburg is one of modern Germany's three city-states, the others being Berlin and Bremen. Since 1937, it has incorporated the cities of Altona and Wandsbek. It is a major port city in northern Germany, sitting on the Elbe River, which connects the city to the North Sea. It now has a population over 1.9 million, making it the second largest city in Germany after Berlin.[476]

There have been Jews recorded in Hamburg since 1590.[477] German Jews settled in the city from around 1600 but were driven out, with only Sephardi Jews allowed to live in Hamburg. Ashkenazi Jews were

---

[476] Federal Statistical Office of Germany homepage
[477] 'Germany: Hamburg', Encyclopedia Judaica, The Gale Group, 2008

Uncovering their Names and Stories:

able to return in 1656.[478] The Sephardi Jews arrived after their expulsion from Spain in 1492, coming to Hamburg via Portugal, Amsterdam and Antwerp in 1577.

The Sephardim notably settled in Altona, just to the west of Hamburg, after high taxation drove them from Hamburg. They established the Portuguese congregation of Altona and continued to speak Portuguese and Spanish for the following 200 years, and even had books published in those languages locally.

The community was growing, and there were already three synagogues in Hamburg by 1611. By 1800, there were about 6,500 Jews living in Hamburg, of whom 6,300 were Ashkenazi, or about 6% of the total population of the city. This was large by the standard of German speaking areas at the time. The Sephardi and Ashkenazi Jews maintain separate congregations. In 1811, the new French masters made Jews equal citizens. But this did not last long. The year after Hamburg became an independent city-state in 1814, the senate removed equality for Jews.

Hamburg is also the birthplace of Reform Judaism, with the first Reform congregation being the Israelitischer Tempelverein in 1818. Its Bauhaus style synagogue was built on Oberstrasse 126, Hamburg in 1931. It was the only synagogue in the city to survive the Nazis.[479]

The Hamburg Jews started to get rights again from 1848, coincidently the year my great grandmother Bella Nathan was born in Hamburg.

Traditionally, in Hamburg and around German-speaking lands, the market square and inn were preferred places to do business. In these venues, Jews mixed with non-Jews, drinking and doing business together. In Hamburg, the Schiffergesellschaft (Shipping Company) was one of those inns.[480] My ancestors may well have been frequenters of inns, and they certainly would have been regulars in

---

[478] 'Germany, Hamburg', Jewish Virtual Library, American-Israeli Cooperative Enterprise, October 2014
[479] Germany for the Jewish Traveller, German National Tourist Board (GNTB), Frankfurt am Main
[480] 'Family and Everyday Life', Dr Stefanie Fischer, Hamburg key documents on German-Jewish history, Institut für die Geschichte der Deutschen Juden, 2016

their local market squares. I visited many of these market squares, some of which are still used for markets, in places like Hamburg, Cologne, Leipzig, Dresden, Halberstadt, Hildesheim and Gröbzig. The Rathaus on the Hamburg Marktplatz is a particularly stunning historic building.

Rathaus on the Marktplatz in central Hamburg
(Photo credit: David Marlow)

On my visit to Hamburg, I found that the Hamburg Municipal History Museum had been closed for renovations for a few years. Contacting them, the very kind librarian at the museum invited me to the library reading room to do some research. She extracted books I requested, and I spent a productive time in the old reading room, which would have been around since my grandparents' day.

While there, I discovered and contacted the Hamburger Gesellschaft für Judische Genealogy,[481] asking for ideas and assistance with finding pictures, graves and documents on my Nathan/Hirsch family from Hamburg. Since then, I have also made contact with the

---

[481] Hamburg Society for Jewish Genealogy

Uncovering their Names and Stories:

Hamburg Genealogical Society and have become a member. They have been very helpful in my research on my Hamburg ancestors.

My earliest identified ancestor in my Nathan/Elkan family was my great (x3) grandfather Natan, who was born around 1790. He was the father of Torah scholar Rabbi Elkan Nathan (-1870). Elkan was born in Hamburg around 1810. The family primarily lived from at least the early 1800s to the early 1900s in Hamburg, before moving to Berlin in the early 1920s. Elkan Nathan derived his surname from his father's first name. His Hebrew name was Elchanan bar Natan.[482] So, the father of my great grandfather Simon Nathan was a rabbi. No wonder that my maternal grandmother Hanni, who married Simon's son Oskar, used to say that her husband's family was religious.

Elkan died in Hamburg in 1870, and was buried in the Jewish Grindelfriedhof, Hamburg. Grindel sits next to the University of Hamburg, about an eight minute drive north from my hotel in Hamburg. Unfortunately, I did not know about him nor my great grandfather Simon Nathan's siblings when I was in Hamburg. I was simply looking for details of Elkan Nathan's son, Simon. Simon was the father of my grandfather Oskar. But if I went to Grindel to look for Elkan, I would have been very disappointed.

The Jewish cemetery in Grindel was built on the corner of the streets An der Verbandsbahn and Rentzelstraße in around 1712, when the Altona cemetery was inaccessible due to a military conflict. In 1835, it became the main cemetery for the High German Israelite Community and the Portuguese Community in Hamburg. The last burial took place in 1909, as the cemetery was full. Like many other Jewish cemeteries, the Grindelfriedhof was devastated by antisemitic attacks under the Nazis. The Nazi regime closed the cemetery in 1937, and contrary to Jewish law, the remains of those buried were exhumed and reburied in Ohlsdorf. About 450 out of 8,000 gravestones were also moved to Ohlsdorf. Apartment buildings have since been built over the site of the old Grindelfriedhof.[483]

---

[482] Elkan Nathan burial record on JewishGen. Please note, Bar (בַּר) means 'son' in Jewish Babylonian Aramaic (בֶּן, ben in Hebrew).
[483] Jüdischer Friedhof Hamburg; 'Friedhöfe', Das Jüdischer Hamburg; and 'Jüdischer Friedhof am Grindel', Wikipedia

We had always wondered where the Elkan surname came from, because of the Nathan family changing their surname to Elkan in 1921. In the Torah, Elkanah was the husband of Hannah and father of the prophet Samuel. Elkanah means 'G-d has purchased'. But as a surname for the family, the Elkan surname would have come from my great (x2) grandfather Rabbi Elkan Nathan. Elkan married my great (x2) grandmother Engel Cohen (-1875) in Varel, Lower Saxony in far northwest Germany, on 7 March 1827. Engel was born around 1805 in Varel. Varel is very near the North Sea and has a population today about 24,000. It has a small Jewish cemetery, and a synagogue (Die Vareler Synagogue) existed from 1848 to 1938. Another loss to Kristallnacht.

Elkan and Engel Nathan seem to have started their family in Varel before moving to Hamburg, and they had five sons and three daughters: Nathan Elkan (1827-) who was born in Varel, David (1831-), Betty Breina (1833-), twins Hanna (1838-) and Jacob (1838-), Marcus (1839-1907), my great grandfather Simon (1841-1929), and Jette (1843-). Simon was the second youngest. They seem to have adopted the Nathan surname soon after their son Nathan Elkan was born.

To date, I have not found out much about Nathan Elkan, David, Betty, Hanna, Jacob and Jette. Though I did find that Nathan Elkan was a typesetter and married Grasse Levin (1826-) in Hamburg on 20 May 1854.

Their brother Marcus Nathan married Minna Fürst (1852-1905) in 1878 in Hamburg. Marcus and Minna's child was Elkan Nathan (1879-1917), who married Emma Florsheim (1874-1924). Their Elkan Nathan died on the Western Front in World War 1 in 1917, serving in the German (Prussian) Army in Oppy, in northeast France, fighting British and Canadian troops. He died on 17 April 1917 and was listed as fallen on 30 May 1917.[484]

My great grandfather Simon Nathan married Bella Hirsch (1848-1919) around 1870. They were both born in and lived their lives in Hamburg, where they had five children, Samuel (1873-1948) who was

---

[484] German Army, Loss lists of World War I, 30 May 1917, page 18729

Uncovering their Names and Stories:

named after Bella's father, Sophie (1874-1942) who was named after Bella's mother, Elkan (1876-1940) who was named after Simon's late father, Hermann (1887-1956), and my grandfather Oskar Nathan (1892-1948).

Bella's parents were Samuel Hirsch and Sophia Ephraim who were born around 1820, Samuel in Hamburg and Sophia in nearby Altona, now part of Hamburg. Altona was under Danish control until 1864. We do not know much more about Bella's parents. Altona and Hamburg are now one, so close together that I easily walked between central Hamburg and Altona on my road trip. I walked the 3 km from the Steigenberger Hotel in central Hamburg to the Jewish cemetery in Altona. And I am not known for my walking.

Interestingly, about half of my walk to Altona was along the Reeperbahn, an infamous and very seedy street of Hamburg, with strip joints and bars leading virtually all the way to the Jewish cemetery.[485] The highlight of the walk was crossing Beatles Platz, and passing the Beatles Platz Hotel, named in honour of the band. That and helping a young African woman carry her baby in its pram down the stairs into the Reeperbahn underground train station. This is the area that the original line-up of the Beatles (pre-Ringo) used to perform frequently in their early days, at various clubs. From this experience as a young man, George Harrison called Hamburg "the naughtiest city in the world."[486]

We know from family photos that Simon Nathan served in the Prussian army, and most likely given his date of birth, fought in the Franco-Prussian War of 1870, and possibly the other German unification wars. He would have been too old to serve in World War 1. In civilian life, Simon was a clothes dealer.

Simon and Bella's son Samuel (1873-1948) worked as an authorised representative, and married the Lutheran Elise Dorothea Martha Deppe (1879-1935) on 4 June 1908. Samuel and Elise had three

---

[485] Travelling west along Reeperbahn, the street changes its name to Königstrasse just before arriving at the old Jewish cemetery in Altona

[486] The Beatles Anthology DVD (2003), Episode 1 - 0:43:05, George Harrison talking about Hamburg, women and sex.

children, all born in Hamburg: Walter (1909-) who worked as a merchant, Helmut (1915-) and Hildegard (1920-). Elise died in Hamburg in 1935. We know that by 1939, Samuel and the children were living at 1 Rossausweg, Hohenfelde Ost, Hamburg. The street name has gone, but it was near the Alster Lake (the Außen-Alster) in central Hamburg. Samuel survived the Holocaust, dying in Hamburg in the same year that his brother Oskar, who died in Melbourne in 1948.

Simon and Bella's son Elkan (also known as Elka) Nathan was a barber by profession, and married Bertha Graff (1871-1932) in Hamburg in 1905. Elkan and Bertha had a daughter Rosa Mina Nathan (1906-1947) but divorced in 1926. Elkan died in Sachsenhausen Concentration Camp in 1940.

But do not feel too sorry for this Elkan Nathan. While my grandfather Oskar was a well-liked, responsible and much-loved husband and father,[487] and I believe his brothers Hermann and Samuel were similar, Elkan was another matter.

Newspaper reports from the Hamburg district court over many years from 1912 to 1925 report that Elkan was a despicable and "dangerous" individual, sexually abusing young teenage girls. He even went so far as to advertise for schoolgirls for light domestic service work, and then sexually abused them. In 1926, he was sentenced to nine years in jail for raping young teenage girls. Overall, he seems to have spent nearly 20 years imprisoned, from three separate convictions. His major conviction in 1926 led to his divorce in the same year.[488] His appalling behaviour may also have been why most of the Nathan family changed their surname to Elkan and moved to Berlin. It would have been unbearable being associated with him, especially while living in the relatively small Jewish community in the same city. The effects on his wife and family must have been terrible. I know every family has a black sheep or two

---

[487] Oskar's death notice read "beloved husband of Hannie Elkan, loved father of Ilse, and loved father-in-law of Henry".

[488] Hamburger Echo Abend-Ausgabe 12 April 1912, p9; Hamburger Fremdenblatt, 12 April 1912, p6; and Hamburger Echo Abend-Ausgabe, 17 June 1925, p7

somewhere in their history, but this discovery surprised and disturbed me.

Sophie Elkan in Berlin

Simon and Bella's daughter Sophie Nathan moved from Hamburg to live in a Jewish community home for the elderly at 26 Grosser Hamburger Strasse in Berlin, which is a five minute walk to the Neue Synagogue on Orienenburgerstrasse. She also changed her surname to Elkan. As a rabbi's granddaughter, she would have taken the short walk down Krausnickstrasse to Orienenburgerstrasse to the synagogue. Coincidently, I parked on the corner of Krausnickstrasse and Orienenburgerstrasse when I visited the synagogue in March. Sophie would have walked that path many times, whether going to shule, for a walk along the nearby Spree River, or for shopping. When her brother and sister-in-law Hermann and Hermine (Nathan) Elkan emigrated to the USA, Hermann put Sophie's name down on the shipping manifest as his closest relative in Germany.

In 1942, the Jewish community home on Grosser Hamburger Strasse was converted into an 'assembly camp' by the Gestapo. The staff of the home were forced to help prepare the transports for the deportation of elderly Jews to Theresienstadt. It operated from 2 June 1942 until 1 March 1944. From May-June 1943 to early 1944 it was the only assembly camp in Berlin. Many overflow assembly camps were set up in Berlin over time, to cope with the number of deportees. About 22,000 people 'were processed' through the Grosser Hamburger Strasse camp alone.[489]

In August 1942, Sophie was moved to 31 Artilleriestrasse in Berlin, which is now renamed and numbered as 40 Tucholskystrasse. The building had been the community centre of the Adass Yisroel congregation in Berlin since 1904 but was closed by the Gestapo in 1939. The Gestapo converted it into an "old people's home as transit point" to Theresienstadt. It was the overflow assembly camp when the Grosser Hamburger Strasse camp was over-stretched. It operated from 17 August 1942 until 3 October 1942 and at least 196 people

---

[489] Stolpersteine-berlin.de/en/glossar

passed through it.[490] Adass Yisroel opened its new synagogue at 40 Tucholskystrasse on 10 March 1990.[491]

Sophie was deported to Theresienstadt on 17 August 1942 on the "First large transport of the elderly" at the age of 68. This was the first of four large transports from Berlin to Theresienstadt and held about 1,000 deportees. The deportees were ordered to appear at the Grosse Hamburger Strasse camp or were taken from their homes by the Gestapo. The Jews were ordered to hand over their apartments after they had paid all their taxes. The Gestapo searched their luggage and the apartments, often taking valuables. At the assembly site the Jews were forced to sign a declaration, transferring their property to the state.

National Cemetery in front of the Small Fortress of Theresienstadt
(Photo credit: David Marlow)

---

[490] ibid.
[491] Adassjisroel.de/en/today/community-center-and-synagogue/

Sophie's train arrived in Theresienstadt the next day. The transport included 997 Jews, of whom 734 were women and 263 were men, with an average age of 75.3.[492]

Many died of hunger and disease in Theresienstadt, while hundreds of others were transferred over time to death camps, such as Treblinka and Auschwitz. Only about 13-16 people from this transport survived.[493] Sophie was transported to Treblinka Concentration Camp the next month on 19 September 1942, where she was murdered.[494]

The Elkans of Cleveland

Oskar's brother Hermann was well off in Germany running a successful furrier boutique, until the Nazi regime took everything from him. He married Hermine Suess (1887-1966) in about 1910, and had a daughter Else Elkan (1914-2001). Else married Rabbi Dr Siegfried Scheuermann (1910-1957) from Frankfurt am Main, on 27 February 1936 in Berlin. So, my mother's great grandfather was a rabbi, and her first cousin Else, was a rebbetzin.[495] Else and Siegfried fled to Cleveland in the USA, where they changed their names to Else and Stephen Sherman, and they were very prominent in the Cleveland Jewish community.

Siegfried (Stephen) was the son of senior cantor Selig Scheuermann (1873-1935) and Marie Hobach (1874-1934), and he attended the University of Berlin. He was ordained at the Theological Seminary in Berlin and commenced as a congregational rabbi in Shivelbein, in what is now northern Poland. He was there for one year, and then became the rabbi in Freiburg im Breisgau from 1936 to 1938. Freiburg is in south-western Germany, near the French and Swiss borders. In Freiburg, he was busy helping community members flee from the Nazi regime. In 1938, he was arrested and sent to Dachau

---

[492] Collections.yadvashem.org/en/deportations/5093025
[493] ibid.
[494] Arolsen Archives records; and Das Bundesarchiv Memorial Book 1933-1945
[495] Rebbetzin = wife of a rabbi or a female religious teacher

Concentration Camp, which was undoubtedly the trigger for Siegfried and Else to quickly leave for the USA.

Else, Hermine and Hermann Elkan walking together in Germany before the war
(Source: Raymon Sherman)

They arrived in New York on 27 January 1939, so were amongst the many Jews who escaped quickly after Kristallnacht. In 1947, they adopted five-day old Raymon Ezra Sherman, born 21 October 1946 in Kenosha, Wisconsin. Ray now lives in Florida, enjoying the much warmer climate. Ray and I have met and talked online, and I am very appreciative for his help with his branch of the Elkan clan. Ray served for three years in the US Navy in the 1960s and married the lovely Donna Giancola in 1969. They have three children, Raymon, Donald and Michelle, as well as seven grandchildren and five great grandchildren.

Rabbi Siegfried (Stephen) became a well-respected rabbi in the USA, working at several synagogues, in Wisconsin, Indiana and Maryland, including the Congregation of Israel in Salisbury, Wicomico in Maryland. He ultimately became the Hillel Director at Western Reserve University in Cleveland. On occasions, he would stand in for the head rabbi at the Reform Temple in Cleveland. He lived in and served the Jewish community of Cleveland for ten years, until his death.

Uncovering their Names and Stories:

Rabbi Siegfried (Stephen), Hermine, little Raymon, Else and Hermann together in Cleveland around 1949

(Source: Raymon Sherman)

When he died early in 1957, Else took over his Hillel position temporarily, to ensure continuation of the religious and cultural activities for the remainder of the year. He is buried in the Mayfield Cemetery in Cleveland. A B'nai B'rith Lodge was named in his honour after his death, and Else helped officiate at the launch of the new Stephen Sherman Lodge in June 1957.[496]

Else became very senior in B'nai B'rith in Chicago (district 2), where she and Ray lived for four years after Stephen and Herman died, and then again when back in Cleveland (district 6) for over 25 years. When Else died, her ashes were buried next to Siegfried (Stephen) in Mayfield, even though she had remarried to Charles Peters in Buffalo New York in 1961. Charles, or Chuck as he was known, was Else's ex-boss and a friend of Stephen.

---

[496] 'New B'nai B'rith Lodge Will Bear Name of Late Rabbi Stephen Sherman', The Jewish Independent, 14 June 1957, front page

Else's parents, Hermann and Hermine, also escaped from Germany to the USA, arriving in 1941, via Nice, France. They had fled Germany some time before World War 2, and finally escaped Europe via a ship departing from Lisbon, Portugal. They also moved to Cleveland and built a life there. They lived with Else and her family, and Ray remembers them at home. He called them Oma and Poppy. Hermann served in the Prussian Army in World War 1 and had lost an arm. Ray remembers that he always had a prosthetic hand. Hermann and Hermine died in Cleveland in 1956 and 1966 respectively. Else died in Sarasota in 2001 after retiring to the much warmer Florida. Coincidently, a cousin from the Kraft side of my family, Jeff Kahane, is the musical director of the Sarasota Music Festival.

I have found Hermann's US Draft Registration Card dated 27 April 1942, though at 54 he was too old to serve, not to mention only having one arm. The card tells me he was 5'7", had blue eyes, a ruddy complexion and 'slightly' grey hair. The 'slightly' is handwritten above the printed grey hair. Most of the men in my family would have been delighted to have any hair.

Oskar and Hanni Elkan of Berlin

Hermann's brother Oskar was 5'5", also had blue eyes and had brown hair according to his immigration statement I found in the National Archives of Australia. Family photos suggest that he did not have much hair, but I gather what little he had was brown. Years ago, I was in the foyer of the old B'nai B'rith building in Melbourne, and I saw that they had a photo of the large group of foundation members on the wall. B'nai B'rith Melbourne had been founded in 1945 by German Jews who had arrived between 1901 and 1939. In the back of the large group of foundation members in the photo, I recognised my grandfather's distinctive bald head and face immediately, despite him being in the back row, amongst dozens of other bald men. The B'nai B'rith Executive Director in Melbourne kindly provided me with a copy of the photo about a decade ago.

Uncovering their Names and Stories:

B'nai B'rith Melbourne foundation members including my maternal grandfather Oskar Elkan - back row in front of second window from left
(Source: B'nai B'rith Melbourne)

Most of the Nathan family changed their surname to Elkan in 1921. At least we know that Simon, Hermann, Sophie and Oskar Nathan did. Most of the family appear to have moved from Hamburg to Berlin. Simon's wife Bella had passed by then, in 1919 in Hamburg. Simon died in Berlin in 1929, at the age of 87.

My maternal grandparents Oskar Elkan (1892 –1948) and Hanni Elkan nee Kraft (1897-1986) lived in Berlin from the early to mid 1920s, where they raised my mother Ilse Bella Elkan (19 November 1926 – 1 October 1997), who inherited her middle name from her grandmother Bella Nathan. Oskar was born in Hamburg, and Hanni was born in Leipzig as part of the Kraft family.

Berlin was the traditional capital of Prussia, and when Germany unified in 1871, it became the capital and largest city of the new German Empire.

Jews are first mentioned in relation to Berlin in 1295, in a Berlin council letter forbidding wool merchants from supplying Jews.[497] Jewish history in Berlin commenced in the 13th century, as Jews fled from persecution and expulsions elsewhere. But Berlin was no

---

[497] 'Berlin', Jewish Virtual Library, jewishvirtualibrary.org/berlin

utopian city for Jews. They were the target of oppression and expulsions, such as the Black Death scapegoating, until 1571. From then, there were virtually no Jews in Berlin until the mid 1600s. They were then allowed in, charged for a residence permit and the growing community built a mikveh, a hospital, and a synagogue (now known as the Old Synagogue).[498]

By the start of the 18th century, there were about 1,000 Jews living in the Jewish ghetto, in the Grosser Judenhof (Great Jew's Court). The Jews of Berlin became successful as merchants, dealing in precious stones, and as bankers. At this time, most of my family were living in smaller cities and often very small towns around the northern and central German states.

In the 19th century, Jews migrated from towns and smaller cities as part of a greater pattern of urbanisation, seeking education and greater wealth for their families. Full equality came to Berlin Jews in 1850, when there were 9,500 Jews in the city. Despite high levels of intermarriage and abandonment of faith, the number of Jews had grown to 108,044 in Berlin by 1890 (5.02% of the population), and 172,672 by 1925 (4.25% of the population).[499]

With the rapid growth in the community, came Jewish communal organisations and a number of Jewish newspapers. The community had grown to 160,000 by 1933, including my mother and her parents. Because of the city's historically large Jewish population, Berlin is home to the largest Jewish cemetery in Europe, Weissensee Cemetery. It was in use from the mid 1800s until the Holocaust and contains over 115,000 Jewish graves.

I did wonder whether my grandfather Oskar Elkan was a member of B'nai B'rith in Berlin as he was later in Melbourne, and lo and behold, I found a record of his membership on the GenTeam German genealogical database. He joined the Timendorfer Jubiläums-Loge of B'nai B'rith in Berlin in 1924, while he was working at M. Müller AG, Pelzwarenfabrik und Rauchwarenhandlung. It was a fur factory and tobacco shop, not so politically correct now, but it was a business for

---

[498] 'Berlin, Germany', Virtual Jewish World, Jewish History Tour
[499] ibid. and 'Berlin', Jewish Virtual Library, jewishvirtuallibrary.org/berlin

Uncovering their Names and Stories:

its time. Except when the Great Depression hit, the company folded in 1930, after 57 years in business.

Oskar and Hanni Elkan on the balcony of their apartment at Kniephofstrasse 53, Berlin in the 1930s (top) and my daughter Brittany out the front of the same apartment building in 2014 (bottom)
(Source: Ilse Marlow family photo and Brittany Marlow Keeghan)

In Berlin, Oskar and Hanni Elkan lived fairly centrally, at Kniephofstrasse 53 in the Steglitz area, with their daughter Ilse (my mother). Luckily, I found a photo of Oskar and Hanni dating from the mid 1930s on the balcony of their apartment, taken from the footpath outside. About 80 years later, my daughter Brittany was on a European holiday and had her photo taken outside my grandparents' old home, which had changed very little. This is the apartment where my mother would have lived as a child until the age of 12. The two photos together are quite a family treasure.

On my road trip, I also visited their old apartment building in Steglitz, just a 20-minute drive southwest from the centre of Berlin, Berlin Mitte. It was a wonderful feeling to see the actual place that my grandparents and mother had successfully fled in 1939. I had butterflies doing aerobics in my stomach on the car ride. Kniephofstrasse is a very narrow street, especially for a two-way street. Being my very first day in Germany, I was not confident enough to find it on my own, so I took a taxi. The driver spoke no English, and we made it thanks a little to my high school German, which is probably the level of a German toddler. The driver laughed along with me at the narrowness of the street.

Only one car could pass through the street with cars parked on both sides. Over the next few weeks, I found many old narrow streets like this in various cities across Germany. Local drivers were very forgiving and patient as I navigated those narrow streets, but I suppose they had little choice.

Mid-sized apartment buildings hovered over both sides of the road all along the street. It was a highly populated area, and most buildings appeared to be equally pre-war constructions. This was where they had lived, slept, had meals, entertained friends and eaten Seder meals at Pesach. My mother would have walked to school, because there was no room anywhere near for a school bus to pass.

The family's eventual apartment in Melbourne, overlooking St Kilda Beach was a definite improvement in terms of location.

I surprisingly felt quite joyous after the visit to the apartment building and seeing where they had lived. I celebrated with a good coffee back on Potsdam Platz in central Berlin, gathered my thoughts and updated my journal. I had always wanted to visit where they had lived in Berlin, and I was delighted to tick it off my bucket list. It helped make my family's history feel much more real and personal. It was also my only taxi ride in Germany. The rest of my family history road trip relied on me driving my rented Opel, and the car's navigation system.[500]

---

[500] Although I did take a tram, underground train and boat on a side trip to Prague.

Uncovering their Names and Stories:

My taxi outside my grandparents' apartment building at Kniephofstrasse 53, Berlin in March 2024

(Photo credit: David Marlow)

Ilse was seven years of age when Hitler came to power, and she had very bad memories of school in Berlin. She remembered and resented, as a Jew having to sit in the back of the class, the Jewish children always having to sit separately, having to wear a yellow star on her clothing, and before too long not being allowed to attend school at all. Hence, her education was very limited.

It should be remembered that issues with Nazis and the far-right did not start with Hitler taking power in 1933. Rosa Luxemburg was murdered in 1919, and antisemitic propaganda escalated from there. The prominent Jewish businessman and politician Walter Rathenau was murdered in 1922. Antisemitic radicals attacked Jews in major Jewish streets in 1923. The virulent antisemite and Nazi leader Joseph Goebbels became Gauleiter[501] of Berlin in 1926, which further encouraged Nazi thuggery. On Kol Nidrei 1931, Jews returning from shule were assaulted by gangs of Nazis. I hope that none of my Kraft,

---

[501] Regional Nazi Party leader

Elkan or Steinthal family living in Berlin were victims of these attacks. The 1931 attacks were organised by Count Wolff Heinrich von Halldorf, the future chief of police under the Nazi regime.[502]

My mother and her parents lived in Berlin until Oskar was arrested, which occurred most likely as part of the Kristallnacht arrests on 9-10 November 1938, like thousands of other Jews.

Today, there are seven synagogues in Berlin, Jewish preschools and a high school. There is also the Berlin Jewish Museum, and the Memorial to the Murdered Jews of Europe and Information Centre (Holocaust Memorial) in the city memorialising and dedicated to the Jews murdered in the Holocaust. The Information Centre is really mis-named, because it is an excellent museum in its own right.

On Kristallnacht, synagogues and shops were vandalised and destroyed like elsewhere in Germany, but the Neue (New) Synagogue, built in 1866, was saved by a police officer, who convinced the fire department to save the building because it was "an officially protected monument".[503] But that did not stop the building being bombed by the Allies in 1943. Nevertheless, the Neue Synagogue remains in Berlin today. It may well have been the synagogue where Oskar, Hanni and daughter Ilse attended services, especially for the Jewish High Holydays. Mum remembered her father as being fairly religious.

Like many other German veterans of World War 1, Oskar may have felt fairly protected from the antisemitism flying around. Veterans were well respected by the public in Germany after the war, regardless of religion. This remained the case largely until 1938, taking a hit when Hindenburg died in 1934, but once World War 2 started any protection from service in the Great War disappeared.[504] Nothing is sadder than the photos of Jewish World War 1 veterans wearing their medals on Kristallnacht in 1938 and the boycott of Jewish businesses on 1 April 1933, expecting that they would provide

---

[502] 'Berlin', Jewish Virtual Library, jewishvirtuallibrary.org/berlin
[503] 'Berlin, Germany', Virtual Jewish World, Jewish History Tour
[504] Comrades Betrayed: Jewish World War I Veterans Under Hitler, Michael Geheran, Cornell University Press, Ithaca New York, 2020 (Kindle version), esp. locations 283-284

Uncovering their Names and Stories:

protection. Though veterans were protected to some extent through the early 1930s. Even Hitler had to step lightly with Jewish veterans in the early years, and especially wounded veterans, until he consolidated power. When Hindenburg announced medals for those who had served, in 1934 on the 20th anniversary of the start of World War 1, Jewish veterans were included. Once Hindenburg passed, so did his protection.[505]

The Nazis initially avoided targeting Jewish veterans in public, not wanting to upset the military leaders and many conservatives who typically supported veterans of any type. But Kristallnacht burst that bubble of perceived safety. And once World War 2 started, the constraints were off. When the wearing of the yellow star became mandatory, Jews were also forbidden from wearing their "medals, decorations, and any other badges."[506] The diarist and philologist Professor Victor Klemperer[507] wrote about the yellow star that everyone wearing it, "carried his ghetto with him, like a snail its house."[508] To make it worse, Jews had to pay for the stars and have multiple of them to be stitched to each piece of outerwear.

The regime even went as far as a major charade with Theresienstadt in Czechoslovakia. They did not want to be seen to deport Jewish veterans to the east, like other Jews, but promoted Theresienstadt as a privileged camp for Jewish veterans. They were sent to Theresienstadt, and the myth was promoted like it was some kind of

---

[505] Comrades Betrayed: Jewish World War I Veterans Under Hitler, Michael Geheran, Cornell University Press, Ithaca New York, 2020 (Kindle version), location 2046ff
[506] ibid. esp. location 3065
[507] Victor Klemperer was born in Landsberg an der Warthe (now Gorzów Wielkopolski) like my great (x5) grandfather Lazarus Philipp. Victor was the first cousin once removed of Werner Klemperer, famous for his widely divergent roles in the TV series 'Hogans Heroes' and the movie 'Judgement at Nuremberg'.
[508] Between Dignity and Despair: Jewish Life in Nazi Germany (Studies in Jewish History), 1st edition, Marion A Kaplan, Oxford University Press, New York, 1999, p.157

retirement village. The retirement village had an 85% mortality rate for German Jews.[509]

I had been told by a German researcher who called me many years ago, that my grandfather Oskar had been arrested and taken to Dachau Concentration Camp, before getting out of Germany. This was possibly Prof Manfred Brusten, who had listened to my father who clearly misremembered in which concentration camp his father-in-law had been imprisoned. Dachau was built in 1933, the first concentration camp established by the Nazi regime. It was built in the town of Dachau, near Munich in northern Bavaria. Unlike other camps, it was relatively much less focused on Jews and was more for political prisoners, including communists, and inmates at various stages included Russian prisoners of war, Roma, homosexuals and others deemed outsiders by the regime.[510]

In Dachau, normal standards of decency and the laws of the land were thrown out. Brutality, torture, starvation, whipping and murder at whim were standard practice of the SS who ran the camp. Inmates were brutalised on arrival, and frequently in camp. Beatings and torture were the norm.[511]

Only about 5,000 Jews became interned there, and about half of those were killed. Jews generally went to other camps, such as Auschwitz, Sachsenhausen and Mauthausen. In the early years of the Nazi regime, Hitler sought to force the Jews out of Germany by encouraging emigration. Later, the focus shifted to extermination. Dachau was eventually liberated by US troops on 29 April 1945. The photographs and videos of the piles of corpses and skeletal survivors they discovered are legendary.

The idea that my maternal grandfather Oskar had been in Dachau, even for a short time, was devastating.

---

[509] Comrades Betrayed: Jewish World War I Veterans Under Hitler, Michael Geheran, Cornell University Press, Ithaca New York, 2020 (Kindle version), esp. location 3935
[510] Histories of the Holocaust – Dachau: State within a State (documentary), 2011
[511] ibid.

Uncovering their Names and Stories:

However, I could never find any documentation that linked Oskar to Dachau, and Dachau down south near Munich was a long way from his home in Berlin, in the east of Germany. The reality is that my grandfather was arrested and sent to Sachsenhausen Concentration Camp, a 45-minute drive north from Berlin, late in 1938.[512] He was 46 years of age. The timing of Kristallnacht being so close to being able to get his family out, suggests that Oskar may have been arrested before Kristallnacht, but it is possible that he was arrested on 9-10 November, like 30,000 other Jewish men.

Documentation from Sachsenhausen shows that his release was authorised on 21 November 1938 for the next day.[513] The political section (Politische Abteilung) of the Gestapo kept meticulous records. By early January, he and his family had already arrived in Australia. They moved very quickly. Oskar, Hanni and young Ilse landed in Melbourne on 9 January 1939.

Sachsenhausen was certainly no improvement over the idea of Dachau. It was established by the SS and was built by internees in 1936. It was the first concentration camp built under direction of the new Chief of the German Police, Heinrich Himmler. It housed over 200,000 internees from 1936 to 1945. Internees included political opponents, Jews, Roma, homosexuals and other targeted groups. Hard work was mandatory. Tens of thousands died from starvation, disease, forced labour, medical experiments, torture, mistreatment or just straight-out SS murders. About 13,000 Soviet prisoners of war were murdered in the autumn of 1941 alone. As in Dachau, brutality, torture and murder were normal. The Russian Army liberated Sachsenhausen on 22 April 1945, a week before the fall of Berlin.[514]

When I discovered that Oskar had been in Sachsenhausen, I was determined to visit the memorial and museum there. As I drove northwards from Berlin to Sachsenhausen Concentration Camp, in Oranienburg, I had big butterflies in my stomach again. This was also

---

[512] 'Sachsenhausen Strength Reports', Holocaust Survivors and Victims Resource Centre, United States Holocaust Memorial Museum
[513] ibid.
[514] ibid.

the place that Hanni's brother Bruno Kraft and Oskar's brother Elkan Nathan were murdered.

Driving through the beautiful German forests on the way to Oranienburg should have been calming, but it did not help. I knew what would be coming and what it meant. On arrival, I steeled myself with a strong black coffee, reading pamphlets on the Sachsenhausen Memorial and Museum, and taking notes in the café of the New Museum building.

Sachsenhausen was meant to be a 'model' concentration camp, but its triangular design did not easily allow for the expansion necessary after the massive increase in Jewish persecution from 1938. Over 200,000 people were imprisoned in Sachsenhausen from 1936 to 1945. Few survived.

Jewish prisoners from November 1938 to October 1942 were held in barracks 37, 38 and 39. Two of those buildings have been reconstructed on the site, after the original buildings were burned down in an arson attack. They now house museum exhibits, which highlight the violence, torture and mistreatment meted out on prisoners, such as Oskar Elkan, Oskar's brother-in-law Bruno Kraft and Oskar's brother Elkan.

It is a dismal place. I thought I might be sick as I walked through the gate with the sign saying 'Arbeit Macht Frei'.[515] The gate passes under a large white building, leading into the main camp. Through the gate, I walked through or by such charming highlights as the site of the gallows, the mass graves of concentration camp victims, the SS troop camp, the execution trench, the site of the first crematorium, the Gestapo prison cells (the prison within a prison), and the Sachsenhausen national memorial at the far end of the camp.

As I walked across the old parade ground, I thought about Harry Naujoks' experience of roll call on the parade ground during his time as a prisoner in the camp (1936-1942), "Many of them are wearing only uniforms of drill (summer clothes). They stand for hours like that on the parade ground, across which an ice-cold wind is blowing. After only a short while the first few prisoners are already lying on the frozen earth, having collapsed through cold and lack of

---

[515] 'Work will make you free'

strength...More and more people collapse; the dead and dying are lying on the ground."[516]

Sachsenhausen Concentration Camp
(Photo credit: David Marlow)

The evils of the Holocaust era weighed heavily on me as I walked around the camp, physically and emotionally. I felt 20kg heavier in the camp. I dreaded walking through the front gate, as I had always avoided visiting Poland or concentration camps generally. I had nothing specifically against the Poles, but Poland as a place meant death-to-Jews for me. Similarly, going through Sachsenhausen, I felt the weight of six million on my shoulders. This was certainly accentuated by my family history research, which had underscored the breadth of devastation the Nazis had inflicted on my family. I had found original documents and discovered the names of over one hundred family members who had been murdered.

This was a time when just being a Jew was enough to be arrested. The fact Oskar had served in the German Army in World War 1 did

---

[516] <u>Sachsenhausen Concentration Camp: Events and Developments 1936-1945</u>, Günter Morsch & Astrid Ley (ed.), Metropol, 2023, p.78

not prevent his arrest, but possibly helped keep him alive long enough to get out of the camp and free from Germany. Military records show that he had served in Prussian Infantry Regiment 175 in World War 1.[517]

Veterans of World War 1, and especially wounded veterans, were held in high regard in Germany through the 1920s and 1930s, at least by the public. Though Jews as a group were severely scapegoated and their military service maligned after 1918 by right wings groups, and most vehemently by Adolf Hitler and the Nazi Party, Jewish veterans were somewhat protected for a time because of public support for veterans, regardless of religion.[518] Also, officers in the German Army often intervened after 1933, to protect or speak up for Jewish veterans with whom they had served.[519]

This was still a time when if you had enough money to pay the emigration (escape) fee and could prove you and your family were leaving Germany, you could get released from a camp. Once the war broke out, those doors would close. Oskar and Hanni had tried various avenues to escape Germany, and could not get out to commonly sought destinations, like the USA and England. They even tried Switzerland but were turned away. Eventually, they found refuge across the world in Australia.

Migration to Palestine was very difficult due to British restrictions on entry of Jews to Mandatory Palestine, made worse by the Arab riots of 1936-1939. Thousands of Jewish refugees still managed to enter, though many had to do so illegally.

My then 41-year-old grandmother Hanni was very brave. She worked hard to get Oskar out of Sachsenhausen, and the family out of Germany. Hanni had to deal with the Gestapo and an emigration office in Berlin, as well as finding a country to where they could escape. She would have booked the ship and arranged it all, while her husband was confronted with the horror of Sachsenhausen. I can only imagine the worry she would have had about Oskar, and about

---

[517] Genealogy.net (compgen.de) German genealogical website
[518] Comrades Betrayed: Jewish World War I Veterans Under Hitler, Michael Geheran, Cornell University Press, Ithaca New York, 2020
[519] ibid.

Uncovering their Names and Stories:

getting all three of them out to freedom. Ultimately, she was very successful.

One observer in a British passport office in Berlin noted, "Families were often represented only by their womenfolk, many of them in tears, while the men of the family waited in concentration camp until some evidence of likelihood of emigration could be shown to the secret police".[520]

How would Oskar have felt on his release? Arrested and locked up in Sachsenhausen, surrounded by torture, brutalisation, mistreatment and overcrowding.

One daughter of a survivor of Sachsenhausen wrote that her father described his experience, "in a low voice, punctuated by the hollow cough that lingered with him for a long time to come, he recounted his terrible experiences. If he hadn't been our own father, a qualified lawyer, and in his right mind, we would never have believed him."[521]

We can look at the thoughts of sociologist Dr Werner J Cahnman, who wrote about his similar experience, but in Dachau, after being arrested on Kristallnacht, "I was released on 16 December 1938. I was called to the central office and told that I had a visa…I was sternly advised that I would be arrested again if I failed to leave the country in due time. I was handed back my civilian suit, shirt, shoes, and other belongings. I arrived at home on a Friday evening, shortly before dinner time. After dinner, I was shown letters from abroad pertaining to emigration, but I felt that I was unable to concentrate on reading them, and I said so. When my father admonished me to try and read the letters nonetheless, I rose from the table, red with anger, and slammed the door. For weeks afterwards I could not even bring myself to read a novel or a detective story. The letters would dance before my eyes, and I would break into a sweat. I was certain that I was hovering on the verge of a serious mental disorder. But I

---

[520] Get the Children Out!: Unsung Heroes of the Kindertransport, Mike Levy, Lemon Soul, London, 2023, p.4
[521] Between Dignity and Despair: Jewish Life in Nazi Germany (Studies in Jewish History), 1st edition, Marion A Kaplan, Oxford University Press, New York, 1999, p.123

finally climbed out of the hole, mentally as well as physically. I left Germany on 20 June 1939. On that day I was born into a new life."[522]

Prof Brusten found that a relative named "Alexander?" in Melbourne had helped Oskar and Hanni arrange the permit to get into Australia.[523] This may well have been young Egon Alexander (1919-1997) from Leipzig who married Henriette Abraham (1925-1991) and was living in Melbourne. Henriette was the daughter of Hanni's first cousin Margarete Abraham nee Kraft (1898-1984) who also emigrated to Melbourne with her husband Herman Abraham (1889-1948).

The Elkans, my maternal grandparents did not take long to leave Germany after Oskar's release. Oskar (age 47), Hanni (41), and daughter Ilse (12), took a train from their hometown Berlin to the Italian port city of Genoa. There, they boarded the Italian ship *Remo* with tickets to Melbourne, Australia. My mother told me that she remembered, carrying her case around Genoa as they waited for the ship to be ready to board. They arrived in Melbourne on 9 January 1939 with £200 and what they carried in their cases.[524]

When Italy entered World War 2 on 10 June 1940, the *Remo* was berthed in Fremantle, Western Australia (WA). The Australian Government seized the *Remo* as a prize of war the next day. The officers and crew were arrested as 'enemy aliens' and placed in internment camps, the crew to nearby Rottnest Island and the officers to the town of Harvey, south of Perth.[525] Australia sold the *Remo* back to the Italian Government in June 1948.[526]

---

[522] <u>German Jewry: Its History & Sociology – Selected Essays of Werner J. Cahnman</u>, Joseph B Maier, Judith Marcus & Zoltan Tarr, Routledge, Oxford, 2019, p.158
[523] Prof Brusten notes to Henry Marlow interview with Prof Manfred Brusten, October 1994
[524] National Archives of Australia
[525] Veneto Market Gardeners 1927 website
[526] Trove online database, National Library of Australia

Uncovering their Names and Stories:

My Elkan grandparents in St Kilda

In Australia, the Elkans settled in the Melbourne beachside suburb of St Kilda, with a nice spacious four-bedroom apartment on the corner of Acland and Fitzroy Streets. Their home was apartment 3 in the Summerland Mansions building, 17A Fitzroy Street, opposite St Kilda beach. I remember it as a fairly dark apartment with dark furniture, with back stairs to a little garden. I often drive past Summerland Mansions and think about the time when Nana lived there, and the terrific views the apartment had of Port Philip Bay, St Kilda Pier, and palm trees.

The building was built in 1920, on the first piece of Crown Land sold in St Kilda in 1854.[527] It was designed by architect Christopher Cowper in a mix of Inter-War Stripped Classical, Inter-War Mediterranean, and Arts and Crafts architectural styles. The interior has stair hallways with timber panelling and gridded glazed walls. Maids and service rooms were included, with rear stairs provided as a tradesmen's entrance. There was a large common area on the rooftop and a common area dining room on Fitzroy Street.

The apartments were quite upmarket for their time, including milk and bread hatches, leadlight windows, built-in dressers, tiled fireplaces and serveries.[528] The old Milk Bar downstairs, which existed from at least the 1970s, has in recent years been replaced by funky cafes with alfresco dining.

The St Kilda Historical Society has said of Summerland Mansions, "It is a type of urbanity, there generally higher rise, which is common in European cities such as London, Paris, Berlin, Vienna or Milan and in Sydney, but rare in Melbourne."[529] It was therefore not surprising that my grandparents, straight from Berlin, selected it as home. It was very much an improvement from their apartment in Berlin.

---

[527] Realestate.com.au
[528] 'Summerland Mansions', Victorian Heritage Database Report, Heritage Victoria
[529] 'Summerland Mansions 17-27 Fitzroy Street, St Kilda', St Kilda Historical Society, skhs.org.au

Summerland Mansions, corner of Acland and Fitzroy Streets, St Kilda

(Photo credit: David Marlow)

The Summerland Mansions apartments have had sympathetic renovations in recent years, but key features have been retained. They are now much brighter, with modern lighting and have a funky vibe to match trendy St Kilda. Some have been used as offices at different times, attracted by the location, with easy access to Acland Street and Fitzroy Street shopping and dining. And the number 96 tram runs right past the apartments on Fitzroy Street, taking passengers north from St Kilda through the Melbourne CBD to Brunswick East.

Oskar and Hanni took in boarders to help make ends meet and immersed themselves in the local community. Ilse worked from a young age, and Oskar was a founding member of the Jewish social and charitable organisation, B'nai B'rith Victoria. Hanni liked feeding the birds from her first-floor balcony, and looking out over the picturesque Catani Gardens, which are opposite their building. Her balcony was second from the left in the picture above.

The Catani Gardens is heritage listed and is named after its 19th century designer Carlo Catani. Still today it has many Canary Island palms, adding a very tropical feel, especially with the backdrop of St Kilda Beach. Though being in Melbourne, the weather is usually far from tropical. I remember often on the weekend as a child, my parents taking me for pony rides in the Catani Gardens, and the pony rides continued to recent times. I have also found a photo of my older brother riding a pony ride there in the late 1940s. If I was lucky, my visit to St Kilda would include a gelati from Leo's Spaghetti Bar on Fitzroy Street.

My grandparents Hanni and Oskar Nathan in the Catani Gardens, St Kilda
(Source: Marlow family photos)

Nana became very close and long-lasting friends with her neighbour across the hall, Mrs Martha Gross, a lovely and friendly grandmother as I remember, who was a similar age to Hanni, and also a widow and German-speaker.

Other neighbours who Nana knew well were Ilse van Engel and Julie van Engel, who lived in Summerland Mansions 1946-1947, who were the mother and grandmother of the later Jewish community leader Vivien Brass OAM.

In later years, Hanni joined WIZO, a Jewish-Zionist women's charitable organisation, which is particularly focused on helping disadvantaged children in Israel. An advertisement in the Australian Jewish News in August 1969, welcomed her as a new member.[530]

When Ilse arrived in Australia, she worked for some time as a milliner, which would contribute to the family income, and helped pay for her cigarettes, which she told me she smoked from the age of 12.[531] The dangers of smoking were not known then, and between growing up under the Nazis, her father being in a concentration camp, emigration and settling in a strange country far across the world, with a foreign language, everything together would have been highly stressful.

Her parents also had clothing industry work experience. Hanni was a clothes-cutter and Oskar had been a manufacturer of professional clothes. In Melbourne, they had boarders and Oskar worked as a commercial traveller.[532]

One evening around 1943, Oskar brought home a young man for dinner, a recent German-Jewish refugee he had met. The young man was Heinz Marowilsky from Wuppertal near Düsseldorf. But he was born in the East Prussian town of Pillau. Heinz was not to see his parents again, and he became very close to Oskar and Hanni. And I think for them, Heinz was like the son they never had.

When Heinz met Oskar's daughter Ilse after his release from the Tatura camp in 1943, they got on very well and they began dating. He was living in an apartment around the corner on Beaconsfield Parade, but later moved to Mitford Street in nearby Elwood. Coincidently, this apartment where my father lived 80 years ago is only a few hundred metres from where I live in Elwood now. I was not aware that he had lived in Elwood when I bought my apartment on Ormond Road, Elwood but I loved the idea of being near the beach and having shops and cafes outside the front door of my

---

[530] <u>Australian Jewish News</u>, 1 August 1969, Trove

[531] My mother told me this when we were out to dinner at a Chinese restaurant on Punt Road, St Kilda as it came to her mind she said, because the restaurant was in the same building as her old employer.

[532] Elkan family records, Australian Jewish Welfare and Relief Society, via United States Holocaust Memorial Museum

apartment building. It is also a great location to walk our dogs, Fred and Mr Chifley.

Heinz and Ilse were married at an Orthodox Jewish synagogue, the prominently located Melbourne Hebrew Congregation, often known in the local Jewish community as 'Toorak Shule', because it sits on Toorak Road, but is not actually in the suburb of Toorak. The wedding took place at 7:30pm on Saturday 14 October 1944 and was officiated by Rabbi Dr Harry Mordecai Freedman (1901-1982) who had arrived in Australia from England in 1938.

On 8 July 1948, Oskar died suddenly. My mother was devastated when she found his body in her parents' apartment building at the age of 21. Oskar was 56. Hanni had lost her life partner and remained an unmarried widow for close to 40 years thereafter. One wonders what the stresses of living as a Jew for six years in Nazi controlled Germany, the anxieties of trying to find a safe haven for his family, combined with the terrible treatment he received in Sachsenhausen had on Oskar's health. He is buried in the Melbourne General Cemetery in Carlton.

My mother's cousin Kate Rotman (1930-2023) was Theodor Kraft's granddaughter, and the mother of my genealogical ally Dan Rotman. In her autobiography, she wrote the following about her father Herman Abraham (1889-1948), who like Oskar had lived in Berlin, served in World War 1, escaped Germany for Australia with his family in 1938, and died of natural causes in 1948 in Melbourne:

"He left the greater part of himself in Germany – a love for his fatherland, his profession, and therefore his business, and his ability to provide for his family, as well as his entire family, his standing in the community, his language! It was a total loss of identity."[533]

Kate's observations relating to her father could be easily about my grandfather Oskar, and the parallels in their life story were amazing. Further, in later life, Oskar's wife Hanni and Herman's wife Margerete (Grete), both widowed in 1948, were for some time both living in Emmy Monash Aged Care in Caulfield North, around the same time, right in the heart of the Jewish community of Melbourne.

---

[533] Kate's Story, the autobiography of Kate Rotman, unpublished manuscript, p2

It was particularly popular with elderly German-speaking Jewish women. I do wonder if they played bridge together, which my Nana loved immensely, or shared gossip in German over a sherry. Nana was unlikely to have shared her Johnny Walker Red Label, which she hid behind her small television, which was for "medicinal purposes only". Nana lived from 1897 to 1986 and Grete from 1898 to 1984.

Oskar's grave is in Jewish section Z of the Melbourne General Cemetery in North Carlton. It is very close to where I used to organise the Jewish Community Council of Victoria's annual Holocaust Commemoration at the Holocaust Memorial in the cemetery. Inscribed on the memorial in Hebrew are the words, "In sacred memory of the six million Jewish Heroes and Martyrs who perished at the hands of the Nazis." Some remains of Holocaust victims are also buried at the memorial, and the services were always very moving. I ran this communal memorial service with my team for several years, when I was Executive Director of the Jewish Community Council of Victoria (JCCV) from 2013 to 2018. It was well attended by Holocaust Survivors, their families and politicians at the time. The major Holocaust commemoration in Melbourne each year was, and still is, run by JCCV on Yom Hashoah.[534]

Hanni lived a good life at Emmy Monash Aged Care, playing bridge, shopping in nearby Glenferrie Road and gossiping in German with her girlfriends. She enjoyed outings with the family, whether with my parents on the weekend or my sister Judy during the week. My other siblings and I would often visit and catch her up on family news. She was pretty strong-minded and healthy, until a series of strokes took affect very late in life. She died aged 88 on 17 May 1986, a week before my 24th birthday. Nana is buried in the Jewish section of the Springvale Botanical Cemetery in Melbourne, very close to a nice big tree, and my parents.

I can still picture the three of them sitting around the big coffee table in our lounge-room at the front of our house on Orrong Crescent in Caulfield, reading magazines and newspapers, while the TV would be on constantly. They would be chatting in English or German, maybe complaining about some member of the British royal family they had read about. World Championship Wrestling or Epic Theatre would

---

[534] Holocaust Remembrance Day

Uncovering their Names and Stories:

be playing on the television, and a little David might be playing with his toy soldiers or Lego on the carpet.

Nana had survived her husband by nearly forty years, lived through two world wars, endured the Great Depression, saw her husband arrested by the Gestapo and be a prisoner in Sachsenhausen, lost her parents and husband, lived through the violently antisemitic Nazi regime, and lived through two of her three siblings murdered by the Nazis, big brother Bruno at Sachsenhausen and sister Else in the Riga ghetto. What a strength of character and resilience a person needs to come through all that, and still be full of love and have a sense of humour.

11.0 The Isensteins

My Isenstein family ancestors came from the cities of Hannover and Hildesheim in northern Germany, and some later lived in Leipzig in the state of Saxony in eastern Germany:

Marcus Salomon
Father of
V
Gütel Isenstein nee Salomon
Mother of
V
Marcus Isenstein (1802-)
Father of
V
Julius Marcus Isenstein (1834-1914)
Father of
V
Frieda Kraft nee Isenstein (1865-1930)
Mother of
V
Hanni Elkan nee Kraft (1897-1986)
Mother of
V
Ilse Bella Marlow nee Elkan (1926-1997)
Father of
V
David Marlow (1962-)

The Isensteins of Hildesheim

Hildesheim is a small city in Lower Saxony, about 30 km southeast of Hannover. It has a population today of just over 100,000 people. It first appears to have had a Jewish community in the middle of the 14th century. Persecutions after scapegoating Jews for the Black Death (1348-1349) led to a decline in the Jewish community, with

Uncovering their Names and Stories:

there being only 80 Jews in town by 1379. In 1457 the Jews were driven out altogether and the synagogue was destroyed.[535]

In the 1600s a couple of Jewish cemeteries were consecrated and a new synagogue built. The Jewish community grew from ten Jewish families in 1634 to 50 families by 1726. By 1812 the Jewish population in Hildesheim had grown to 380, and 513 by 1880. A new synagogue was built in 1849 but was burned down on Kristallnacht. This community included several of my Isenstein family ancestors.[536]

My great (x5) grandfather Marcus Salomon is my earliest known relative in my Isenstein clan. He was born around 1740-1750 in Hildesheim.

Marcus Salomon had a daughter Gütel in Hildesheim around 1770, the same year that English explorer Captain James Cook arrived in Australia on the Endeavour, an event that led to the British colonisation of the continent, which commenced in practice with the First Fleet in 1788. Gütel Salomon married Israel Isenstein in about 1800, having three sons and a daughter. Their children were Liebmann (Lippmann), Salomon, my great (x3) grandfather Marcus (1802-) and Rebecca Friederike Isenstein (1816-1900).

Rebecca Isenstein married Jacob Buchholz (1789-1860), and they had two sons, Victor (1858-1938) and Jacob Julius (1861-1942). Jacob ended up emigrating to England.

Salomon Isenstein and his wife Minna had five children, Adolf (1835-1892) who moved to New York, Jenny, Johanna, Rosalie and Julius S Isenstein (1837-1882).

Salomon's son Adolf Isenstein married Saleska Kayser (1839-1898) and had four children, Max (1862-1915), Martha (1867-1964), Otto George (1869-1959) and Anna (1871-). Max married Bertha Neugass (1870-) in New York in 1887, and they had a daughter Jessie (1889-) and a son Walter (1892-1961) who served in the US Army in an artillery battery (company) in World War 1 as a Private. Walter served overseas from July 1916 to April 1919. I do hope he was not shooting at my relatives in the German Army, nor them at him. Max's sister

---

[535] 'Hildesheim, Germany', Jewish Virtual Library
[536] ibid.

Martha married Dr Willy Herman Davidsohn (1862-), and Anna married Hermann Borchert (1872-1947), having a daughter Grace Borchert (1904-1923).

Salomon's brother Marcus Isenstein (1802-) married Caroline Wolff (1810-) around 1830, in Hildesheim, and they had six sons and a daughter. Their children were George (1832-1902), my great (x2) grandfather Julius Marcus (1834-1914), Moritz (1838-), Gustav (1841-1920), Eduard (1842-1923), Wilhelm, and Emilie (1837-1890).

Marcus' son Gustav Isenstein married Franziska Sichel (1845-1895) and had four children, Rudolph, Thekia, Paul (1881-1943) and Wolfgang Karl (1877-). Paul had a son Rolf in 1930 with his wife Johanna Schiblbach (1903-). Paul was one of many Jews who committed suicide during the Holocaust, on 24 March 1943 in Leipzig.

Many Jews committed suicide during the years of the Nazi regime, and especially once the deportations to concentration camps commenced seriously from 1941. But were they really suicides, when driven by persecution, dehumanisation, property theft, loss of identity as Germans, and fear of a worse death in cattle cars, in ghettos or death camps? Author Christian Goschel suggests, "The wave of deportations of German Jews from 1941 until 1943 prompted about 3,000 to 4,000 suicides ... After the deportations commenced, Jewish suicides made up roughly half of all suicides in Berlin and, at times, considerably more than that."[537] There were 811 suicides buried in the Weissensee Jewish Cemetery in Berlin in 1942 alone.[538]

Gustav and Franziska's son Wolfgang Karl married Rosalie Schlesinger (1878-1947) and had three children, two of whom died very young, Harald (1898-), Helmuth (1905-1908) and Martha (1913-1915). Wolfgang and Rosalie were deported in 1943 to Theresienstadt, but amazingly both survived the Holocaust.

---

[537] <u>Suicide in Nazi Germany</u>, Christian Goeschel, Oxford University Press, Oxford, 2009, p.107-108
[538] ibid. p.106

Uncovering their Names and Stories:

Marcus' son Moritz married Regina (1837-) from Bavaria and migrated to England. Moritz worked as an importer and warehouseman in London.

Otto George Isenstein married Minnie Sidenberg (1877-1939) moved to New York before World War 1, and raised three children in Manhattan, Helen (1905-1993) who married Joseph Goldsmith (1901-1990), Richard Otto (1908-2000) who married Eileen Stern, and James William (1913-1967) who married Ellen Louise Ridout. James changed his surname to Innes, served in the US Army in World War 2, and rose to the rank of colonel, serving in China, Burma and India in the Judge Advocate General's Office. He was a graduate of both Yale Law School and Harvard Business School.[539]

Only about 210 Jews were still in Hildesheim by May 1939. Most of them were deported to Theresienstadt. This may have included some of my relatives, if they had not fled to safety, but they needed to move far away to be safe, and even then, fate could intervene. For example, Marcus' daughter Emelie Isenstein had moved to Kassel in central Germany. Her daughter Henriette Gotthelft (1872-1943) was deported and murdered at Theresienstadt aged 71, and her other daughter Jula Gotthelft (1878-1941) died in Buenos Aires, Argentina aged 63.

There were only eight Jews in Hildesheim by 1970, but it has regrown a Jewish community again after the immigration of Jews from the former USSR.[540]

Captain George Isenstein goes to America

George Isenstein is of particular interest because of the unusual directions his life took. It is thought that about 10,000-12,000 Jews fought with the Union Army in the American Civil War.[541] George

---

[539] 'James W Innes', <u>The Reporter Dispatch</u>, 9 August 1967, page 2 obituary
[540] ibid.
[541] <u>The American Jew as Patriot, Soldier and Citizen</u>, Simon Wolf, The Levytype Company, 1895 (republished New York University Press, New York, 18 October 2014) Kindle edition location 2014.

Isenstein, uncle of my great grandmother Frieda Kraft nee Isenstein, was one of them.

I was not expecting to find a relative that fought in the Civil War. The thought had never occurred to me. But when I Googled George Isenstein's name, he came up on the Shapell Roster of Jewish Service in the American Civil War website, which is run by the Shapell Manuscript Foundation. This is a reminder to always do a Google search on a person or unusual family name, as you never know what resources it might bring into play.

I knew it was the right George Isenstein, because his file on the Shapell website included documents relating to George's parents back in Germany, my great (x3) grandparents Marcus and Caroline Isenstein, and his grand-nephew Bruno Kraft.

Shapell is an organisation dedicated to documenting the lives of Jews who fought in the Civil War. It is a pretty new source of information, and it held quite a treasure trove of material and documents relating to George.

George was born on Christmas Day 1832 in Hildesheim. Like many Germans of the time, he emigrated to the United States by ship in 1854. In the USA, he worked at various times as a theatre director, actor, cigar manufacturer and later a postmaster in Clarkesville, Tennessee. But on 22 September 1861, he enlisted in the US Army as a First Lieutenant to fight in the American Civil War, serving in the 15th Regiment, Missouri Infantry. He rose to the rank of Captain of Company E in January 1962 but spent most of his military career on detachment from December 1862, largely in quartermaster roles.

In the early days of its formation, the 15th Regiment, Missouri Infantry was known as the 'Swiss Rifles', though its German volunteers significantly outnumbered the Swiss volunteers. Nevertheless, with the Swiss Cross on its regimental flag and its prominent Swiss born commander, Colonel Francis Joliat, the name stuck for a while. But it was a truly German-American regiment, with close to 75% of its men being German born or of German parentage,

---

George Isenstein is actually mentioned in the book, locations 5436 and 16849.

Uncovering their Names and Stories:

including George Isenstein.[542] While George was with the regiment, they fought in the Battles of Pea Ridge and Chaplin Hills. Over 12% of the men of the 15th died in combat.[543]

Captain George married Sarah (Sallie Linn) Wood (1831-) in Virginia on 23 November 1863, in front of a Justice of the Peace. They raised three sons, Carl, Julius (1857-) and John (1860-).

Captain George Isenstein in his Union Army uniform
(Photo credit: Wallis Brothers, Premium Photograph Gallery, Chicago via Shapell Roster of Jewish Service in the American Civil War)

---

[542] Long Road to Liberty: The Odyssey of a German Regiment in the Yankee Army: The 15th Missouri Volunteer Infantry, Donald Allendorf, The Kent State University Press, Kent OH, 2014, Kindle edition, location 694

[543] ibid. location 247

The war ended on 9 April 1865, and George was honourably discharged in March 1866, after nearly five years of military service.[544]

After discharge, they lived in Tennessee and later settled in Chicago. George pursued his career in theatre management after the war, being involved with various dramatic and theatrical productions, such as the Mikado in German.[545]

Gradually, George became very unwell, and a letter from his friend and old comrade in arms Samuel Rexinger described briefly serving with George and his seeing George's health problems, from first-hand experience. George was so sick that he had difficulty speaking.[546] Rexinger and George were fellow Jewish officers who both joined the 15th Regiment, Missouri Infantry, in September 1861.

Rexinger himself was a colourful and entrepreneurial officer, having been charged as a Lieutenant with setting up a poker game for the men and selling them liquor at what seems inflated prices. He was charged, but nothing eventuated from the charges, and he eventually became a captain, and second in command of the regiment in 1863.[547]

By 1877, George was already seriously unwell, and a vaudeville benefit 'Der Loewe Des Tages!' was held for him, organised by his friends and colleagues in the New Chicago Theatre on 6 May 1877.[548]

Because of his deteriorating health condition, he applied for an invalid pension. In support of the application, his parents Marcus Isenstein and Caroline Isenstein nee Wolff both signed an affidavit in Germany, certifying that, "George Isenstein, formerly Captain U.S.A is our first born lawful son. Hannover the 20th of February

---

[544] George Isenstein record, ID 11494, The Shapell Roster, Shapell Manuscript Foundation
[545] Cincinnati Daily Star, 20 August 1878 p1 and Illinois Staats-Zeitung, Chicago, 3 January 1888
[546] Letter from Samuel Rexinger, The Shapell Roster, Shapell Manuscript Foundation
[547] Long Road to Liberty: The Odyssey of a German Regiment in the Yankee Army: The 15th Missouri Volunteer Infantry, Donald Allendorf, The Kent State University Press, Kent OH, 2014, Kindle edition, locations 993-994 and 3302
[548] Chicago Daily Tribune, 6 May 1877, p16

Uncovering their Names and Stories:

1875".⁵⁴⁹ Given the date, the process must have taken some time. The affidavit was certified by the US Consul for the District and Duchy of Brunswick, Germany. Germany had been unified for four years by then. I appreciated finding the affidavit, as it provided me with copies of the signatures of Marcus and Caroline, my great (x3) grandparents.

With declining health, George moved into the National Soldiers Home in Milwaukee, Wisconsin, where he died on 22 October 1902 aged 69. He is buried in the Wood National Cemetery in Milwaukee.

The Isensteins in Hannover

George's brother Julius Marcus Isenstein was born in the city of Hannover, where he married Anna Rosenhain (1839-1916) around 1860. My great (x2) grandparents Julius and Anna lived long lives for their time, to age 81 and 77 respectively. So far, I have not uncovered any information relating to Anna's parents.

Hannover is about a 30-minute drive north of Hildesheim. Julius and Anna owned a factory and lived in Hannover, raising five daughters and one son, Oskar Isenstein (1874-1943) who died in the Riga Ghetto with his wife Valeska (1892-1942). Oskar and Valeska's sons Julius Bernd (1926-1944) and Otto Hans (1928-1944) were murdered in Auschwitz.

Julius and Anna's daughters were Carola (Carole) (1873-1923) who married Adolf Weiss, Milli who married David Katz (1864-1916), my great grandmother Frieda Isenstein (1865-1930) who married Selmar Kraft, Elsa (1868-1923) who married Eduard Kraft (1855-1916), and Adele (1870-1949) who married Ferdinand Heinemann (1868-1936).

Adele's husband Ferdinand Heinemann looks surprisingly like my great grandfather Selmar. They both had a similar curly moustache and a roundish, bald head. You must carefully check family photos to distinguish between the two.

---

⁵⁴⁹ George Isenstein record, ID 11494, The Shapell Roster, Shapell Manuscript Foundation, affidavit from Marcus and Caroline Isenstein

Ferdinand and Adele had two children, Walter (1895-1957) and Ilse (1898-). Walter served in the military and eventually died in Florida. Ilse married Max Simon (1883-1954) and had a son Heinz Simon (1923-1992). Ferdinand died in Germany, but the rest of his family appear to have moved to Israel, where Adele died in 1949.

Hannover is the capital of the modern state of Lower Saxony in northern Germany and has a population of over 532,163.[550] Jews were present in the old city from 1292.[551] The Jewish population ebbed and flowed, as persecution, scapegoating for the Black Death and financial needs pushed and pulled the Jewish population pendulum.

Isenstein – Kraft family photo
(Source: Dan Rotman)

Left to right: Adele Heinemann nee Isenstein and Ferdinand Heinemann, Selmar Kraft and Frieda Kraft nee Isenstein, Milli Katz nee Isenstein and David Katz, Carole Weis nee Isenstein and Adolf Weis, and the then widow Elsa Kraft nee Isenstein.

---

[550] United Nations Eurostat
[551] Encyclopedia Judaica, The Gale Group, 2007

Uncovering their Names and Stories:

However, no Jews lived in Hannover's old city from 1588 until the 19th century, as they had moved out to the then independent Calenberger Neustadt. In 1588, antisemitic sermons by Protestant clergy led to riots, and trade between Christians and Jews was banned. Calenberger Neustadt is now part of the city of Hannover and is just a 15-minute walk across the River Leine to the centre of the city.

By the beginning of the 19th century, there were 500 Jews in Hannover.[552] This had grown to 5,000 Jews by the beginning of the 20th century. But by 1939, there were only 2,271 Jews left, which was still the tenth largest Jewish community in Germany at the time.[553]

On Kristallnacht in Hannover, the synagogue was burned down, 94 Jewish businesses and 27 homes were destroyed, the mikveh was destroyed and 334 local Jews were sent to Buchenwald Concentration Camp. By World War 2, between Jews fleeing the persecution and arrests, there were only about 2,000 Jews remaining. Of those remaining, 1,200 were squeezed into 'Judenhäuser', as the regime got ready to murder as many of them as possible in camps and ghettos. The deportations took place from 1941 to 1945. Only 68 survived from the first transport of 1,001 Jews[554].

Frieda Isenstein was born in Hannover and married Selmar Kraft (1863-1935), and they moved to and lived together in Leipzig, where they raised four children, including my grandmother Hanni Elkan nee Kraft (1897-1986), better known to me as 'Nana'.

Interestingly, Frieda's younger sister Elsa Isenstein (1868-1923) also married a Kraft. Elsa married Selmar's older brother Eduard Kraft (1855-1916). They had two sons, Fritz (1894-1917) and Werner (1896-1991). Werner married Erna Halle (1897-1991), and both lived long lives, dying within a few months of each other in Israel.

On my family research road trip, I arrived in Hannover after the 30-minute drive from Hildesheim. My first stop was the Jewish Cemetery an der Strangriede, which is a smallish, very old cemetery. I did not identify any family members. Nevertheless, it was

---

[552] 'History of the Jews in Hannover', Wikipedia
[553] 'Hannover', Encyclopedia Judaica, The Gale Group, 2007
[554] 'History of the Jews in Hannover', Wikipedia

interesting walking around this raised old cemetery, surrounded by a tall brick wall, amid a very built-up part of Hannover.

My great grandmother Frieda Kraft nee Isenstein
(Source: Dan Rotman)

Onwards, I drove to my hotel, the Central Hotel Kaiserhof, located centrally so it's true to its name. It sits on the very large square named Ernst-August-Platz, which is dominated by the Hannover main railway station. The square is the centre of action in Hannover, and is named after Ernst August I, who was the first King of Hannover. A statue of the king on his horse sits proudly and prominently outside the station.

Near my hotel in Hannover were many Turkish owned cafes, restaurants and shops. People of Turkish descent is the largest minority ethnic group in Germany, being 3% to 4% of the population. They are very noticeable in larger cities, such as Berlin, Cologne and Hamburg. Turkish restaurants and shops were prominent in all those cities when I visited. It was no different in Hannover. And I had a terrific Turkish lunch in a family run café when I visited Wuppertal. Most ethnic Turks in Germany trace their ancestry back to the German guest worker programs of the 1960s and 1970s.[555]

---

[555] 'Turks in Germany', Wikipedia

Uncovering their Names and Stories:

I walked through the square, through central Hannover to Altstadt, with many old timber and medieval buildings. After walking across a footbridge to cross the rapidly flowing River Leine, I passed into an area with many churches and Christian religious buildings. I was here to see what was left of the Alte Synagogue and Neue Synagogue, destroyed on Kristallnacht. The sites now include a memorial to those lost in the great pogrom.

On the walk there and back, I thought of my Isenstein relatives, who may have prayed in these synagogues, who worked in Hannover, who shopped in the markets, went to school somewhere nearby and were surrounded by friends and family. All long gone. Hopefully more escaped the Holocaust than I know.

The next day, I visited the huge non-Jewish Stadtfriedhof Stöcken cemetery in Hannover. The cemetery opened in 1891 as the city's second municipal cemetery. It is huge, covering 55 hectares, and containing 170,000 graves.

I was looking for the grave of my ancestor Julius L Isenstein (1856-1929). He is a first cousin of my great (x2) grandfather Julius Marcus Isenstein (1834-1915), and I had found the location of his grave online. His father was Liebmann Isenstein, a brother of my great (x3) grandfather Marcus Isenstein (1802-), and his mother was Elise Isenstein nee Güdemann. I felt that if I was going to be in Hannover, then I should try to find him. You also never know who might by resting nearby, or what information his gravestone might reveal.

Julius L Isenstein married Sophie Gotthelft (1869-1913) from Kassel, in Kassel in 1890. He was a prominent banker who led the Hannover branch of the Dresdner Bank from 1901 to 1926. By 1908, Julius was a member of the German Jewish Aid Association. He was also an active representative of the Jewish community in Hannover. During his life, he was a prominent chairman / board member of various company boards in Lower Saxony. Under his leadership, the Alexander Simon Bank and the Niedersächsische Bank were merged into the Dresdner Bank. He retired in 1926 but continued to live in the bank building at Rathenauplatz 4, Hannover, where he died in 1929.

It was interesting that each branch of the Isenstein family tree had a Julius, or someone with Julius as a middle name, in the same generation. I have found nineteen relatives with a first name of Julius in the family tree, including four Julius Isensteins.

The cemetery is extensive, beautiful and very well cared for, with its own light rail stop. I walked and searched for a long time without success, having not yet found a map of the cemetery. There were also few people around to ask. But, thanks to finding a determined, very dedicated and enormously helpful groundskeeper, I found the physical location of Julius' grave. The groundskeeper set out on his tractor, and sometimes on foot, looking for the location, while I followed on foot behind. But there is no gravestone, possibly there never was one according to the cemetery administrator, who I met later back in the cemetery office.

Nevertheless, I was able to walk around the section where Julius rests. And it is a lovely location, surrounded by trees and well-manicured bushes, close to views of a very large lake, complete with many swans and ducks. With the beautiful green gardens around, including large sections of rhododendron plants, it is more like a botanical garden than a cemetery. My new groundskeeper friend, who speaks not a word of English, takes his work very seriously.

Stadtfriedhof Stöcken cemetery in Hannover
(Photo credit: David Marlow)

Uncovering their Names and Stories:

Several months after my visit I found that there is a significant tomb and monument dedicated to Julius and his wife Sophie in the cemetery, despite what the cemetery administrator told me. It is a shame that we did not find it on my visit to the cemetery in March.

Julius purchased the plot for the tomb in 1913 when Sophie died, and commissioned architect Albrecht Haupt to design the tomb monument, which evidently still stands on the bank of the pond, under pine trees and amongst the rhododendron bushes I saw on my visit. It was restored in 2006-2008 thanks to historian Peter Schulze, the Falkenreck Foundation and a 10,000 Euro donation from the Dresdner Bank.

12.0 The Krafts

My Kraft family lived for many years in and around the modern German state of Saxony-Anhalt, and in particular the towns of Calbe (Saale), Stassfurt and Magdeburg, as well as the city of Leipzig in Saxony, and later in Berlin:

Herman Kraft
Father of
V
Bernhardt Kraft (1820-1882)
Father of
V
Selmar Kraft (1863-1935)
Father of
V
Hanni Elkan nee Kraft (1897-1986)
Mother of
V
Ilse Bella Marlow nee Elkan (1926-1997)
Father of
V
David Marlow (1962-)

The Krafts of Calbe (Saale)

My family history in the town of Calbe commenced in 1810, with the arrival of my great (x3) grandfather, merchant Hermann Kraft.[556] Hermann established a "cloth, pattern and fashion goods shop" on what is now Friedensplatz in Calbe and, according to the 'Patriotic Volksblatt', he later relocated the business to Querstrasse 295, or what was later known as Kriebel Strasse.[557]

I arrived in Calbe, having driven from beautiful and historic Halberstadt. The towns could not be more different from each other. Calbe has unfortunately lost much of its historical charm. It is a small

---

[556] 'We remember Theodor Kraft and his son Walter', Gegen Dasver Gessen, Informationsstand, November 2020
[557] *Beitrage zur Geschichte de Juden in Calbe (Saale)*, Hanns Schwachenwalde, Manuskriptabzug, 1988, p.9

Uncovering their Names and Stories:

town in the current state of Saxony-Anhalt on the Saale River, about 25 km southeast of the city of Magdeburg. Modern Calbe has a population of just over 8,000. Historically it was a railway junction. Today there are still open paddocks a few hundred metres from the centre of town. It is not a big place.

There have been Jews, though not continuously, living in Calbe since the 14th century. The Jewish school and synagogue were eventually built on Tuchmacherstrasse and Am Wassertor Alley, but in 1495 almost all the Jews were expelled from the Archbishopric of Magdeburg, including in Calbe, by Archbishop Ernst. A few Jews stayed temporarily over the following centuries. By the end of the 18th century, there were probably no Jews living in the town.[558]

Through the civil upheaval in German-speaking lands initiated by Napoleon, German Jews received civil rights. For example, they no longer had to live in ghettos and could pursue middle-class jobs. Thereafter, there was a small wave of immigration of Jews into Calbe between 1808 and 1812 and again in 1822. They took the oath of citizenship and paid "6 thalers, 12 silver groschen [559] and 6 pfennigs".[560]

These new Jewish citizens in town included two merchants, Lazarus Steinthal, possibly from my Steinthal family in Gröbzig, and my great (x3) grandfather Hermann Kraft.[561] Within a decade, Hermann had met and married Johanna Beer (1791-)[562] and together they had a son, my great (x2) grandfather Bernhardt Kraft (1820-1882) who became a successful merchant in Calbe, and a daughter Fanny Kraft (1830-1911).

---

[558] 'Calbe (Sachsen-Anhalt)', xn--jdische-gemeinden-22b.de/index.php/gemeinden/c-d/75-calbe-sachsen-anhalt
[559] Groschen were a monetary unit in Austria until introduction of the Euro in 2002 and thalers were a German silver coin
[560] Historischer rundgang Calbe ladenapotheke (Historical tour of Calbe pharmacy) website (historischerrundgangcalbe.keepfree.de/4ladenapotheke.htm)
[561] ibid. and Hanns Schwachenwalde (1988)
[562] This marriage needs 100% confirmation, but it seems very likely given the evidence to date

There is not much to be found about Herman and Johanna's life in Calbe. But Fanny's gravestone identifies her as 'Fräulein' which is an 'unmarried woman', confirming what I had previously understood, that she had never married. I found Fanny's grave in Leipzig, by accident, as I was looking for my great grandparents' graves in the Alte Jüdische Friedhof. Her gravestone also included the epithet in German 'Here lies our beloved Auntie'. This suggests that the gravestone was most likely arranged by her nephew Selmar, as he lived with his family in Leipzig at the time, most likely with input from his siblings. Fanny was probably living with Selmar and Frieda in her later years.

The 1857 census counted 35 Jews in Calbe, but these were probably the heads of households, so the total Jewish population was likely to have been significantly higher. The community had increased to 48 members of the local synagogue congregation by 1880.[563]

My great (x2) grandfather Bernhardt Kraft
(Source: Dan Rotman)

Bernhardt Kraft (1820-1882) married Helena Steinthal (1824-1871) from Gröbzig between the late 1840s and early 1850s, establishing a home in Calbe. They may have met through Helena's possible

---

[563] Hanns Schwachenwalde (1988)

Uncovering their Names and Stories:

relative Lazarus Steinthal who arrived in Calbe about the same time as Hermann.[564] Helena Kraft's mother was Chaichen Samson, and her father was Moses Steinthal from the Lazarus-Steinthal family from Gröbzig. Thankfully, most of Bernhardt and Helena's children were a generation too far away to have suffered from the Nazi regime, except for their second youngest child Theodor.

Bernhardt and Helena had eight children in Calbe, Therese (1853-), Bertha (1854-1913), Edmund (Eduard 1855-1916), Emma (1857-1935), Max (1861-1901), Selmar (1863-1935), Theodor (1864-1943) and Richard (1867-). Selmar was my great grandfather, and as mentioned above, he later moved to and lived most of his life in Leipzig, a much larger city.

My great (x2) grandmother Helena Kraft nee Steinthal
(Source: Dan Rotman)

Bernhardt and Helena and all their children are listed in the 1867 Prussian census for Calbe. It is a substantial household with their eight children, and an "unrelated" young woman Johanne Würfel aged 23, who may have been a live-in housekeeper or nanny. The same 1867 census identifies Bernhardt's mother Johanna and his sister Fanny living together at another residence, but no Hermann.

---

[564] ibid.

He had probably passed away by then and would have been buried in the Calbe Jewish cemetery.[565]

My great grandparents, Selmar Kraft and Frieda Kraft nee Isenstein (1865-1930) owned and ran a department store business in Leipzig. It was based at 10 Lindenauer Markt with his office and warehouse on the ground floor and included his home upstairs on the first floor. The building still exists in place having undergone a lovely sympathetic renovation, and it sits opposite the open-air fresh food market in the Lindenauer Markt square. Trams travel past the building, as they have on Lindenauer Markt since 1881. My experience with trams back home in Melbourne, helped keep me safe while I was taking photos of the old Kraft family building from across the road.

Selmar's sister Emma married Adolf Hassmann (1867-) and had three children, Margarethe Käthe (1893-1943), Alphons (1888-1974) and Dr Bruno Hassmann (-1917). Alphons worked as a fur merchant, married Hedwig (1877-) and had a son Sigurt Hassmann (-1952). Margarethe Käthe married a man named Ehrenfried and they moved to Breslau and then Amsterdam. Dr Bruno married non-Jew Gertrude Glaesser (1895-1988) from Königsberg, East Prussia. Margarethe Käthe, Alphons and Dr Bruno were some of my maternal grandmother's first cousins.

Dr Bruno Hassmann served as a medical officer in World War 1 and was killed serving his country in 1917. His name appears on the large 1914-1918 memorial in the New Jewish cemetery in Leipzig, which I saw on my visit in March 2024. Margarethe Käthe was deported from Amsterdam to be murdered in Sobibor, and her son Günther Ehrenfried (1921-1941) was murdered at Mauthausen. Alphons survived, escaping to England where he lived to the age of 86, although he did visit New York and Rio de Janeiro in 1962-63.

Through my research, I found my Canadian cousin Prof Rhoda Hassmann (1948-), who is the granddaughter of Dr Bruno Hassmann. Her father was Bruno's son Helmut Hassmann (1913-1998), who married Mary Byrne (1920-1989), a non-Jewish Scot.

---

[565] Bernhardt Kraft and Johanna Kraft census documents obtained from FamilySearch

Uncovering their Names and Stories:

Helmut changed his name to Michael Howard in 1947 to escape his German-Jewish past and potential racism or antisemitism. Though, like my father, his accent would have given him away immediately. Helmut escaped Germany in 1938 with the Gestapo on his tail because he had evidently criticised Hitler at a company dinner. He used a forged passport to escape, spent time in prisons in Yugoslavia and Italy, and ended up finding safety in England, thanks to a helpful Swiss Quaker. Also like my father, safety in England was far from perfect. He was interned as an enemy alien on the Isle of Mann and then in Canada. He served in the British Pioneer Corps, and the family moved to Canada from Britain in 1951.[566]

Rhoda, a sociologist with a specialty in human rights, changed her surname back to Hassmann from Howard after her father's passing. He had always hidden his past from people outside the family, and she did not want to distress him. She wrote, "I want to die as who I am."[567] Unsurprisingly, he had post-traumatic stress disorder from his experiences, having nightmares, and hid his Jewish background. Rhoda remembered that her father also felt guilty about not being able to save his favourite Jewish aunt, who must have been Margarethe Käthe Hassmann, who was murdered in Sobibor.

Selmar's sister, Bertha, married Max Jacobi around 1880 and had two children, Helen (1882-1948) and Julius (1883-). Julius married Margarete Reichmann (1884-) from the little town of Fannygrube, southern Poland in 1913. Helen married Adolf Weinschenker (1879-) from Russia, and they emigrated to the USA, having two children in New York City, Mary (1908-) and Leo (1916-1991). Leo married and had a son Lawrence. Emigrating to the USA around the start of the 20th century was a fortuitous move, which saved their children and future generations from the Holocaust.

The Jewish cemetery in Calbe was inaugurated on 7 May 1863, by Rabbi Dr Güdemann from Magdeburg. The land for the cemetery was purchased by a local farmer. I found the small Jewish Cemetery after an extensive search of the area but could not gain access. It is not signposted nor is its location particularly well-known. It is across

---

[566] 'Changing my Name', Rhoda Hassmann, The Globe and Mail (Toronto), 24 May 2000, pA20
[567] ibid.

the narrow street from the very large non-Jewish cemetery, which I walked around just in case I might stumble across the gravestone of a long lost relative. The Jewish Cemetery is surrounded by a high brick fence with a locked high cast iron gate, which were erected after the land was acquired for the cemetery in 1862.[568]

The cemetery was devastated, and gravestones destroyed in 1938. It was partially restored after 1945, but only eight gravestones were said to exist recently, "in a narrow row in the middle of the property."[569] I was still trying to find records of the remaining gravestones to see if they include family members. It seemed that any grave records or gravestones of my ancestors in Calbe had been lost to time and the devastation of Kristallnacht.

But I kept searching for records of my family in Calbe and for information on the gravestones in what remains of the Jewish Cemetery. When I approached the Calbe (Saale) City Council, they advised that the Jewish cemetery "no longer exists" and that they have very little archival material. After all, it is a very small town. They referred me to the nearby Schönebeck City archive, which holds regional records. The hunt continued.

Many very small towns in Germany have all or part of their council administration centralised to larger provincial or regional towns. For example, Gröbzig has been part of the town of Südliches Anhalt since 2010. Südliches Anhalt was formed from the merger of over 20 former municipalities/towns in Saxony-Anhalt.

Archivist Mathias Hille from the Schönebeck City Archives (Elbe) advised me that there are no official lists for the graves in the Calbe Jewish Cemetery, no registration books for the Schönebeck synagogue community, nor records for the cemetery. He further told me that "according to contemporary witnesses, around 40 people were buried in the cemetery between 1862/68 and 1939. Of the remaining gravestones, one is of Hugo Steiner, one of Jakob and one of Peter Zuckerberg."[570] The old cemetery is now private property.

---

[568] Alemannia-judaica.de/calbe_friedhof.htm
[569] ibid.
[570] Email from Mathias Hille from the Schönebeck City Archives (Elbe) 25 April 2024

Uncovering their Names and Stories:

Mathias, my new best friend in Schönebeck, literally went the extra mile and kindly drove 14 km down the road to Calbe and took photos inside the cemetery and the few surviving gravestones. Only a few are at all readable, and all are surrounded, and sometimes very much covered, neatly by flowers and shrubs. None appear to relate to my family, but undoubtedly, I have ancestors under the garden there, though unmarked. I seem unlikely to determine which family members lie hidden there.

My great (x3) grandparents Hermann and Johanna Kraft, and my great (x2) grandparents Bernhardt and Helena Kraft are quite likely buried in the Calbe Jewish cemetery. They died in Calbe, but I cannot yet definitively prove where they were laid to rest. At least I found Bernhardt's sister Fanny's grave in Leipzig.

Doing this family research, I sometimes feel that I am a poor detective. Columbo, Endeavour Morse, Jessica Fletcher and Vera Stanhope can all solve the most complex of mysteries in an hour, while taking breaks to smoke a cigar, have a cup of tea or stare at the scenery. It can take me months to unravel the smallest of clues. When stuck on a research path, I sometimes feel more like Scooby Doo than Hercule Poirot.

Theodor Kraft in Magdeburg

Magdeburg is the capital of the modern German state of Saxony-Anhalt. It is in eastern-central Germany on the Elbe River, with a population today of nearly quarter of a million people.[571] It was heavily bombed by the allies in World War 2 and spent the Cold War as part of East Germany.

There were Jews in Magdeburg as early as 965 CE. A Jewish religious school was established in 1834, and a Jewish burial society (Chevra Kadisha) began in 1839, signifying a serious Jewish community was in place. The Jewish community gradually grew from 330 in 1817 to 1,000 in 1859, and 1,815 by 1885, growing to about 3,200 by 1928. The synagogue was built in 1851 and destroyed on Kristallnacht. But

---

[571] 'Magdeburg', Gotthard Deutsch and Max Schlossinger, JewishEncyclopedia.com

by May 1939, there were only 679 Jews left. Some Jews married to Christians survived, but those who could not flee Germany, usually ended up in tragic places like the Buchenwald Concentration Camp near Weimar in central Germany, Theresienstadt or Auschwitz.[572]

Selmar's brother Theodor Kraft was born in Calbe but raised his family in Magdeburg. He married Kathinka Sonder (1870-1935) from Magdeburg in 1895. She was the orphaned daughter of a Stadtlengsfeld cattle dealer, Abraham Sonder (1823-1884) and Sara Sonder nee Ruppel (1826-1884). Theodor and Kathinka married in Magdeburg and had four children, Else (1895-1995), Walther (1897-1943), Margrete (1898-1984), and Gertrude (1902-1972). Theodor was murdered in Theresienstadt during the Holocaust, but Kathinka died a few years before the war.

Their son Walther was murdered in Auschwitz in 1943, but luckily their three daughters survived to live longer lives, especially Else who nearly reached 100.

Else Kraft married the widower Alfred Schäfer (1884-1955) in Magdeburg in 1920. They escaped with their family to the USA, eventually settling in Los Angeles. Alfred had three sons with his first wife, Klaus (1913-1981), Fritz (1914-2014) and Horst (1918-1918). Alfred's first wife was Hedwig Frankenstein (1889-1918) who sadly died giving birth to Horst, and Horst only survived a few days. Else and Alfred had two children together, Hannelore (1921-2010) and Rudolf Leo (1924-2020).

Rudolph emigrated to the USA in 1939, settling in Los Angeles, along with most of the Schäfer family, including his parents and sister Hannelore. He married Rhoda Jean Lushing (1927-) from Los Angeles in 1949 and worked as a construction estimator.

Hannelore escaped Germany in January 1939, on the *SS Orinoco*, arriving in Los Angeles in October 1939 via Havana, where her family awaited approval to enter the USA.[573] Hannelore married New

---

[572] 'Magdeburg', Jewish Virtual Library, A Project of AICE
[573] 'Orinoco Sketches', Gabriel Kahane, Content.thespco.org/music/concert-library/composition/orinoco-sketches-for-string-orchestra-gabriel-kahane; and 'An Aural Family

Uncovering their Names and Stories:

Yorker Murray Kahane (1922-1993) in Brooklyn, New York in 1945, but they lived most of the rest of their lives in Los Angeles. They had three children, Daniel (1952-), Jeffrey (1956-) and Debbie (1957-). I have met Jeffrey online, thanks to his being my number three match on Ancestry DNA. Jeffrey is a classical concert pianist and former musical director of the Los Angeles Chamber Orchestra, and current music director of the Sarasota Music Festival. He and his wife Martha, who he met when they were both aged ten at a 'sleep-away camp', have a daughter Annie (1981-) and a son Gabriel (1981-), who is also a prominent musician, and a singer-songwriter.

I was delighted in August 2024 to be able to meet our newly discovered cousin Gabriel, when he performed in the beautiful Melbourne Recital Centre, at the start of his latest international tour. Catching up online is terrific, but nothing can replace a face-to-face meeting, which we did after his show, along with my Melbourne-based cousin Dan Rotman, and his wife Julie. And the show was amazing. Gabriel and his on-stage partner Pekka Kuusisto performed remarkable pieces, with brilliant chemistry, including their entertaining banter. Whether by design or by coincidence, one song they performed was actually titled 'Cousins'.

Last year, Jeffrey Kahane and the Kansas City Symphony performed 'Heirloom', a concerto written by Jeff's son Gabriel. Gabriel described it as an "aural family scrapbook, exploring, in its three movements, a series of inheritances".[574] In his work, Gabriel explores the emotional impact of his grandmother being torn between her love of German music and literature, and the devastation of the Holocaust, as well as how those emotions can be transmitted across generations. This is another way of exploring the intergenerational trauma affecting many families of Holocaust survivors.

Theodor Kraft's daughter Margarete and her Poland-born husband Herman Abraham (1889-1948) moved to my hometown of Melbourne, Australia with their two daughters Henriette Ruth (1925-1991) and Kathlyn (Kate) (1930-2023) just before the war. Kathlyn died only recently, having married Louis Rotman (1929-2017) from

---

Scrapbook: Gabriel Kahane's *Heirloom*', The Saint Paul Chamber Orchestra Blog, 22 November 2023
[574] 'Heirloom', Gabriel Kahane on Tumbler, 2023

Melbourne, building a life in Australia, and raising three children, including my friend, cousin and fellow genealogical junkie Dan Rotman.

Dan is number four in my matches on Ancestry DNA and my top DNA match on MyHeritage. He is my friend, cousin and genealogical comrade in crime. A lot of what I have in the Kraft family tree comes from extensive work by Dan over a couple of decades. Having someone you can share research discoveries and workload with is a tremendous benefit in collating a family history. A team can achieve so much more than a solo effort. Dan has also collated a great collection of photos of relatives in the Kraft and Rotman families.

Theodor's youngest child Gertrude Kraft married Otto Konirsch (1898-1974) from Chomutov in Bohemia, Czechoslovakia. Gertrude and Otto had two children, Ruth (1931-) and Gershon (1935-), who were both born in Berlin. The family escaped Germany, moving to Rio de Janeiro and eventually settled in what is now Israel. Ruth married Fritz Moses (1925-) from Berlin and had three children who all ended up raising families in Australia. Gershon married Loretta Simon (1936-) from Modena, Italy. They also had three children who raised families of their own. Gertrude lived to the age of 70 and died in Nahariya in northern Israel. I have lucky to have met Gershon (Gert) Konirsch online, who lives on a kibbutz, and some of the Moses family descendants including Ruben and Arie, who are now living in Melbourne.

Theodor Kraft became a prominent businessman in Calbe, advertising in local newspapers, selling products like scarves, shawls and other clothing items. But from 1880, Jews were often leaving Calbe for the much larger city of Magdeburg, which provided better economic prospects. Theodor and his brother Max both left Calbe for Magdeburg, most likely in the mid-1880s. Theodor opened fashion shops, moving into shoes, furs and hats, as well as other clothing.[575]

Max Kraft had a manufactured goods and clothing store, but sadly died in 1901 at the age of 40. His wife Elise Simon (1865-1894) only

---

[575] 'We remember Theodor Kraft and his son Walter', Gegen Dasver Gessen, Informationsstand, November 2020

Uncovering their Names and Stories:

lived to the age of 29, leaving behind two of their children Leonhard (1890-) aged four and Helena (1888-) aged six. Max married Elise's sister Emmi in 1895. Max and Emmi's son was the poet Paul Kraft (1896-1922), some of whose work is still available despite his dying at the age of 26. Sadly, Emmi was murdered by the Nazis in Riga, Latvia in 1942.[576] Helene married Max Sternfeld (1878-1944).

Theodor and his son Walther were both operating similar businesses in Magdeburg by the 1930s. The anti-Jewish laws under the Nazi regime gradually took away their home, businesses and livelihoods, as well as their identity as Germans. Kathinka died on 1 September 1935 at the age of 65, and her husband and son were forced by the Nazi regime to move in with a married couple.

Sadly, Theodor was deported on 25 November 1942 and murdered on 9 March 1943 in Theresienstadt. Theodor's son Walther was deported via Berlin to Auschwitz on 23 February 1943, where he was murdered. 'Stolpersteine' memorials have been dedicated to Theodor and Walther in Magdeburg by an anonymous donor, and they lie outside the 'Judenhaus' from where they were deported.[577]

When I visited Magdeburg, I took photos of their (Walter and Theodor's) Stolpersteine, the Judenhaus where they were forced to live, and the building at 119 Halberstädter Strasse where I saw Theodor and Kathinka with their family in a lovely family photo, which their great grandson Dan Rotman had kindly provided to me.

The lovely people at the Magdeburg City Library extracted a rare manuscript from their archives (from 1988, so not ancient), which I was desperately after, on the history of the Jews in Calbe, 'Beitrage zur Geschichte de Juden in Calbe (Saale)' by Hanns Schwachenwalde. It is a typed document, and I had found it very difficult to source. I had contacted many libraries, museums and archives around the world looking for a copy, as it was referenced in various articles that talked about the Jews of Calbe. The manuscript mentions my great (x3) grandfather Hermann Kraft's (Selmar and Theodor's grandfather) arrival in Calbe, and his business interests in the early to

---

[576] ibid.
[577] 'We remember Theodor Kraft and his son Walter', Gegen Dasver Gessen, Informationsstand, November 2020

mid 1800s. It was very useful. I read through it on the first floor of the library. Notes taken. Copies made.

Theodor Kraft and family at home - 119 Halberstädter Strasse, Magdeburg in 1916 – left to right Trude, Grete, Kathinka, Theodor and Else Kraft
(Source: Dan Rotman)

Germany dealing with its past

There were at one time about 30 Jewish congregations across what is now the German state of Saxony-Anhalt. Many of my Steinthal and Kraft family ancestors came from this area, including from Calbe, Gröbzig, Magdeburg, Stassfurt and Bernburg. Only 119 Jews survived the Holocaust in the city of Magdeburg, out of a pre-war Jewish population of 2,300. The only synagogues in Saxony-Anhalt to survive the Holocaust, were in Wörlitz and Gröbzig.[578] I visited both on my research road trip.

---

[578] 'Jewish Communities in Saxony-Anhalt', Dr Marc Jarzebowski, DMJ website, 27 April 2021

Uncovering their Names and Stories:

The two synagogues both now house small museums. The Wörlitz Synagogue was built by the Duke of Anhalt-Dessau in 1790 as a symbol of tolerance, and acts as an ornament in the beautiful Dessau-Wörlitz Garden Realm, on the Wörlitzer See, a very pretty lake. The synagogue was attacked on Kristallnacht and has since been converted into a museum. The Garden Realm is now a UNESCO World Heritage site. The synagogue is somewhere my local ancestors may have occasionally attended, at least until the Gröbzig Synagogue was completed a few years later.

The Gröbzig Synagogue was consecrated in 1796, and its surrounding buildings were expanded continuously from 1858.

Martin Luther was renowned for his role in the Protestant Enlightenment, Lutheranism and his antisemitism, especially later in life. The Nazis used Luther's antisemitism as a justification for the regime's Jewish persecution. Luther's 65,000-word book "Von den Juden und Ihren Lügen" (On the Jews and their Lies), originally published in 1543, was republished many times from 1933 onwards and was used by the Nazi's to justify their racial agenda.[579]

The Nazis exploited Martin Luther's 450th birthday on November 10, 1933, celebrating Luther's milestone birthday with a national 'German Luther Day'. A plaque specially minted for the day, quotes Martin Luther from 1521, "I was born for my Germans, I want to serve them". The plaque was one of about 180 exhibits in a 2018 exhibition on Luther, which explored his dark side.[580]

At the rear of the Stadtkirche (City Church) in Wittenberg in Saxony-Anhalt, famous for Martin Luther, is a carved sandstone sculpture depicting a Rabbi "lifting the tail of a pig to look for his Talmud".[581]

---

[579] 'Luther's dark side - and how the Nazis abused it for their ideology' article on "Luther's Words Everywhere... - Martin Luther in National Socialism" exhibition, which opened on February 25, 2018 in Saarbrücken's Ludwigskirche,
luther2017.de/neuigkeiten/luthers-dunkle-seite-und-wie-die-nazis-sie-fuer-ihre-ideologie-missbrauchten/index.html
[580] ibid.
[581] 'Hatred in Plain Sight', Carol Schaefer, <u>Smithsonian Magazine</u>, October 2020

Other Jews are around the sow to suckle. This is the site of the first celebration of Mass in German, which was traditionally in Latin. This Judensau (Jewish Sow) was a common antisemitic depiction of Jews by Christians on churches in cities around Germany, notably in Saxony-Anhalt in Magdeburg, Calbe and Zerbst.[582]

The Judensau was a common form of medieval iconography. Sculptures of Jews and pigs started appearing in architecture in the 1300s. Still today, between twenty and forty Judensau sculptures still exist on German churches, despite efforts by some to have them removed.[583]

In recent years, there has been debate in Germany about these antisemitic sculptures, which you would have thought would not take much debate to remove. After all, Germany has taken many steps since the war to repair its image.

After the war, Nazi swastikas (Hakenkreuz), Nazi flags and other symbols of the regime were removed. Germany paid nearly US$90 billion in reparations, mainly to Jewish Holocaust survivors. Museums, monuments and memorials across Germany were built to commemorate the murdered Jews, including the relatively new Holocaust Memorial and Jewish Museum in Berlin. Nazi salutes are illegal in Germany, and so is calling someone a 'Judensau'.

The impressive Berlin Jewish Museum was opened in 2001 and Berlin's Memorial to the Murdered Jews of Europe, with its underground information centre was opened in 2005. Its exhibition on the Holocaust attracts half a million visitors annually.

There are also 'Stolpersteine' in 500 German towns and cities. These are small (10 cm) brass cube plaques recognising Jewish Holocaust victims, set into the ground outside the buildings from which they were taken.[584] While visiting Magdeburg, I took photos of

---

[582] 'Jewish Communities in Saxony-Anhalt', Dr Marc Jarzebowski, DMJ website, 27 April 2021
[583] 'German church goes to high court to take down perverse anti-Semitic carvings', Toby Axelrod, <u>Times of Israel</u>, 26 June 2020
[584] 'Hatred in Plain Sight', Carol Schaefer, <u>Smithsonian Magazine</u>, October 2020

Uncovering their Names and Stories:

Stolpersteine for a friend and a cousin in Australia, commemorating their lost family members.

The Stolpersteine project was initiated by the non-Jewish artist Gunter Demnig in 1992, aiming to commemorate individuals who fell victim to the Nazi regime at their last home or workplace, including those who suffered forced euthanasia, deportation to concentration camps, or escaped by emigration or suicide. About 100,000 Stolpersteine have been installed up to mid 2023 around Europe.[585] The majority commemorate Jewish victims, but many have been installed for Sinti and Romani, Poles, homosexuals, disabled people and many others who were persecuted, tortured and/or murdered by the Nazi regime.

The Stolpersteine Project is an important and wonderful initiative. As Gunter Demnig himself said, "A person is only forgotten when his or her name is forgotten."[586]

But despite these efforts, across the country, and especially in Saxony-Anhalt, far-right nationalism has been rising. In one antisemitic attack, a Jewish business owner said dozens of far-right thugs threw rocks and bottles at his business, and shouted, "Get out of Germany, you Judensau!".[587]

In the 2016 Saxony-Anhalt election, the ultra-nationalist party Alternative für Deutschland (AfD) achieved 24.2 percent of the vote. And the AfD have had some electoral successes in various German states during 2024.

In October 2019, a far-right gunman attacked a synagogue in Halle, killing two people and wounding two others.[588] On my road trip, I stopped in Halle, just northwest of Leipzig, to visit the lovely Halle synagogue. But I did not visit because the synagogue was lovely. I

---

[585] 'In Nürnberg liegt jetzt Europas 100,.000 Stolperstein', NN.de, Retrieved 2 October 2023.
[586] Quoted in 'I can't forget what the Nazis did to my family, but I can be grateful to a repentant Germany', Rabbi Michael Meyerstein, JTA, 12 April 2023
[587] 'Hatred in Plain Sight', Carol Schaefer, Smithsonian Magazine, October 2020
[588] ibid.

wanted to pay my respects, because the Halle synagogue was the scene of that horrific right-wing extremist attack. Luckily the attacker was prevented from entering the building. The perpetrator expressed no remorse and was a Holocaust denier. The judge described it as a "cowardly attack" and he was given a life sentence.[589] As I walked around the area, I found a memorial plaque dedicated to the victims, Jana Lange and Kevin Schwarze, on the brick fence surrounding the shule. One victim was simply a passer-by and the other was in a nearby kebab shop, murdered because the attacker could not access the synagogue.

More recently, on Tuesday 25 June 2024, Felix Klein, Germany's commissioner for fighting antisemitism, reported that hate crimes against Jews in Germany had increased 83% year on year in 2023, to 4,782 incidents. Most of this was hate speech, but there were hundreds of cases of "physical violence to people and property". Klein described this as a "catastrophic rise in hate crimes against Jews".[590]

But things are very different to the 1930s. Now, the German government opposes the antisemites, rather than leading them. It has declared a zero tolerance for antisemitism. On Thursday 26 June 2024, it was reported in the Financial Times that Germany would now be requiring that applicants for citizenship declare that Israel has a right to exist, as well as requiring declarations on antisemitism and Jewish life in Germany.[591] This was already being discussed in Germany when I visited in March.

Meanwhile, the Judensau sculptures remain. Petitions and calls for their removal have failed to date. Opponents of the Judensau have tried using defamation laws to remove the sculptures, arguing that they defame the Jewish community.

The court in Wittenberg found that an explanatory memorial plaque added in the 1980s, and signage about Martin Luther and medieval

---

[589] 'Life sentence for Halle synagogue shooter who killed 2 in Yom Kippur rampage', Times of Israel, 21 December 2020

[590] 'New German citizens must declare Israel's right to exist', Sam Jones, Financial Times, 26 June 2024

[591] ibid.

antisemitism offset the inherent antisemitism of the sculpture. The judges said, "You can neutralize the original intent with commentary on the historical context…This is the case with the Wittenberg sculpture."[592] This can be paralleled to arguments in the USA where some people argue that explanatory information on signage can offset the negative messages inherent in glorifying a Confederate general or a slave-owner with a statue.

This has also been a similar issue in Bernhardt Kraft's hometown of Calbe in recent years. Calbe's St Stephani Church removed a sculpture of a Judensau for restoration, "but decided to retire it altogether".[593] Judges ordered that the sculpture be reinstalled. The parish complied but covered the sculpture instead of adding apologetic or explanatory signage. As the town mayor Sven Hause said, "I don't think anyone really wanted to have to see this chimera again."[594] This solution in Calbe may be seen as a metaphor for the strategy of parts of Central and Eastern Europe who seek to cover up some of their antisemitic histories, rather than come to terms with the reality.[595]

Selmar and Frieda Kraft in Leipzig

My great grandfather Selmar Kraft married Frieda Isenstein (1865-1930) in Leipzig in the late 1880s. They then lived in Stassfurt near Calbe for some time, and had four children, Bruno Bernhard (1890-1940), Helene (1891-1970), Else (1892-1942) and my grandmother Hanni (1897-1986) who was born in Leipzig. The family settled in Leipzig between 1892 and 1897, where they raised their family and grew the family business.

The formal Jewish community of Leipzig was only founded in 1847. Documents over the centuries mention Jews in Leipzig since the Middle Ages, however it has only been since the mid 1800s that Jews

---

[592] 'Hatred in Plain Sight', Carol Schaefer, <u>Smithsonian Magazine</u>, October 2020
[593] ibid.
[594] ibid.
[595] 'German church goes to high court to take down perverse anti-Semitic carvings', Toby Axelrod, <u>Times of Israel</u>, 26 June 2020

were allowed to settle there. Before that time, Jews mainly visited Leipzig as attendees of the local trade fair. There were Jews living in the city at various times over history, but they came and went with political circumstances and local discriminatory laws. [596]

My great grandparents Frieda and Selmar Kraft
(Source: Dan Rotman)

Within a century, Leipzig had the largest Jewish community in Saxony and the sixth largest in Germany, complete with synagogues and Jewish schools. However, by the end of World War 2, emigration and the Holocaust had slashed Leipzig's Jewish population from 13,000 to just 24. A few returned after the liberation of the

---

[596] Das Jüdisches Leipzig: Ein Kleiner Stadtführer, (Jewish Leipzig: A Short City Guide), Christian Böwe, Leipzig, 2013

Uncovering their Names and Stories:

concentration camps, but many later headed west after 1950 as Leipzig fell into East Germany (GDR), and the numbers dwindled to only 30 by 1990. More recently, immigration from the former USSR has given the city a Jewish population injection with the reunification of Germany.[597] Today, Leipzig has a general population over half a million.

Selmar Kraft had his department store at 10 Lindenauer Markt, Leipzig where he lived and operated his business from 1900 until at least 1933.[598] Lindenauer Markt is in Lindenau, which is on the western side of inner Leipzig. Selmar and Frieda lived on the first floor of the four-storey building with their family from 1900 until their deaths. Their department store was on the ground floor. Reading the Leipziger Volkszeitung local paper from 19 July 1909, one can see an advertisement for Selmar's store offering real new beds.[599] He advertised frequently in local newspapers.

The building was built in 1900, and still houses commercial premises on the ground floor, with 22 apartments on the upper three floors. It is a Wilhelmian[600] style building as are many surrounding buildings, and it was extensively renovated in 2010-2012. It has a red-brown clinker brick façade and many opulent ornamental details and highlights.[601]

Selmar died of natural causes in 1935 in Leipzig, and Frieda died in 1930 in Bad Salzungen, 228 km east of Leipzig. This was documented in the local Jewish community newspaper, the Gemeindeblatt der Israelitischen Religionsgemeinde zu Leipzig.[602] At least they were not personally inflicted with the worst of the Nazi era. Formal

---

[597] ibid.
[598] Ortsblatt-Leipzig – Leipziger westen, (Leipzig local newspaper - Leipzig west), January 2016, p3
[599] Reelle neue Betten
[600] The Wilhelmian era covers the period from 1890 to 1918, comprising the reign of Kaiser Wilhelm II from the resignation of Bismarck until the end of World War 1.
[601] Iks-holding.de/referenzen/historisches-wohnensemble/
[602] Community newsletter of the Israelite religious community in Leipzig, 13 June 1930 p7 and 16 August 1935 p 4

deportations of Leipzig Jews commenced on 21 January 1941 and continued into 1945.

10 Lindenauer Markt, Leipzig - once housed the home and department store of Selmar & Frieda Kraft:
(Photo credit: David Marlow)

I was delighted when I finally found their graves in the Neue Jüdische Friedhof in Leipzig on my road trip, confirming their dates of birth and death, as well as their final place of rest. I took photos of my great grandparents' gravestones and placed small stones on their gravestones. It was quite an emotional experience, after walking for hours around many graves in Leipzig, falling over old tree roots and

Uncovering their Names and Stories:

uneven ground, not sure I would find them. The Neue Jüdische Friedhof was only opened in 1928, so they were amongst the first to be buried there. It is currently still used for funerals.

It is an old custom in Judaism, dating back to at least medieval times, to place small stones on gravestones rather than flowers.[603] I always liked this, as flowers wilt but stones last. Finding a stone on a family member's gravestone can provide some comfort, as it tells you that someone visited, mourned and cared for that person. I travelled around Germany with a small number of stones in my cargo pants, picking up a few small stones here and there along my travels.

As one Jewish American memorial company nicely states it, "The Hebrew word for pebble is also a word that means 'bond.' By placing a stone on the headstone, it bonds the deceased with the visitors. Some people take extra care in choosing the right stone. It's possible that it may have special significance or that it came from a place that reminds them of their loved one."[604] I put small stones on quite a few family gravestones across Germany as I found them, including on the gravestones of four of my great grandparents: Frieda & Selmar Kraft in Leipzig and Adolf & Sophie Lennhoff in Wuppertal.

Meanwhile, in the Alte Jüdische Friedhof in Leipzig, I found the graves of Fanny Kraft, the sister of my great (x2) grandfather Bernhardt Kraft, and the grave of Eduard Isenstein (1842-1923) from Hannover. He was Frieda's uncle, and I thought he had died in Berlin, but here he was. Eduard is also a brother of Captain George Isenstein who fought in the American Civil War.

While in Leipzig, I remembered that my mother, Ilse held a long-lasting grudge against her grandfather Selmar Kraft. She told the story to me a couple of times that as a child, she was visiting his store with her favourite doll, and a customer told Selmar how much they liked her doll. As my mother remembered it, Selmar took the doll from my mother and sold it to the customer.

---

[603]'Why do Jews put stones on graves?', Yehuda Shurpin, Chabad.org, chabad.org/library/article_cdo/aid/3002484/jewish/Why-Do-Jews-Put-Stones-on-Graves.htm
[604] Foxmemorials.com/placing-a-stone-on-a-loved-ones-grave/

Selmar and Frieda's fourth child, baby Hanni was the grandmother I grew up with, known as 'Nana' to me and my siblings. Two of their children escaped the Nazis, Helene escaping to New York and Hanni to Melbourne, Australia. Both lived long lives. Two unfortunately, were not so lucky. Their big brother Bruno was murdered at Sachsenhausen Concentration Camp in January 1940, after being arrested in May 1939. Else was deported in 1942 to the Riga Ghetto in Latvia, where she was murdered by the Nazis. Their mother Frieda, and Else and Hanni bore striking resemblances to each other, especially around the eyes.

The tragic life of Uncle Bruno Kraft

My grand uncle Bruno Bernard Kraft (1890-1940) was the oldest child and only son of my great grandparents Selmar and Frieda Kraft. Like his sisters Helene and Else, he was born in Stassfurt, while his baby sister Hanni (my Nana) was born in Leipzig. Stassfurt is nearly 100 km northwest of Leipzig but only 19 km southwest of Calbe, where Selmar was born. It currently has a population of about 30,000.

Stassfurt is of note, apart for my grand uncle Bruno, because it is one of the places that the Nazis hid artwork to protect them from Allied bombing. The collection of the Kaiser-Friedrich Museum (now the Kulturhistorisches Museum) in Magdeburg was hidden in a salt mine in Stassfurt. The art was stored 460m down a shaft of the Neu-Stassfurt salt mine. Hidden in a separate shaft, was a BMW jet engine factory making engines for the Luftwaffe. Most of the artwork was destroyed in a sequence of fires, some say to cover up thefts of some of the art.[605]

Bruno would have had his barmitzvah in Leipzig in 1903. I have a photo of him as a young man, dressed very smartly in a dinner suit, attending a family wedding.

Professionally, Bruno worked as a sales representative, likely working some time for the Kraft family business until the early 1930s. After

---

[605] Monumentsmenandwomenfnd.org/join-the-hunt/wwii-most-wanted-van-gogh

Uncovering their Names and Stories:

that, the business would have been Aryanized like other Jewish businesses across Germany.

Bruno Kraft as a young man
(Source: Dan Rotman)

Bruno served on the frontline in the German army in World War 1 and was a proud veteran, being a member of the RjF: the German Union of Jewish Front Soldiers.[606] He served in the Prussian Army's Infantry Liebregiment 117 and was reported wounded in December 1914 at the age of 24. It is likely he was wounded in the First Battle of the Marne, east of Paris, in September 1914, which is where his regiment was fighting at the time. About 250,000 troops were killed, wounded or taken prisoner on both sides in that battle. In 1917, he was listed as captured, so he would have spent time as a POW as well.

He married Erna Knöfel (1893-) in 1924 and they had a baby Johann Günter Kraft in 1923, but little Johann only survived until 16 June 1924.[607]

Bruno lost his mother Frieda in 1930 and his father Selmar in 1935. He lived as a Jew under the Nazi regime from 1933, with all the persecution, alienation and dehumanisation that entailed. By the age of 45, he had lost his parents and his only child.

---

[606] Reichsbund Jüdischer Frontsoldaten
[607] Saale Zeitung: allgemeine Zeitung fur Mitteldeutschland, 8 June 1924, page 12

On 22 September 1938, less than two months before Kristallnacht, Bruno wrote a letter to the US Veterans Administration through the German Consulate in St Louis Missouri, trying to find the descendants of his 'Uncle' George Isenstein in the USA. George had signed-up in St Louis.

Captain George Isenstein was a brother of Bruno's maternal grandfather Julius Marcus Isenstein (1834-1914), so George was really the uncle of Bruno's mother Frieda, and thus Bruno's great-uncle.[608]

Bruno wrote, "I am anxious to find out whether sons and daughters or grandchildren of George Isenstein still live in the USA. Isenstein was my great-uncle. You will be rendering your assistance to a 'Jewish soldier of German Army in War 1914-18'."[609]

Clearly, Bruno was seeking an American relative to help sponsor his and his wife's emigration / escape from Nazi Germany. His parents were already gone, and Uncle George had died in the USA in 1902.

These were desperate times, and only became worse with the great pogrom two months later. To their credit, the German Consul did write to the US Veterans Administration trying to find George's relatives, but they could not provide any assistance.[610]

George's three sons Carl, Julius and John Isenstein, would have been in their mid to late 70s, if they were still alive, so the chances of finding them were limited. No American relatives were found, and Bruno's fate was sealed.

The Mapping the Lives records show that Bruno was arrested by the Gestapo in May 1939 and imprisoned briefly at Prison 1, 47 Moltkestrasse, Leipzig.[611] In 1933, it had been an early concentration

---

[608] Bruno Kraft letter and responses in the Captain George Isenstein files in the Shapell Roster of Jewish Service in the American Civil War, Shapell Manuscript Foundation
[609] ibid. Translated by the US Veterans Administration 17 October 1938.
[610] ibid.
[611] 'Early concentration camp Prison I in Leipzig', gedenkplaetze.info

camp for political opponents, but was now being used as a general prison, as well as for other purposes. Today, it is a residential building in Leipzig.

Bruno was soon transferred to the Sachsenhausen Concentration Camp.[612] The Sachsenhausen records in the Arolsen Archives and the Mapping the Lives records show that Bruno was imprisoned in Sachsenhausen in May 1939.[613] He was killed on 31 January 1940, but his official death record in the Arolsen Archives reports his cause of death as "physical weakness". He may have been worked to death. But death from torture, starvation, and straight-out murder were common at Sachsenhausen, as the museum there makes very clear. He was 49 years of age and had survived being wounded on the frontline in World War 1, only to have his country turn against him.

Helene Kraft Deutsch's family in the USA

Selmar and Frieda Kraft's second child and oldest daughter Helene (1891-1970) married Alfred Deutsch (1875-1936) in Leipzig on 7 August 1910. They had two daughters, Ilse (1911-1991) and Margot (1915-2006), both born in Leipzig. Helene moved to the USA in 1937, the year after her husband of 25 years Alfred died. She lived in New York until she died at the age of 79 in 1970.

Helene's daughter Ilse Deutsch married Erwin Krongold (1903-) in 1935 in Dresden. Ilse and Erwin lived in England for a while, where they had my cousin Prof Ralph Krongold (1944-) who now lives in Los Angeles. From England, the family moved to the USA.

Ralph and I have recently reconnected online, after not seeing each other for a couple of decades. Our grandmothers were sisters, and both our mothers were named Ilse.

Ilse Deutsch Krongold also had a daughter, Barbara Kanter Simon, who has a daughter Rachel (1992-). They live in New York City, which I have visited many times, visiting the US Book Fair almost annually when I was in the book business in Australia from 2003 to 2012. Unfortunately, I didn't know about them at the time. I

---

[612] Mappingthelives.org
[613] ibid. and Arolsen Archives.

connected with Barbara online after our Ancestry DNA hit a strong connection. She is my number two DNA match.

Helene's other daughter Margot married twice, first to Hans Newman (1906-1988) in Prague, and later to Barand Bromet (1906-) from the Netherlands. She lived in New York for most of her life, and had two children, Joan Bromet (1938-) and Jerry Bromet (1949-). Margot passed away in Palm Beach, Florida after a long life in 2006, aged 91. My sister Helen remembers meeting 'Joanie', who adopted many children, building a big family.

Else Kraft and the Krebs family

Selmar and Frieda Kraft's second daughter, Else (1892-1942) married Fedor Krebs (1883-1942) in Leipzig.[614] Else was one of my Nana's sisters. Fedor was born in Tarnowitz, Poland. Fedor and Else had two daughters Ann Siera nee Krebs (1921-2007) and Edith Bertha Leisner nee Krebs (1924-2010). Else and Fedor lived with the Krafts at 10 Lindenauer Markt in the 1920s. Ann and Edith both escaped the Holocaust on a Kindertransport, and never saw their parents again.[615]

Ann Krebs was married three times, firstly to a man with the surname Adler briefly in England, for about 35 years to Moritz Sieradzki (Mark or Moshe Siera: 1908-), and later in life to Heinz Fleischer (1911-). She had no children but was very close to her stepson Dan Eshel and her nephew David Leisner.

Ann's sister Edith Krebs married Elkan Leisner (1924-1976) from Halberstadt, and they had a few children, including David Leisner (1953-), who is now a friend, as well as a cousin. David is a musician, a leading classical guitarist and composer. He is "among the finest guitarists of all time", according to American Record Guide.[616] David

---

[614] It is important to note that there were two Else Krafts. Selmar's brother Theodor also named his eldest daughter Else (1895-1995).
[615] Email from David Leisner, grandson of Fedor and Else Krebs, 29 April 2024.
[616] 'World Renowned Guitarist, David Leisner, to Give Public Workshop', news.uark.edu/, University of Arkansas, April 24, 2017

Uncovering their Names and Stories:

is married to Ralph Jackson (1952-) and they live together in New York City with their new puppy Tofu.

Ann, Elkan and Edith all survived the war and lived in the USA until the end of their lives. Unfortunately, Else and Fedor were both deported from Leipzig to the Riga Ghetto on 21 January 1942, where they were murdered in the Holocaust.

Fedor Krebs came from a big family in Tarnowitz (Tworog) in Poland. His parents, the innkeeper and merchant Simon Krebs and Bertha Krebs nee Kallman, had eight children, Siegfried, Max (1871-1944), Herman (1873-1957), Salo, Else (1875-), Dorothea (1877-), Frieda (1878-) and Fedor.

Max married the successful businesswoman and shoe store owner Natalie Salzman (1882-1944), and they had a daughter Susi (1913-2000) in Glogau. Their shoe business at 49 Preussische Strasse was prominent and successful in Glogau (now Glogow in Poland), until antisemitism and boycotting of Jewish businesses drove them away. In 1937, Max and Natalie moved to 13 Gasteiner Strasse, Berlin. Their belongings in Glogau and the business were sold at fire-sale prices and Aryanized.[617]

Max and Natalie were murdered in the Treblinka Concentration Camp after being initially deported from Berlin to the Theresienstadt Ghetto where they were only held for a week, while Susi Glaser nee Krebs managed to escape Germany for Sao Paulo, Brazil with her husband. A Stolpersteine marks the memory of Max and Natalie outside where they lived in Berlin.[618]

The master tailor Herman Krebs married Paula Reis (1881-1957), raising two sons, Hans (1904-) and Horst Simon (1909-1953) in Berlin. Herman, Paula and Hans escaped to the UK, adopting the surname Keith, while Horst went to the Netherlands. In the UK,

---

[617] 'Stolpersteininitiative Charlottenburg – Wilmersdorf', Karin Sievert, District office Charlottenburg-Wilmersdorf, Berlin, berlin.de/ba-charlottenburg-wilmersdorf/ueber-den-bezirk/geschichte/stolpersteine/artikel.1207718.php
[618] ibid.

Herman became Uncle Howard Keith. Hans married Hilda Herman (1903-).

The travelling salesman Horst married Dorothea Biallosterski (1908-), having two children, Guus and Paul Krebs (-2012). Paul's son Mark Krebs is my cousin and my Krebs family adviser, who now lives in the Netherlands, after studying, working and living in several countries.

Dorothea Krebs married Eduard Adler. Frieda married Benjamin (Benno) Hurtig (-1930), and they had a son Rudolph Hurtig. The Hurtigs emigrated to Johannesburg, South Africa.

Krebs family photo featuring Else Krebs nee Kraft and her husband Fedor Krebs (centre back)

(Source: Mark Krebs)

The brothers Dr Werner and Fritz Kraft[619]

Selmar's older brother Eduard Kraft (1855-1916) married Elsa Kraft nee Isenstein (1868-1923) and had two sons, Dr Werner Kraft (1896-

---

[619] Email from Mathias Hille, Schönebeck City Archives (Elbe), 25 April 2024

Uncovering their Names and Stories:

1991) and Fritz Kraft (1894-1917). They were nephews of my great grandparents Selmar and Frieda Kraft.

Eduard and Elsa's family lived initially in Braunschweig but moved 67 km northwest to Hannover in 1901. The boys attended primary and secondary school on Wolfstrasse in Braunschweig.[620]

Fritz died as a young man, at the age of 23, in World War 1 near Jerusalem, while serving as a deputy sergeant in the Levante Corps in the German Imperial Army.

His younger brother Werner lived a long life and is an example of what can be achieved if you have talent, and are lucky enough to survive World War 1, and being Jewish under the Nazi regime.

Werner had a significant career as a librarian, which helped fund his extensive work as a writer, poet and literary scholar.

He worked as an apprentice for a short time at Dresdner Bank in Hannover for his cousin on his mother's side Julius L Isenstein (1856-1929). He studied at the University of Berlin in Philology, Romance Studies and Philosophy during 1914-1915 with his first cousin Paul Kraft (1896-1922). He served in the military from 1916-1919, working as a nurse in Ilten, just 17 km southeast of Hannover.

In 1920-1928 Werner undertook library training in Berlin and Leipzig. He worked in the German Library, now the German National Library, from 1922 to 1926.[621] He was a key librarian at the Gottfried Wilhelm Leibniz Library - Lower Saxony State Library from 1928 during the Weimar Republic period.

He later studied in Freiburg and Hamburg with his wife-to-be Erna Halle. The future leader of the German Jewish community under the Nazi regime, theologian, and leader of Reform Judaism Rabbi Leo Baeck (1873-1956) married Werner and Erna in Berlin in 1922, the same year Rabbi Baeck was elected President of the General German Rabbinical association.[622]

---

[620] ibid.
[621] 'Werner Kraft', Wikipedia
[622] 'Leo Baeck', Gedenkstätte Deutscher Widerstand, gdw-berlin.de

They moved to Leipzig and had two children, Paul Caspar (later Sha'ul) Kraft (1923) and Elsa (Alissa) Kraft (1929-). Werner's mother Elsa had died six years earlier, and Paul was likely named after Werner's cousin Paul Kraft, who had died in 1922.

In 1925, Werner completed his doctorate in Frankfurt am Main on "Investigation into the history of motives about Pope Joan in German literature". From 1928 to 1933 he became a library councillor, a senior position, in Hannover. He worked as a library councillor in the 'Formerly Royal and Provincial Library' from 1928. During this period, he had interactions with Bertolt Brecht and other important German literary figures.

He was dismissed in 1933 because he was Jewish. He evaluated his options and fled via Sweden in 1933 to Palestine in 1934. Werner emigrated to Jerusalem with his family shortly thereafter in 1934 and lived as a German-language writer in Palestine - Israel until his death in 1991.[623] In exile, Werner worked as a librarian for a couple of decades, largely in Jerusalem, while being keenly involved in his writing and publishing. He also maintained correspondence and relationships with Martin Buber and Bertolt Brecht.

As I was walking around Jewish sites in Hannover, I was surprised to see a picture of my grandmother's first cousin Werner Kraft staring back at me. On the information board on the site of the Neue Synagogue 1870-1938 on Rote Reihe (Red Row), is a section featuring fourteen "Daughters and Sons of the Jewish Community". One of those sons' faces looking back at was "Werner Kraft, Librarian". Others, surrounding Werner, included political scientist Hannah Arendt, Nobel Prize winner Otto Meyerhof, philosopher Theodor Lessing and Joseph Berliner, co-founder with his brother of Deutsche Grammophon. He was in illustrious company.

---

[623] Email from Mathias Hille, Schönebeck City Archives (Elbe), 25 April 2024

Uncovering their Names and Stories:

Dr Werner Kraft (bottom row, second from the left) in prestigious company on the information board on the site of the Neue Synagogue (1870-1938) in Hannover

(Photo credit: David Marlow)

Werner's influence was underlined by the presence of a quote of his at the Berlin Jewish Museum, which I was surprised to discover, from 9 August 1933, "Welch eine Hölle ist in Deutschland. What a hell Germany has become." Any love he may ever have had for Germany had clearly ended by then.

Werner later wrote in his diary, "It was only after 1933 that I finally and forever knew that I was not a German, that I was a Jew. He was now dictated by a criminal force that the Jews belong to the German people only through language. What a sign on the wall that was already smeared with blood! Just through the language that murdered violence before it murdered people! I have never given up this language, I have always considered it to be a commission to which there was no objection, to lead my life within the German spirit."[624]

---

[624] 'Werner Kraft', Wikipedia

Dr Werner Kraft quoted on the wall inside the Berlin Jewish Museum
(Photo credit: David Marlow)

> **Werner Kraft, 37 Jahre | Werner Kraft, aged 37**
> **9. AUGUST | 9 AUGUST 1933**
>
> *Welch eine Hölle ist in Deutschland.*
>
> *What a hell Germany has become.*

Werner retired as a librarian in 1956 and was a freelance writer until his death in 1991. He was awarded an amazing array of prizes and honours through his career until his death, including the Literature Prize of the Bavarian Academy of Fine Arts, the Sigmund Freud Prize for scientific prose, the German Academy for Language and Poetry in Darmstadt, an Honorary doctorate from the University of Freiburg, the Goethe Medal, the Wilhelm Heinse Medal of the Academy of Sciences, the Cross of Merit of the Federal Republic Germany, and the Lower Saxony Artist Scholarship for Literature.[625]

The Schiller National Museum in Marbach am Neckar and the Lower Saxony State Library dedicated exhibitions to Werner in honour of his 100th birthday in 1996, just a few years after his passing. The Lower Saxony exhibition was on display by the Deutsche Bücherei Leipzig from 11 November 2000 to 14 January 2001.[626]

The Gottfried Wilhelm Leibniz Library held an exhibition from 9 September 2008 to 9 April 2009 under the title: "My employment was for life and ended in 1933" - Werner Kraft – librarian, poet, literary critic in Hannover. Ten display boards and ten display cases presented information about his life and work.

The Werner Kraft Archive was founded in 1983 in Cologne. He died on 14 June 1991 in Jerusalem and is buried in the cemetery in Kibbutz

---

[625] Email from Mathias Hille, Schönebeck City Archives (Elbe), 25 April 2024
[626] ibid.

Uncovering their Names and Stories:

Tzora, a 30-minute drive west of Jerusalem.[627] It is ironic that he lived so much of his life in Jerusalem, given that his big brother Fritz died nearby in World War 1.

Werner and Erna have many descendants through their son Paul Kraft (1923-2003) and daughter Alisa Tibon nee Kraft (1929-). There are three generations currently living their lives in Israel, with their grandson retired Major General Noam Tibon (1962-) and his son, the writer and journalist Amir Tibon being the most prominent. But there are many successful members of the family, including CEO and CFO Eran Tibon (1959-) and authors amongst the clan. Noam, Amir and their family became globally known, after surviving the tragic October 7 attack on Amir's kibbutz. Their story is theirs to tell, and a Google or newspaper search will uncover many details of what the family endured.

I did not expect to find family in Israel. I had never heard of any, but I have now been in contact with numerous members of the Tibon family, and introduced them to our mutual cousins in Israel, the Konirsch family, as well as cousins in the USA. We are all descendants of the Kraft family from Calbe. I am also related to the Tibon family through the Isenstein family of Hannover. My great grandmother Frieda Kraft nee Isenstein was a sister of Eran, Noam and Yael Tibon's great grandmother Elsa Kraft nee Isenstein. Frieda and Elsa had married brothers Selmar and Eduard Kraft respectively. In fact, Eran's middle name is Edward, named after his great grandfather Eduard.

---

[627] ibid.

13.0 The Marlows – Australia

My family's story in Australia started when my parents Ilse Marlow nee Elkan and Heinz Marowilsky (later Henry Marlow) arrived on separate ships. My mother and her parents arrived on the *Remo* in 1939, and my father arrived on the *HMT Dunera* in 1940. Neither had really planned to come here, and both had no choice in the matter, but here they came. Dad said that he thought he was going to Canada. After the displacement of forced emigration, leaving so much family behind and arriving in a foreign land, they found a foreign culture and a foreign language. At least Dad had some experience speaking English in England, and Mum was with her parents.

My parents Ilse and Heinz Marowilsky as a young couple
(Source: Marlow family photo album)

You can take the boy out of the Rhineland

Though my parents tried very hard to assimilate in Australia, they were also always very German and very Jewish simultaneously. But they never made any pretence of being very religiously observant. Dad would eat hot cross buns and matzah when Easter and Pesach

Uncovering their Names and Stories:

coincided. Mum played Bingo often, enjoyed doing tapestry work as a hobby as she became older, and in later life would have a small Christmas tree on the dining room table in their home in Caulfield. I am not sure what the Chanukiah[628] displayed in the dining room felt about that Treyfe intruder.

Dad often played what I called 'oompah' music in the car, which should be better called polka music I suppose. I found it enormously embarrassing at the time, and I probably still do. Nevertheless, his favourite songs were Edelweiss (not the Elvis version) and Spanish Eyes, based on his requests to bands at German and Austrian restaurants. He also sought out tapes of German music wherever he could, whether in local record stores or from Germany. Now, the memory of this always reminds me of a photo of Dad as a teenager holding an accordion. I do not know if he could play it, but he evidently used to play the violin as a youngster. The only musical instrument I ever saw him play were the cymbals, which he played with the German band at the Hofbräuhaus in Melbourne as a regular dinner patron. I certainly did not inherit any musical ability. His father, Hermann Marowilsky had played the violin in the evenings, after dinner. I think the musical skills skipped a generation to my younger son Josh, who played the guitar in high school. Nevertheless, I still have Dad's cymbals, which the Hofbräuhaus band presented to him for his 50th birthday in 1971.

Dad kept his old violin on the wall of his 'den' (study) as he called it. The room held his large collection of alcohol and very small collection of (unread) books. On display on small tables and the large bookshelves were a range of beer steins, a yard glass and various exotic looking fancy bottles of various types of spirits. There was also a cigarette lighter shaped like a gun, his collection of matchbooks from restaurants across the country, and a radio shaped like a globe. A very man-cave of a room, which he later doubled in size by knocking out a wall to incorporate the next room, after my sister Helen married and moved out. A small desk and never-to-be-used running machine were added to the room much later.

Mum on the other hand, liked to collect spoons from her travels, small crystal ornaments, Lladro figurines and particularly after I

---

[628] Chanukkah festival menorah or candelabra

moved out, an ever-increasing range of dolls. She accumulated quite a large collection of dolls, which she kept in my old bedroom. This may have been to compensate for the doll taken away from her and sold by her grandfather Selmar Kraft.

At a fairly young age, my parents outfitted me with lederhosen,[629] and sent me to learn German 'slap-dancing' as I called it. It is properly known as Schuhplattler, which is a traditional German style of folk dance especially popular in Upper Bavaria, Tyrol and Salzburg. The performers stomp, clap and slap the soles of their shoes (schuhe), thighs and knees with their hands held flat (platt). Though the other children were friendly, I was not impressed, and it felt quite alien to me, but I had no say in the matter. Eventually their delusion of me becoming a world-class 'slap-dancer' disappeared, like I disappeared the lederhosen.

My parents had four children, Peter (1945-), Judy (1949-), Helen (1951-) and me, David (1962-). We were all born in Melbourne, the second largest city in Australia with the largest Jewish community in the country.

I arrived about ten years after my 'baby' sister Helen. The family legend is that my parents gave my siblings (or at least Peter) the choice of a holiday in Japan or another baby in the family. They chose to have another sibling, but they may have voted differently if they had known it was going to be me. I used to tease my mother that I only came about because of a "bottle of Brandavino in the backseat of the Dodge". My mother was horrified and would retell the Japan holiday story. She would also ask how I knew about the Dodge, which they only had until I was very young. The suggestion of Brandavino was a little anachronistic. It was a blend of brandy and wine, which was very popular in Australia in the 1970s and 1980s. And I was born in 1962. But I liked to tease.

My brother also tells the same Japan holiday story as the family legend, but my sister Helen and I have doubts. We can never remember Dad being so democratic and he never boarded a ship for

---

[629] Lederhosen are the traditional leather breeches that were worn in Austria, Upper Bavaria and South Tyrol – the uniform also for male 'slap-dancers'.

travel after his *Dunera* experience, and avoided flying like the plague, especially until his later years. He would typically take the overnight train to Sydney or Brisbane, while the plane trips were much quicker, one to two hours. He only took two overseas flights that we can remember, and those were two relatively short flight to Vanuatu, which is much less than 4 hours.

Me in my lederhosen
(Source: Marlow family photos)

My siblings and I were largely unaware of our parents' change of surname until I was preparing to get married in the 1980s. I needed documentation for the rabbi to proceed with the wedding, and one of the documents identified that Henry Marlow, as we knew him, had been Heinz Günther Marowilsky until officially changing his name in 1947. My brother seemed unaware that for a short time, he too had been a Marowilsky, before his surname was changed as a small child.

Many Dunera Boys had also changed their names, aiming to better fit into the very Anglo-Australian community and probably partly to avoid some of the antisemitism and anti-German sentiment of the post-war years. Of course, as soon as they opened their mouths, their German accents made their 'foreign-ness" an open secret.

Even St Kilda Hebrew Congregation was very Anglo or British at the time, with the leadership wearing top hats. The congregation only ended the tradition of the president and vice president wearing top hat and tails in synagogue in 2010. Even then, the president and senior rabbi at the time opposed the move.[630] The president's top hat can still be seen amongst the museum pieces on display in the synagogue's boardroom. Another of the top hats is on display in the nearby Jewish Museum of Australia.

Dad's naturalisation certificate came through in September 1946, only six years after arriving in Australia.[631] It was formally signed on 30 July 1946.[632] Not much later, he officially changed his name to Henry Marlow by deed poll on 22 May 1947.[633] From trying to assimilate into Germany, German Jews around the world who had escaped to English-speaking countries, were changing their names to better fit-in to their adopted countries. A Chaim or Aron became Heinz or Adolf to become more German, and after arriving in places like the USA, UK or Australia were becoming Henry or Ken.

Despite this, when my parents were talking in German to each other when I was around as a child and teenager, which I expect they did to ensure I would not know what they were talking about, Mum always called Dad 'Heinz', not Henry. I studied German for a few years at Melbourne High School to help understand what they were saying, while my parents thought they could talk in German without

---

[630] 'St Kilda shelves its top hats and tails', Naomi Levin, Australian Jewish News, 16 September 2010.
[631] Certificates of Naturalisation, 5 September 1946, Trove online database, National Library of Australia
[632] Certificate of Naturalisation for Heinz Gunther Marowilsky, National Archives of Australia
[633] Noted on attachment to naturalization documents of Heinz Gunther Marowilsky, National Archives of Australia

Uncovering their Names and Stories:

me understanding. They were not far wrong, as I was not a natural with languages.

Soon after Dad was released from internment, he started working in sales, including jewellery, shirts and toys, selling from his suitcase. He started specialising in electrical sales and then built an electrical wholesale business, creatively called 'Henry Marlow' which he said he founded in 1947. But initially he was in partnership with Walter Lippmann in F. B. Lippmann and Co, until they had a falling out.

In the early days of the business, Mum worked in the business too. The business thrived on the post-war building boom in Australia, and they ended up with many stores all around Victoria, mostly in country towns including Ballarat, Horsham, Mildura, Morwell, Reservoir, Shepparton, Swan Hill and Wangaratta, as well as Five Dock in NSW. As house building in the country slowed, the country stores were closed to focus on the main, large shopfront at 895 High Street, Armadale in Melbourne. It was a mecca for electricians needing supplies, such as electrical cable, ceiling fans and switchgear, and householders needing light globes, light fittings and extension leads. By 1994, he had sixty staff and a turnover of A$2.5m per month.

Customers included Australian rock legend Molly Meldrum because his electrician Jimmy was a regular, and former Prime Minister Malcolm Frazer and his wife Tammy, because Tammy's mother evidently lived close to the shop. I can remember one day when Malcolm and Tammy, and their large security detail, came into the store when he was Prime Minister, and he hit his head on light fittings because he was so tall. My father did not believe the light fittings were hanging low, because he was more vertically challenged.

Dad was very active in several community organisations and clubs, including Prahran Rotary, the businessmen's club the BRIEF Club, the Wineologists (which my mother called the 'Boozers Lunch') and for some time in the 1960s-1970s held Christmas parties for children from the local Catholic orphanage at his shop in Armadale. I can still remember seeing the nuns in their habits at the parties. Family members would often help with Rotary fundraising events, and I remember as a 19-year-old driving the rented stick-shift truck at a fete, because I was the only one who could drive it.

By the 1960s, the family were living at 70 Orrong Crescent in North Caulfield, which was renumbered to number 54 in the early 1970s. It was a five-bedroom, brick veneer house, a short walk from Caulfield Synagogue, one of the three major synagogues in Melbourne. After most of their children had left home, Dad combined two of the bedrooms into a 'den' for himself, where he kept his reel-to-reel tape deck, bar and never-to-be-used running machine. Mum and Dad lived there until they died. Despite the proximity to Caulfield Synagogue, we attended the major Progressive synagogue in Melbourne, Temple Beth Israel in St Kilda.

Mum continued to work in the family business until she became quite ill while pregnant with me in 1961-1962. She was bedridden for much of the pregnancy, and a housekeeper was hired to help with chores at home. Our second housekeeper Noela Begbie was with us for many years, and she became very close and a good long-term friend of the family, especially my mother. I remember well Noela trying to get me to eat vegetables as a small child, saying, "you don't have to bloody like 'em, just bloody eat 'em". Noela passed away in June 2008.

Mum and Dad grandiosely called the rumpus room at the back of their house, the 'ballroom'. I remember helping with my sister's 21st birthday party, when I would have been 11, making the punch, including plenty of vodka and vermouth. I think my later brother-in-law Graeme Nathan (1950-2020) taught me, and I still make a decent punch today.

At some stage, probably in the 1960s, my parents bought a holiday house on Fig Street in Dromana, a seaside suburb on the Mornington Peninsula. In the early days, it was surrounded by paddocks, with a few houses scattered around here and there, amongst a lot of open land. It was a timber house, with a very large weeping willow tree out the front. The house would often be used on long weekends, such as Easter and Cup Day weekends. From here, my brother-in-law Graeme Nathan taught me to fish on Port Philip Bay, drive a small boat and clean & fillet fish, on the rare times we caught anything. My parents eventually sold the house because of lack of use in the later 1970s. Dromana was replaced by holidays in Surfers Paradise on Queensland's Gold Coast. These days Dromana is very built-up and

Uncovering their Names and Stories:

suburban, and the site of the old house is a stone's throw from the freeway.

David, Ilse and Henry Marlow circa 1970
(Source: Marlow family photos)

I do not think that my siblings and I have a great connection in any way to being 'German', though I think we all like a schnitzel, but we certainly do connect closely to being Jewish. Though we all went to state school, rather than a Jewish day school, our Jewish connection was probably reinforced by three of the four of us having Jewish partners. And the same three were married in synagogues and sent our children, at least to some level, to Jewish schools, notably Mount Scopus Memorial College, Leibler Yavneh College and King David School.

Those three Marlow siblings are very connected to the Jewish community. My sister Judy is the exception. Between us, we had thirteen wonderful children and innumerable beautiful grandchildren, all full of personality. The family continues to grow and thrive in Melbourne, Australia.

Mum was always fond of travel (when not playing her beloved bingo or doing her tapestry craftwork) and went on many cruises to the Pacific Islands and fly-out holidays to South-East Asia. Before Helen married, she sometimes accompanied Mum on her cruises. Helen now has re-caught the cruising bug, and it is not unusual for her to go on a few cruises in a year. Dad did not go, as he was not a fan of ships or planes. On a trip to Thailand, Mum's minibus rolled over and she was badly injured. She gradually recovered, but between heart and kidney issues, by-pass surgery and diabetes, she aged well before her time.

At 70, she was more like a very sickly 90-year-old. Diabetes, especially type 2 but also type 1, are common amongst the family. The diabetes badly affected her ability to heal from surgeries, and she died from a combination of factors in her bed at home on 1 October 1997, at the age of 70. My then wife Sharon and I built a house in 1997, but Mum was never able to see it from the inside. Diabetes also caused the death of my young niece, Kylie Lightfoot (1982-2007), who sometimes babysat my children.

During his business career, Dad built a parallel family business called Endex Agencies to supply light fittings to retailers, like Myer department stores, McEwans Hardware and many lighting shops around Australia. This was set up initially in inner-city Prahran in what had previously been a large toy warehouse. I remember being the beneficiary as a child, of numerous toys which had been left behind in the warehouse, including a great farm set including a wide variety of plastic animals.

After a few years, Endex Agencies was moved to a larger and more cost-effective warehouse in Keys Road, Moorabbin. Branch operations were also established in Sydney and Brisbane to serve its national customers. Years later, as Dad started thinking begrudgingly about retirement, he finally accepted an offer to sell Endex Agencies and ended up having to close the Henry Marlow business, as it was harder to sell. Thankfully, he owned the Henry Marlow building and accumulated little debt, as he was always highly debt averse, so he was in a comfortable financial position for retirement.

I think Dad felt successful when he bought his Mercedes-Benz sedan. He always looked at the car lovingly when the Mercedes-Benz

Uncovering their Names and Stories:

featured on Sale of The Century on TV. When he finally bought one, he was delighted. His interest in cars was reflected in the number of photos of him posing with cars or photos he took of cars in his childhood photo album. But his love of cars was only matched by his poor driving skills. He became close with his local panel beater. He also had no mechanical ability or interest. He could not even change a tyre, and I would often get called to change a tyre when he hit another curb or a nail on the road.

Dad retired in 1998, enjoying seeing his grandchildren grow, and was still very attached to his television remote. When I was young, before the remote arrived in the later 1970s, he used to call me from the other end of the house to change the channel. I loved that remote. He gradually deteriorated physically and mentally after retirement, and despite his cigar smoking for most of his life, his fondness for Black Forest Cherry-Cake, a solid history of enjoying a tipple, and his terrible driving, he lived to be more than ten years older than Mum managed to reach. There was often a heavy cloud of cigar smoke in the house when I was a youngster. The old cigar boxes were very handy for storing my toy soldiers.

He had been planning to visit Wuppertal with my brother Peter for the 75th anniversary of the amalgamation of Wuppertal. Unfortunately, he was not well enough, so Peter and his wife Helen attended, representing Dad at the anniversary celebration. It is unlikely that Dad really would have attended anyway, as he was highly averse to long flights, experiencing bad vertigo on ships and planes. The only time the family can remember Dad going overseas since he arrived in Australia, were two holidays Mum talked him into going to in Vanuatu. They liked it so much that they went twice in three months and continued to send gifts and toys to a family in Vanuatu thereafter. Four hours to Vanuatu is very different to flying about 30 hours to Germany.

When asked whether his children ever asked about his past and origins, Dad told Prof Brusten, "Yes, they have, but we have only talked about it very little; not even as much as we talk about it now in the interview. Thank God our children didn't have to go through all that, so why should we burden them with it? Peter recently had a very serious operation; when I visited him at home for this reason, I spent a whole evening telling him a lot about our German past.

Otherwise, we hardly spoke to our children about it, just a word here and there. All they really know is that my parents and almost all my relatives died in Nazi Germany; that's all."[634] In reality, he never even told me that much.

As his mental health declined dramatically due to Alzheimer's, Dad was in high-care aged care. He became particularly ill in 2002 while I was working in Singapore and Kuala Lumpur (KL). I received a call in my office in KL to "get home quick" from my then wife Sharon. I caught the next plane home and managed to see Dad that evening and talked to him for quite a while, though he was asleep the whole time and snoring heavily as always. As a child, I could always hear his snoring from the other end of the house. It was a one-sided conversation, but I was very relieved to see him one more time. He died that night, 14 December 2002, aged 81.

Both my parents are buried in the Jewish section, which was called the Rose Garden, in the Springvale Botanical Cemetery. Mum's mother Hanni is also buried only a few metres away in the same section. I like to think they are keeping each other company, with Nana adjusting her hearing aid so she can keep up with the conversation.

Personally, I have been active in a number of roles in the Jewish community in Melbourne, including the Jewish Community Council of Victoria as Executive Director, the Australian Jewish Historical Society Victoria (AJHS Vic) as Honorary Secretary, J-Wire online news service as a regular contributor, in volunteer leadership roles with the Jewish Christian Muslim Association, and St Kilda Hebrew Congregation as Executive Director and then as a volunteer. Being a family history guru, my partner Dr Erica Cervini sits on the committee of the AJHS Vic with me. She is also an award-winning journalist, regular writer for Eureka Steet, sessional academic and has been a frequent speaker on family history for ABC radio.[635]

My relationship with Erica and the connection with her family is a story in spooky coincidence. When we started seeing each other over

---

[634] Henry Marlow interview with Prof Manfred Brusten, October 1994

[635] ABC is the government-owned national broadcaster in Australia

Uncovering their Names and Stories:

nine years ago, we did not know about any connections between our families. One day, Erica was working on her PhD on life-writing and family history, focusing on the story of her great grandmother Rose Pearlman. We were sitting in Erica's living room, at her old house in Fitzroy. As part of her research, Erica had been collecting family photos from various family members. She showed me photos of Rose and some of her children but skipped over a few with the quip, "Oh, it's just my parents, Faye and Ken who you have already seen pics of, and people I don't know."

Not long afterwards, her cousin Lynda Fridman asked Erica if she had shown me the photo of her parents and Erica's parents, who weren't married at the time, at the Samuel Meyers Hall at St Kilda Shule. Lynda had a feeling that the other couple in the photo, who Erica didn't know, were friends of her father, Ken Green. "I think his name was Henry Marlow. Ask David if he is any relation to him?" Erica did ask me and showed me the photo. Incredibly, the man and the woman sitting with Erica's and Lynda's parents were my parents. The hall opened in 1940. What were they doing there together? We knew of no connection between the families.

We later discovered that my father had been best friends with Ken Green (Kurt Grünbaum), from when they had been interned together and into the 1950s. Ken married Erica's great aunt Faye Pearlman, who was very close to Erica's mother, a young Roberta Cervini. There was more to come. After this surprising discovery, Lynda Fridman sent Erica a wedding photo of her parents, Ken and Faye who married in 1950. Beside the bride and groom on the left were Erica's uncle Barry Josephs and Ken's sister Elsa. On the right were Erica's mother, Roberta, arm-in-arm with my father.

Roberta does not remember Dad, but did remember the surname 'Marlow' vaguely from the past. Newspaper clippings of the wedding announcement confirmed that Dad had been Ken's best man when he married Faye. I was now partnered with Faye's great niece, after the Marlow and Green families had lost connection for over 50 years.

Before the communal roles, I ran call centres in four different countries,[636] founded and run a bookshop business with a couple of

---

[636] Australia, New Zealand, Singapore and Malaysia

stores for nearly a decade and worked in banking and finance for ANZ Banking Group for 18 years. For several years, I arranged heart surgeries in Australia for patients from East Timor, as well as organising other medical services and medical supplies as CEO of East Timor Hearts Fund. This included arranging cardiac telehealth services, portable echocardiograph machines and personal protective equipment during the COVID pandemic, when we could not transport patients to Australia nor cardiologists to East Timor. Despite the difficulties during COVID, this was one of my more rewarding roles in my career.

My children Bradley (1991-), Joshua (1993-) and Brittany (1996-) are all married to lovely partners (Sonja, Sharon, and Andrew better known in the family as 'Keegs', respectively) with a beautiful young child each, Zander (2022-), Issy (2021-) and Ava (2021-), and are very successful in their careers. Brad is a structural engineer / project manager who works for a construction company that builds apartment buildings, Josh is a post-doctoral scientist and science teacher, and my daughter Britt is a solicitor cum recruitment specialist, who works with her mother Sharon in their recruitment business. All three are wonderful children and parents with good hearts.

My brother Peter Marlow and my sister Helen Nathan are retired and have both been very involved in the Jewish community in Melbourne, for example with Peter being an active member of B'nai B'rith like our grandfather Oskar, and Peter's wife Helen Marlow (yes, two Helens in the family) enjoying Israeli dancing for many years. Peter worked in the family electrical wholesale business from university to retirement, very much focused on the lighting side of the business.

My sister Helen has been active with various Jewish community organisations, including years ago being a Progressive youth group leader with her late husband Graeme, who was also very involved with Jewish Scouts for decades, in Ezra the Jewish women's organisation until it folded, and working with elderly citizens through the National Council of Jewish Women for many years, after retiring from being a primary school teacher.

Uncovering their Names and Stories:

14.0 Glossary[637]

Aliyah	Honour when someone is called-up in synagogue on Shabbat, or when a Jew returns to Israel to live. It literally means ascent or rise in Hebrew.
Alte	German for old.
Aryanization	The Nazi term for seizure of property and businesses from Jews and its transfer to non-Jews.[638]
Ashkenazi	Jews from Central or Eastern Europe, including Poland, Lithuania and Germany. Askenaz means 'Germany' in Medieval Hebrew.
Bar Mitzvah	First call-up of a boy (13) in synagogue signifying adulthood.
Bat Mitzvah	Modern equivalent of Bar Mitzvah for a girl (12).
Berliner	German for doughnut, though parts of Germany call them Pfannkuchen (pancakes)
Bibliothek	German for library.
B'nai B'rith	Jewish fraternal order founded in New York in 1843 which organises social activities, education and charitable work.
Bocher	Unmarried yeshivah student.
Brücke	Bridge in German.

---

[637] Adapted from <u>Jewish Life in Germany: Memoirs from Three Centuries</u>, Monika Richarz (Ed), Indiana University Press, 1991 pp.475-478; Oxford Languages (languages.oup.com); and Britannica.com

[638] 'A 1938 Nazi Law Forced Jews to Register Their Wealth – Making It Easier to Steal', <u>Smithsonian Magazine</u>, Lorraine Boissoneault, 26 April 2018

Bücherei	Library in German.
Bundesarchiv	German national archives.
Cantor	Person who leads the singing or sometimes prayer in synagogue (especially Reform or Progressive).
Challah	Twisted bread traditionally eaten at Friday night dinner.
Chanukiah	Nine-armed menorah or candelabrum used for the festival of Hanukkah.
Chazzan	Person who leads synagogue services and singing of prayers in synagogue, especially as a profession (especially Orthodox).
Chevra Kadisha	Jewish burial society that organises funerals.
Enkeln	Grandchildren
Fräulein	An unmarried woman.
Friedhof	Cemetery in German.
Frontsoldaten	Frontline soldiers in German.
Gedenkplaetze	Memorials
Gemeinde	Community in German.
Genealogy	The study of the history of families, especially through studying historical documents to discover the relationships between people and their families.[639]
Gesellschaft	Society in German.
Geschichte	Story or history.
Gestapo	Geheime Staatspolizei, the secret state police of Nazi Germany, which was established by Hermann Göring in 1933, and transferred to the SS in April 1934.

---

[639] Collinsdictionary.com

Uncovering their Names and Stories:

Grabsteine	Gravestones in German.
Halachic	According to Jewish law.
Haskalah	Jewish enlightenment.
Holocaust	The Nazi state-sponsored systematic murder of six million Jews.
Jekke (Yekke)	A German Jew or Jew of German-speaking origin..
Judenhaus	Literally 'Jewish house', were houses or apartments where Jews were concentrated into prior to deportation to concentration camps.
Jüdisches	Jewish in German.
Kaddish	Prayer praising G-d and prayer for the dead.
Kehilla	A local Jewish community leadership organisation.
Ketubah	Jewish marriage contract.
Kiddush	Sanctification blessing over wine or the small meal after Shabbat or festival morning services.
Kindertransport	Literally children's transport; program of rescuing Jewish children from Nazi Germany, Austria and Czechoslovakia.
Konzentrationslager	Concentration camp.
Kosher	In accordance with the Jewish dietary laws
Kristallnacht	Known as the "Night of broken glass" due to the broken glass from the windows of Jewish–owned buildings that littered the streets, on 9-10 November 1938. It was a nation-wide pogrom targeting Jews led by the SA and SS.
Lager	Camp in German.

Landesarchiv	State archives
Marranos	Spanish and Portuguese Jews who converted or were forced to convert to Christianity during the 15th and 16th centuries.
Matzah	Unleavened bread eaten during Pesach.
Mikveh	Ritual bath house; women and men bathe in separate Mikveot.
Minchah	Afternoon prayers.
Mishpacha	Yiddish for the entire family network of relatives by blood or marriage.[640]
Mitzvah	Commandment or good deed.
Nazi	A member of the far-right National Socialist German Workers' Party.
Neue	German for new.
Ostjuden	East European Jews.
Pesach (Passover)	Festival celebrating exodus of the Jews from Egypt.
Pogrom	An organised massacre of a particular ethnic group, particularly the Jewish people in Russia and Eastern Europe.
Rabbi	Qualified Jewish religious leader.
Rathaus	German for town hall.
Reb	Respectful form of address for a man.
Rebbe	A person's main Yeshivah teacher or mentor who provides religious guidance.
Rebbetzin	Wife of a rabbi or a female religious teacher.
Rosh Hashanah	Jewish New Year.

---

[640] Vocabulary.com

Uncovering their Names and Stories:

SA	Nazi Sturmabteilung (Storm Division) paramilitary (colloquially Brownshirts because of the colour of their uniforms).
Schloss	German for castle.
Schul or shule	Traditional expression for a synagogue.
Schutzjude	Protected Jew, having a status granted by the imperial, princely or similar court.
Seder	The ceremony or order of the dinner during Pesach.
Sephardi	Jews who came from the Spanish peninsula.
Shabbat (Sabbath)	Jewish day of rest, from sunset Friday to sunset Saturday.
Shacharit	Morning prayers.
Simcha	Celebration (such as weddings, batmitzvahs or barmitzvahs) or joyfulness.
SS	Nazi Schutzstaffel paramilitary (colloquially Blackshirts because of the colour of their uniforms).
Staatarchiv	State archives.
Stadtarchiv	City archives.
Stiftung	Foundation or endowment in German
Stolpersteine	Literally stumbling blocks, which are memorial brass blocks set into the ground outside the homes where Jews were deported from, in honour of Holocaust victims.
Stormtroops	Sturmabteilung - see SA above.
Strasse (Straße)	German for street.
Sufganiyot	Doughnuts in Hebrew.
Synagogue	Jewish communal house of prayer.

Talmud	Compilation of the teachings and traditions of Judaism.
Torah	The five books of the Old Testament or Hebrew Bible.
Treyfe	Not kosher.
Untersuchungsgefängnis	Detention centre.
Urenkeln	Great grandchildren.
Yad Vashem	Israeli museum and monument to the six million Jews murdered in the Holocaust, based in Jerusalem, established in 1953.
Yarmulke	Jewish religious skullcap, also known as a kippah.
Yeshivah	Talmudic study academy.
Yom Kippur	Jewish Day of Atonement, holiest day of the Jewish year.
Zeitung	Newspaper in German.

Uncovering their Names and Stories:

15.0 Bibliography

15.1 Archives and archival sources

Allenstein[641] State Archives, Poland

Arolsen Archives, International Centre on Nazi Persecution

Bundesarchiv (German Federal Archives), Koblenz, Germany

Central Archives for the History of the Jewish People, Jerusalem

Center for Jewish History, New York

Esther Elbin Family Collection, Leo Baeck Institute, New York

Jewish Museum Berlin Archives

German Army, Loss lists of World War I

German Propaganda Archive, Calvin University, Grand Rapids, Michigan, USA

Landesarchiv Berlin (Berlin Provincial Archives)

LASA, Landesarchiv Sachsen-Anhalt (Saxony-Anhalt State Archives), Dessau-Roßlau

LASA, Landesarchiv Sachsen-Anhalt (Saxony-Anhalt State Archives), Magdeburg

Leo Baeck Institute, Berlin

Leo Baeck Institute, New York

Memorial book: 'Victims of the Persecution of Jews under the National Socialist Tyranny in Germany 1933 – 1945' prepared by the German Federal Archives, Das Bundesarchiv

Military Archives Department, Bundesarchiv

Moses Mendelssohn Centre Archives, Dessau-Roßlau

National Archives of Australia

National Archives and Records Administration, Washington DC, USA

---

[641] Olsztyn

National Archives, United Kingdom

New York State Archives, USA

Public Records Office Victoria (PROV), Australia

Shapell Roster of Jewish Service in the American Civil War, Shapell Manuscript Foundation

Staatsarchiv Hamburg (Hamburg State Archives)

Staatsarchiv Bremen (Bremen State Archives)

Staatsarchiv Leipzig (Leipzig State Archives)

Stadtarchiv Leipzig (Leipzig City Archives)

Stadtarchiv Schönebeck (Elbe) (Schönebeck City Archives)

Stadtarchiv Wuppertal (Wuppertal City Archives)

Trove, National Library of Australia

United States Holocaust Memorial Museum

Werner Kraft-Archiv, Rheinbach-Todenfeld

Wiener Holocaust Library, London[642]

World Jewish Relief (formerly known as The Central British Fund)

15.2 Books and articles

<u>7 Essential Tips for Starting German Genealogy Handout</u>, Katherine Schober, Germanology Unlocked, 2024

'The 7 Largest Cemeteries in the World', Billiongraves.com

'8 Tallest Cathedrals in the World', SAHC Histructural, 8 November 2018

'15 Facts About Yekkes, the Jews of Germany', Rabbi Menachem Posner, Chabad.org

---

[642] Founded by Dr Alfred Wiener in 1933 and originally named the Jewish Central Information Office (JCIO)

Uncovering their Names and Stories:

'A 1938 Nazi Law Forced Jews to Register Their Wealth – Making It Easier to Steal', Smithsonian Magazine, Lorraine Boissoneault, 26 April 2018

1,700 Years of Jewish Life in Germany, Leo Baeck Institute, New York, 2021

Accommodating People Since 1934: The Story of the Wernick Group, Nigel Watson, St Matthew's Press, Leyburn, 2023

'Ach Du Lieber', Pauline Loewenhardt, Lucy Loewenhardt, and Prof John Löwenhardt, Löwenhardt Foundation, The Netherlands, 12 September 2013

'Achnebbisj, a self-analysis', Prof John Löwenhardt, Löwenhardt Foundation, The Netherlands, September 2021

Advanced Genealogy Research Techniques, George G. Morgan & Drew Smith, McGraw Hill Education, New York, 2013

'After 60-plus Years, Local War Hero Gets His Due', Jean-Paul Salamanca, The Forum Newsgroup, 2nd February 2012

'The Alien Enemy', La Trobe University students, Making History blog, Melbourne

Aliens: The Chequered History of Britain's Wartime Refugees, Paul Dowswell, Biteback Publishing, London, 2023

The Alteneuland (The Old New Land), Theodor Herzl, Sakuramachi shoin, 2017

The American Jew as Patriot, Soldier and Citizen, Simon Wolf, The Levytype Company, 1895 (republished New York University Press, New York, 18 October 2014)

Annäherungan eine Jüdische Geschichte Lindenaus (Approaching a Jewish history in Lindenau), Lindenau District Association, work status: 10 December 2023

Anti-Semitism: A History and Psychoanalysis of Contemporary Hatred, Avner Falk, Praeger, Westport, 2008

Antique Maps of the 19th Century World, R. Montgomery Martin (ed.), Portland House, New York, 1989

'An Aural Family Scrapbook: Gabriel Kahane's *Heirloom*', The Saint Paul Chamber Orchestra Blog, 22 November 2023

Atlas des Deutschen Reich, Ludwig Ravenstein, Bibliographisches Institut, Leipzig, 1883

'Aus den Jugenderinnerungen Steinthals mit einer Vorbemerkung von Leo Baeck', Der Morgen, Heymann Steinthal, pp. 141-146, 8. Jahrgang, June 1932, 2. Heft

'Aus der Geschichte der jüdischen Gemeinden im deutschen Sprachraum', Gröbzig (Saxony-Anhalt), Gröbzig Synagogue Museum

'Avant la letter: Chajjim Steinthal (1823-1899) as a linguist of Chinese revisited', Wolfgang Behr, keynote presentation, 6th Conference of the European Association of Chinese Linguistics, Adam Mickiewicz University, Poznan Poland, 26 August 2009

'A Year after the attack, Israeli couple recounts trying to get to their son on Oct 7', M Gutman, M Abramoff, J Schlosberg and M Deliso, ABC News, 8 Oct 2024

'Being a Yekke is a really big deal for my mum! On the intergenerational transmission of Germanness amongst German Jews in Israel', Dani Kranz, Austausch, Vol. 2, Issue 1, July 2013

Belzec, Sobibor, Treblinka: The Operation Reinhard Death Camps, Yitzhak Arad, Indiana University Press, Bloomington, 1987

"Be patient and reasonable!': The internment of German - Jewish refugees in Australia', Konrad Kwiet, Australian Journal of Politics & History, pp.61-77, Vol. 31, Issue 1, 1985

'Berlin', Jewish Virtual Library, jewishvirtuallibrary.org/berlin

'Berlin, the Jewish Museum and the Holocaust Memorial', Isabella Pezzini, chapter 5, Reading Memory Sites through Signs: Hiding into Landscape, Cristina Demaria & Violi Patrizia (eds.), Amsterdam University Press, Amsterdam, 2023

Berlin Diary: The Journal of a Foreign Correspondent, William L Shirer, Hamish Hamilton, London, 1942

Berlin: The Downfall 1945, Antony Beevor, Penguin, London, 2007

Uncovering their Names and Stories:

<u>Berlin's Grand Hotels and the Crisis of German Democracy</u>, Adam Bisno, Perspectivia.net/servlets/MCRFileNodeServlet/pnet_derivate_000 02120/27_bisno_hotels.pdf

<u>Beitrage zur Geschichte de Juden in Calbe (Saale)</u>, Hanns Schwachenwalde, manuscript, 1988[643]

<u>Between Dignity and Despair: Jewish Life in Nazi Germany (Studies in Jewish History)</u>, 1st edition, Marion A Kaplan, Oxford University Press, New York, 1999

'Blessing hands in Plettenberg', Prof John Löwenhardt, Löwenhardt Foundation, The Netherlands

'Book Burning Memorial at Bebelplatz', Visitberlin.de/

<u>Bound upon a Wheel of Fire</u>, John V. H. Dippel, Basic Books, New York, 1996

'Calbe (Sachsen-Anhalt)', xn--jdische-gemeinden-22b.de/index.php/gemeinden/c-d/75-calbe-sachsen-anhalt

Certified Award on the Account of Max Steinthal, Claim Number 501712/HB/AC, Claims Resolution Tribunal, 12 October 2007

'Chajim Steinthal' by Friedrich Ekkehard Vollbach, Sachsen-Lese.de

'Changing my Name', Rhoda Hassmann, The Globe and Mail (Toronto), 24 May 2000, pA20

'Cologne Cathedral and 'The Jews'', Harald Schlüter, Kölner Dom (Cologne Cathedral) website, Koelner-dom.de/en/tour/cologne-cathedral-and-the-jews

<u>Colonels in Blue - U.S. Colored Troops, U.S. Armed Forces, Staff Officers and Special Units,</u> Roger D Hunt, McFarland, New York, 2022

<u>The Coming of the Third Reich: How the Nazis Destroyed Democracy and Seized Power in Germany</u>, Richard J Evans, Penguin, London, 9 August 2012

---

[643] copy held in Magdeburg City Library archives

'Community Centre and Synagogue', Jewish Congregation Adass Yisroel, Berlin, Adassjisroel.de/en/today/community-center-and-synagogue/

Comrades Betrayed: Jewish World War I Veterans Under Hitler, Michael Geheran, Cornell University Press, Ithaca New York, 2020

'Conservation Project Beaufort', Australian War Memorial

'Culture and Exchange: The Jews of Königsberg, 1700-1820', Jill Storm, PhD dissertation, Washington University, St. Louis Missouri, May 2010. All Theses and Dissertations (ETDs). 335, openscholarship.wustl.edu/etd/335

'Dessau', Richard Gottheil, Siegmund Salfeld, Isaac Broyde and Joseph Jacobs, JewishEncyclopedia.com, 2002-2021

The Diary of Anne Frank, Anne Frank, Avarang Books, 2023

Die Juden in Hamburg 1590-1990, Saskia Rohde, Doelling Und Galitz Verla, Hamburg, 1991

Division of Labour among the Perpetrators in Sachsenhausen Concentration Camp, Günter Morsch, Metropol, Berlin, 2018

'Do remember the past, but do not be held captive by it', Rabbi Jonathan Sacks, The Rabbi Sacks Legacy, from The Times, 17 July 2004

Dunera Boys, Defining Moments, National Museum Australia

'The Dunera Boys in History and Memory', Ken Inglis, Australian Jewish Historical Society Journal, November 2013, Vol. XXI

'The Dunera Incident', Albert Isaacs, presentation prepared for U3A Banyule, 18 May 2022

The Dunera Internees, Benzion Patkin, Cassell Australia, 1979

Dunera Lives: A Visual History, Ken Inglis, Seumas Spark, Jay Winter & Carol Bunyan, Monash University Publishing, Clayton, 2018

Encyclopedia Judaica, The Gale Group, 2007

'The End of the Holy Roman Empire', Richard Cavendish, History Today, Volume 56, Issue 7, July 2006

Uncovering their Names and Stories:

'Enemy Aliens', Kate Garrett, Andrew McNamara & Seumas Spark, State Library of NSW, 2022

Erinnerungsort Alter Schlachthof Ausstellungskatalog /Alter Schlachthof Memorial Centre Exhibition Catalogue, Dr Joachim Schröder, Droste-Verlag, Düsseldorf, 2019

'Family and Everyday Life', Dr Stefanie Fischer, Hamburg key documents on German-Jewish history, Institut für die Geschichte der Deutschen Juden, 2016

'Family get-together with two dogs', Prof John Löwenhardt, Löwenhardt Foundation, The Netherlands

'Family History and the Leo Baeck Institute', Frank Mecklenburg, in Jewish Families and Kinship in the Early Modern and Modern Eras, (PaRDeS; 26), University of Potsdam, Potsdam, 2020, S. 51-57

'Family Relationship Terms', Ancestry.com, Support.ancestry.co.uk/s/article/Understanding-Kinship-Terms#

Family Research notes on Steinthal family in register books of 'Protected Jews' in Gröbzig, Anke Boeck, Landesarchiv Sachsen-Anhalt, Dessau-Roßlau, 19 March 2024

Family Tree Historical Atlas of Germany, James M Beidler, Family Tree Books, 2019

Fatherland and the Jews: Two Pamphlets by Alfred Wiener, 1919 and 1924, Alfred Wiener, Granta, London, 2022

Field of Stelae and Information Centre, Uwe Neumärker, Memorial to the Murdered Jews of Europe, 2017

'The forgotten haven: Kent camp that saved 4,000 German Jews', Harriet Sherwood, The Guardian, 24 August 2019

'The Former Wolverhampton Synagogue & Jewish Community', Wolverhampton, West Midlands, JCR-UK (Jewish Communities & Records)

'Fritz Pfeffer', Anne Frank House, annefrank.org/en/anne-frank/main-characters/fritz-pfeffer/

'From Berlin to the Bush', Ken Inglis, The Monthly, August 2010

Gedenkbuch Wuppertal, (Memorial book Wuppertal), 2019

Gemeindeblatt der Israelitisches Religionsgemeinde zu Leipzig,[644] 13 June 1930 and 16 August 1935

'Genealogical Resources for German Jewish Ancestry' by George E Arnstein PhD, chapter VII, Germanic Genealogy, A Guide to Worldwide Sources and Migration Patterns, Dr Edward R Brandt et.al., Germanic Genealogy Society, St Paul MN, April 1995

'German church goes to high court to take down perverse anti-Semitic carvings', Toby Axelrod, Times of Israel, 26 June 2020

'German court affirms ruling synagogue arson not anti-Semitic', JTA, The Time of Israel, 15 January 2017

'These German Jewish Baby Names Honor Yekke Heritage', Naomi Kaye Honova, Kveller, 8 August 2023

German Jewry: Its History & Sociology – Selected Essays of Werner J. Cahnman, Joseph B Maier, Judith Marcus & Zoltan Tarr, Routledge, Oxford, 2019

Germany for the Jewish Traveller, German National Tourist Board (GNTB), Frankfurt am Main

'The German Rabbinate Abroad – Australia', Rabbi Dr Raymond Apple, European Judaism, Berghahn Books, Volume 45 No. 2 Autumn 2012

German Rabbis in British Exile and their influence on Judaism in Britain, D. Phil thesis, Astrid Zajdband, University of Sussex, December 2014

'German Jewish Refugees, 1933-1939', Holocaust Encyclopedia, United States Holocaust Memorial Museum

German Virtual Jewish History Tour, David Shyovitz and Mitchell Bard, The Virtual Jewish World, A Project of AICE, 2023

'Germany: 1750-1945', Associate Professor Sharon Gillerman, The Shalvi/Hyman Encyclopedia of Jewish Women, Jewish Women's Archive, 31 December 1999

---

[644] Community Newsletter of the Israelite Religious Community in Leipzig

Uncovering their Names and Stories:

'Germany Handwriting', FamilySearch

Get the Children out!: Unsung heroes of the Kindertransport, Mike Levy, Lemon Soul, London, 2023

'Global Jewish population hits 15.7 million ahead of new year, 46% of them in Israel', Times of Israel Staff, Times of Israel, 15 September 2023

Good Living Street: The fortunes of my Viennese family, Tim Bonyhady, Allen & Unwin, Sydney, 2011

'Gorzów Wielkopolski: Lubusz', International Jewish Cemetery Project, International Association of Jewish Genealogical Societies

'Government Gazette' ("Reichs-Anzeiger") of 5 April 1893

'Grossbritannien und Belgien als aufnahmelan der Judischer Kinder und Jugendlicher aus dem Nationalsozialistischen "Grossdeutschen Reich"', Dr Ursula Reuter, in Kindertransporte 1938/38, Dr Ulrike Schrader (ed.), Begegnungsstätte Alte Synagoge in Wuppertal, Wuppertal, pp.233-243

Guide to Die Famalie Steinthal von Jahre 1720 bis 1935, 1935-1961, AR1393, Leo Baeck Institute

'A Guide to the United States' History of Recognition, Diplomatic, and Consular Relations, by Country, since 1776: North German Confederation', Office of the Historian, US Department of State

'Halberstadt, Germany', Jewish Virtual Library

'Hamburg's Hidden Jewish Heritage', Bill Echikson & Justus Becker, EUPJ News, 15 February 2021

'Handwriting Guide: German Gothic', Resource Guide, Family History Library, Salt Lake City Utah

'Hatred in Plain Sight', Carol Schaefer, Smithsonian Magazine, October 2020

'Heaven on the verge of Hell', Jessica Abelsohn, Australian Jewish News, 11 Oct 2024

'Henry Marlow (Heinz Marowilsky)', transcript of interview with Prof Manfred Brusten, Armadale, 4 October 1994, edited version 6 - 2001

'Hildesheim', JewishEncyclopedia.com

'History in the House of the Hangman: How Postwar Germany Became a Key Site for the Study of Jewish History', Steven E Aschheim and Vivian Liska eds., The German-Jewish Experience Revisited, de Gruyter, Berlin, 2015, pp.171-192

'The history of Jewish families in early modern and modern times', Mirjam Thulin & Marcus Krah, in Jewish Families and Kinship in the Early Modern and Modern Eras, (PaRDeS; 26), University of Potsdam, Potsdam, 2020, S. 13-23

A History of the Jews, Paul Johnson, Harper Collins, 2009

'The History of Old German Cursive Alphabet and Typefaces', Karen Lodder, Germangirlinamerica.com

'History of the Holy Roman Empire', Holy Roman Empire Association, holyromanempireassociation.com

History on our Doorstep: Harwich & the Kindertransport, Sian Allpress, New Heritage Solutions CIC, London, 2020

Hitler's Empire: Nazi Rule in Occupied Europe, Prof Mark Mazower, Allen Lane, London, 2008 (Uncorrected Proof Copy)

'Hitler shot himself 75 years ago, ending an era of war, genocide and destruction, Michael E. Ruane, The Washington Post, 30 April 2020

Holocaust Encyclopedia, United States Holocaust Memorial Museum, Washington DC

The Holocaust, Laurence Rees, Viking, London, 2017

The Holocaust and Australia: Refugees, Rejection and Memory, Prof Paul Bartrop, Bloomsbury, London, 2022

The Holocaust: The Jewish Tragedy, Sir Martin Gilbert, Harper Collins, London, 1987

The Holocaust: Voices of Scholars, Jolanta Ambrosewicz-Jacobs (ed.), Centre for Holocaust Studies, Jagiellonian University, Auschwitz-Birkenau State Museum, Krakow, 2009

'How did the children get a place?', National Holocaust Centre and Museum (UK), Journey.holocaust.org.uk/

Uncovering their Names and Stories:

'How to Find a Jewish Grave', Nolan Altman, My Jewish Learning website

<u>How to Trace your German Ancestors: A Guide for Australians and New Zealanders</u>, Owen Mützelburg, Hale & Iremonger, Sydney, 1989

'How to trace Jewish ancestors and find their family records', The Findmypast Team, Find my Past, 3 April 2020

<u>How to Write Your Personal or Family History</u>, Katie Funk Wiebe, Good Books, 2017

'I can't forget what the Nazis did to my family, but I can be grateful to a repentant Germany', Rabbi Michael Meyerstein, JTA, 12 April 2023

'In Berlin, Teaching Germany's Jewish History', Edward Rothstein, New York Times, 1 May 2009

'Introduction on Yiddish', Aya Elyada, <u>Naharaim</u> (journal), 10(2) pp 169-173, 30 November 2016, in <u>De Gruyter</u>

'Izbica', Holocaust Historical Society, holocausthistoricalsociety.org.uk, 2016

<u>Izbica: A Story of a Place</u>, Robert Kuwałek and Weronika Litwin, Foundation for the Preservation of Jewish Heritage in Poland, Poland, 2012

<u>Jews and the Civil War: A Reader</u>, Jonathan D. Sarna and Adam D Mendelsohn (eds.), New York University Press, New York, 2011

'Jewish Communities in Saxony-Anhalt', Dr Marc Jarzebowski, DMJ website, 27 April 2021

<u>Jewish Daily Life in Germany, 1618-1945</u>, Marion Kaplan (ed.), Oxford University Press, 2005

<u>Jews in Germany: From Roman Times to the Weimar Republic</u>, Nachum T. Gidal, Könemann, Cologne, 1988

<u>Jewish Life in Germany: Memoirs from Three Centuries</u>, Monika Richarz (ed.), Indiana University Press, 1991

<u>Jewish Life in Halberstadt</u>, Jutta Dick, Berend Lehmann Museum, Halberstadt

'The Jewish orphanage for Westfalia & Rhineland', Prof John Löwenhardt, Löwenhardt Foundation, The Netherlands, 24 December 2012

'Jews in Saxony-Anhalt: History and Present', Ursulahomann.de/ copied from Tribune: Magazine for Understanding Judaism, 39th year, issue 154, 2bd quarter 2000

The Jewish Response to German Culture, J. Reinharz & W. Schatzberg (eds.), University Press of New England, Hanover, 1985

The Jews of Germany, Ruth Gay, Yale University Press, New Haven, 1992

Jews of Vistytis, Dr Vilius Kočiubaitis,[645] translated by Ralph Salinger

Juden in Halberstadt, W Hartmann, Druckerei Lüders, Halberstadt, 2005

Die Juden in Hamburg 1590 bis 1990, Arno Herzig (ed.) with Saskia Rohde, Dölling and Galitz Verlag, 1991

'Judeo-German (West Yiddish)', Yaron Matras, Archive of Endangered and Smaller Languages

Jüdisches Hamburg, Erika Hirsch, Landeszentrale für Poliitische Bildung Hamburg, Hamburg, 2021

Jüdisches Identität in Deutschland und im Exil: der Lebensweg des Wissenschaftlerehepaars Hans und Rahel Liebeschütz, Silke Kaiser, Hamburg University Press, Hamburg, 2021

Jüdisches Leben in Ostpreußen: Geschichte und Untergang einer großen Kultur, Brigitte Jager-Dabek, neobooks, Germany, 25 September 2013

Das Jüdisches Leipzig: Ein Kleiner Stadtführer, (Jewish Leipzig: A Short City Guide), Christian Böwe, Leipzig

Jüdisches Leipzig, Nora Pester, Hentrich & Hentrich, Germany, 1 December 2022

Jüdisches Museum Berlin, Marie Naumann & Katharina Wulffius, Stiftung Jüdisches Museum, Berlin, 2020

---

[645] medical doctor from the village of Vistytis

Uncovering their Names and Stories:

'Die jüdische Volksschule in Anhalt von 1830 – 1840', H. Steinthal, <u>Zeitschrift für die Geschichte der Juden in Deutschland,</u> 1890, Band IV. (1890) Heft 1, page 66-74, Germany

<u>Kate's Story</u>, the autobiography of Kate Rotman, unpublished manuscript

'Kindertransport 1938-1940', <u>Holocaust Encyclopedia</u>, US Holocaust Memorial Museum

<u>Die Kindertransporte 1938/39: von Wuppertal nach England</u>, Anna Ruhland, unpublished master's thesis, Universität zu Köln, Cologne, 29 July 2005[646]

'The Kindertransport and Refugees', Learning about the Holocaust and Genocides, Holocaust Memorial Day Trust

<u>The Kindertransport: Contesting Memory</u>, Jennifer Craig-Norton, Indiana University Press, Bloomington, 2019

'Kindertransporte (Children's Transports) 1938/39', Jüdisches Museum Berlin, Jmberlin.de/en/topic-kindertransport-1938-39

'Kindertransport: History and Memory', Rebekka Göpfert (ed.) & Andrea Hammel (trans.), in <u>Shofar: An Interdisciplinary Journal of Jewish Studies,</u> Vol 23, No.1, Fall 2004, pp.21-27, Purdue University Press, West Lafayette

<u>Der Kölner Dom und die Juden</u>, Peter Füssenich und Klaus Hardering (eds.), Verlag Kölner Dom, Köln, 2018

'Landsberg an der Warthe (Brandenburg Neumark) – today in Poland', Benjamin Rosendahl, Germanysynagogues.com

'Law on Alteration of Family and Personal Names', <u>Holocaust Encyclopedia</u>, United States Holocaust Memorial Museum

'Learn the History – Why did Jews not leave Germany when the Nazis came to power?', Konrad Kwiet, Sydney Jewish Museum blog, Sydney, 19 September 2019

---

[646] copy held by Begegnungsstätte Alte Synagoge Wuppertal

'Levi Löwenhardt', Prof John Löwenhardt, Löwenhardt Foundation, The Netherlands

'Life sentence for Halle synagogue shooter who killed 2 in Yom Kippur rampage', Times of Israel, 21 December 2020

Life Under Siege: The Jews of Magdeburg under Nazi Rule, Michael E Abrahams-Sprod, PhD. thesis, University of Sydney, 2006

Lonely Planet Germany, Marc Di Duca et.al., Lonely Planet, 10th edition, 2021

Long Road to Liberty: The Odyssey of a German Regiment in the Yankee Army: The 15th Missouri Volunteer Infantry, Donald Allendorf, The Kent State University Press, Kent OH, 2014

'Löwenhardt children in Hörde', Löwenhardt Foundation, The Netherlands

'Luther's dark side - and how the Nazis abused it for their ideology' article on "Luther's Words Everywhere... - Martin Luther in National Socialism" exhibition, which opened on February 25, 2018 in Saarbrücken's Ludwigskirche, Luther2017.de/neuigkeiten/luthers-dunkle-seite-und-wie-die-nazis-sie-fuer-ihre-ideologie-missbrauchten/index.html

Maria Blitz: Final Days in East Prussia: An Unspoken Chapter of the Holocaust, Uwe Neumärker, Foundation Memorial to the Murdered Jews of Europe, 2019

'Many anti-semitic artefacts in Cologne Cathedral', CNE News, Christian Network Europe, 27 September 2023

'Maritime tales – tragedy of the Arandora Star', Stephen Guy, National Museums Liverpool

'Marking the 80th anniversary of the Dambusters Raid', Department of Veterans' Affairs, Australian Government, 16 May 2023

'May 1939: new light on the Kindertransport story', Tim Locke, 10 May 2020, Ephraimneumeyer.wordpress.com/2020/05/10/may-1939-new-light-on-the-kindertransport-story/

Memorial to the Murdered Jews of Europe: Field of Stelae and Information Centre, Uwe Neumärker (EIC), Foundation Memorial to the Murdered Jews of Europe, Berlin, 2017

Uncovering their Names and Stories:

'Milakowo Jewish Cemetery', ESJF Cemeteries, Esjf-cemeteries.org/survey/milakowo-jewish-cemetery/

'Milakowo', Virtual Shtetl, Polin Museum of the History of Polish Jews, Sztetl.org.pl/en/towns/m/743-milakowo/99-history/137684-history-of-community

'Minsk', Holocaust Encyclopedia, United States Holocaust Memorial Museum

'Mistake', Prof John Löwenhardt, Löwenhardt Foundation, The Netherlands, 13 March 2024

Monuments Men, Robert M. Edsel with Bret Witter, Arrow Books, 2013

'My Name Change: A Story About Genocide and Racism', Dr Rhoda Hassmann, 3 October 2014, rhodahassmann.blogspot.com

'Nazi Looted Art: The Holocaust Records Preservation Project', Anne Rothfeld, Prologue Magazine, National Archives, Summer 2002, Vol. 34, No. 2

'New German citizens must declare Israel's right to exist', Sam Jones, Financial Times, 26 June 2024

'The Nine Löwenhardt brothers in World War One', Prof John Löwenhardt, Löwenhardt Foundation, The Netherlands

'Orinoco Sketches', Gabriel Kahane, Content.thespco.org/music/concert-library/composition/orinoco-sketches-for-string-orchestra-gabriel-kahane

Ortsblatt-Leipzig – Leipziger westen, (Leipzig local newspaper - Leipzig west), January 2016

'Palestinians admit attack on Wuppertal synagogue', DPA/The Local Germany, 14 January 2015

'Pauline Löwenhardt, 1934 – 2024', Prof John Löwenhardt, Löwenhardt Foundation, The Netherlands, 10 July 2024

Personal search and Jewish genealogy (bibliography), Judith Kessler, Jewish Community of Berlin

'Persons Holocaust History Tracing – External Resource Links', Melbourne Holocaust Museum,

The Pity of It All: A Portrait of Jews in Germany 1743-1933, Amos Elon, Penguin, 2002

'Plettenberg (North Rhine-Westphalia)', Aus der Geschichte der jüdischen Gemeinden im deutschen Sprachraum, xn--jdische-gemeinden-22b.de/index.php/gemeinden/p-r/1582-plettenberg-nordrhein-westfalen

Der Pogrom Gegen Die Juden in Wuppertal Im November 1938, Ulrike Schrader, Begegnungsstätte Alte Synagoge Wuppertal, Wuppertal, 2018

'Polizeiverordnung Uber die Kennzeichnung der Juden', Verfassungen der Welt, 1 September 1941

'Provenance Research on Judaica and other holdings in the Museum Synagogue Gröbzig since 1933', Tim Schauer, Museum Synagogue Gröbzig, 29 June 2020

A Recipe for Writing Family History, Devon Noel Lee & Andrew Lee, FHF Group LLC, 2018

'A remembrance', Gabriel Kahane, memorial for his grandmother, 16 May 2010, Gabrielkahane.tumblr.com/post/604974726/a-remembrance

Retterwiderstand in Wuppertal während des Nationalsozialismus, Inauguraldissertation zur Erlangung des Grades eines Doktors der Philosophie in der Philosophischen Fakultät (Fach Geschichte) der Heinrich-Heine-Universität Düsseldorf vorgelegt, von Frank Friedhelm Homber

'Quantifying the Holocaust: Hyperintense kill rates during the Nazi genocide', Lewi Stone, Science Advances, January 2019

'Rabbi Zimmels and the Dunera', Rabbi Raymond Apple, Australian Jewish Historical Society Journal, 2022, Vol 26, Issue Part 1, p9

'Reading Hebrew Tombstones', Warren Blatt, 2013, JewishGen

'Refugees: Hitler's Loss, Our Gain', Brian Fitzpatrick & Noel Counihan, Jewish Council to Combat Fascism and Antisemitism, Melbourne, 1944

'Representative Edith Nourse Rogers: A Beacon of Light in America's Darkest Moral Hour', Elazar Cramer, 2019 Winning Essay

Uncovering their Names and Stories:

John F Kennedy Profile in Courage Essay Contest for High School Students, jfklibrary.org, 2019

The Routledge History of the Holocaust, Jonathan C Friedman (ed.), Routledge, Oxford, 2011

'Rural German museum hustles for funding here', The Jewish News of Northern California, 18 June 1999

Sachsenhausen Concentration Camp: Events and Developments 1936-1945, Günter Morsch & Astrid Ley (ed.), Metropol, 2023

'Sachsenhausen Memorial and Museum' (visitor pamphlet), Friedheim Hoffmann and Volker Kreidler, Brandenburg Memorials Foundation, Oranienburg, 2023

'Salomon-Georg Löwenhardt', Prof John Löwenhardt, Löwenhardt Foundation, The Netherlands, 18 February 2023

'Schutzjude', Joseph Jacobs, JewishEncyclopedia.com

'Schutzjuden', Encyclopedia.com

'Small Fortress Terezin', Terezin memorial leaflet, Terezin Small Fortress, Terezin

'Spiritual Heroes of the Dunera Affair', Debbie Maimon, Yated Ne'eman, 13 April 2022

'Stolpersteininitiative Charlottenburg – Wilmersdorf', Karin Sievert, District office Charlottenburg-Wilmersdorf, Berlin, berlin.de/ba-charlottenburg-wilmersdorf/ueber-den-bezirk/geschichte/stolpersteine/artikel.1207718.php

'The Story of the Dambusters: Operation Chastise, May 1943', The Historic England Blog, 15 May 2023

'The Story of the Yekkes – Jewish Germans in the Land of Israel', ANU – Museum of the Jewish People, 30 April 2018

Suicide in Nazi Germany, Christian Goeschel, Oxford University Press, Oxford, 2009

'Summerland Mansions', National Trust Victoria

'Summerland Mansions 17-27 Fitzroy Street, St Kilda', St Kilda Historical Society, skhs.org.au extracted from Richard Peterson, A

Place of Sensuous Resort: Buildings of St Kilda and their People, chapter 15, St Kilda Historical Society Inc, 2005

'Summerland Mansions', Victorian Heritage Database Report, Heritage Victoria, November 1999

'Swiss in the American Civil War: A Forgotten Chapter of our Military History', David Vogelsanger, Swiss American Historical Society Review, Vol.51 No.3 Article 5, 2015

'Tax lists from the first half of the 19th century as sources for family and community research', Dr Ruth Leiserowitz, Presentation to the 43rd IAJGS, London, 2 August 2023

'Terezin Concentration Camp: History & Overview', Jewish Virtual Library

'Theresienstadt', Yad Vashem – The World Holocaust Remembrance Center, yadvashem.org/holocaust/about/ghettos/theresienstadt.html

Topography of Terror: Gestapo, SS and Reichssicherheitshauptamt, Reinhardt Rürup (ed.), Verag Willmuth Arenhövel, Berlin, 2000

'Touring Present Day Vistytis', Howard Sandys, Howard.sandys.ca/, 2005

Trace your German roots online: A complete guide to German genealogy websites, James M. Beidler, Family Tree Books, 2016

Tracing your Jewish ancestors: A guide for family historians, Rosemary Wenzerul, Pen & Sword, 2008

'The Traders of Wyshtyten: The Border as a Modernization Factor for Litvaks in Transnational Space in 19th Century', Dr Ruth Leizerowitz, pp319-331, in Central and European Jews at the Crossroads of Tradition and Modernity, Jurgita Siauciunaite-Verbickiene and Larisa Lempertiene (eds.), Vilnius: Centre for Studies of the Culture of East European Jews, 2006

Uncovering their Names and Stories:

'Transport I/46, Train Da 502 from Berlin, Berlin (Berlin), City of Berlin, Germany to Theresienstadt, Ghetto, Czechoslovakia on 17/08/1942', Yad Vashem, Collections.yadvashem.org/en/deportations/5093025

Traveller's Guide to Jewish Germany, Billie Ann Lopez & Peter Hirsch, Pelican Publishing, 1998

'Über Botschaften', Sophie Blasberg, Fabian Maruschat et.al., Zeit Fur Wuppertal, July 2014

'The Ultimate Refuge: Suicide in the Jewish Community under the Nazis', Prof Konrad Kwiet, The Leo Baeck Institute Year Book, Vol 29, Issue 1

'US-Auszeichnung für deutschen Einwanderer: Wie Arno Heller gegen Hitler kämpfte', Johannes Korge, Der Spiegel, 3 February 2012

'Vater und neun Jungen', Der Schild, Journal of the German Union of Jewish Front Soldiers (Reichsbund Jüdischer Frontsoldaten, 1922-1938), 6 March 1936

'Virtual Jewish World: Gorzów Wielkopolski, Poland', Jewish Virtual Library, Encyclopaedia Judaica, 2008

'Vishtinetz, Lithuania: A visit to Vistytis', 1994, Bert Oppenheim, JewishGen

'Vistytis' chapter, Encyclopedia of Jewish Communities in Lithuania, Josef Rosin, Yad Vashem, 1996

'Vistytis, Lithuania: Autobiography of Jacob Hyam Rubenstein 1890-1963', Jacob Hyam Rubenstein, JewishGen

Vzpominsky – Memories, Ludek Sladek, Terezin, 2018

'Der Weg zur Löwenhardts', Sebastian Zimmer, Löwenhardt Foundation, The Netherlands, 26 September 2021

'We remember Theodor Kraft and his son Walter', Gegen Dasver Gessen, Informationsstand, November 2020

What They Saved: Pieces of a Jewish Past, Nancy K Miller, University of Nebraska Press, Lincoln, 2011

'Women's Lives: Work and Impact of Jewish Women in Hamburg', Hamburg key documents on German-Jewish history, Institut für die Geschichte der Deutschen Juden, 2016

'World Renowned Guitarist, David Leisner, to Give Public Workshop', News.uark.edu/, University of Arkansas, April 24, 2017

'Why do Jews put stones on graves?', Yehuda Shurpin, Lifecycle Events, Chabad.org, Chabad.org/library/article_cdo/aid/3002484/jewish/Why-Do-Jews-Put-Stones-on-Graves.htm

'Why was Nazi Germany called the Third Reich?', Michael Ray, Britannica.com

'Yiddish', BJE: NSW Board of Jewish Education, Bje.org.au/knowledge-centre/jewish-languages/non-hebrew/yiddish/

Yizkor for Rose: A Life Lost and Found, Dr Erica Cervini, Kindle Book, Melbourne, 2020

'You can't run away from Izbica. Jan Karski's story', Przemyslaw Batorski, The Emanuel Ringelblum Jewish Historical Institute, Warsaw

Zerbrochene Zukunft: Der Pogrom Gegen Die Juden in Wuppertal Im November 1938, Dr Ulrike Schrader, Begegnungsstätte Alte Synagoge Wuppertal, Wuppertal, 2018

Zwanzig Jahre Hamburger Gesellschaft für Jüdische Geneaologie, Jürgen Sielemann, GeistigeR Schopferln, Hamburg, 2016

15.3 Databases, websites and social media

Academia.edu

Alemannia-judaica.de

Ancestry DNA

Annefrank.org

Avenza Maps app

Britannica.com

Uncovering their Names and Stories:

Bterezin.org.il (Beit Terezin)

Cindislist.com

Compgen, Verein für Computergenealogie (Association for Computer Genealogy)

Datenbank Judische Verfolgte in Wuppertal, Bergische Universität Wuppertal

Deutsches Zeitungsportal (German newspapers)

Encyclopedia.com

Eisenman Architects website

Ephraimneumeyer.wordpress.com (Kindertransport related blogsite)

Familysearch.org

Findagrave.com

Former Jewish Leipzigers and their Descendants

Gedenkbuch, Bundesarchiv.de

Genealogyindexer.org

Genealogical Translations Facebook Group[647]

Geneanet.org

Geneteka, Genenteka.genealodzy.pl

Geni World Family Tree[648]

GenTeam, Die genealogische Datenbank

Geogen.stoepel.net/ (Geogen)

Germanology Unlocked

Germanroots.com/germandata.html

---

[647] Please be aware that they provide a great free service but are very strict about their rules.

[648] Useful for hypothesis building, but it includes a lot of questionable and not well substantiated information, so content should be tested against actual evidence and historical records.

GerSIG: German Jewish Genealogy Special Interest Group Facebook Group

Google Lens

Harwichhavenhistory.co.uk/sanctuary/ (Harwich Haven Surrender and Sanctuary website)

Institut für die Gesichte der deutschen Juden (Institute for the History of German Jews)

Jewish Genealogy in Latvia and Lithuania Facebook Group

JewishGen.org which is part of the Museum of Jewish Heritage in New York City

Jewish Genealogy Portal Facebook Group

Jewish Records Indexing (JRI) Poland Database

Jewish Virtual Library: A Project of AICE

JEWS – Jekkes Engaged Worldwide in Social Networking Facebook Group

Jüdische Familienforschung in Berlin / Jewish Genealogy in Berlin Facebook Group

Kindertransporte aus Nordrhein-Westfälische, JAWNE Place of Learning and Memorial, kindertransporte-nrw.eu/projekt_3.html

Kitchener Camp – 1939 Register, Kitchenercamp.co.uk/list-of-names/

Löwenhardt Foundation, The Netherlands

Litvak SIG, Lithuanian Special Interest Group All Lithuania Database

Mapchart app

Mapping the Lives: A Central Memorial for the Persecuted in Europe 1933-1945

Mindat.org

MyHeritage.com

Namensindex, der Ost und Westpreußichen Standesamtsregistrar

Uncovering their Names and Stories:

Newspapers.com

OldNews.com

Picryl.com

Pixabay.com

Refugeemap.org (The Wiener Holocaust Library)

Sammlungen.ub.uni-frankfurt.de/ (especially for newspapers and journal articles)

Shapell Roster of Jewish Service in the American Civil War, Shapell Manuscript Foundation

Stolpersteine-berlin.de/en/glossar

Studio Libeskind website

Tracing the Tribe – Jewish Genealogy on Facebook Group

Transkribus.ai

Trove online database, National Library of Australia (Australian newspapers)

Veneto Market Gardeners 1927 website

Verein für Familienforschung in Ost- und Westpreußen e.V. (Association for Family Research in East and West Prussia)

Vistytis New Jewish Cemetery digitised documents, Litvak Cemetery Catalogue, Maceva

WHC.unesco.org (UNESCO World Heritage Sites)

Wirtualny Sztetl, Sztetl.org.pl (Virtual Shtetl Poland)

Woollcombe.co.uk – Woollcombe family tree

Yad Vashem Central Database of Shoah Victims' Names

YIVO Institute for Jewish Research Facebook page

YIVO Institute for Jewish Research website

15.4 Genealogical and historical societies

Australian Jewish Genealogical Society Victoria

Australian Jewish Historical Society Victoria

Bergische Geschichtsverein e.V., Wuppertal

Dunera Association, Melbourne

Dunera Interest Group, UK

Genealogische Gesellschaft Hamburg e.V. (Hamburg Genealogical Society)

GerSIG: German Jewish Genealogy Special Interest Group

Hamburger Gesellschaft für jüdische Genealogie e.V., Hamburg (Hamburg Jewish Genealogical Society)

Historische Gesellschaft der Deutschen Bank e.V., Frankfurt am Main

Israel Genealogy Research Association

JewishGen German Jewish Special Interest Group

Jewish Genealogical Society, Colorado

Jewish Genealogy Society of Cleveland

Jewish Genealogy Society of Pittsburgh

Jews in East Prussia, History and Culture Society (Juden in Ostpreussen)

Jews – Jekkes Engaged Worldwide in Social Networking

Lithuanian – Jewish Special Interest Group

15.5 Museums and libraries

Anne Frank House, Amsterdam

ANU – Museum of the Jewish People, Tel Aviv

Begegnungsstätte Alte Synagoge Museum, Wuppertal

Berend Lehman Museum, Halberstadt

Bernburg Castle Museum

Erinnerungsort Alter Schlachthof, (Old Slaughterhouse Memorial Centre), Düsseldorf University

Uncovering their Names and Stories:

Germania Judaica library, Cologne

Gröbzig Synagogue Museum, Germany

Hamburg Museum of History library and reading room

Heinrich Heine Universität Düsseldorf, Universitäts-Und Landesbibliothek, Düsseldorf

House of the Wannsee Conference Memorial and Education Centre, Berlin

Jewish Museum of Australia, St Kilda

Jüdisches Museum Berlin, Germany

Klaus Synagogue, Halberstadt

Lamm Jewish Library of Australia, Caulfield

Landeshauptstadt Magdeburg Stadtbibliothek (City Library Magdeburg), Sachsen-Anhalt

Library of Congress, Washington DC

Melbourne Holocaust Museum, Elsternwick

Memorial to the Murdered Jews of Europe and Information Centre, Berlin

MiQua, LVR - Jewish Museum in the Archaeological Quarter, Cologne

Museum of Jewish Heritage – A Living Memorial to the Holocaust, New York

Museum Neue Synagoge Kaliningrad

National Library of Australia, Canberra

The National Library of Israel, Jerusalem

National Museum of Australia, Canberra

NS (National Socialism) Documentation Centre of the City of Cologne

Prague Jewish Museum, Josefov, Prague

Sachsenhausen Gedenkstatte (state memorial) und Museum, Oranienburg

Saxony-Anhalt Museum Association

Stadtmuseum Düsseldorf

State Library of Victoria, Melbourne

Stiftung Moses Mendelssohn Akademie, Halberstadt

Terezin Concentration Camp Memorial and Ghetto Museum (Památník Terezín), Czech Republic

Topography of Terror History Museum, Berlin

United States Holocaust Memorial Museum, Washington DC

Universitätsbibliotek (University Library), Goethe Universität, Frankfurt am Main

USC Shoah Foundation, Los Angeles

Yad Vashem, Jerusalem

15.6 Video resources

7 Essential Tips for Starting German Genealogy, Katherine Schober, Germanology Unlocked, FamilySearch, Youtube, 2 March 2024

Arno Heller Holocaust Survivor testimony,[649] Interviewed by Ellen Adler, Rego Park New York, USC Shoah Foundation, 12 September 1996

The Auctioneers: Profiting from the Holocaust, documentary, Jan N. Lorenzen and Michael Schönherr, 2018

A Beginner's Guide to German Jewish Genealogy in North Rhine-Westphalia, webinar, Jeanette Rosenberg, IGRA, 3 April 2022

Brigitte Steele nee Meyer's Holocaust testimony, Holocaust Museum Houston, 9 July 2004

Führerbunker: Adolf Hitler's Final Days, documentary, 2020

---

[649] Arno was my father's first cousin.

Uncovering their Names and Stories:

Henri Korn Holocaust Survivor testimony,[650] Melbourne Holocaust Museum, 2012

Histories of the Holocaust – Dachau: State within a State, documentary, 2011

Into the Arms of Strangers: Stories of the Kindertransport, Documentary, Warner Bros., 2000

Izbica – Drehkreuz des Todes, Frank Gutermuth and Wolfgang Schoen, documentary, 2007

Jewish Genealogy in the Germanies, Roger Lustig, JewishGen Youtube, 25 May 2022

Jewish Surnames and Patronymics - Tracing Your Ancestors before they had Surnames, Dr Thomas Fürth, JewishGen Youtube, 2 June 2022

Das Landesarchiv Sachsen-Anhalt und seine Bestände für Familenforschende, Landesarchiv Sachsen-Anhalt

Locating German Records: Beyond Family Search and Ancestry, Katherine Schober Germanology Unlocked, Zoom, 9 April 2024

One Life, movie about Nicholas Winton and the Czech Kindertransport, 2023

Sherman's History: A Brief History of Steve Sherman and Elsa Elkan, Raymon Sherman, Youtube, 2024

Tour Across the Jewish cemetery of Gröbzig, Gröbzig Synagogue Museum, Youtube, 12 November 2020

Tour of the Synagogue of Gröbzig Germany, Gröbzig Synagogue Museum, Youtube, 15 November 2020

Die Wannseekonferenz, docudrama, 2020

15.7 Cemeteries

Alter Israelitischer Friedhof, Leipzig

---

[650] Henri Korn was born in Wuppertal and witnessed Kristallnacht in Elberfeld-Wuppertal, Germany.

Alte Jüdischer Friedhof Dresden (thanks to Hatikvah, Dresden)

Findagrave.com

Friedhof Calbe, Germany

Friedhof Liebstadt, Germany

Friedhof Sessenhausen, Germany

JewishGen Online Worldwide Burial Registry (JOWBR), JewishGen

Jüdischer-friedhof-altona.de/datenbank.html

Jüdische Friedhöfe[651] in Deutschland und Angrenzenden Ländern[652]

Jüdischer Friedhof An Der Strangriede, Hannover

Jüdischer Friedhof Bernburg

Jüdischer Friedhof Calbe

Jüdischer Friedhof Dierdorf

Jüdischer Friedhof Fröndenberg

Jüdischer Friedhof Gröbzig

Jüdischer Friedhof Hennen

Jüdischer Friedhof Königstrasse, Altona, Hamburg

Jüdischer Friedhof Lenhausen

Jüdischer Friedhof Moritzberg, Hildesheim

Jüdischer Friedhof Plettenberg, Freiligrathstraße, Plettenberg

Jüdischer Friedhof an der Strangriede, Hannover

Jüdischer Friedhof Weinbergstrasse, Wuppertal

Jüdischer Friedhof Werl

Melbourne General Cemetery, Carlton North

---

[651] Jüdischer Friedhof = Jewish Cemetery
[652] Jewish cemeteries in Germany and neighbouring countries (online)

Uncovering their Names and Stories:

National Cemetery, Theresienstadt Concentration Camp, Czech Republic

Neue Israelitische Friedhof, Leipzig

Neue Jüdischer Friedhof Dresden

Ohlsdorf Jüdischer Friedhof Ilandkoppel Strasse, Ohlsdorf, Hamburg

Springvale Botanical Cemetery, Melbourne

Stadtfriedhof Stöcken, Hannover

Vistytis New Jewish Cemetery digitised documents, Litvak Cemetery Catalogue, Maceva

Weissensee Jüdischer Friedhof, Berlin

15.8 Synagogues or remains of synagogues

Alte Synagogue, Hannover

Alte Synagogue Memorial, Dessau-Roßlau

Begegnungstätte Alte Synagogue, Wuppertal

Bergische Synagogue & Judische Kultusgemeinde, Wuppertal

Brodyer Synagogue, Leipzig

Halle Synagogue, Halle

Klaus Synagogue, Halberstadt

Melbourne Hebrew Congregation, South Yarra

Neue Synagogue, Oranienburger Strasse, Berlin

Neue Synagogue, Hannover

Neue Synagogue, Dessau-Roßlau

Old Gröbzig Synagogue, Gröbzig

Pinkas Synagogue, Prague

Poolstrasse Synagogue, Hamburg

Roonstrasse Synagogue, Cologne

Schwerin Synagogue, Schwerin

Spanish Synagogue, Prague

St Kilda Hebrew Congregation, St Kilda

Temple Beth Israel, St Kilda

Wörlitz Synagogue, Wörlitz

15.9 Presentations

'The Dunera Incident', Albert Isaacs, presentation prepared for U3A Banyule, 18 May 2022.

'The Holocaust and Australia: Refugees, Rejection and Memory', Prof Paul Bartrop, presentation to the Australian Jewish Historical Society Vic, 23 March 2023.

'How to use Genetic Genealogy', Lawrence Fagan PhD, JewishGen Talks, 24 July 2024.

'Introduction to Jewish Genealogy', Liz James, presentation to the Australian Jewish Genealogical Society Vic, Glen Eira Town Hall, 4 February 2024.

'Introduction to JewishGen & Jewish Genealogy', Avraham Groll, JewishGen, presentation to the Jewish Genealogy Society of Cleveland, 5 June 2024.[653]

'Locating German Records: Beyond FamilySearch and Ancestry', Katherine Schober presentation, Germanology, 17 July 2024.

'Navigating Displacement – Archiving the Dunera Collection', presentation by Louise Anemaat, Executive Director Library Services & Dixson Librarian, State Library of New South Wales, at the Lamm Jewish Library, 29 May 2024.

---

[653] Avraham Groll is Vice President for JewishGen at the Museum of Jewish Heritage – A Living Memorial to the Holocaust, New York

Uncovering their Names and Stories:

'Rabbis, Innkeepers, Tricksters: Jewish Life in Poland – Lithuania', presentation by Zachary Mazur, to the Jewish Genealogy Society of Pittsburgh, 7 July 2024.

'A Sacred Bond: How the story of Moritz and Henriette Mandelkern's survival during the Holocaust has transformed lives', Prof Leon Mann AO and Dr Danny Mann-Segal, presentation to the Australian Jewish Historical Society Vic, 18 July 2024.

'Tracing the story of the HMT Dunera in the archives of The Wiener Holocaust Library', presentation by Dr Barbara Warnock to the UK Dunera Interest Group and the Association of Jewish Refugees, 20 May 2024.

'What was it like to be a Jewish soldier in Lincoln's armies?', Prof Adam Mendelsohn, presentation to the Jewish Genealogical Society Colorado, 4 February 2024.[654]

---

[654] Prof Adam Mendelsohn is Director of Kaplan Centre for Jewish Studies, Cape Town and author of Jewish Soldiers in the Civil War: The Union Army, New York University Press, New York, 2022

16.0 Acknowledgements

It is said that it takes a village to raise a child, and so it is with this book. Any significant project, such as a family history research project or writing a non-fiction book, requires the input, cooperation, expertise, local knowledge and professionalism of many people. Everything good about this book is thanks to the amazing friendships, partnerships and collaborations formed through the course of my research.

I am particularly thankful for the kindness, assistance and support from the many German archivists, historians, librarians, genealogists, researchers and museum staff who assisted with my research. Thank you for helping beyond my expectations and being such passionate contributors to this work. Your Gemütlichkeit is greatly appreciated.

When I started this research work, it was like putting together a jigsaw puzzle where there is no picture of the finished puzzle and almost all the pieces were upside down. Maybe a couple of pieces were right side up, giving a few clues to what the whole picture might look like, but the full picture would only reveal itself with time and effort. The people I thank here, helped turn the pieces over, revealing a piece or in some cases several pieces of the full puzzle.

Along the way, I have made some assumptions, hoping that future finds would confirm or disprove the hypotheses made, based on incomplete data. In some cases, census records, archive discoveries or marriage records helped prove or disprove several assumptions. In some cases, the assumptions remain in my family tree, ready to be corrected if need be. Any failures or incorrect assumptions are to be blamed on me, and me alone.

As the author of this work, I deserve all blame and take full responsibility for any errors, inconsistencies, poor assumptions or omissions. Nevertheless, this book would not have been possible without the generous and expert advice, research support, openness and assistance from many dedicated, welcoming and selfless people and organisations.

My thanks are also extended to all the dedicated volunteers who scan records and photograph gravestones, who preserve documents, and who record and digitise the very footprints of our ancestors. Your

Uncovering their Names and Stories:

work helps keep the history of our forefathers maintained and accessible.

I thank *everyone* that has good-heartedly helped bring this book to fruition, including the great people at JewishGen Press, most notably the following who went out of their way to assist, contributing more than they know, from Bensberg, Berlin, Calbe, Canberra, Cleveland, Cologne, Colorado, Dessau-Roßlau, Düsseldorf, East Sussex, Essex, Florida, Frankfurt am Main, Gröbzig, Hamburg, Hoisdorf, Leipzig, London, Los Angeles, Magdeburg, Melbourne, The Netherlands, New Jersey, New York, Oregon, Oxfordshire, San Diego, Sao Paulo, Schönebeck, South Carolina, Tel Aviv, Toronto, Warsaw, Wuppertal and several Kibbutzim in Israel. I owe you all a great debt of gratitude:

- Dr Erica Cervini, my partner in life, award winning journalist, family history researcher, sessional academic at the University of Melbourne, frequent speaker on family history on ABC Radio, chief motivator and adviser, research role model, and fellow committee member of the Australian Jewish Historical Society Vic,

- Ellana Aarons, CEO, B'nai B'rith Victoria and Assoc Prof Peter Schattner, President, B'nai B'rith Victoria for permission to use photos,

- Frau Anke Boeck, Landesarchiv Sachsen-Anhalt, Dessau-Roßlau for her amazing work collating historical Steinthal-Lazarus family records and very generous assistance, her wonderful suggestions, and for being a creative and proactive discoverer of primary resources relating to the Steinthal-Lazarus family,

- Gunther Boss, cousin living in Sao Paulo, Brazil – related through the Steinthal family,

- Prof Dr Manfred Brusten, criminal sociologist and leader of the Stolpersteine project in Wuppertal,

- Carol Bunyan OAM, originally from Hay and now Canberra, Carol is a *Dunera* researcher and writer extraordinaire, for her dedication, amazing *Dunera* knowledge and recall,

- Prof Randall L Bytwerk, German Propaganda Archive, Calvin University, USA for permission to use photos,

- Todd Cohn, CEO, Hate Ends Now which sends a cattle car with exhibits around the US, educating Americans about the Holocaust, for permission to use photos,

- Dr Christoph Danelzik-Brueggemann, DGPh, Head of Collections - 19th Century/Photographic Collections, Stadtmuseum Düsseldorf, for his support and permission to use photos,

- Eitan Drori, Chair and Founder Global Israeli Leadership, for his terrific advice and suggestions regarding people and experts to meet in various parts of Germany during my 'road trip',

- Rodney Eisfelder, the bulldozer clearing away my genealogical roadblocks, President and German genealogy specialist in the Australian Jewish Genealogical Society Vic, I appreciate greatly for his persistence, expertise and advice, and special thanks for kindly finding so many members and details of my Leipzig and Hamburg ancestors,

- Jessica Feinstein, Managing Editor, JewishGen Press, UK who was a delight to work with and helped make this book happen,

- Tanya Fox, Archive Volunteer, World Jewish Relief and the rest of the archives team in the UK for access to their records on my Marowilsky family,

- Reinhard Frost, Deutsche Bank Historical Institute, Frankfurt am Main, for permission to use photos,

- Kim Gasperino, marketing and graphic design guru in Melbourne, for her help with the design of my family trees in this book,

Uncovering their Names and Stories:

- Dr Carlo Gentile, historian and researcher, Martin Buber Institute for Jewish Studies, University of Cologne for our very informative and interesting discussion over coffee,

- Anett Gottschalk, Museum Director, Gröbzig Synagogue Museum for her assistance, advice and very knowledgeable personal tour of the Jewish Cemetery in Gröbzig,

- Mrs M Graham nee Rollinghof, my German teacher at Melbourne High School in the 1970s. My high school German became very useful in my research, reviewing documents, and on my research road-trip,

- The Haarburger brothers for permission to use their father Werner's journal of the *Dunera* voyage,

- Noè Harsel, Museum Director & CEO, Jewish Museum of Australia, St Kilda, for permission to use photos,

- Christine Hartung, Deputy Head, Begegnungsstätte Alte Synagoge, Wuppertal for her very kind assistance with the Jewish history of Wuppertal, including Kristallnacht and the Kindertransport,

- Prof Rhoda Hassmann, my Canadian cousin from my extended Kraft family,

- Katrin Heil, Staatsarchiv Leipzig, for her assistance and for pointing me in the right direction,

- Peter Heller, from New York, a cousin and sharer of information on his Heller and Lennhoff family,

- Mathias Hille, Schönebeck City Archives (Elbe) for his wonderful assistance on the Kraft family, personally providing photos, and sourcing records of the Jews of Calbe for me, and for permission to use photos,

- Claudia Hinze, Clerk in the Office for Digitisation and Organisation, Stadtarchiv Leipzig,

- Dr Anna Hirsch, Manager of Collections & Research, Melbourne Holocaust Museum,

- Dr Simon Holloway, Manager of Adult Education and Academic Engagement, Melbourne Holocaust Museum,

- Eva Hussain, Director at Polaron for her suggestions,

- Tsur Israel, a quite distant but very helpful cousin in Israel who is related through my Neufeld-Denneboom-Vyth ancestors, for his help with my Neufeld family,

- Nancy Ittenson, Head of Department, Security and Order/Building and Urban Development, City of Calbe (Saale),

- Liz James OAM, Librarian and Archivist, Australian Jewish Genealogical Society Vic, and fellow committee member of the Australian Jewish Historical Society Vic. Liz's parents were also friends of my parents, her father John Mense and my father did business together, and Liz's brother Rob Mense was my scout leader at 3rd St. Kilda Scouts for several years,

- Gabriel Kahane, Kraft family cousin from Oregon, via Brooklyn and Los Angeles, and son of Jeffrey Kahane,

- Jeffrey Kahane, Los Angeles-based cousin through my Kraft family,

- Leah Komesaroff, my niece and provider of clues,

- Gershon (Gert) Konirsch (born 1935) who is nearly ninety and living in Israel, He is a grandson of my great granduncle Theodor Kraft,

- Mark Krebs from the Netherlands, a cousin and sharer of information on his Krebs family ancestors,

- Prof Ralph Krongold, Los Angeles-based cousin through my Kraft family,

Uncovering their Names and Stories:

- Michael Leiserowitz, volunteer with the Jews in East Prussia, Berlin and Guide at the POLIN Museum of the History of Polish Jews, Warsaw,

- Prof Dr Ruth Leiserowitz, Chairwoman and Historian at the Jews in East Prussia, Berlin,

- David Leisner from New York, a cousin and sharer of information on his Krebs family ancestors,

- Rabbi Dr John Levi AC, Emeritus Rabbi Temple Beth Israel, well-respected community leader and renowned Australian Jewish author and historian,

- Tim Locke, Ephraims and Neumeyers website, Lewes, East Sussex, for permission to use photos,

- Prof John Löwenhardt, Löwenhardt Foundation, The Netherlands – cousin through my Lennhoff family and Löwenhardt family historian, thanks especially for your extensive work on the Löwenhardt family history and the excellent photographs provided, and for permission to use photos,

- Dorisz Macher, Museum Educator, from the Gröbzig Synagogue Museum, for her research assistance, information sharing and very educational tour of the beautifully restored Gröbzig Synagogue,

- Russ Maurer, Research Chair, Jewish Genealogy Society of Cleveland, for very kindly helping me with my Cleveland family connections,

- Helen Marlow (my sister-in-law), for our memory-enhancing discussions,

- Peter Marlow (my brother), for our sharing of memories and historical family revelations,

- Fabian Mauruschat, Wuppertal-based journalist, friend and author for our catch-up in Wuppertal and for the signed copy of his book on Friedrich Engels,

- Dr Frank Mecklenburg, Mark M. and Lottie Salton Senior Historian, and Director of Research and Chief Archivist, Leo Baeck Institute, New York,

- Garry Meller, nephew of Ken Green, for our discussion and sharing of ideas in Elwood,

- Helen Nathan (my sister), for our many memory-enhancing discussions, and special thanks for being a provider of family photographs, including Dad's (Heinz Marowilsky's) childhood photo album from the 1930s, and for permission to use photos,

- Katja Niemann, Bibliothek, Stiftung Historische Museum Hamburg for her welcoming and kind assistance,

- Katrin Oschmann, Landeshauptstadt Magdeburg Stadtbibliothek (City Library Magdeburg) for her very kind assistance,

- Jeffrey Pfeffer, from New Jersey, a cousin and sharer of information on his Pfeffer and Lennhoff family,

- Aubrey Pomerance, Chief Archivist, Jewish Museum Berlin,

- Dr Ursula Reuter, Director Germania Judaica Library and Member Lern- und Gedenkort JAWNE for her generous advice and pointing me towards some great sources of information,

- Elisa Ronzoni, Curator, Collections, Jewish Museum of Australia, St Kilda,

- Susan Rosin, Publications Manager, JewishGen Press,

- Dan Rotman, interviews and meetings with my cousin through my mother's Kraft family, provider of photographs and family

Uncovering their Names and Stories:

> history researcher, especially for his generous advice and sharing of his extensive work on the extended Kraft family,

- Judith Roudman, Israeli-based cousin through my Steinthal family,

- Anna Ruhland, history teacher in Bensberg, for finding and providing the transcript of my father's interview with Prof Manfred Brusten in 1994 and other Marowilsky family documents,

- Ralph Salinger, volunteer for Maceva, and guru on Lithuanian Jewish family history, for his terrific assistance on Vistytis history and sourcing cemetery records from the New Jewish Cemetery of Vistytis, and for permission to use photos,

- Gary Samenfeld, a distant relative and DNA match from Greenville, South Carolina, for his help with some descendants of Jacob Lennhoff,

- Steven Sasso, cousin from California and family history researcher of his related Lennhoff and Sasso family, with an additional thanks to his wife Patricia,

- Julia Schmidt, Archivist, Centre for Urban History and Industrial Culture, Stadtarchiv Wuppertal for providing copies of the Marowilsky documents,

- Dr Joachim Schröder, Head of the Erinnerungsort Alter Schlachthof (Old Slaughterhouse Memorial Centre), Düsseldorf University for his wonderful advice and suggestions, for the approval to use the brilliant photos, as well as providing the story of deportations processed in Düsseldorf in 1942,

- Raymon Sherman, cousin through my Elkan family from Florida via Cleveland, for providing valuable information and photos relating to the Elkan family,

- Michael Simonson, Director of Public Outreach, Dr. Robert Ira Lewy Reference Service, Leo Baeck Institute, New York for his very kid help, including providing access and permission to use LBI records and images,

- Dr Seumas Spark, Adjunct Research Fellow in History at Monash University, *Dunera* researcher and President of the Dunera Association in Melbourne for his expertise and assistance,

- Our Tibon family cousins, notably siblings Eran, Noam and Yael, who are part of our extended Kraft and Isenstein family in Israel,

- Dr Christiane Twiehaus, Head of Department of Jewish History and Culture, MiQua, LVR - Jewish Museum in the Archaeological Quarter, Cologne who very kindly gave me a personal guided tour of Jewish Cologne and has been a great source of advice and suggestions,

- David Wernick, Executive Chairman of The Wernick Group, for his kind assistance and provision of a copy of the book on his family's and family company's history, and for permission to use photos,

- Corinna Wöhrl, Genealogische Gesellschaft Hamburg, for her very kind and generous assistance researching my Nathan – Elkan ancestors and for correcting some of my flawed assumptions,

- Anna Wolf, Dunera Association, Melbourne for her kind assistance, and

- Sebastian Zimmer, Berlin-based cousin through my Lennhoff and Löwenhardt family, and contributor to the Löwenhardt Foundation, The Netherlands.

www.ingramcontent.com/pod-product-compliance
Lightning Source LLC
Chambersburg PA
CBHW072118290426
44111CB00012B/1697